RELIGION AND CHANGE

RELIGION AND CHANGE

by

DAVID L. EDWARDS

Fellow and Dean of
King's College, Cambridge

HARPER & ROW, PUBLISHERS
New York and Evanston

FIRST EDITION

LIBRARY OF CONGRESS CATALOG CARD NUMBER: 69-19778

To

HILARY

Preface

In this book I try to consider the challenges to religion which have resulted from changes in the twentieth century. These changes have, I think, made our time the *secular* century, in a sense which is without precedent in history. Many people draw the conclusion that the religion which survives is doomed to disappear. In my introductory chapter, I try to consider the challenge of the current feeling that man is "coming of age", and the challenge of the growing unity of the world. Will the one world of the future be completely secular?

Since I maintain that these matters should not be treated in a bloodlessly intellectual way, I begin my more detailed chapters by studying the social character of traditional religion and the social character of traditional religion's defeat in industrial Europe, Russia, China and some other areas; but I note that the impact of this century has not led to religion's complete defeat. On the contrary, religion— or at least churchgoing—flourishes in the United States of America, and an examination of American religion may suggest some lessons which could be studied with profit by religious bodies in modern "pluralist" societies elsewhere (for example, in Britain). Then I turn to the psychological impact of secularisation, and I try to illustrate this both from the writings of Sigmund Freud and from the perplexities of some religious writers, Muslim or Jewish as well as Christian; but I note that even under this impact the religious passion has survived rather strongly. Perhaps, then, the "death of God" is an exaggerated report? After these sociological and psychological observations, I at length feel free to turn to the intellectual challenge to religious doctrine. I take as the key example the challenge to Christian dogmatism, briefly recording and assessing some of the responses of Christian theologians during the twentieth century. This theological quest for truth is, I think, a moving and impressive, if inconclusive, story.

My own conclusion is that the old shape of Christian life and thought—as in Protestant Fundamentalism, for example, or in conservative Catholicism—is not likely to become again the powerful religion of the West. But although many of the old customs and images of religion are dead, I regard the "post-Christian" West as a society which is still in search of an object to worship, and in two chapters I examine the possibilities that the old religions of the East, specially Hinduism and Buddhism, may come to the rescue, or that a new and more or less secular kind of "religion" without the traditional God may be evolved within the West. The evidence seems to suggest that, great as are Christianity's current problems, the problems faced by Westerners who try to find a religious (or quasireligious) substitute for Christianity are at present greater. Both the religious missionaries from the East and the West's own humanist have a long way to go before they can close down the churches. I believe, therefore, that Christianity still has a chance of filling the religious vacuum in the West, and of expanding its world-wide influence, if Christianity will accept the necessary changes.

In my last two chapters, Part Two of the book, I try to be constructive rather than analytic, for I attempt to discuss what these necessary changes in Christianity may be—while recognising that major changes in such a sphere must have origins beyond the reach of any commentator who is not a prophetic genius. Because of my emphasis on the social character of religion, I try to summarise first the very extensive discussion which has already taken place about a new shape for the Christian Church. This involves some detailed reforms which may seem out of keeping with the broad sweep of the other chapters, but I do not believe that the spiritual power of Christianity can be reborn unless its human embodiment is renewed for in practice believers hold a religious faith within a human fellowship. Finally, although still disclaiming the role of a religious prophet I offer an outline of a restatement of Christian belief. This restatement tries to take into account the criticisms of Christianity mentioned earlier in the book, but I claim that what I am struggling to say in a new way, while we all await a new prophet, is *not* a new religion: on the contrary, it is a restatement for our time of the essence of the New Testament. In a period of great confusion in Christian theology, I am traditional enough to think that if a message is to be worth calling Christian it must be a message about the eternal God who is other than man, and about the hope and the patience which we may gain from faith in this God. The outline here offered is too brief to be satisfactory to unbelievers (or to believers); that I know. On the other hand, I do try to tackle some of the problems involved—relating the integrity to the communication of the Christian message, relating religion to science, relating God to evil, relating the ideas of the fir century A.D. to our time—and no worthwhile discussion of these important problems can be other than difficult. The central question for me is whether a recognisably Christian faith in God can be held healthily and maturely by honest and intelligent people who know why Christianity has seemed incredible or repulsive to so many in the twentieth century. In asking for the reader's patience, I must simply say that at every stage of a long argument I have tried to sum up the truth as I see it, and that I know that the full truth cannot yet be seen.

These chapters are, therefore, only an introduction to a vast field of study, which I want to explore and which I invite others to explore with me. The chapters were delivered in an abbreviated form as eight Hulsean Lectures in the University of Cambridge in the Michaelmas Term, 1967. I am grateful to the Vice-Chancellor and to my senior colleagues in the Faculty of Divinity at Cambridge for the high honour which they conferred on me by electing me to stand in the succession of Lecturers since the benefaction by the Reverend John Hulse in 1777.

This book, short as it is, could not have been written had I not been forced to think about these things by seven years as a Fellow of All Souls College, Oxford, by eleven years in the service of the Student Christian Movement of Great Britain and Ireland (partly in its work for students but mainly as the Editor and Managing Director of its publishing house) and by some participation in the activities of the World Council of Churches and the World Student Christian Federation. Nor could the book have been completed without the time for independent work which I have enjoyed at King's College, Cambridge. Therefore, to many colleagues, old and new, I owe and offer thanks.

It was absurdly audacious to try to survey both the social and the intellectual forces in world-wide twentieth-century religion, and to assess them, in one book. No other book with such a comprehensive scope and restricted length is known to me, although that may suggest only that this book should never have been attempted. The ambition might not have occurred to me without an invitation from my Editor before the possibility of the Hulsean Lectureship arose. In my footnotes I have mentioned some of the books which would be most useful in further study, but obviously a complete bibliography would make a very large book in itself. To many authors I am indebted in ways which these pages do not fully reveal.

I am also indebted to friends who have commented on these pages

without necessarily agreeing with them. In particular I thar
Professor D. E. Nineham and Professor Norman Pittenger for the
labours. My friends John Bowden, Stephen Sykes and Max Warre
read the proofs. The Archbishop of Canterbury kindly included
draft of part of the last chapter among the preparatory essays for tl
Lambeth Conference of 1968, with the result that a number ◦
helpful comments reached me.

D.L.

August 1968

The author is grateful to the following for permission to u
material from their publications:

Faber and Faber Ltd., for material from *The Sacred Canopy* by Pet
    Berger.
George Allen & Unwin Ltd., for material from *A Preface to More*
    by Walter Lippman.
Harper & Row, Publishers, Incorporated, for material from *T*
    Eclipse of God by Martin Buber.
Marvell Press, Hessle, Yorks., for lines from "Church Going" in *T*
    Less Deceived by Philip Larkin.
SCM Press Ltd., for material from *The Reality of God* by Schubert N
    Ogden.
Mr. M. B. Yeats and Macmillan & Co. Ltd., for lines from "Tl
    Circus-Animals' Desertion" from *Collected Poems of W. B. Yea*

Contents

PART ONE

PART TWO

RELIGION AND CHANGE

CHAPTER ONE

Religion and the World's Coming of Age

Secularisation

If space were even more limited than it is in this book, and if we were asked to produce one word which would characterise the twentieth century, we should indeed despair. But if circumstances forced us either to produce one word or else to accept some horrific punishment (such as having to keep silent), we should eventually utter—but in how great an anxiety lest we should be misunderstood!—the one word *secular*. The twentieth century, we should say, is the secular century. Originally, in Latin, this word meant no more than that the thing being described belonged to its own time. However, something more than a glimpse of the obvious is being attempted when the twentieth century is described as secular.

Secularism as a word seems to have been coined by George Jacob Holyoake, who once spent six months in an English prison for public blasphemy and who died in 1906. For him it was "the doctrine that morality should be based on regard to the well-being of mankind in the present life, to the exclusion of all considerations drawn from belief in God or a future state". This definition is quoted by the *Oxford English Dictionary*; and it implies the doctrine which used to be called "atheism" and which, since it has become established and respectable, is now usually known as "humanism". *Secularisation*, however, is a word which may be used to describe a situation when "the exclusion of all considerations drawn from belief in God or a future state" reflects the main emphasis in a society, but not necessarily the opinions of all its members. Secularisation, it can be argued, does not necessarily make everyone embrace atheistic doctrines with all his heart and mind and strength. Thus Professor Gregor Smith, a theologian who applauds secularisation and what he calls "secularity", tells us that "modern secularism is not secular enough".[1] He means that secularisation ought not to lead to *any*

---

[1] Ronald Gregor Smith, *Secular Christianity* (London, 1966), p. 172. Professor Gregor Smith here develops themes propounded in the 1950s by the German theologian, Friedrich Gogarton, for which see Larry Shiner, *The Secularization of History* (Nashville, 1966).

doctrine—not even to secularism. Secularisation ought to emphasise
the worldly and the human, but leave people free to think their own
thoughts about God, in a liberal type of society which may be described as "open" or "pluralistic". A suspicion at once crosses the mind.
Is this distinction between the process of "secularisation" and the
doctrine of "secularism" more than a clever theologian's play with
words? It will be our task in this book to see, but at least we can agree
now that secularisation means the displacement from a society's
centre of belief in the eternal God, in the "after-life" as man's great
hope, and in supernatural force as man's great ally. *Secularisation
occurs when supernatural religion—that is, religion based on "belief in God
or a future state"—becomes private, optional and problematic.*

We cannot put it more simply than that, by saying that under the
impact of secularisation all religion disappears. Professor Gregor
Smith's warning against assuming the necessity of secularism in a
secularised age may be rather abstruse, but some solid evidence that
secularisation need *not* mean "no religion at all" can be produced
from the contemporary world. Many secularists (and even many
theologians such as Professor Gregor Smith) have not been down-to-
earth or "empirical" enough: they have not given due weight to the
survival of supernatural religion in our time. A great many people
still do participate in religious ceremonies. They do so in African
villages, in the deserts of Arabia, on the banks of the Ganges; they
even do so in London and Moscow. In the 1960s Buddhist monks
burned themselves to death in Vietnam; they were protesting against
a corrupt local Catholicism and against the American way of life.
The American way of life, we must add, has a definitely religious
content—for the United States, the most modern country in the
world, is also the country most addicted to churchgoing. And all this
religious observance certainly indicates some religious belief, which is
probably more widespread than the statistics of the observance
suggest. Christianity, Islam, Hinduism and Buddhism all continue to
command great popular respect, which can flame into enthusiastic
devotion in exceptional circumstances and which normally results in
the steady influence of religious beliefs and values on the psychology
of the masses.

Stalin's only daughter, who was baptised as an adult into the
Russian Orthodox Church and who fled to the United States saying
that religion had changed her outlook on life, may be a figure more
typical of our time than many would suppose. She was impressed by
a husband's Hindu background, and she by no means appears as a

orthodox Christian believer, but she has voiced a strong feeling that she could not live without God and that the true religious spirit makes for unity and love. At least, we may conclude from her story, in her eyes true religion does not bear such fruits as her father's tyranny and her mother's suicide; what it does produce is her own present spirit of forgiveness, understanding and peace (a spirit which her more sophisticated Western reviewers have found it hard to forgive).[1] With Stalin's daughter as a witness, it could indeed be argued that *religion occurs when secularisation occurs*. By this attempt at an epigram we should mean that when religion becomes private, optional and problematic it also becomes more self-conscious, articulate and militant. When the tradition is challenged, it comes alive. The young Stalin was trained for the priesthood of the Russian Orthodox Church, before he became the persecuting high priest of the Communist Party; and it was perhaps only natural that his daughter should have her attention turned to the age-old religious mysteries of Russia, and of the world, as she found her own identity and moved out of his shadow—just as it was perhaps only natural that the greatest novel to come out of Soviet Russia should be by a poet who, appalled by the human cost of the Revolution, had turned back to the Christian images of human and divine love.[2] The testing and purifying challenge of secularisation has brought the religious reply.

Nevertheless, the fact remains that in many countries of the modern world, and conspicuously in Soviet Russia, the elite does not allow itself to be much influenced by this continuing or reviving religion. The intellectuals are often the heirs of Holyoake's militant type of secularism. They are openly cynical about religious customs, contemptuous about theological claims and hostile to ecclesiastical institutions. And in a million subtle ways the media of mass communication and of public instruction spread a secular emphasis, even if this lacks the philosophising of the intellectuals. Although time may be given to religious worship and teaching, the mass-media and the schools excite worldly curiosity and desire. In addition to intellectual and cultural awakenings, people are encouraged in "the lust of the flesh, the lust of the eyes and the pride of life", in the New Testament's ancient but accurate phrase; and the activities of organised religion are not connected with the things which matter most. The thinking of the people is influenced, however obscurely and slowly. All over the modern world the sea of traditional faith in the supernatural God

[1] Svetlana Alliluyeva, *Twenty Letters to a Friend* (Eng. trans., New York, 1967).
[2] Boris Pasternak, *Dr. Zhivago* (Eng. trans., London, 1958).

or gods seems to be ebbing. Even in the great plains of India, million
hear the "melancholy, long, withdrawing roar" which in Victoria
England sounded for Matthew Arnold on Dover beach. Many
modern people are, however, fascinated by a more cheerful spectacle
Before their delighted eyes, the mainstream of modern life appears to
flow from its own inexhaustible sources and at its own irresistible pace
towards an ocean which may even now be glimpsed, serene and shin
ing—the ocean of human health, freedom, dignity and dominance
over the earth and over space. This mainstream of secular energy i
what really excites many people today. They judge themselves and
others basically by their ability to take part in the progress to secula
knowledge and secular prosperity. Here is the system of beliefs and
values into which even the churchgoing of the United States may
have to be fitted; for it has been suggested that if the real attitudes c
most American churchgoers are to be reflected, the motto which i
familiar on United States dollar notes should be expanded to read
"*In God we trust*—all others pay cash." Thus the fascination of ou
study lies in the question: *will the religion which survives in this maint*
secular century disappear before too long? The question is crucial and
urgent, for—whatever the theologians may now say—many observer
of contemporary trends are convinced that secularism will graduall
prove to be the universal consequence of secularisation.

Before we try to answer that central question, however, we mus
ask another of almost equal interest: *Is this degree of secularisation a new
phenomenon?* Is this century in fact the first secular century?

There are no clean breaks in history. Just as religion has not in fac
disappeared from our largely secular civilisation, so also the secula
emphasis was in fact prominant in past ages which we regard a
heavily religious. According to the evidence of history, there hav
been no ages of faith—if we have in mind a whole society's acceptance
of a religious faith, and if we define religious faith as the deliberate
subjection by a freely acting individual of his whole personality
thought and conduct to the dominance of "belief in God or a futur
state". In every age both the clever and the rich have often been
critical of religion, and again and again—as in the poetry of Lucretius
who died half a century before the birth of Jesus, or amid th
"Enlightenment" of eighteenth-century Europe and America—th
death certificate of the God of popular religion has been signed b
the elite with a flourish. Among the masses the observance of religiou
ceremonies and the profession of religious beliefs would often seem t
have been more or less unthinking. Popular religion was largely th

product of convention, inspired by the wish to be like others rather than to be like God; and popular religion was limited even in its popularity. Where reliable records of popular religion can be recovered (for example, statistics of church attendance) we discover that in times or areas which appear to have been heavily religious (for example, Victorian England), in fact considerable numbers had few or no connections with organised religion. On Sunday, 30 March, 1851, a census of places of worship in England, the last of its kind to be taken, indicated that only about thirty-six per cent of the population attended services.[1] It is a mistake to suppose that there has ever existed a large society of saints, or that mass movements of intense religious belief have been anything other than freaks. Most people, for most of the time, have preferred to concentrate not on unseen powers but on the everyday powers of earth and flesh and mind. When people have turned in large numbers to religion, it has often been in order to use religion for secular aims. Religion has meant to them the solidarity of their clan or class or nation, in contrast with others; and religion has enabled them to express the loyalty and the hatred in their hearts. Human nature being what it is, crusades of righteous indignation have been specially liable to use the weapons of excommunication, mob fanaticism, oppressive legislation and violence in order to impose their visions on lesser breeds. The inevitable consequence of this intense form taken by the internal secularisation of religion has been a revulsion. Men have been revolted by the foul corruption of the religious idea, and have turned back to the enjoyment of life without raising dangerous questions of theology. The religious vision of the saints, we may conclude, has scarcely been glimpsed by the mass of mankind. Religion, like music, has been a bond of unity for human societies, and a basic religious sense, like a simple pleasure in tunes, is human; but a deeply religious sense, like a deep appreciation of music, has been for the few. Most history, including most religious history, was secular.

However, the secularisation of our time seems to be novel in two ways: (1) in its conviction that *the world is "coming of age"*, and (2) in its conviction that *the world is becoming one*. We must consider these two features of the twentieth century in turn; for, between them, they have produced, if not a totally new situation of universal secularism, then at least a world-wide challenge to religion from a new power of secularisation.

[1] The studies of W. S. F. Pickering were summed up by David Martin, *A Sociology of English Religion* (London, 1967), p. 19.

Coming of Age

The idea of the world's "coming of age" has a long history, for the comparison of the life of mankind with the life of an individual has been a stock theme in literature and rhetoric. To cite a fairly modern use of the idea: Pope Leo XIII, when he condemned "Americanism" in 1899, linked that heretical tendency with the suggestion that "the Church should adapt herself more to the civilisation of a world that has reached the age of manhood". But the use of the "coming of age" catchword by the German Protestant theologian Dietrich Bonhoeffer in a letter on 8 June, 1944,[1] has made it echo in many places, and the discussion has shown that many interpretations can be given to it.[2]

The best interpretation makes "the world's coming of age" refer to modern man's sense that his powers are increasing, and that, however inadequate they may be at present, his only real hope lies in their increase, for no greater power will help him. In the last 150 years or so, the technical and social revolutions have created a new psychological situation. This climate of opinion has given an unprecedented encouragement to the intoxicating sense of freedom, power and progress. Even before the technical and social revolutions of the nineteenth century began, optimism already marked in their different ways the Renaissance in Italy, the political revolutions in America and France, the intellectual revolutions of idealism and romanticism in Germany, and almost the whole life of an England whose revolutions were (after the execution of Charles I) a fairly painless evolution in prosperity. Again and again during the nineteenth century, from the defeat of Napoleon to the Golden Jubilee of Queen Victoria, progress in peace to greater and greater riches seemed inevitable for an England, a Europe and a North America reaping the new harvests of the industrial factories and the illimitable prairies. Optimism has continued to be the prevailing note of the West in the twentieth century. Exuberant proclamations of self-confidence marked the birth of the century. Around 1910 there was the "great unrest" because new powers were stirring in the industrial society. After the catastrophe of the Great War, optimism revived in the reconstruction of a world "safe for democracy"; and many clung to this optimism through the 1930s. Optimism grew as never before in the 1950s, with

[1] *Letters and Papers from Prison* (1951; Eng. trans., London, 1953, revd. 1966), pp. 177-82.
[2] Two volumes of essays are available in English: *The Place of Bonhoeffer*, ed. M. E. Marty (New York, 1963), and *The World's Coming of Age*, ed. R. Gregor Smith (London, 1967). Dr. Eberhard Bethge's lectures published in the latter volume provide readers of English with the best discussion until his full biography is translated from the German. Many other recent theological books are substantially concerned with Bonhoeffer.

their vision of affluence in the West; and this vision has not been contradicted in the chastened 1960s.

The intoxication has now spread to Asia and Africa, where hundreds of millions have celebrated independence and a new chance to reach Europe's living standards (by a colossal effort, it is admitted). And running beneath the official rhetoric of triumph there has been the assumption of increasing numbers of people, in increasing numbers of moods, that things have been getting better—and will get better still. Nor has this quieter optimism lacked solid justification. Diseases have been tamed; crops have been blessed by science and given vastly greater markets; democracy has moved its objective from the vote for all to security for all; women are being emancipated, and children educated. And for the first time in his history, man is becoming predominantly a city dweller. In vast conurbations such as Tokyo, man has had to adapt himself to a new civilisation. Despite all the squalor which he has created in the cities, and despite all the misery which he has experienced there, urban man has grown increasingly independent of the elemental forces of nature. The fruits of nature have become the raw material of manufacturing. Apart from the sky, some decorative gardens and some natural food, everything around the city dweller has been man-made. Even his children have been planned. The dream has grown of the city as a place fully adequate to man's dignity, from its skyscrapers to its subways; that dream has been the magnet to the paupers of Calcutta or the shanty-dwellers of Rio; and that dream has begun to come true. Villagers the world over also share in this dream, looking up at aeroplanes, listening to the radio, tasting the first trickle of the amenities of modern life. Even simple people nowadays regard science as magic and salvation, creating the good life in the City of Man.

If the menace of famine can be met by birth control and increased food production and if the Southern world can be admitted to the feast of the North, the next centuries will enjoy a prosperity more brilliant than can now be conceived, but it is difficult to imagine that our successors will be called upon to make quite the same dramatic change as our time has made in its revolution of expectations. It seems probable that the twentieth century, with its thrilling first promise of wealth for the masses, will be remembered as one of the decisive moments in the story of man.[1]

[1] The perspectives of history are in Carleton S. Coon, *The History of Man* (revd. ed., New York, 1962) and Ritchie Calder, *The Inheritors: The Story of Man and the World He Made* (London, 1961). The background to the technical and social revolutions of modern times was outlined in Carl Becker's brilliant study of *The Heavenly City of the Eighteenth-*

This century has, of course, witnessed many setbacks to the realisation of its dream. That prince of English secular humanists, Professor Gilbert Murray (a scholar who attributed the rise of the "mystery" religions, including Christianity, to a "failure of nerve" among the ancient Greeks), lived to see his daughter Rosalind a convert to Roman Catholicism and the author of *The Good Pagan's Failure*.[1] Led by Oswald Spengler with his turgid lament for *The Decline of the West*,[2] innumerable prophets have arisen to proclaim the end of the modern era of optimism and energy. Apparently overwhelming problems have been posed by man's inability to civilise the contacts between nations and races, to relate his breeding capacity to the availability of food, and to control economic advance so as to secure fair shares for all. The gap between the rich and the poor nations has widened tragically, and by the 1960s it was still unclear how Asia, Africa and Latin America would be admitted to that Northern feast; the twentieth century may be recorded as the prelude to an explosion of hungry anger from the poor two-thirds of mankind. Wars and political fanaticisms, famines and economic depressions have brought tragedies to millions in Europe and even in North America, so that a harsh disillusionment has followed the agonies of the rich society during and since 1914. In the trenches of France and Flanders, in the Wall Street crash of 1929, in the British queues for the unemployment dole, in the ruin of central Europe under the Kaiser or the Führer, in Auschwitz and Hiroshima, in Stalin's Russia, in the Vietnam war and the riots in American cities, many false optimisms have been buried, and today—as we are so often told—the mushroom cloud of nuclear annihilation casts its shadow over all civilisation.

Yet many of the prophecies of doom have been falsified, for progress has continued. Many millions, greatly shocked but not crushed by our time of troubles, have insisted on making *this* "the century of hope" (the label which was attached to the nineteenth century). In the United States the early prophets of prosperity have been outdistanced by the speed of the actual growth in the country's economy. Elsewhere, hopes have often been very modest—a cure for

Century Philosophers (New Haven, 1932), which may now be supplemented by Charles Vereker, *Eighteenth-Century Optimism* (Liverpool, 1967). The historical significance of those revolutions was suggested by J. B. Bury's classic *The Idea of Progress* (London, 1928), to which John Baillie added a theological critique in *Belief in Progress* (London, 1950). Kenneth Boulding offered a summary of the more recent "great transition" in *The Meaning of the Twentieth Century* (New York, 1964).

[1] London, 1939.
[2] 2 vols., 1918-22; Eng. trans., New York, 1926-8.

an eye disease, regular meals instead of empty bellies, a home with
a minimum of security, a better chance for the children. But many of
these hopes have actually come true before men's eyes in our time.
The economic recovery of Europe with a speed which no one prophesied in 1945 has been a symbol of the whole century's resilience.
Twice over, Europe has bled itself white, yet from somewhere fresh
blood has come, and Europe enters the 1970s immensely stronger
than the continent was in the fateful summer of 1914. For all
Spengler's gloom, in the long run the West has *not* declined. It has
staggered, it has picked itself up, and it has run on. "Man," Professor
Bateson once told the scientists assembled in the British Association,
"is just beginning to know himself for what he is—a rather long-lived
animal with great powers of enjoyment if he does not deliberately
forego them. Hitherto superstition and mythical ideas of sin have
predominantly controlled these powers."[1] That address was delivered
in August, 1914. A half-century followed of bloody tragedies with an
inter-war "waste-land"; sin became not a "mythical idea" but a
thing of steel and fire, bayonets, mud and poison gas; yet at the end
of this ordeal of the West the optimistic professor's words seemed
plausible again.[2] The East has kept much of its own pessimism, but
that has been a pessimism about the basic condition of man, a despair
inherited from the ages. For the East, this century began with
Japan's defeat of Russia, a momentous symbol of what modernised
Asians could do. Since then the East has known, amid its often overwhelming material problems and its continuing fatalism of the
spirit, that famine is not inevitable; in other words, the East has
known a hope so great and so new that the masses have felt that they
have entered history for the first time since the golden ages of their
half-legendary past.

This is, therefore, a time of *humanism*. In many previous ages the
arts which ease, illuminate and adorn life flourished for the few, and
the twentieth century has seldom reached the standards of excellence
then established. Many Muslims look to the past for the glory of
Islam, and many Chinese or Indians confess that the twentieth
century cannot match the high culture of their vanished empires.
Modern Europe has not produced a Shakespeare or a Beethoven, an
Athens or a Florence. Below that level of excellence, middle-class
culture as a whole has not reached the solid strength which it knew
in nineteenth-century England, France and Germany. But the

---

[1] Quoted in S. Rhadakrishnan, *An Idealist View of Life* (London, 1932), p. 43.
[2] See, e.g., Charles Frankel, *The Case for Modern Man* (New York, 1956).

achievement of our time—most dramatic in Russian and Chinese Communism's liberation of the peasants, but most powerful in the growth of American capitalism—has been the extension of humanism to include humanity. Although many forms of privilege remain in the world, excluding the masses from the good things of life and challenging reformers to fights enough for many centuries, yet popular expectation and popular education have made immense advances already, and all the signs are that their progress will accelerate. This means that teaching, travel, television and radio, printing and other forms of preservation and reproduction can now place the sublime achievements of genius within the reach of the people. Above all, it means that men, women and children are now valued more highly *for themselves.* Increasingly the individual is courted as an elector by politicians; he is caressed by doctors, dentists, oculists and psychiatrists; he is pampered by merchants whose sole hope of fortune lies in attractively feeding, clothing, transporting and amusing the customer with money in his pocket, in his millions. Increasingly the individual is tolerated even when in character or in opinion he is not normal within his society. The quest for human dignity is what is vital—more vital even than economic motivation. Our age is accordingly the age of the revolt of the poor against the rich; of the coloured against the white; of the women against the men; of the deviants against the respectable. It means something that fully a quarter of all the human beings who have ever survived infancy are alive in the 1960s—thanks to the fact that over ninety per cent of all the scientists who have ever lived are living now. But it means more that in the unprecedented social response to the unprecedented economic change, the masses grasp at an equality of respect.

What has survived from the prophecies of doom, and from the facts of many disasters, has been a sense that progress to an equal prosperity for all is not automatic. And this sense of ambiguity and danger, so clear in the political and economic worlds, is another key to what the unprecedented "coming of age" means spiritually. Dietrich Bonhoeffer, the Christian pastor who was writing in a Nazi prison cell ten months before his execution, would have been the last person to endorse all the inane prophecies of inevitable human progress. (He had been repelled by his personal experience of American religious optimism.) But exactly in its ambiguity and danger has lain our time's resemblance with the coming of age of an individual. New powers stir; they can lead either to fantastic progress or to utter catastrophe. That is the thrill, and when things go wrong that is the poignancy. "Coming of age" is the beginning of battle, not the consummation of victory; it is promise, not perfection. The power is there; if disaster comes, it will be because the power was not used in a sufficiently intelligent plan. The great transition into modernity comes through the loss of that sense of intellectual and physical powerlessness which in the past accompanied man's dependence on God or the gods. Now that man is powerfully—and perhaps tragically—mature, there is no going back to any Paradise which existed before man defied the divine prohibition and ate the fruit of knowledge. "The future cannot be predicted," writes Dennis Gabor, "but futures can be invented . . . We cannot stop inventing because we are riding on a tiger. We must now start thinking of social inventions to anaesthetise the tiger, so that we can get off its back."[1]

Above all, a society, like an individual, can feel that now, if things do go wrong, if the tiger-ride out of Paradise does end in catastrophe, there is no one else to blame. This is a sober thought, often forgotten as the champagne for independence flows, but when the party is over the thought remains, to give a society, like an individual, an adult pride in taking responsibility, even for mistakes. Even if ballistic missiles with nuclear warheads horrifically devastate our civilisation and pollute the earth, it will remain true that with unprecedented skills twentieth-century men made them and sent them on their journeys. And here lies the transforming element in this "coming of age" for the future of religion. As man's consciousness of his powers, or at least of his potential, has grown, so his reliance on supernatural force has shrunk, or at least has been seen to need a radical readjustment and restatement.

In history, the beating heart of religion has lain deeper than the intellect, deeper even than the conscience. The heart of religion has been that primal sense of awe before a tremendous and fascinating mystery, that sense of absolute dependence on the mercy of a power infinitely greater than man, which may still be experienced among Africans or Indians, and which has been expounded by Western theologians such as Friedrich Schleiermacher[2] and Rudolf Otto.[3] And the essence of practical religion has been petitionary prayer. A villager knowing that he was really empty-handed but burning a little incense or leaving a few flowers before an idol, with a petition

[1] *Inventing the Future* (London, 1963), pp. 185-6.
[2] *On Religion: Speeches to Its Cultured Despisers* (1799; Eng. trans., London, 1893).
[3] *The Idea of the Holy* (1917; Eng. trans., Oxford, 1923).

for a crop or a son, has been the typically religious man. This has been the case even in India, where the official philosophy has been based on the eternal identity of *Atman* and *Brahman*, the human and divine spirits. Even Buddhism, which in its founder's intention was a godless philosophy, has largely become in subsequent practice an emotion surrounding a request for supernatural aid in the affairs of this life—which means that it has become a practical religion. Even Confucianism and Taoism, which originally were philosophies of the good life in the family and society and in communion with nature, with references to "Heaven" (*tien*) so vague that they have won the approval of modern Western atheists, became in Chinese history religions to some extent like the practical religion of India: systems of petitionary prayer sliding quite easily into magic. And even in Islam, where prayer is meant to be adoring submission to the will of Allah, men in practice ask for things. We stand in caves painted by primitive men and we know that their beliefs cannot be recovered by us, despite the ingenuity of the anthropologists; yet one psychological reality we think we can often recognise in the scenes of hunting and of pregnancy preserved on the amazing walls of those caves— and that is, a confession that already, when nature had scarcely yet turned into history, *homo sapiens* was *homo religiosus*, for he needed supernatural help to survive, to hunt animals and to rear offspring. From primitive magic to the prayer of the Christian to the heavenly Father for daily bread, the central theme of religion could be expressed as a cry for help.

In the nineteenth and twentieth centuries of the Christian era, increasing numbers of people have either experienced no such need of supernatural force, or else they have believed that it would be futile to expect their need to be satisfied as a consequence of petitionary prayer. Of course, the situation is often confused, with the old and the new mingling, the old surviving, the new failing. But that there has been a shift of emphasis in modern civilisation can scarcely be doubted. When modern people feel sick, they want medicine when their crops are poor, they want fertilisers; when they are ignorant, they want education; when their relationships are entangled, they know that they ought to profit by a cool, scientific study of the underlying economic or emotional problems. And when they want rain, they do not beat drums. At least to the unreflective, all this seems a world away from the Church of England's Litany which echoed in the language of the Tudor age the petitions of all the religious centuries to the God of a thousand names:

That it may please thee to succour, help, and comfort, all that
are in danger, necessity, and tribulation;
We beseech thee to hear us, good Lord.

What is strong in the modern world seems to have come by the
exploitation of man's inherent powers, not by a gift from God. The
prayer of the religious centuries was for illumination. Out of illusions
they asked to be led into reality, out of darkness into light, and thus
out of death into life; and to this day the Latin motto of the University
of Oxford affirms that the Lord is its light. But now the vast conquests
of science have been won without any reference to a supernatural
source of illumination. Indeed, it has been of the essence of the
scientific method that every object, however impressive, should be
analysed as just one object in nature, and that supernatural causes
should not be ascribed to any event in the universe. To many in this
age of science, God has been the great illusion, and the worship of
God has seemed a cause of darkness and death to the mind of man.
Even religious believers have had to do their science as if God did
not exist. The activity of God, as the astronomer Laplace remarked
to Napoleon, is a hypothesis of which the scientist has "no need";
and "to bring religion into it" has seemed the chief of sins in the age
of science. Thus scientific man seems to have understood nature as
merely natural. Without supernatural illumination, he can boast that
he has created our glittering and hugely pregnant civilisation.

To secularists it does not seem to be conclusive evidence against
"man's coming of age" to say that the achievements of the scientific
civilisation matter little in comparison with the continuing tragedy
of the human situation taken as a whole. The common argument
designed to overthrow humanist arrogance and to commend religious
humility—the argument used by many religious conservatives against
Bonhoeffer—rests on the point that man's basic problem remains his
finitude, experienced through his deep loneliness, his disappointments
with the good things of life, his exposure to accidents and diseases, and
his inevitable aging to death. It is urged that man's basic problem can
be overcome only through religious faith, for it is only by such faith
that man feels himself to be in touch with a power which, being
supernatural and immortal, sustains him through all the losses
inflicted by chance and decay. All other happiness, it is suggested, is
unsubstantial and transitory. The vitality of religious life and
thought in the twentieth century has shown that many people still
find truth in that religious analysis of the condition of man. Many

humanist advertisements of the glories of life in the age of science
seem, in comparison with that ancient vision, brash and trivial
Twentieth-century life is often still tragic, and for everyone life is in
one way or another frustrated. Everyone dies. Further advances in
technology or in the humane and social sciences will cure few of such
complaints. But it is crucial for the future of religion that its defender
should see that the main weight of their case can no longer rest on the
weakness of man; instead, most of the case for religion must now be
built on the recognition of man's great strength. The Litany already
referred to contains the prayer: "In all time of our tribulation; in
all time of our wealth . . . *Good Lord, deliver us*"; and for all it
tribulations, ours is a time of wealth. Many twentieth-century people
have succeeded, to a greater or lesser extent, in pushing their mor
tality to the back of their minds. Life for them is ultimately death, bu
they think that there is nothing that they can do about this unfortu
nate circumstance, and meanwhile they are merry enough, with many
duties to perform and many enjoyments to explore in this teeming
and fascinating world. All their important things are the thing
before the last things. Against all the abstractions of the metaphysica
philosophies and against all the hell-fire or angel-voices of the "old
time" religion, this physical joy, this earthiness, has usually been the
position on which the average sensual man has taken his stand; and
in the twentieth century the earth's consolations for the absurdity o
man's ultimate place in the scheme of things have multiplied. Amid
the surrounding wilderness and the silence of the infinite spaces, this
earth has become more of a garden of delights.

Admittedly, some sensitive artists and intellectuals have gon
deeper than that. They have explored the full, sad consequences o
atheism. Thomas Hardy and A. E. Housman did it in England; sex
brought misery to them, and in their misery they saw the tragedy o
all our days. Jean Paul Sartre and Albert Camus did it more
thoroughly, when French intellectuals had to rebuild their whol
view of the world under the pressure of the ethical dilemmas posed
by three appalling problems: the necessity of committing evil in orde
to resist the Nazis, the necessity of countenancing evil in order to
support social justice through Communism's appeal to the working
class, and the necessity of denouncing one's own country as th
French empire sank into ruin amid futile cruelties in South Eas
Asia and North Africa.

As the depths of the human situation have been probed by Hard
or Housman, Sartre or Camus, man has been seen as thrown int

the world without an explanation, compelled to make decisions but not allowed long satisfactions, subjected to passions with no hope of peace while in that bondage, experiencing guilt but not forgiveness, drawn to the grave with all his dreams. That tragic vision has produced "nausea"; and the right response to the "absurdity" has seemed not acceptance but rebellion. Yet many have refused to escape from the "nausea" by the method adopted by Housman when he buried himself in pedantic scholarship—or by Sartre when he chose the cause of Soviet Russia. On the contrary, Camus before his accidental death in 1960 spoke for many in our generation with his profounder analysis of the proper task and scope of the human rebellion. Rebellion there must be, but Camus taught that the real rebellion against the real enemies of man is betrayed if the mind and conscience capitulate to a political creed of fanaticism and violence. Modern man must be a rebel; but just as he betrays his body if he commits suicide, so he betrays and kills his intelligence if he embraces the consolations of religion or of the Marxist substitute for religion. In an absurd world, we must learn to live with a lucid authenticity, to think and to feel among our fellow-men—to think and to feel, *but not to hope*. In the plague of life, man must be a doctor, but a doctor without heroics.[1]

Camus saw modern man as being like Prometheus, who stole fire from the Greek gods—but also like another mythological hero, Sisyphus, who in Hades was doomed to roll a stone to the top of a hill and see it always roll down again. The necessity of rebellion, with its hopelessness, were expressed for our time in Franz Kafka's novel *The Castle*;[2] and the anxiety of guilt with its permanence had been put a year before, in Kafka's *The Trial*.[3] Can human nature assert its own dignity under such anguishing conditions? Is it possible in such a tragic solitude *to be a man?* Kafka seems merely to have asked the question; and Sartre has given an ambiguous reply, for Sartre's individualism needed to be rescued by his Communism. Camus (like Freud) showed his undeterred humanism by his disillusioned *yes*. But, we may add, Camus (like Freud) saw how difficult it is for the vital energies of man to accept a civilisation which renounces both the passions which energise and the illusions which console; he saw how difficult it was for others to say *yes*. On the first page of *The Rebel*,[4] Camus recorded his sympathy (although also his disagreement)

---

[1] This is taught in the great novel or allegory by Albert Camus, *The Plague* (1947; Eng. trans., London, 1948). The best study of Camus is by Philip Thody (London, 1964).
[2] 1926; Eng. trans., London, 1930.   [3] 1925; Eng. trans., London, 1937.
[4] 1951; Eng. trans., London, 1953.

with the violence of the revolts against modern man's fate. "One might think that a period which, within fifty years, uproots, enslaves, or kills 70 million human beings, should only, and forthwith, be condemned," he wrote, adding: "But also its guilt must be understood." The violence in modern man's rebellion against his destiny was understood by Camus—understood, but not endorsed, for whether or not men could say *yes* to the human situation, they must renounce illusions about it.

Existentialism such as that of Camus sounds differently from an earlier optimism, for it is fully atheistic. Hegel in 1802 observed that the religion of modern times rested on the feeling that God himself is dead, and Feuerbach's *Essence of Christianity* (1841), which George Eliot translated in 1854, publicly celebrated the fact that the feeling was true, so that at last man could come into his own. But it needed genius of the stature of Nietzsche and Dostoevsky to begin to probe the consequences in the depths of the emotional life. "God is dead! God remains dead!" cried the madman in Nietzsche's *Joyful Wisdom* (1882) to those scoffers in the market-place who merely did not believe in God.[1] "And we have killed him! The holiest and the mightiest that the world has hitherto possessed has bled to death under our knife . . . Is not the magnitude of the deed too great for us? Shall we not ourselves have to become Gods, merely to seem worthy of it? There never was a greater event, and on account of it, all who are born after us belong to a higher history than any history hitherto!" So Superman could come—when "everything is permitted", as Ivan Karamazov said in Dostoevsky's last book.

Nietzsche's madman concluded that he had shouted too early about the murder, for "this deed is as yet further from them than the furthest stars—*and yet they have done it!*" But the twentieth century has been the time of the widespread experience of the "death" of God. That experience has seemed to many a liberation, so that what the madman said sounds like the Gospel of life. Millions have felt some of the excitement of the liberation; they have felt godlike, because now, like a man come of age, they could do things which are not done in the nursery or at school. This has, however, not been the predominant mood in the great artists, poets, dramatists and novelists. These have often known despair. Nietzsche himself went mad; Dostoevsky dreamed of a resurrection into purity and peace; other artists have chosen other ways to protest against the emptiness of life. In a crudely materialist and commercial society, many artists

[1] Translated in the *Complete Works*, vol. x (Edinburgh, 1910), p. 168.

have projected their own feeling of alienation, and have made out of
their personal sorrows works of art which state that when everything
is possible, little is achieved; when everything is permitted, little is
enjoyed. While the main note of public opinion in the twentieth
century has been a note of hope, or at least of adult pride in responsibility, we should also reckon with the conviction of these artists that
man's hope is (like everything else) chiefly an illusion, and that his
lonely responsibility is a tragedy. As Nietzsche's *Joyful Wisdom* put it:
"The total nature of the world . . . is to all eternity chaos."[1]

Some twentieth-century secularists, sensitive to the anxiety of man
after the "death" of God, have expressed sympathy with religion.
These thinkers have appreciated religion's age-old and continuing
attempt to comfort the heart's sufferings in this plague which is life,
and to raise the mind's vision to a destiny above the long littleness of
our days. They have been patient with religion's difficulties as it has
struggled to convey its vision through imperfect symbols, for to a
considerable extent they look on religion's problems from inside—
not from the superior point of view of outside critics who can afford
to sneer and to destroy without needing to replace. Thus we find
Sir Julian Huxley, the eminent zoologist who was Director-General
of UNESCO, editing *The Humanist Frame* (London, 1961). This
book was a collection of extracts from the works of atheists or agnostics
ancient or modern, and might be regarded as some sort of secular
Bible. The extracts advocated many moral attitudes which many
religious believers would heartily endorse, and in his Introduction to
the volume Sir Julian summed up criticisms of religion which many
believers would admit to be valid. But he believed that "what the
world now needs is not merely a rationalist denial of the old but a
religious affirmation of the new", for he saw clearly the strength and
value of religion. "All religions," he wrote, "involve the emotion of
sacred mystery . . ., the sense of right and wrong; and feelings of
guilt, shame, or sin. They are always concerned in one way or another
with the relation between the individual and the community, and
with the possibility of his escaping from the prisoning immediacies
of space, time and selfhood by relating himself to some broader frame

---

[1] *The Joyful Wisdom* seems to have been inspired in part by Nietzsche's bitterness that
Lou Salomé had refused to marry him. (She lived to become a friend of Freud.) A few
months after its composition Nietzsche wrote to a friend: "I have suffered from the
disgraceful and anguishing recollections of this summer as from a kind of madness." But
these psychological origins do not lessen the significance of his great vision. See R. J.
Hollingdale, *Nietzsche: The Man and his Philosophy* (London, 1965); and for a sympathetic
Christian comment on this whole movement, Henri de Lubac, *The Drama of Atheist
Humanism* (1947; Eng. trans., London, 1949).

of reference, or in some self-transcending experience of union or communion with a larger reality."

This is an estimate of religion which is far more positive than was the attitude of the critics who reduced religion to "nothing but" ignorance, superstition, illusion or nonsense. This is an estimate which sympathises more deeply with the efforts of past ages than do many reformers within organised religion today. At a time when a theo logian such as Professor Gregor Smith believes that "modern secu larism is not secular enough", we find an atheist such as Sir Julian Huxley calling for a new religion to clothe the insights of the age of science. "This reformulation of traditional religious concepts and beliefs and ceremonies," Huxley writes, "their translation into a new terminology and a new framework of ideas, is a major task for Humanism."[1]

Here is an important plea. In this book we must be preoccupied with many secular substitutes for the old religious beliefs, and Sir Julian Huxley's will be among the efforts demanding our attention. We must note that the "new religion" which has dominated history since 1914 has been militantly political and defiantly irrational—it has been the European militarism of 1914 or the Nazism of 1939, it has been the imperialism of the 1900s or the Afro-Asian nationalism of the 1950s; and in the 1960s a third of the world's population live under fourteen governments which subscribe to the Communist doctrines. In our age of violence, it is a "rough beast" who (as in that famous nightmare, *The Second Coming*, of W. B. Yeats) "slouches towards Bethlehem to be born". But perhaps in the more peaceful future man will reconstruct religion on a scientific basis, as Sir Julian Huxley advises. At any rate, it is vital that we should appreciate the force of this demand for a new religion, whether irrational or scientific. We should not be unduly impressed by the fact that the philosophy of religion is often written by men who, having renounced the orthodox Christianity or Judaism taught in their homes or schools, have found their own fulfilment through work as university teachers. A university teacher is encouraged by his whole environment to keep an open mind and to regard a reasonable discussion of a well-put question as the chief end of man. We need not belittle the value of such intel lectual activities if we observe that the atmosphere of the study or lecture-room is rarified. Most people living outside universities believe that, in order to live effectively, they have to make up their

[1] *The Humanist Frame*, p. 43.
[2] See below, pp. 237-243.

minds about what are the values (or gods) they will serve—and almost always they make up their minds by agreeing on these points with their group or class or church or nation, often without giving the matter a great deal of thought. In one sense, it might be right to define secularisation as the replacement of an old religion by a new one in the allegiance of the millions. At any rate, it is clear that many of the secularised people of our time do *not* feel "not secular enough"; for they want a quasi-religious substitute for the "dead" God.

Yet there is a real danger in speaking about Huxley's evolutionism (or Stalin's Communism or any other secular creed) as a "religion"— and that is, the danger of tempting believers in the old religions to minimise the threat offered by the new belief to the old. At most a secular creed is, in Paul Tillich's phrase, a "quasi-religion". We cannot call it simply a "religion" unless we are to agree on a definition of religion which represents a clean break with the past. When a humanist such as Sir Julian Huxley witnesses to the importance, indeed to the necessity, of religion in history and in the future, he is of course resolute to avoid any endorsement of what has been the heart of religion: "belief in God or a future state". He writes, clearly enough: "Religious experiences such as those of communion with some higher reality, or inspiration from outside the personality, or a sense of transcendent power or glory, or sudden conversion, or apparently supernormal beauty or ineffable sacredness, or the healing power of prayer, or repentant adoration, or, above all, the deep sense of inner peace and assurance in spite of disorder and suffering, can no longer be interpreted in the traditional terms of communication with a personal God or with a supernatural realm of being ... They are the outcome of human minds in their strange commerce with outer reality and in the still stranger and often unconscious internal struggle between their components."[1]

Many nowadays share this sympathetic scepticism towards the claims of supernatural religion to be true. In the heyday of rationalism, it was fashionable to reduce religion to "nothing but" a pre-scientific attempt to cope with nature, or to "nothing but" a social discipline, or to "nothing but" repressed sex. Today that crudely secularist reductionism still lingers on in some quarters. It is aided to some extent by the fervour with which theologians still tend to denounce those varieties of religion to which they owe no allegiance. Karl Barth, in particular, has claimed that God's Word comes as "the abolition of religion" as he defines "religion", and Bonhoeffer's

[1] *The Humanist Frame*, p. 45.

speculation that the day of *homo religiosus* might be over had some of its roots in this Barthian polemic.) But many who have pondered the significance of religion in history and in human nature today seem to be agreed that both the rationalists and the theologians were wrong in their contempt for the phenomenon of religion, which is in truth central to the whole story of *homo sapiens*. Religion has roots in nature, in society and in sex, but it is concerned primarily with the attempt to pierce the mystery which surrounds man and which conceals his destiny from him. It should not be reduced to one simple element and then dismissed as illusory apart from that element; it should be taken much more seriously. Indeed, it is widely agreed that religion is to a certain extent self-authenticating. Many millions of lives, producing many millions of words of recorded testimony, have borne witness that through religion men experience a power which produces not only righteousness but also love, joy and peace. F. H. Bradley, a philosopher who was superior enough to the "appearances of the Absolute" which are honoured in popular religion, once remarked that the man who asks for a reality more solid than that given in religious experience does not know what he is seeking.[1]

But what *is* "the Absolute" which we experience in religion? A common attitude among the thoughtful in our time combines with a seriousness in appreciating the psychological reality of religious experience a scepticism, greater or less, about the extent to which the power or "Absolute" experienced is really supernatural, really absolute. At least, it is agreed that if some part of the power experienced in religion extends beyond nature, the existence of that transcendent power is a matter not of direct experience but of what William James called "over-belief". At the very end of his widely influential *The Varieties of Religious Experience* (London, 1902), a book based on Gifford Lectures which set for our century a new standard of sympathetic seriousness in religious studies, James said: "The idea power with which we find ourselves in connection, the 'God' of ordinary men, is . . . assumed as a matter of course to be 'one and only' and to be 'infinite' . . . Nevertheless in the interests of intellectual clearness, I feel bound to say that religious experience, as we have studied it, cannot be cited as unequivocally supporting the infinitist belief. The only thing that it unequivocally testifies to is that we can experience union with *something* larger than ourselves and in that unity find our greatest peace." If the tendency grows to separate the experience of this "something" from the "infinitist" belief in the

[1] *Appearance and Reality* (Oxford, 1893), p. 449.

eternal God, then the future of traditional religion is plainly dubious. In a brilliant essay of 1897 James described the "will to believe", but it may be doubted whether modern men are likely to wish to believe in this "something" which is vaguely "larger". The God of traditional religion—at least among Jews, Christians, Muslims and many Hindus and Buddhists—was certainly more than the "Absolute" of the metaphysical philosophers, for he had a personal character and will; but he was also more than the "something" of the mystical consensus, for religious believers found their peace in his infinite power. William James was primarily a psychologist, not a propagandist, but the belief in "something" which he advocated with great modesty and courtesy may not be far removed from Sir Julian Huxley's more brutal dismissal of the "dead" God in favour of a new, secular "religion". It can be said about William James (as Heine said about Kant) that he brought the sacraments to a dying God.[1]

The lack of truth in the old, supernatural religion arouses in some twentieth-century people *The Tragic Sense of Life*—to use the title of Miguel de Unamuno's great book of 1912.[2] Man's heart, Unamuno declared, craves God and immortality, but his intellect is sceptical. Unamuno's solution is that "the man of flesh and bone" should so live that if, after all, it is annihilation that finally awaits him, that will be an injustice. "What, then, is the new mission of Don Quixote, today, in this world? To cry aloud, to cry aloud in the wilderness." This is the quasi-religious philosophy of "as if", and it is a recurrent theme in the thought of our time. Whatever our doubts, we should behave *as if* supernatural religion were true. But Freud remembered a child of his who turned away in disdain from fairy stories, and he commented: "We may expect that people will soon behave in a similar way towards the fairy tales of religion, despite the advocacy of 'as if'."[3] Many thinkers less involved than Unamuno was in the religious craving have agreed with Albert Camus that it is necessary to think clearly and not to hope. They have drawn a sadly clear distinction between the truth of traditional religion's diagnosis of human need, its mapping of the wilderness of life, and the falsity of its offer to meet that need and to make the wilderness blossom. Such

---

[1] In the last chapter of his *A Pluralistic Universe* (London, 1909), James more clearly stated belief in a God who is "finite, either in power or in knowledge, or in both at once", as the "line of least resistance" for philosophers, adding: "These, I need hardly tell you, are the terms in which active men have usually carried on their commerce with God" (p. 311).
[2] Eng. trans., London, 1921. See José Ferrater Mora, *Unamuno: A Philosophy of Tragedy* (Berkeley, 1962).
[3] *The Future of an Illusion* (1927; revd. Eng. trans., London, 1962), p. 25.

sad sceptics believe it to be wrong, however tempting, to embrace an illusion for the sake of its comfort. They believe it to be better to die on one's feet than to live on one's knees. Their one hope is that much of the passion of religion may be rescued from the "death" of God and applied to our earthly life, understood on an openly atheistic basis. Instead of petitioning the supernatural, religion in their view should inspire and consecrate human effort in this difficult and tragic world. So they seek a quasi-religion of humanity—not a tawdry glorification of Superman, but a quasi-religion for the time when the "death" of God has really sunk into men's minds, a quasi-religion to give men some guidance and comfort as they enjoy a short day of frost and sun during the winter.

No writer in our time has expressed this attitude more powerfully than Bertrand Russell. He has shown a profoundly mystical or quasi-religious feeling for life. The first volume of his *Autobiography* (London, 1967) made that clear, if it was ever obscure. The integrity of his devotion to truth shines through his self-revelation; and Russell is like another mathematical genius, Blaise Pascal, for it is the truth about man that concerns him most. He has plainly been moved to his depths by the finitude of man, by the mystery of man's brief existence in this universe, and by man's self-inflicted miseries. When Russell tells us of his compassion for humanity he clearly speaks the truth, and he has further demonstrated that he does so by his passionate involvement in so many protests against injustice and war, against the subjection of women and against a woodenly unimaginative educational system. Here may have been the makings of our century's greatest religious leader. The unhappiness which he has caused to others, specially to women, in the private life which he reveals so candidly, and the vanity and folly of many of his interventions in political or educational debates, should not be allowed to outweigh these signs of a great, quasi-religious prophet. But rightly or wrongly Bertrand Russell has allowed his youthful agnosticism and contempt for institutional religion to stay as the verdict of his maturity. He has remained happily ignorant of most current movements in religion and theology.[1] Religion has seemed to him to be rightly concerned about the mysteries and miseries of our existence, but the falsity of the claims of all existing religions to supply information about the real world has seemed so obvious that it has not seemed worth a thinker's time to enquire more deeply into the mystery.

[1] As may be seen from the collection of essays called *Why I am Not a Christian* (London, 1957).

What will be the end of a secularism such as Russell's? In his "Church Going"[1] the English poet, Philip Larkin, wondered

> When churches fall completely out of use
> What we shall turn them into . . .

For

> . . . superstition, like belief, must die
> And what remains when disbelief has gone?
> Grass, weedy pavements, brambles, buttress, sky,
> A shape less recognisable every week,
> A purpose more obscure.

Yet a church does mean something to this secularised humanist:

> A serious house on serious earth it is,
> In whose blent air all our compulsions meet,
> Are recognised, and robed as destinies.
> And that much never can be obsolete,
> Since someone will forever be surprising
> A hunger in himself to be more serious . . .

The probability is, however, that if secularisation completely empties the churches of worshippers—we think of many of the great churches of Soviet Russia, or of the Byzantine Hagia Sophia which is now a museum in the half-Muslim, half-secular city of Istanbul—men will choose other places in which to be "serious" about their "compulsions" and "destinies", in quasi-religions uncontaminated by the supernatural ideas of the traditional religions. The English novelist, Kingsley Amis, has told us that the Russian poet, Yevgeny Yevtushenko, once asked him whether he was an atheist. "Well, yes," was the reply, "but it's more that I hate him." Yevtushenko seemed to understand what still troubled Amis about the death of God in England, but he himself voiced the more thoroughly secular side of life in the Soviet Union. The Russian poet and the English novelist were conversing in King's College Chapel, Cambridge, and Amis tells us how in that great church Yevtushenko at this point delivered himself of a comprehensive verdict on the history of religion, after a friendly grin. " 'Me,' he said, pointing to himself, then gesturing more vaguely towards the roof, the other people there, the Rubens, but also seeming to include the being I had just mentioned, 'me . . . means nothing'."[2]

[1] In *The Less Deceived* (1955).
[2] Quoted by Martin Jarrett-Kerr in his useful study of the contemporary mood, *The Secular Promise* (London, 1964), p. 48.

To sum up: the "coming of age" of mankind, the sense that man i
"on his own now", may be seen from a religious angle in two way:
First, it is the sense, so widespread in our time, that men can do wha
previously was impossible; *men can celebrate the power and responsibilit*
of adulthood. Second, it is the sense, so noticeable in the smalle
company of the sensitive, that men have to reconcile themselves witl
the fact that, because they cannot do everything, everything will no
be done; *men must accept tragedy maturely.*

So the debate about the validity of religion in the modern worl
continues. It is a wider debate, and in places a deeper debate, tha
the nineteenth century or any previous century knew. At least w
must say that the debate aroused by a secularism which is so cocksur
sometimes, so poignant sometimes, has created a massive sense c
uncertainty among religious believers. Will the future of religion li
in a humanism which will replace belief in a supernatural realm
Will the religion of tomorrow worship evolution or "somethin
larger" which is not God? Or can belief in, and worship of, the On
who is eternal and divine survive the "coming of age" of mankind–
and even benefit from it? Has belief in God a stature sufficient t
exceed the height of man's new powers, and a truth able to commen
itself to the full exercise of man's free intelligence? Can belief in Go
flourish not at the frontiers of man's dominion and in the gaps of hi
knowledge, but at the very centre of his strength? Can its psycholog
be the psychology of maturity? Whatever answers it gives to sucl
questions, religion over all the modern world is compelled to respon
to the challenge of secularisation, which brings the impact of man'
"coming of age".

One World

The second main feature which is new in the contemporar
world, viewed from the angle of the student of religion, is i
unification.

When the twentieth century dawned, railways and steamships ha
only begun the conquest of distance; and, reflecting the grea
difficulties in secular communications, the age-old isolation of on
religious tradition from another still prevailed to a large exten
Most of the tribes of Africa performed their ancestral rites. The masse
of India were largely undisturbed in their Hinduism. China, a
empire older than Rome, knew some excitements, but was in it
depths stagnant. Buddhism, which seeks serenity, to a large exten

knew it in "the unchanging East". Islam was fundamentally one society, with one Prophet and one Law from the Atlantic to Indonesia and just as the Chinese traditionally distinguished between their "Middle Kingdom" and the foreign barbarians, so the Muslims divided mankind into *dar-al-Islam* (the Household of Submission) and *dar-al-harb* (the Household of War). There were millions of Jews in Eastern Europe, and some elsewhere, who despite persecution and temptation were proudly loyal to a timeless orthodoxy; they were the People of the God of Abraham, Isaac and Jacob.

Christianity was troubled by the alienation of many among the intellectuals and in the industrial cities, but few whose background was Christian doubted the superiority of their civilisation in Europe and America over all others. Many, perhaps most, Christians believed as late as 1900 in "salvation" through the Church alone, or in "justification" through faith alone, with the consequence that many, perhaps all, non-Christians would be punished everlastingly in hell. Moreover, the three main branches of the Christian Church were scarcely in communication with their critics or with each other. The Eastern Orthodox Churches maintained their hierarchies and recited their liturgies with a complacent traditionalism. The Roman Catholic Church was defiantly conservative. In the remarkably effective Papal thunder against French "modernist" theology in 1907-10 may be heard an echo of Pius IX's solemn denunciation of the error that "the Roman Pontiff can, and ought to, reconcile himself and come to terms with progress, liberalism and modern civilisation" (1864). Among Protestants, complacency took a different form. A more positive emphasis was placed on modern progress, but this was seen as "building the Kingdom of God". German Protestantism seemed to dominate the intellectual and cultural centre of the world; the American Churches were abounding with energy; the last of Britain's religious revivals swept Wales in 1904-5; and at this height of the British Empire an Archbishop of Canterbury, E. W. Benson, had recently declared that the Church of England was "charged with the world's Christianity". Among Protestant students a movement arose which would send from the colleges many thousands of missionaries pledged to "the evangelization of the world in this generation" (to quote the watchword popularised by John R. Mott, an American Methodist who applied the energy of the YMCA to all the problems of churches and nations). Here was a movement which was more globally minded than any previous movement in religious history, but the World Missionary Conference in Edinburgh in 1910

demonstrated that the missionaries under Mott were not daunted by
the variety to be found in the world. They were resolved to give to
the world the benefit of their superior culture as well as of the final
religion. In the very passage of their Conference Report in which they
pleaded for sympathy with non-Christian religions, they declared:
"all these religions without exception disclose elemental needs of the
human soul which Christianity alone can satisfy". And in this
Edinburgh conference on the world mission of Christianity, only
seventeen non-westerners sat among the 1,200 delegates.

Today we see the religions plunged into the ferment of a revolutionary world.[1] Nowhere has the change been more conspicuous than
in the recession of Christian missionary fervour. The survey by
American laymen published in 1932 under the title *Rethinking
Missions* rested on convictions that the heathen were not going to
hell, and that Christians must learn to talk with them in a common
search for truth. The chairman of that group was Professor W. E.
Hocking, whose personal statement on *Living Religions and a World
Faith* (New York, 1940) was to argue that "Christianity is not yet
ready to serve as a world religion" and that "our present Christianity
does not include all that other religions have". "It is right, and indeed
necessary, for the good of men, that the non-Christian religions should
hold to their own, at least until they find themselves in fact understood, translated, and included in the growing power of a religion
which, in achieving its own potentiality, achieves theirs also."[2] Paul
Tillich's *Christianity and the Encounter of the World's Religions* (New York,
1963) shows one of the greatest theologians of the century saying
openly that the aim of the Christian approach must now be conversation, not conversion.

A dialogue between the religions is slowly beginning, and the
fundamental cause of this new flexibility has been the common
exposure of the religions to the challenge of secularisation. Is this
challenge to be welcomed, so that all religions must be reshaped to
serve a new age? Or is the challenge of the secular world to arouse
a firmly negative reply, so that all religions must ally in the defence
of God or of spiritual values? Or if our revolutionary world is more
complex in its significance for the different religions, should we at
least welcome the highly dramatic increases in communications, so

[1] A comprehensive summary of the nineteenth and twentieth centuries, with bibliog
raphies, was offered by K. S. Latourette, *Christianity in a Revolutionary Age*, 4 vols. (New
York, 1951-62). Some literature about the other religions will be mentioned in the course
of this book.
[2] See p. 262.

that the religions can learn from one another? Such questions have been asked by many in our time. The comparison of religions has been developed as a science, and broadcasts or books have familiarised millions with at least the outlines of other creeds. "Dialogue in a plural world" has begun to be a *cliché*, at least among the sophisticated. Religions, like political creeds, learn to make the best of coexistence.

Although this encounter of the world's religions has scarcely begun to influence the actual beliefs and customs of the masses, we can see more clearly the effect of the revolution in communications, and of the wider challenge of our time, in the simpler process of unifying each religion internally. In part, this process may be seen by studying the great religious conferences of the twentieth century. The Buddhist Congress in Rangoon, 1954-6, which was only the sixth in Buddhism's history, and which celebrated the 2,500th anniversary of the Buddha's entry into Nirvana, was by no means exceptional in its desire to unite all the adherents of a faith. Hinduism, Islam and Judaism have produced similar movements—most easily on the basis of charitable or political co-operation. Christianity, the most sharply divided religion in history, has now put its extraordinary energies into the cause of reconciliation. The ecumenical movement around the World Council of Churches, constituted in 1948, has involved Protestants, Orthodox and Anglicans in a strenuous process of reunion and renewal. The Second Vatican Council of 1962-5 showed against all previous expectation that the Roman Catholic Church was willing to participate in this new pilgrimage—even if as yet largely in its own way and in loyalty to its own doctrines. But more influential still in destroying the old isolationism of the religions, and of the denominations within them, has been the less organised movement of study, thought and discussion fed by education, broadcasting and writing. Many millions of individuals have attempted to relate their inherited scriptures and religious traditions to the scientific outlook and to life in a modern nation. The great religious conferences are thus part of a much wider ferment of religious thought, responding to the secular challenge of the twentieth century.

Our mention of the revolution in communications has more significance than is exhausted by saying that delegates can now travel to international, interdenominational and interfaith meetings, while books reflecting these encounters can now be printed for distribution throughout the world. The real point is that all peoples of the world

are now being drawn into a single stream of history.[1] The age of the
jet, succeeding to the age of the steamship, symbolises the Western
isation of the world, and the long-term trend to the West is no
effectively halted when (in religion as in politics and economics
African, Asian or Latin American pride flings the arrogance o
colonialism back in the West's teeth. By its own action or by arousin
reaction, it is the West that sets the pace. Admittedly, East and Wes
have not yet finally settled their accounts. Later chapters in this boo
will mention some aspects of the challenge or offer in the spiritual lif
now being made to the West by Africa and Asia. But the Westernisa
tion of the world is a great and growing fact. Even at this stage of th
transition we can already study much in this world-wide debate abou
religion if we approach it as an almost infinitely varied series o
reactions to the "coming of age" experienced by Western man in h
scientific civilisation. Thus a treatment of the religions of the worl
does not make itself nonsensical, however inadequate it may be, if :
concentrates on Christianity's own response to the scientific revolu
tion which arose in a Europe which had been Christendom. If th
impact of the secularisation brought about by Western science an
technology is to result in a universal secularism, in "no religion a
all", it will be thanks mainly to Christianity's defeat in the West. An
if a mature religion is recognised to be possible in the modern worlc
this place for belief may result from a conviction in the West that th
essence of Christianity is credible by rational adults, more than fror
any other factor.

But perhaps we should try to avoid comparing the *religions* as such
In a discussion of *The Meaning and End of Religion* (New York, 1964
Professor Cantwell Smith of Harvard, who is one of the world
leading experts in the comparison of religions, pleaded that the wor
"religion" should now be used as little as possible, because it is a
idea which inclines men to attack or defend a set of other idea
associated with "religion". Professor Cantwell Smith does indee
show that "religion" in its modern sense is a product of the moder
West. Other civilisations have had no exactly equivalent word i
their languages: Ancient India did not, and Ancient Israel did no
The Latin *religio* did not have the full meaning of the moder
"religion", although it is the origin of our word. Many of the nam

---

[1] I take this opportunity of acknowledging my indebtedness to two books on this then
by Dr. Lesslie Newbigin, a leader of the World Council of Churches who is now Bishop
Madras: *A Faith for This One World?* (London, 1961) and *Honest Religion for Secular M*
(London, 1966); and to two books by a Roman Catholic scholar who is now Professor
Eastern Religions and Ethics at Oxford: R. C. Zaehner, *The Convergent Spirit* (New Yor
1963) and *The Catholic Church and the World Religions* (London, 1964).

of the "other religions"—Buddhism, Hinduism, etc.—were developed by Westerners in the nineteenth century. We may add that it has been in dialogue with the West during the twentieth century that these "other religions" have become more self-conscious and articulate than they were before the impact of the West. Muslim apologists commonly write with an eye on attacks by Christian missionaries and by Westernising secularists; world-wide Buddhism's first creed was written in 1945 by a convert who is an English judge, Christmas Humphreys;[1] and Hinduism has simplified its theology in order to reply to Christians in India, and in order to counter-attack through its own missions in the West. The idea of "religion" has encouraged Christians themselves to defend "Christianity" (and has encouraged secularists to attack it), although the Bible knows no such abstractions, preferring to speak about the whole of life being given direction through a covenant between God and man, or through a way of discipleship by which men can know and obey God. Professor Cantwell Smith validly points out that this alleged necessity to attack or defend a whole religion such as "Christianity" frequently distorts our understanding of real life, and hinders us from learning from each other as we share our visions of the mystery of man's place in the universe.

"It is what the Hindu is able to see, by being a Hindu, that is significant," he writes. "And we may be sure that, as he looks around him, he does not see 'Hinduism'. Like the rest of us, he sees his wife's death, his child's minor and major aspirations, his moneylender's mercilessness, the calm of a starlit evening, his own mortality. He sees these things through coloured glasses, if one will, of a 'Hindu' brand. He sees also certain gods and institutions that may carry this label, though the deeper and more sophisticated his faith, the more he sees through these. His neighbour, also a Hindu, sees the foreground differently; if their vision finally converges, it is because both have been sufficiently penetrating to see through and beyond their foreground to a reality that, if not altogether attributeless, is certainly quite without the attribute of being in any sense *Hindu*."[2]

This is the approach which more and more people are coming to see is needed if man is to make religious progress in the period into which he is now moving. It is unrealistic to expect Christian missions, for example, to convert or even to "evangelise" in the world if their

[1] For the "Twelve Principles", see Christmas Humphreys, *Buddhism* (London, 1951; revd. edn., 1962), pp. 73-6.
[2] *The Meaning and End of Religion*, p. 127. See also his *Questions of Religious Truth* (New York, 1967).

emphasis is on the propagation of all the institutions and intellectual expressions of present-day Christianity. The only realistic hope for Christians is that, partly through the contribution of missionaries but mainly through larger forces which have no "Christian" label, the essential vision of man and of God taught by what Jesus has been, said and done will be accepted by more and more of those who are now—and who will always in some sense remain—Hindus, Buddhists, Muslims, etc. This development is unlikely unless those who are now Christians strengthen their own grasp of that vision, if need be letting go many of the outworn traditions of Christianity. This "reconception" of the religions (to use W. E. Hocking's phrase) through the testing of abstractions by realities is a development which may be heard as the music of the future.

However, the future is not the present, and the world is not yet one. It is premature to ask men to forget about "religion" or "the religions" at a stage when (as we have already noted) it is precisely the challenge of the new secular pressures that makes some of them more sharply aware of the questions raised for them personally by the religious tradition of an area. At present, the single stream of history into which the peoples of the world are being drawn is a single stream of questions, not of answers; and what unites the peoples is their common experience that their own societies are breaking up. What exists now is a supply of differently coloured spectacles through which the reality of God and the world may be viewed. Whether or not we regret this, what actually exists now is a plurality of religions. This has its parallel in the political sphere, where a world order including a world police force and some degree of world government is so clearly the long-term necessity, yet what exists now is a plurality of national states. To ask the religions to lose their self-consciousness in the face of secularisation is like asking the peoples to abandon their nationalisms while their pride still seems under challenge. The energy of what remains of the twentieth century will be absorbed by the relationships of the religions (and of the nations) to each other and to the pressure of the emerging future (spiritual and social). And in the religious as in the political sphere, it tests all of a commentator's intelligence to discern one pattern of response to these challenges in the separated parts of our world.

CHAPTER TWO

The Social Impact of the Secular Century

The Social Character of Religion

Before religion is thought of as a creed, it is offered as a prayer; and before it is offered as a prayer, it is experienced as a community. *Religio*, as the most probable interpretation of the Latin word suggests, is what "binds" a group. *Religare* in Latin means "to bind" (although some scholars dispute whether *religio* comes from *religare*).

It is necessary to set religion (and also irreligion) in this social context because believers (or unbelievers) sometimes suppose or pretend that their acceptance (or rejection) of religious belief was produced solely by personal meditation on the true, the beautiful and the good. An individual may indeed accept (or reject) his religious tradition in an intimately personal way—in extreme cases, in a mystical vision which leaves him confident that he knows the character of ultimate reality. But the individual is likely to reach a conclusion, or to receive a vision, which is directly related to the tradition of his community and to the whole pattern of his life. Within this century a number of Roman Catholics have claimed that the glory of heaven has been revealed to them, notably in the visions which three children saw of the Virgin Mary at Fatima in Portugal in 1917. We need not cast doubt on the sincerity of these visionaries, if we observe that the content of the visions and of the accompanying messages from heaven has corresponded with the expectations of the Church to whose members they occurred—or if we add that many non-Christians have received visions of the divine. Ramakrishna, for example, who died in 1886, and who is usually reckoned the greatest mystic of modern India, repeatedly entered *samadhi* (the bliss of enlightenment). In these trances he saw and talked with his "Mother". But his "Mother" was the goddess Kali, who is usually imagined amid blood and skulls; she is the goddess of destruction, and must be worshipped as such (in the old days, by human sacrifice) before she will give the blessing of new life.[1]

[1] See Christopher Isherwood, *Ramakrishna and his Disciples* (New York, 1964). Such a

How are we to understand the connections and contrasts between the visions at Fatima and the visions of Ramakrishna? Many of the psychological experiences and effects of mysticism seem to be closely similar in Portugal and India. Nor need we confine our study to the stranger experiences of the acknowledged saints. Similar, although less dramatic, moments of vision are known by many religious believers—and by many others also. Mystical, or at least ecstatic, experiences have been reported by pantheists who worship nature, or who call nature God—and by atheists who remain atheists, and for whom mysticism may feed Sir Julian Huxley's secular "religion" of humanism.[1] We are confronted here by *a basic religious sense* which seems to be innate in all (or almost all) people, whatever their theologies. This sense should not be reduced to an "essence" consisting of morality (as the high-minded eighteenth-century Enlightenment maintained), or the herd-instinct or sex (as in the more cynical atheism of our own century). This religious sense seems to be the raw material both of believing religion and of the reverent unbelief which has been called "religious atheism"; and if it is totally lacking—if an individual feels that in no sense does he belong in the world around him—then suicide may come. We may add that the connections between the religions at this level of man's basic religious sense are usually accepted by the religions themselves. Thus the children of Fatima, had they known about Ramakrishna, would have been good Catholics if they had commented that Kali, if she was not an appearance of Satan, was an appearance of the Virgin distorted by Ramakrishna's heathen ignorance; and Ramakrishna, had he lived to hear about Fatima, would have displayed the Hindu respect for all the images under which the divine One appears or is conceived. And not all atheistic humanists would wish the Catholic visionaries or the Hindu saint to be certified as insane; they would respect the mystics' moments of human glory, amid the sad state of the economy in Portugal and India.[2]

But we shall not get very far in our assessment of religion if we confine ourselves to this basic agreement and exchange of compliments. The mystical ecstasies by themselves, stripped of all more

---

presentation of Eastern spirituality may be compared with the discussion of Catholic European marvels in, e.g., Herbert Thurston, *The Physical Phenomena of Mysticism* (London 1952).

[1] In *Ecstasy* (London, 1961) an atheist, Marghanita Laski, collected memories of such experiences from many of her friends.

[2] One of the most confidently brash of the reductionists was James H. Leuba, *The Psychology of Religious Mysticism* (New York, 1926). For a more generous assessment, see W. T. Stace, *Mysticism and Philosophy* (New York, 1960).

contentious interpretations, seem to suggest no more than that the mind of man is related to the universe and can experience the universe intensely. Insanity or drug-taking can produce similar feelings.[1] Any further interpretation immediately plunges us into disputes, for any further interpretation involves a very substantial and controversial element of choice or faith. It is important to remember this universal testimony of the mystics to "something larger than ourselves" when we study the critics of religion, but it is also important to consider whether we may legitimately go beyond such a banal conclusion and say more about the significance of religious experience. "Mysticism," Bertrand Russell once wrote, "is in its essence little more than a certain intensity and depth of feeling in regard to what is believed about the universe";[2] but many people want to insist that the phenomenon of religious experience in its total context should not be analysed *only* as insanity or drug-taking is analysed, for they attach great significance to what they believe about the universe. The trouble is that people's beliefs are so varied that, as we have already noted, if we are to be realistic we have to speak not about man's *religion* but about the world's many religions and quasi-religions. The veneration of the Virgin Mary, and the worship of Kali, and Sir Julian Huxley's quasi-religion of evolution are (to put it mildly) different—for they arise not from the mystic experience themselves, but from the interpretations given to these experiences by the faiths of complex human beings.[3]

Thus both the basically similar experiences and the different interpretations, both the ecstasies and the churches, both religion and the religions, should be given due weight in our assessment. On the one hand religious believers, and even religiously-minded atheists, do experience visions or ecstasies which are extremely hard to define or assess—and which it is unscientific to deny. Any student who acknowledges this fact must find much of the origin of religion at that fundamental level, in man's basic religious sense. On the other hand, the individual involved is not likely to be content with a vague feeling that he "belongs" or that he is in touch with "something

[1] See R. C. Zaehner, *Mysticism, Sacred and Profane* (Oxford, 1957).
[2] *Mysticism and Logic* (London, 1917), p. 3.
[3] Articles in which he has already indicated his line of thought suggest that Professor Ninian Smart's forthcoming book on *The Religious Experience of Mankind* will be a useful assessment. At present (1968) the books which may be recommended on the phenomenon of religion as a whole have the disadvantage of resembling catalogues, although they are comprehensive, learned and sympathetic: Gerardus van der Leeuw, *Religion in Essence and Manifestation* (1935; Eng. trans., London, 1938), and Joachim Wach, *Sociology of Religion* (Chicago 1944; British edn., London, 1947).

larger". He tries to interpret his experience more fully to himself and to others. And here is the point: when a person makes this attempt, when he undertakes one more crack at the riddle of the universe, *he does so almost entirely within the context provided by his community.* Catholicism suggests an interpretation in the shape of the Blessed Virgin; Hinduism suggests an interpretation in the shape of another Mother; modern secularism suggests a psychological explanation such as Sir Julian Huxley's (and perhaps the gentle charm of Harvard University suggests a religious moderation such as that of William James). The spectacles with which a religious believer (or an atheist) views reality are usually spectacles provided by his society.

This understanding of religion (and irreligion) as *an experience interpreted by the faith of a society* has come to be fairly widely shared by thoughtful people—with consequences which have not only influenced the academic study of religion, but which have also affected the position of the living religions in the modern world. On the one hand, the recognition of the reality of the mysticism behind religion has checked the confident dogmas of rationalism. It is now commonly acknowledged that a secularist who attempts to reduce religious experience to "nothing but" this, that or the next "essence" which can be fitted into his reasoning is not able to abolish the fundamental fact of man's religious sense—or the "ecstatic reason" as Paul Tillich called it—but is simply offering one debatable interpretation of it, since any assessment of this strange and ambiguous phenomenon in the experience of mankind will be an interpretation linked with the observer's total response to the mystery of life. On the other hand, the recognition of what might be called the sociology of mysticism provides part of our century's challenge to religious belief, for nowadays only the naïve are willing to accept religious visions at their face values, without considering the total situation of the mystic.

Of course, the social context of a mystical vision or religious crisis is an extreme case to show the importance of a study of society in religious studies. A far more typical case would be provided by an individual whose religious convictions were never fortified or displaced by a dramatic crisis but either matured gradually or vanished gradually. An immense amount of work has been done in this century to observe, classify and interpret religious behaviour with a scientific attempt at objectivity. Some of this work has been flavoured with hostility towards religion; such "positivist" hostility, we may add, has marked "sociology" as a self-consciously secular discipline ever since Auguste Comte, who invented the word in the nineteenth century. But some sociologists have been more sympathetic with the phenomena which they were examining, more modest about their competence to judge the truth of the beliefs involved, and thus better qualified to penetrate into the life of religion.[1]

What is clear from these studies (and, of course, from personal observation also) is that in every case the community—the home, the school, the adult world or the religious group itself—deeply influences the individual's religion. The influence may be conveyed through formal instruction, through public or domestic ceremonies, through private conversations in families or among friends, or through behaviour which has little or no explicitly religious content. Religion is normally caught like a children's epidemic, in the tender years. It is often brought to a crisis by a conversion in adolescence, related to the crisis of sexual growth—but this religious decision is usually related closely to the experiences of childhood, and is taken at any age when the adolescent who gives his allegiance to a religion is not qualified to vote for a politician. When questioned in maturity, religious believers tend to base their answers on the faith of their fathers. They take their stand within a tradition. A Muslim, for example, is likely to intend to be loyal to Islam, however careless he may be in discharging the obligations of his religion, for the religion of Islam represents an important part of his heritage, and probably constitutes an important element in his identification of himself. Without this religion, he would feel cut off from his roots. Strongly as reformers in every generation regret this, it is inevitable that religion, where it flourishes, is usually conservative; for religion is usually associated with sentiments of gratitude to parents and teachers and with affection for the sights and sounds of childhood. If religious influences have been weak in childhood, or if the religion of child-hood seems to have been defeated by stronger social forces, the

[1] For the background, see Peter Berger, *Invitation to Sociology* (New York, 1963; Pelican Books edn., London, 1966), and *The Sacred Canopy: Elements of a Sociological Theory of Religion* (New York, 1967). Two books by Roman Catholic priests offer convenient summaries of the most advanced investigation and discussion, which have been French: Fernand Boulard, *An Introduction to Religious Sociology* (1954; Eng. trans., London, 1960) and Hervé Carrier, *The Sociology of Religious Belonging* (1961; Eng. trans., New York, 1965). The most lively American introductions are Will Herberg, *Protestant, Catholic, Jew* (New York, 1955; revd. edn., 1960), which analyses the contemporary scene, and the more academic J. M. Yinger, *Religion, Society and the Individual* (New York, 1957), which combines a systematic treatise with selected readings from other authorities. For England, see Michael Argyle, *Religious Behaviour* (London, 1958), and David Martin, *A Sociology of English Religion*. Books of a similar quality on the non-Christian religions are needed. A beginning was made in Max Weber's essays, specially in those translated as *The Sociology of Religion* (1922; Eng. trans., Boston, 1963), and followed up in, e.g., the papers by Cambridge anthropologists collected as *Dialectic in Practical Religion*, ed. E. R. Leach (Cambridge, 1968).

acceptance of a religion is usually bound up with the desire of the adult to improve himself and to become a respectable member of a society which has a religious tradition accumulated over the centuries. If an individual is in revolt against his society, or against life in general, but adheres to a religious sect, one explanation can be that the individual has found his identity within the fellowship of that sect. He can now voice his protest through the sect's disapproval of society. A religious conversion, whatever else it may be, almost always includes the individual's acceptance of a social role proposed by a religious group.

The habits of irreligion in a society also deserve to be analysed sociologically. If a Muslim rejects the faith of his fathers, it is likely to be because of the attraction of the secular West through education and technology, not because of deep studies in philosophy or in "comparative religion". If a Frenchman is contemptuous of priests and churches, it is likely to be because his *milieu* is traditionally anti-clerical; for a map can be drawn of religious as of political electorates. Unbelief can be as irrational as any religious faith, because its social and psychological roots go just as deep; and, like a popular religious movement, atheism can be spread by a fashion.[1]

Both the power of religion and its eclipse therefore need to be studied in the context of the whole life of society. The ideas and the society need to be taken together. In passing we may observe that far too many theologians seem remote from the real world when they state their reasons why their particular religious theory has appealed or ought to appeal; and many secular humanists talk like shallow rationalists, naïvely over-emphasising the place of reason in human behaviour, as they state their reasons why religion has declined or ought to decline. Some of those theologians who have attempted to mediate between belief and unbelief have perhaps been the most absurdly intellectual of all. Their books sometimes seem to treat the contemporary society as a by-product of European philosophy or fiction, and seem to assume that the religious destinies of peoples hang on the lectures of theologians. Such intellectualist fancies will have to be abandoned if the serious study of religion is to make progress. David Hume once observed that "reason is, and ought to be, the slave of the passions". The famous saying applies with equal strength to religion—and to its rejection. Religion (or its rejection) is a psychological phenomenon which shows with special clarity how

---

[1] For two psychologists' essays in this field which deserves fuller study, see H. C. Runcke, *The Psychology of Unbelief* (1949; Eng. trans., London, 1952), and Ignace Lepp, *Atheism in Our Time* (1961; Eng. trans., New York, 1963).

man, although fundamentally mysterious specially in his basic religious sense, can be analysed with far-reaching success as a creature of circumstance, as a social animal, as the slave of the passions of the group into which he is thrown by the accidents of birth and upbringing. A realistic assessment of religion (or of atheism) must begin where people begin—not with ideas but with emotions, shaped as these have been by everyday experiences and by all the subtle influences of home and school, work and friends. Many definitions of religion have been proposed, but one of the best has been that put forward by the American sociologist, Dr. Gerhard Lenski: "a system of beliefs about the nature of the force(s) ultimately shaping a man's destiny, and the practices associated therewith, shared by the members of a group."[1]

What *are* the forces which ultimately shape our destinies? The sociologist, unfortunately, must himself make an act of belief in a social context if he attempts to answer this philosophical question. Here he is just like the rest of us; for the sociologist does not *know* in a scientific sense. "Sociological theory must, by its own logic, view religion as a human projection, and by the same logic can have nothing to say about the possibility that this projection may refer to something other than the being of the projector. In other words, to say that religion is a human projection does not logically preclude the possibility that the projected meanings may have an ultimate status independent of man."[2] What sociology can show is that the replacement of one religion by another may usually be interpreted as a shift in the psychological forces of society, encouraging a new belief about the ultimate forces of the universe; and sociology can also explain secularisation itself not as a mainly intellectual movement but as the process by which the beliefs and practices of all available religions are rejected by a group because they do not correspond with that group's present vision of its destiny. Religions, or secular substitutes for them, are projections which groups think plausible. A particular religion loses its grip on the hearts and minds of a society by losing its plausibility or its power to symbolise that society's corporate passions. We shall study the key area in modern secularisation, which is Europe in the nineteenth century; but first we may remind ourselves of the previous unification of society through religion. Religious unity may be seen most clearly in the life of primitive peoples, to which we now turn.

[1] *The Religious Factor* (New York, 1961; revd. edn., 1963), p. 331.
[2] Peter Berger, *The Sacred Canopy*, pp. 180-1.

Primitive Religion

Much attention has been given in this century to the study of the role
of religion in primitive societies, but confusion has been caused
because, mixed with the solid research and sober interpretation,
there has been a good deal of fanciful speculation, inspired by one or
more of three motives: (1) the wish to recover the historical origins
of religion, (2) the wish to see the essence of religion in those origins
and (3) the wish to show that religion, having such origins and such
an essence, rests on an illusion. The speculation has been in vain,
because the origins and essence of the religious life of mankind cannot
be recovered by a strictly, scientifically historical method. The
evidence is far too obscure, and its interpretation always demands
the expression of a deeply personal faith or of a deeply personal
unbelief. Religious experience cannot be *proved* to be illusory—any
more than it can be proved to reveal a supernatural reality.

Sir James Frazer's great study of primitive magic and religion may
be mentioned as a mixture of fact and fantasy typical of the brilliantly
speculative generation of the "arm-chair" anthropologists. *The Golden
Bough* assembled from all over the world, including the literature of
Greece and Rome, a mass of evidence about magicians and priests,
the deities of the hunt and the harvest, sacred kings and scapegoats,
sacraments and myths, taboos and festivals, and it brought all these
curious phenomena together in one argument. "We shall perhaps be
disposed to conclude," wrote Frazer at the end of his work, "that the
movement of higher thought, so far as we can trace it, has on the
whole been from magic through religion to science. In magic man
depends on his own strength to meet the difficulties and dangers that
beset him on every side. He believes in a certain established order of
nature on which he can surely count, and which he can manipulate
for his own ends. When he discovers his mistake, he . . . throws himself humbly on the mercy of certain great invisible beings behind the
veil of nature, to which he now ascribes all those far-reaching powers
which he once arrogated to himself. But as time goes on this explanation in its turn proves to be unsatisfactory. For it assumes that the
succession of natural events is not determined by immutable laws . . .
Thus the keener minds . . . revert in a measure to the older stand-
point of magic by postulating explicitly, what in magic had only
been implicitly assumed, to wit, an inflexible regularity in the order
of natural events which, if carefully observed, enables us to foresee
their course with certainty and to act accordingly. In short, religion,

regarded as an explanation of nature, is displaced by science."[1]

That clear distinction between magic, religion and science has now been generally abandoned. It was part of the whole speculative approach. The basic trouble about Frazer's analysis was that he had no personal experience of "savages" but, instead, relied on reading and on introspection to try and understand beliefs which he found very strange, so that he failed to do justice to the mixture of magical manipulation, religious awe and down-to-earth matter-of-factness which later anthropologists have found to be the actual mentality of primitive peoples still surviving. Frazer was too intellectualist in his emphasis on the theories of nature worked out by the "keener minds" —and his intellectualism was dominated by the evolutionism of that age of Darwin.

A more promising approach was made by Emile Durkheim in his very influential discussion of *The Elementary Forms of the Religious Life.*[2] Durkheim, like Frazer, was in religion an unbeliever, and his primary interest in anthropology seems to have been to expose the origins and essence of religion. He maintained that when a primitive group worshipped a god it was really worshipping itself, or at least its own traditional morality or collective conscience; it was building up its solidarity by its religious enthusiasm. He illustrated this theory by reports of the worship of totems by clans among the aborigines of Australia. However, Durkheim was another anthropologist who did no field-research among the primitive people whom he described. Had he done so, he would have discovered that the custom of totem-worship in Australia was not so simple as he thought, and that there was no evidence to show that this particular custom, in itself not very impressively religious, provided an explanation of all religious beliefs and practices. Durkheim's theory *may* be correct, but it cannot be demonstrated scientifically. In fact, the origins of primitive religion cannot be recovered, and any attempt to describe its essence needs to be treated cautiously, for beliefs and practices vary greatly from one group to another, from one period to another, from one individual temperament to another, and from one social situation to another.

It is true to say with Frazer that primitive man wishes to manipulate nature by magical rituals, and it is true to add with Durkheim that "a religion is a unified system of beliefs and practices relative to sacred things, that is to say, things set apart and forbidden—beliefs and practices which unite, into one single moral community called a

[1] *The Golden Bough* (12 vols., London, 1900-15), abridged into one vol. (London, 1922), pp. 711-12.
[2] 1912; Eng. trans., New York, 1915.

Church, all those who adhere to them".[1] But to add that these are the *only* origins of religion, and that all religion rests on the fantasies produced by these attempts of ignorant savages to do scientific and political jobs, so that "the idea of society is the soul of religion",[2] is merely to state one's own philosophy of life. The evidence is equally compatible with another suggestion: namely, that primitive men have responded to a reality which civilised men have also experienced —and to which civilised men have responded in ways not radically different. Both in primitive and in civilised societies, "the idea of society" and "the soul of religion" may be viewed as two ways of establishing a society's total view of the world. This total view of the world comes before both the politics and the religion. "It must be stressed very strongly," writes one of the best of recent sociologists to discuss religion, "that what is being said here does *not* imply a sociologically deterministic theory of religion. It is *not* implied that any particular religious system is nothing but the effect or 'reflection' of social processes. Rather, the point is that the *same* human activity that produces human society also produces religion, with the relation between the two products always being a dialectical one. Thus it is just as possible that, in a particular historical development, a social process is the effect of religious ideation, while in another development the reverse may be the case."[3]

Many of the speculations of the "arm-chair" anthropologists such as Frazer and Durkheim about primitive religion's origins and essence have been held up to deserved ridicule by Professor E. E. Evans-Pritchard—an anthropologist whose own field work provides a model of humble study of the primitive peoples whose superstitious savagery the earlier theorists despised.[4] Through the work of such recent anthropologists a less highly coloured, but also more accurate, picture is emerging. In this picture, the valid part of Durkheim's analysis is preserved: namely, his suggestion that a religion, whatever may be its origins and essence in man's basic religious sense, is usually interpreted in a way which binds a group. Here we offer only a crude outline of current study of primitive religion, as this is relevant to the wider discussion of the role of religion in society.

In primitive religion is to be found not only the fear of the dead— which Frazer regarded as "probably the most powerful force in the

[1] *The Elementary Forms of the Religious Life* (Collier Books edn.), p. 62.
[2] *Ibid.*, p. 466.
[3] Peter Berger, *The Sacred Canopy*, p. 48.
[4] See the essay on "Religion and the Anthropologists" in E. E. Evans-Pritchard, *Essays in Social Anthropology* (London, 1962), and his *Theories of Primitive Religion* (Oxford, 1965).

making of primitive religion"—but often also a glad communion with the dead. The present members of a village or tribe are united with their ancestors in a living fellowship. This communion symbolises and increases both their pride in membership of a society which goes back far into time, and also their ability to draw on the wisdom of the past for guidance in their problems. And it offers them this encouragement, that when they are dead, they will be remembered as they now remember. The inhabitants of a modern industrial city are indeed rootless in comparison. But communion with the past is not the only use of religion to primitive peoples. Regular participation in ceremonies such as dances immensely strengthen the solidarity of the living. Drinks or drugs may be used to intensify the group's experiences in these ceremonies, but the religion matters more in creating the party spirit. All the members of a tribe or a village have their parts to play, as actors or involved spectators, and the profound enjoyment with which they take part has often aroused the envy of their civilised, lonely guests. "Savage religion," in one anthropologist's famous phrase, "is something not so much thought out as danced out."[1]

Primitive religion has the further merit—in the eyes of observers who are most sensitive to their own civilisation's discontents—of putting each stage of the individual's life in a social, and even cosmic, setting. The ruler of the tribe or the village is a legitimate, and indeed sacred, ruler—almost one of the gods from whom he is expected to derive wisdom. The taboos of religion surround and safeguard (usually with hygenic consequences, if not motives) sexual intercourse, pregnancy, birth and weaning. The lore and rites of religion educate and initiate a young person into adult responsibilities. Daily work in the fields or at home is given significance and even holiness because religion provides both teachings about the duties involved, and customs which are vivid reminders of these teachings. Some rituals directly suggest moral duties, and even when what is specifically religious seems to be unrelated to normal conduct, the rituals still have the function of expressing the group's life *as a group*— a life which in every primitive society leads to a more or less elaborate code about what is permitted and what is prohibited. When a tribe fights, its priests assure it that its gods fight with it. When a member of the group falls sick, religious belief either heals or consoles him. A dying person is told by religion where he is going, and religion helps the survivors both to express and to overcome their grief. Religion

[1] R. B. Marett, *The Threshold of Religion* (London, 1909), p. xxi.

performs these services from the cradle to the grave not only by
linking each crisis or duty with the total life of the group, but also by
linking it with the whole of nature. Rocks or trees or other objects
in nature are felt intensely, almost as if they were brothers. For
primitive peoples nature is alive, extending punishment to those who
defy it and friendship to those who live in obedience to its laws.
What human beings do and think matters to the universe; man and
nature are bound in a bundle. Here is one meaning of the stories of
the world's creation, which at first strike a modern critic as mere
legends. In primitive religion, the essential fact is the integration of
man with himself and his environment, and "myth, ritual and ethics
are definitely but three facets of the same essential fact."[1]

The primitive world-view is, paradoxically, more familiar to many
in contemporary Europe and North America than is the rather
similar world-view which was held during most of European history.
This is because anthropological studies of primitive peoples have
been supplemented for our civilisation by a popular fascination with
Africa. When an African leader such as President Senghor of Senegal
speaks about the deep meaning of *négritude*, Western people can
understand something of his emotion, for they seek to share it through
their own enthusiasm for primitive art, and above all for African
music as this has been preserved from the pagan past and given new
life by the (often deeply and actively religious) Negroes of the United
States. Thus the sophisticates of New York turn for spiritual food to
the remnants of African religion at a time when the Negroes themselves are in deep confusion about the motives in their demands for
human rights in the United States—and when in Africa's own cities
the pagan survivals have been almost overwhelmed by the cultural
impact of the West.[2]

The paradox is great, but significant. *The West destroys primitive
religion, but the West believes that it needs primitive religion.* Indeed, Africa,
with its sense of the unity and meaningfulness of life, occupies in the
imagination of the West in our time a status similar to the appeal of
China to the eighteenth century, when by its order, rationality and
elegance the more ancient civilisation fascinated a Europe emerging

[1] Bronislaw Malinowski, *The Foundations of Faith and Morals* (London, 1936), p. 25.
[2] The spiritual history of Africa in the New World has been told by Ruby F. Johnston, *The Development of Negro Religion* (New York, 1954) and *The Religion of Negro Protestants* (New York, 1956). See also Joseph Washington, *Black Religion* (Boston, 1964). A study of Ibadan, Nigeria, was made by Geoffrey Parrinder, *Religion in an African City* (London, 1953). The same author has provided a summary of *African Traditional Religion* (2nd edn., London, 1962). Some recent novels by Africans have illustrated the anxiety produced by the conflict of cultures. See, e.g., Chinua Achebe, *Things Fall Apart* (London, 1958).

from the barbarities of the Wars of Religion. If so, the appeal of Africa is a sign of the West's growing awareness of the disintegration of its own culture, and it may be also a confession that the West seeks not only an injection of primitive vitality but also an initiation into the mysteries of religion.[1] The anthropologist Lucien Lévy-Bruhl used to speak about the *participation mystique* in nature and in society which is provided by primitive religion, and he would add that the need for participation remains more pressing, even in modern societies, than the need for knowledge or for conforming to logical exigencies, for it comes from the depths.[2]

Christendom in Europe

For many Europeans in our time, special study and a scholarly imagination are needed in order to recapture something of the religious pattern which constituted Europe during the Byzantine Empire and during the Middle Ages in the West, although this pattern remained largely intact in the social conservatism of the mainstream of the Protestant Reformation and survived in a semi-secularised form into the recent past. One of Shakespeare's central themes was the importance of "degree" if "discord" was not to ruin society. The order of society—with rulers, barons, churchmen of various grades, merchants, craftsmen, apprentices, peasants and other groups all discharging their distinct duties—was upheld by the crown and by the feudal system, by civic guilds and by manorial courts; but at bottom it was upheld by religion. It was God who decreed the acceptance of the rights and duties of each grade in society. Indeed, a sacred order or a "hierarchy" was thought to exist in the whole of God's creation, from the archangels to the dust out of which man had been created "a little lower than the angels". In the fourth century, under the Emperors Constantine and Theodosius, Christianity took over this insistence on order from the

---

[1] All this is suggested in John Taylor's moving introduction to African religion, *The Primal Vision* (London, 1963).

[2] See, e.g., his *The "Soul" of the Primitive* (1927; Eng. trans., 1928). His posthumous *Carnets* (Paris, 1949) show that Lévy-Bruhl was later prepared to modify his stress on the distinctiveness of the pre-logical or irrational "mysticism" of primitive peoples. Recent anthropologists, e.g. Claude Lévi-Strauss in *Totemism* (1962; Eng. trans., London, 1964) and *The Savage Mind* (1963; Eng. trans., London, 1966), have attributed a subtly logical, not mystical, thinking to primitive peoples. Lévi-Strauss therefore deplores Durkheim's whole approach. "It is the obsession with religious matters which caused totemism to be placed in religion" (*Totemism*, p. 103). But if "mysticism" and "religion" are not defined too narrowly, Lévy-Bruhl's contrast between the primitive and secular mentalities seems generally valid. A good general introduction to *Social Anthropology* was provided by Godfrey Leinhardt (London, 1964).

Roman state religion, connecting it with many teachings already to be found in the Bible. As the supernatural side of religion grew dimmer in the seventeenth and eighteenth centuries, this hierarchy of heaven and earth under God became a "great chain of being", still keeping everything in the universe and in society in its proper place—a semi-secular version of St Paul's "the powers that be".[1]

This hierarchical vision in Christendom and "post-Christian" Europe has been so frequently described that it might seem redundant to offer even this brief reminder, had not influence recently been secured by a Dutch scholar, Professor Arend van Leeuwen, who in his book *Christianity in World History* (London, 1964) has maintained that the culture of Europe, based on the Bible, was essentially exempt from what he calls "ontocracy". He means by "ontocracy" a rigidly ordered society, structured according to a religious under-standing of "Being", of the kind which he observed both in primitive paganism and in Islam while he was a missionary in Indonesia, and which he explored further as he studied the religious cultures of India and China. *Christianity in World History* was a massively learned book, and the contrast which it drew between the message of the Bible and the normal type of religious society in history is of crucial significance. Christianity has been a faith restlessly and explosively dynamic, boldly and dangerously personal, and many in West and East have rebelled against their societies in the name of Christ, the divine outcast. Yet Professor van Leeuwen's readers will observe that a lack of understanding of medieval society indicates one of the few gaps in this Dutch Protestant's scholarly equipment. For medieval society *was* an "ontocracy". Radicals have been a small minority in most periods of Christian history, and in the Middle Ages few indeed were the Christians who offered a really radical opposition to their society. The great fact of the Middle Ages was the fact of a sacred society—a society which was unified almost as completely as the sacred societies of the East. It was the Christendom of the cathedrals and the crusades, and its aftermath lasted for a long time.[2]

[1] A. O. Lovejoy, *The Great Chain of Being* (New Haven, 1936), is one of the classics in the history of ideas. *Romans* 13 records St Paul's teaching on the "powers".

[2] A recent collection of evidence about the "established religion" of Christendom is Werner Stark, *The Sociology of Religion*, vol. ii (London, 1966). H. Richard Niebuhr, *Christ and Culture* (New York, 1953), has become the standard introduction to the vast discussion among Christians about whether Christ is "against" human culture, or is "for" human culture, or is the ruler and transformer of human culture. For the early centuries, see C. N. Cochrane, *Christianity and Classical Culture* (London, 1940). Christopher Dawson's Gifford Lectures on *Religion and Culture* and *Religion and the Rise of Western Culture* (London, 1949-50) discussed the dynamic role of Christianity in European history, as did J. B. Morrell, *The Medieval Imprint*, published by the Rationalist Press Association (London, 1967).

Indeed, the legacy of Christendom is still alive among Christians, however little the European public may recognise this. As if in comment on Professor van Leeuwen's argument about the Christian missionary movement as the enemy of "ontocracy", Professor N. Q. King in a recent study of *The Emperor Theodosius and the Establishment of Christianity* saw that the influence of that distant Roman emperor was still effective among Christian missionary work in West Africa (in Ghana), where he was writing. "In giving Christianity to new peoples how easily missionaries since Theodosius' day have found themselves asking their converts to accept their view that one group of Christians (their own of course) is the only true Church! . . . We now all accept the view that church affairs ultimately depend on a material prosperity and a sound organizational and legal basis . . . Too easily in our relationships with other religions our politeness is a matter of biding our time till we can get at their throats."[1]

Frequently in the twentieth century Christian thinkers have expressed their hopes for Europe in a language about a recovery of Christendom. Many Lutherans have sought to recover the reality of the "Folk Church". A vocal group in the Church of England was called the "Christendom" group (V. A. Demant, Maurice Reckitt, T. S. Eliot, etc.).[2] More influential were Popes Pius XI and XII in repeated warnings against secularisation, and Roman Catholic writers such as G. K. Chesterton and Hilaire Belloc among the popularisers and Jacques Maritain and Christopher Dawson among the philosophers. Their vision of an England which was merry when it was Catholic, and their equation of Europe with the Faith, had many antecedents among Christians or romanticists of the nineteenth century, but in our age it has had this strong appeal, that sometimes the only alternative seemed to be Hitler or Stalin. Thus nostalgia for the Middle Ages has lingered on. When John XXIII addressed a Papal Encyclical to the world about its social problems, that document took its title from its first words, *Mater et Magistra*. The Roman Catholic Church was still in 1961 the "Mother and Mistress", the teacher of the world—or at least it was to its Pope.[3]

But the religious pattern of medieval Christendom could not hold

[1] (London, 1961), p. 10.
[2] See *The Return of Christendom* by "A Group of Churchmen" (London, 1922) and *Prospect for Christendom*, ed. M. B. Reckitt (London, 1945).
[3] See, e.g., Jacques Maritain, *True Humanism* (1936; Eng. trans., London, 1938). In the Roman Catholic context, Maritain has been conspicuous for his distrust of clericalism and his advocacy of religious liberty; but in a broader setting what has been noticeable has been his belief that against the Nazi and Marxist challenges a "new Christendom" must be built on the basis of a revived Catholic (i.e. Thomist) philosophy about man's "supernatural end".

together. As it flew apart, each fragment tried to preserve religious uniformity and social hierarchy. The emergent nation states of Europe were Catholic or Protestant according to the ruler's choice; *cuius regio eius religio* ("he who controls the country, controls the religion") was the principle on which the Wars of Religion ended in Germany in 1648. German "Culture-Protestantism" expressed the idea of a Christian society with a confident energy right up to 1918. In the Catholic countries of Europe the alliance of throne and altar was a powerful theme of the nineteenth century, with echoes into our own time through the sanctified dictatorships of Franco and Salazar. Still in 1900 the Church of England educated more school children than did the state; and Russia was Holy Russia until the Orthodox Church fell with the last of the Tsars in 1917. However, religious minorities obstinately survived, notably the English Nonconformists, and in the course of the nineteenth century the repeal of the "tests" (religious qualifications for public office) indicated the gradual and partial erosion of the old identification of Church and State. Political and economic realities dictated first the practice and then the principle of religious pluralism and toleration, whether or not the National Church was formally disestablished. Four centuries after the Reformation, and three centuries after John Locke's great plea for toleration in England, the Roman Catholic Church conceded the principle of religious liberty at the Second Vatican Council in 1965. But even after tracing the rise of religious liberty in Europe, we have still not accounted for the most important cause of the end of the old identification of Church and State. For we have to remember that the Nonconformist religious bodies by no means included all the groups arising in society to disrupt its old patterns. In England they were only partially successful in their evangelism; on the Continent, they were often socially insignificant. The main attack on the religious establishment came from people whose hearts belonged to no church at all.

The Renaissance has often been regarded as the time when the Middle Ages ended and "humanism" began. Obviously, no one denies that there was a flowering of humanism then, but the Renaissance had its roots deep in the medieval culture—and, even more important, it did not produce many Machiavellis who entirely dismissed Christianity. All the tendency among recent historians is to see the end of the medieval religious pattern in the scientific revolution among intellectuals, and in the popular revulsion against the Wars of Religion, in the seventeenth century. But even this end of the medieval religious pattern was not the end of widespread Christian belief. The eighteenth century was the Age of Enlightenment in that most of the leading thinkers had by now rejected orthodox Catholicism or Protestantism, and in the parishes the flame of faith burned low. But the influence of the religious movement known as Pietism in Europe, the success of Methodism and Evangelicalism in England, and the Awakenings across the Atlantic, showed how much of Christianity was left, awaiting revival. Thus religious enthusiasm still could flare up. The religious establishments of Europe were still maintained in the official alliances of throne and altar, or of the manor house and the rectory, until the French Revolution; and although the Catholic Church in France suffered very severely through its identification with the monarchy and the *ancien régime*, the extreme anti-clericalism of the Revolution was shrewdly modified by Napoleon in his Concordat with the Papacy in 1802, for Napoleon knew that French unity could not be built on an anti-clerical basis. And the forces marshalled against the Revolution and Napoleon thought of themselves as defending religion. We may say that Europe was, in a real sense, a Christian continent into the nineteenth century.

Religion in the Industrial Revolution

The greatest defeat of modern Christianity was *its failure in the industrial revolution*. Pope Pius XI was right to call this the "great scandal" of the nineteenth century, for the failure not only brought about the ruin of the Christian Church in the Europe which had been its home; it also provided a precedent for the decline of religion amid industrialisation elsewhere. And nowhere were this defeat and "scandal" more evident than in England, the world's first industrial country. What was involved was more than shortages in the provision of church buildings and clergy in England's new industrial towns.

It was a defeat in theology. When the children sang their notorious hymn (first published in 1848) about

> The rich man in his castle,
> The poor man at his gate,
> God made them high or lowly,
> And orderd their estate.

they were echoing the social philosophy of Christendom; but that philosophy infuriated the new industrial masses. For, whatever may have been the case with the feudal barons or the aristocratic land-owners or the squires of the old agricultural society, the rich man in the new industrial society clearly did *not* owe his wealth to his position in a timeless scheme of things. He owed it to his control of some financial capital, which he had increased by retaining profits instead of paying a just wage to the workers. The God who was the "Lord of lords" among the gentry in the ordered countryside might be taken to town by the capitalists as their celestial mascot, who rewarded their thrift and energy with profits now and heaven hereafter; but in the factories and sordid tenements of the industrial age this God seemed a positive menace to the progress of the people. The social philosophy founded on the theology about this rural or capitalistic God taught that the division of rich and poor was inevitable, at a time when—precisely because of the novelty of industrial society—the masses were for the first time beginning to think that this might not always be the case. "To the conservative," wrote Horace Greely in 1868 in the midst of the industrialisation of the United States, "Religion would often seem a part of the sub-ordinate machinery of Police, having for its main object the instilling of proper humility into the abject, of contentment into the breasts of the down-trodden, and endowing with a sacred reverence for Property those who have no personal reason to think well of the distinction between Mine and Thine."[1] Twenty years before, in *Politics for the People*, Charles Kingsley had told his English readers "We have used the Bible as if it were a mere special constable's handbook—an opium-dose for keeping beasts of burden patient while they were being overloaded—a mere book to keep the poor in order." Similar quotations could be multiplied endlessly from the records of nineteenth-century English religion.[2]

Society was mobile, but the social philosophy implied by official religion was not. Here was the basic defeat of religion—a defeat for which there was no adequate compensation in the prestige rightly acquired by the philanthropic energy or the reforming zeal of many individual Christians. The working class in its day of need might accept charity or patronage or education from religious bodies, but it would not take doctrines from them and it would not give them its heart. This alienation of the working class from the churches, although

[1] Quoted by H. J. Laski, *The American Democracy* (London, 1949), p. 271. For a history see Henry F. May, *Protestant Churches and Industrial America* (New York, 1949).

[2] A modern classic is Bishop E. R. Wickham's study of nineteenth-century Sheffield *Church and People in an Industrial City* (London, 1954). See also K. S. Inglis, *Churches and the Working Classes in Victorian England* (London, 1963), and Stephen Mayor, *The Churches and the Labour Movement* (London, 1967).

normally producing a silent belief that religion was "not for us", might easily explode into bitterness. Many capitalists who exploited the workers, or who were believed to exploit them, were regular churchgoers—as were many of the bourgeois who also profited out of the workers, or whose comfort aroused their envy. Some ecclesiastics (bishops in particular) seemed rich and reactionary; and ministers of religion without wealth could still be resented, as being hypocritical or stupid in their "soft jobs". Both the institutions and the personnel of religion became the targets of criticism and sometimes of abuse. This spelt disaster for Christianity in an increasingly industrial Europe. And it was virtually a new problem. As Max Weber pointed out, "Christianity began its course as a doctrine of itinerant artisan journeymen. During all periods of its mighty external and internal development it has been a quite specifically urban, and above all a civic, religion. This was true during Antiquity, during the Middle Ages, and in Puritanism. The city of the Occident . . . has been the major theatre for Christianity."[1] Weber quoted a point often made by the church historian Adolf von Harnack: the success of Christianity in any particular city in ancient times was in direct proportion to the size of that city, for it was in the city that old customs and castes were broken down and the ground prepared for a new brotherhood of faith.[2] But in the nineteenth century the most genuine brotherhood in an industrial city was the brotherhood of the oppressed against their oppressors. The churches seemed to be lined up with the city's oppressors. So it is that in the twentieth century, Christianity's institutional failure is likely to vary with the size of the city: the bigger the city, the smaller the congregation. A visitor wishing to see the continuing strength of the ecclesiastical tradition should go to Herefordshire and not to Birmingham, to Brittany and not to Paris, to the Middle West and not to New York. And in its own social life, "the city of the Occident" seems to have become the secular city.

That, in a rapid summary, is the story of the churches amid the industrial revolution. The summary is, of course, over-simplified. A fuller account would make us give more attention to the probability that the new industrial workers (or their parents) had not been enthusiastic churchgoers during their years in the countryside; and more attention, too, to the fact that many of the industrial workers

[1] *From Max Weber*, essays translated and edited by H. H. Gerth and C. Wright Mills (London, 1947), p. 269. This essay on "The Social Psychology of the World Religions", written in 1913, was perhaps the peak of Weber's achievement.
[2] See, e.g., the essay on "Castes, Estates, Classes and Religion" in Max Weber, *The Sociology of Religion*.

were willing to use the churches as their allies in social and educational progress, while some people in industrial areas, usually in the
class immediately above the proletariat, actually belonged to the
churches—in England, specially to the Nonconformist chapels. The
material position of many of the industrial workers can be shown to
have been an improvement on their status in the agricultural society;
and the numerical strength of the churches in the cities and towns
can be shown to have been better than much anti-clerical propaganda
or ecclesiastical lamentation would suggest. Yet the summary just
given seems to be a true enough account of the basic psychological
consequences of the shift from rural to industrial work. It was a
crisis; and the churches were not the same, before and after that
crisis. And more than nineteenth-century churchgoing suffered in
the crisis. The African pagan lived in an enchanted forest. It was
enchanted because its gods were honorary senior members of his
tribe, because his rulers were the friends of those gods, because his
whole life was ordered under the gods and the rulers, in a sacred
society. Now in the industrial city, life was (to use one of Max
Weber's favourite expressions) *disenchanted*. This was not only because
the city was often very ugly, and often very unpleasant. The basic
disenchantment came in the worker's realisation that society was a
struggle, not an already ordered structure. In the city the rich
exploited the poor, and all too often the poor had to compete with
each other; and no gods controlled these battles. Karl Marx used the
term "alienation" to describe the profound lack of satisfaction in his
work and his society which the nineteenth-century industrial worker
experienced. This "alienation" could not be overcome except by a
kind of religion—by a vision of man in society, past, present and
future. But Marx believed that traditional religion was disastrous
because it stressed the social hierarchy at the expense of human
equality. In one of the supreme ironies of modern history, the found-
ing prophet of Communism believed that the humanistic religion
which was needed could be provided by his own understanding of
human equality; and Marx proclaimed the coming of the Kingdom
of Man.[1]

Two Communist States: Russia and China

The writings of Karl Marx still form a monument to the nineteenth-
century revolt against religion, and the monument has cast its shadow

[1] The key texts were gathered in *K. Marx and F. Engels on Religion* (Moscow and London
1957) and Erich Fromm, *Marx's Concept of Man* (New York, 1961). A good, brief survey
is H. B. Acton, *What Marx Really Said* (London, 1967).

over many houses of prayer in our time. Marx argued that all religion, like every other system of ideas or "ideology", arises out of the economic structure of society. The religion which Marx knew was for him the "opium of the people", because it was used by exploiters to drug the exploited into believing that their lot was inevitable, and that they must wait for the next world before seeking justice.[1] Even for Marx, religion was also something deeper. Not for nothing was he the grandson of a Jewish rabbi. Religion was "the cry of the oppressed, the heart of a heartless world"; as the comforting illusion that there was a God who cared for the poor, it was opium self-administered. He wrote in such terms about Hinduism as well as about Christianity. But this did not commend religion to Marx. On the contrary, he believed that "all criticism begins with the criticism of religion"; and he was confident that when the poor came into their own economically, religion would be seen to be unnecessary as well as false. Marx hated the churches. As a political revolutionary, he hated them for their conservatism, one of the factors which disappointed the high hopes of 1848 in Germany. As an observer of the misery of the working class, specially in England, he hated them for their irrelevance to the social crisis. As an individual, he hated them because they were a particularly hollow and rotten part of the hypocrisy of unreformed society—as he had experienced when his Jewish father had thought it socially desirable to have the young Karl baptised a Christian.

This Marxist critique of religion has often seemed to belong to the very spirit of the twentieth century. Curiously enough, it has not had much influence on England, where it was largely formulated; English working-class anti-clericalism has found its own voices (Holyoake, Bradlaugh, Bottomley, Blatchford). But elsewhere it has stimulated the whole modern movement analysing the social character of religion (for example, the challenge of Marx lay behind the analysis of the German "history of religions" school, although Ernst Troeltsch, its leading exponent, subtly stressed the fact that religious ideas also influence social changes). And what is infinitely more important than any analysis: Marxism has changed the destinies of great countries. In these countries there was little industry and public opinion was conservatively religious; but an elite was determined to drag the masses into the modern world, forcing them by propaganda or political pressure to adopt the secular outlook of the

[1] The famous "opium of the people" phrase was first published in 1844, two years before Charles Kingsley's use of it.

Western European masses. Marx's posthumous career has indeed been astonishing. From the grave in Highgate Cemetery where he was buried in 1883 surrounded by crosses, Marx has by his philosophy changed the religious world. He has persecuted the Orthodox Church in Russia, he has discredited the three religions which had covered China for more than two millenia, and he has even overthrown the Lamaist palace-monasteries of Tibet. What Russia and China (and Tibet) shared in common with industrial Europe in the nineteenth century was the freezing of their official religions in rituals and doctrines which supported a social order doomed to disappear. Popular as such religion often was, it was incapable of internal reform on a scale large enough to meet the challenge of Westernisation.

In Russia, most of the Orthodox Church seemed completely identified with the stagnation of rural society, and with the Tsarist empire which was tyrannical and yet was unable to cope with modern challenges even before its wartime catastrophes. Priests were poor and ill-educated, their standards scarcely above those of the peasants among whom they lived. But this did not identify them with the people's cause, for they were under the detailed control of the bishops, and the bishops in their turn were controlled by the state-dominated Holy Synod. The Church's own central council had not been allowed to meet since 1721. The system made churchmen, in Lenin's famous phrase, "defenders of serfdom in cassocks"—as was shown by the hierarchy's reactions to the 1905 revolution. Some Christians in Russia saw the need of the people and struggled ineffectively to break out of the Church's disastrous position; and their vision of a Christian society honouring freedom and personality was developed later by the philosopher, Nicolas Berdyaev. But before the 1917 revolutions neither the hierarchy nor the bulk of the believers sympathised with the cause of radical change in this unjust society, and in the civil war to 1921 much of the Orthodox Church was openly identified with the White counter-revolution. The Christians of Russia have paid dearly for the social orientation of their leadership.

The Bolsheviks decreed the confiscation of all church property. During and after 1922 they imprisoned or shot many thousands of bishops and priests, they set up the "Living Church" movement to gain control of the parishes, they closed down the seminaries, the church schools, the church hospitals and almost all the churches. Step by step they prohibited all forms of spreading religion, and they co-ordinated atheistic propaganda through the League of the Militant Godless. Intensified when Stalin came into full power and collectivised the peasants in 1928-9, this was probably the most savage and prolonged persecution ever faced by a large Christian community. Only the constitutional right to assemble for worship remained to churchpeople, and in practice this liberty was often denied. Sunday was abolished as a public holiday. In 1917 there were about 51,000 priests active in Russia; by 1939 there were only 5,000. A miracle was needed to save this remnant—and a miracle came, when Hitler invaded Russia and Stalin needed all the help he could get.

The persecution of the Russian Orthodox Church was called off by Stalin in 1943 in exchange for the bishops' support of the war effort. Religious liberty was also seen as a useful emphasis in Communist international propaganda and as a good basis for the Russian Church's attempt to become the leader of all Eastern Orthodoxy. The League of the Militant Godless was now dissolved. The key position of Patriarch of Moscow, which had been virtually in suspense since the arrest of Tikhon in 1921, was filled by Sergius (who, acting as *Locum Tenens* of the Patriarchate, had announced his loyalty to the Soviet government in 1927), and after his death by Alexis (in 1968 still the head of the Russian Orthodox Church). Under this leadership a vigorous Russian foreign policy was conducted in the sphere of religion. Orthodox church conferences were convened in Moscow, and Russian church leaders became prominent in the "peace" campaigns. Within Russia a modest revival took place in church attendance. This revival seems to have alarmed those who took over after Stalin's death. Khruschev's denunciation of Stalin in 1956 shook Marxist dogmatism to its foundations, but brought no blessing to the Orthodox Church (or to the smaller religious groups in the Soviet Union). From 1959 the anti-religious campaign grew hot again, although the methods used were now more subtle than before the war. The Russian Orthodox Church has been allowed to join the World Council of Churches, but what its future is no one can tell, for no one can say what has been the real effect of the exclusion of religion from education since 1918.[1]

In China, the primary Confucianist virtue had always been filial piety, ritualised in ancestor worship; yet economic progress in China was impossible unless sons were to be educated above their fathers

[1] The history was presented by J. S. Curtiss in *Church and State in Russia, 1900-17* (New York, 1944), and *The Russian Church and the Soviet State, 1917-50* (Boston, 1953). See also William Fletcher, *A Study in Survival* (London, 1965). For recent assessments of the Orthodox Church, see Nicholas Struve, *Christians in Contemporary Russia* (1963; Eng. trans., London, 1966), and Michael Bordeaux, *Opium of the People* (London, 1965). For other religious bodies, see Walter Kolarz, *Religion in the Soviet Union* (London, 1961).

and were to be prepared to defy and even to abandon them. Th
stability of the family had been set in an empire which was stabl
because the emperor's ritual and moral behaviour was in accordanc
with the "way of heaven"; yet the Manchu empire was unable t
give efficient government to a country in desperate need of it, an
the ancient examination system for civil servants, based entirely o
the Confucian classics, was abolished in 1905. For all the attempts a
renewal by Neo-Confucians and Neo-neo-Confucians, the last of th
great reformers, Chu-hsi, had died 700 years before. The irrelevanc
of Confucian etiquette to the needs of the people had accounted fc
the rise of Buddhism—despite Buddhism's other-worldliness, s
uncongenial to the Chinese mind. The last of the Buddhist leade:
with some hope of influencing China, Tai-hsu, died in 194'
Confucianism's failure had, however, mainly resulted in magic amon
the masses, as the peasants attempted to manipulate nature in th
style of Sir James Frazer's primitive peoples. The less anxious eli
in Chinese society turned to the nature mysticism of Taoism, with i
philosophy of the simple life lived in accordance with nature's gent
decrees. Taoism certainly had its charm, and incidentally its enth
siasm for nature encouraged the early rise of Chinese science. B
Taoism had a darker side also; the elite was encouraged to withdra
from all useful involvement in social life, and when Taoism reache
the hungry masses what it produced was a further wave of mag
(since nature, if it was unsatisfactory, might be adjusted). Thus I
the nineteenth century A.D. none of China's religions—whe
pursued separately or (as was more usual) when fused together in
tolerant syncretism—possessed the dynamic power needed to unit
inspire, energise and transform the Chinese people. They we
religions for gentlemen, and they provided the opium of magic fo
the masses.

There was a time when, in the search for a religious power to matc
China's time of crisis, Christianity seemed a live option. Protected (
least to some extent) by the extra-territorial privileges yielded
foreigners after the Opium War, missionaries poured into China. A
unexpected result was the mixture of crusading Protestantism wi
popular Confucianism which inspired the Tai-ping rebellion in tl
1850s. Christianity was never a popular movement after the crushir
of that rebellion (by the devoutly Protestant General Gordon amor
others), but the Chinese elite did use the schools and colleges est
blished by the missionaries. The result was another chance f
Christianity: the Kuomintang when it emerged under Sun Yat-se

and Chiang Kai-shek, and founded the Chinese Republic in 1912, was to a considerable extent Christian in its leadership and inspiration. But the reliance of the Christians on American and other foreign patrons was always a great embarrassment among a people so intensely patriotic as the Chinese. The Boxer Rebellion which was crushed by the Western powers and Japan in 1900, and followed by a crippling fine on the Chinese nation, was only the most violent of many protests against foreign interference symbolised by the hated missionaries; and actions such as those of the Roman Catholic hierarchy after the Rebellion did little to end the resentment. (The bishops used the compensation which was paid to them for murders of Roman Catholics to purchase land, adding to the Church's already conspicuous wealth and entanglement in the decaying social order.) When in 1919 the Western powers betrayed China in favour of Japan (over the claim to Shantung), anti-foreign feeling again flared up, and again turned against the missionaries, now known as the "running dogs of capitalism".[1]

Nationalism, socialism and democracy were the great passions, and the main intellectual impact of the West on the elite of the Chinese Republic was through atheists such as Bertrand Russell, John Dewey and the Communists. Many Buddhist and Taoist temples were turned into secular schools. The moving spirit behind the "Chinese Renaissance" in the 1920s and 1930s, Hu Shih, declared that "the most important contribution that the religions of the world could make to modern societies in the world today would be to commit suicide".[2] The "Liberation" of 1947-9 clinched the answer to China's problem; but this answer had been probable since Sun Yat-sen's appeal to Soviet Russia for help in 1919. The religions, if they failed to commit suicide, would be slowly murdered, for only atheist Marxism provided a viable alternative to the corruption of the old society. Mao Tse-tung's "long march" of 1934-5 went further han from Kiangsi to Yenan; it went from the old to the new. The constitution of 1954 provided for freedom of religious belief in the People's Republic, and for a time religious organisations and buildings enjoyed some patronage from the regime, on condition that hey freed themselves from all foreign interference (the "Three-Self Movement"). Missionaries were expelled, and Chinese who had

[1] The American Protestants were studied by Paul A. Varg, *Missionaries, Chinese and Diplomats* (Princeton, 1958).
[2] B. E. Meland, *The Secularization of Modern Cultures* (New York, 1966), p. 22. For the background, see Hu Shih, *The Chinese Renaissance* (Chicago, 1934); Wing Tsit-chan, *Religious Trends in Modern China* (New York, 1954); Chow Tse-tsung, *The May Fourth Movement: Intellectual Revolution in Modern China* (Cambridge, Mass., 1960).

collaborated with them were "re-educated", often violently. And then the pace of the march of secularism quickened. The Cultural Revolution of 1966 threw the Red Guards against all religion, closing almost all the temples and churches and humiliating such open believers as were left after two decades of Communism.[1]

Three Lay Republics: France, Mexico, Turkey

Russia and China were two great peoples with essentially irrelevant, or even harmful, religions; their religions were broken, often brutally, by Marxism. But the twentieth century has provided many examples of countries where the grip of religion was ended by forces which were not Marxist in character. What these countries had in common with each other (and with the Marxist lands) was that in them all religion was identified with a doomed social order, and secularisation was the fruit of social protest.

France is the classic case. Through much of the nineteenth century the fate of the Catholic Church hung in the balance. Widespread intellectual rejection of Christianity was certainly an element in the danger which the Church faced. From Renan's *Vie de Jésus* in 1863 to the death of Anatole France in 1924 the current in French literary life was against religion, and the intellectual response of French Catholicism was inadequate. But in the history of French *laïcité* leading to open anti-clericalism, social factors mattered decisively. First the aristocracy returning after the Revolution and then the middle classes enriched by the new industries favoured the Church (with the American capitalist's blessing on religion as "a part of the subordinate machinery of Police"); but when the Republicans triumphed in the elections of 1876 the doom of the Church was sealed with that of the monarchy which most vocal Catholics had supported. Specially through newspapers such as *L'Univers* or *La Croix*, churchmen openly and violently played at party politics, and the lower middle and the working-classes were out for vengeance. They were led by anti-clerical politicians of the stamp of Emile Combes. Combes had been trained for the priesthood but, after losing his faith, he was driven by the determination to take education out of the hands of priests and nuns and to transfer wealth from the maintenance of the religious hierarchy to the progress of the people.

[1] For two sympathetic Christians' views of the Communist Liberation, see Katharine Hockin, *Servants of God in People's China* (New York, 1962), and C. R. Hensman, *China: Yellow Peril? Red Hope?* (London, 1968); and for a general assessment, Joseph Levenson, *Confucian China and its Modern Fate*, 2 vols. (Los Angeles, 1959).

The political life of the Third Republic was dominated by religious issues, right up to the war of 1914; urgent social reforms were neglected because the overthrow and defence of Catholicism aroused the most ardent passions. The affair of Alfred Dreyfus, an army officer of Jewish descent who in 1894 was unjustly sentenced for selling secrets to Germany, was used to discredit the Church as well as the army. Religion was excluded from the state schools, and the Church's own schools were penalised. The religious orders were forbidden to do either teaching or pastoral work, and many religious houses were closed by the police. The government broke off diplomatic relations with the Papacy (under Leo XIII the Papacy had made some efforts to rally Catholics to compromise with the Republic, but under Pius X it was completely hostile). Finally in 1905 the separation of Church and State in France ended the large financial grants, the public privileges and the prestige which the Church had enjoyed since Napoleon's Concordat in 1802.

Much turned on the question of the use of the church buildings. Unlike the Russian Communists or the Red Guards in China, the French anti-clericals were not prepared simply to close all these down. But the position was dangerous for the French Church. Since 1790 the church buildings had been owned by the French state; the 1802 Concordat had left this arrangement intact, but the state had provided grants to the Church out of taxes, partly as a compensation for ownership of the buildings. Now the grants were abolished, other buildings might be used for a variety of purposes, and the churches themselves could be leased from the state for use in worship by *Associations Cultuelles*. For a time anti-clericals nursed the hope that Catholicism might split up in schisms, as isolated priests, wishing to use particular buildings, made their peace with the state without reference to the bishops. Such hopes were not realised. In a series of negotiations which were not concluded until 1943 the authorities of Church and State agreed to the use of almost all the buildings for religious purposes by leasing them to diocesan "associations" formed under the bishops for the purpose, and Pope Pius XI accepted this principle in 1924. In its essentials, however, the 1905 separation of Church and State in France has proved permanent, despite many Papal thunders. It has been more than a matter of taking the crucifix out of the courtroom. The schools of France have taught ethics instead of any religious doctrine; there have been Catholic schools, there have been some Christian teachers in the state system, there have been many teachers who have been genuinely neutral in their attitude to religion, but there have also been many anti-clerical teachers who have taught, or at least implied, that all religious doctrines are false. In many French villages there was no longer a resident *curé* to take care of the parish church; and in these and many other villages a teacher who might be contemptuous of Christianity became the leading man. Between 1901 and 1913, both the number of ordinations and the proportion of ecclesiastical to civil marriages fell by about a half. Many of the parish clergy were reduced to poverty by the withdrawal of the state grants, and in the expanding industrial cities the shortage of clergy and of money in the Church meant that the working-class suburbs were virtually wildernesses in religious observance. Durkheim and many others wanted sociology with its anti-religious conclusions made a compulsory subject for the training of teachers in France's schools, but Durkheim's analysis of the centrality of religion in past societies had ceased to be true for his own country. The French Republic had turned to other totems.

The cause of religion in France has been damaged very severely not only by such frontal assaults but also by the mood of reaction which has gripped many who wished to defend Catholicism. The ending of the Concordat with the State meant it was now the Papacy that appointed all the bishops; Pius X favoured reactionaries and stopped the hierarchy from taking any concerted initiative. But the coldness in the intellectual atmosphere had causes subtler than the bishops' dislike of anything which might be termed liberalism. The stark alternative of atheism or "fideism" (the willingness to believe anything because it is taught by the Church) has been prominent in French intellectual life, with the Catholic believers in the minority. In 1907 Pius X violently condemned the "modernism" of Alfred Loisy, Edouard Le Roy, and a small circle around them. This was a group of French religious thinkers who, for all their liability to error, were at that stage intelligent and honest sons of the Church, prepared to accept the Church's teachings whatever interpretations they might put on them. Given time, such theologians might have worked out a modern Catholicism, but the Vatican announced that they erred in separating Church and State, as well as in separating faith and science. After the condemnation of "modernism" there followed a virtual reign of terror among intellectual Catholics. For many years a tendency prevailed to avoid real thought lest it lead to heresy and condemnation. Many Catholics flirted with the militantly reactionary (although personally agnostic) Charles Maurras and his *Action Française*, at least until Pius XI condemned that semi-Fascist movement in 1926. When the experiment of the worker-priests going into factories was condemned by Pius XII, the scars of former conflicts still showed, for these priests had been driven to incur the wrath of the Vatican by their conviction that if they were to make contact with the dechristianised working class they must abandon most of the traditional discipline of a Catholic priest (not least his distinctive dress, the *soutane*) and must embrace the militant politics of the Left. All this took place in a France which had once been known as the 'eldest daughter" of the Catholic Church—and the canonisation of Joan of Arc as a saint in 1920 was a pointed reminder of that past. The diary of a country priest was now likely to be the record of a slow crucifixion, and the France of the "Most Christian" monarchy had become, to use the title of Godin's book which shocked and excited Catholics when it appeared in 1943, *pays de mission.*[1]

A mission field France might be (Godin reckoned that only ten per cent of the population regularly practised their religion—but his statistics were criticised as unduly alarmist). However, Catholicism retained enough influence in France, and enough moderation, to prevent a complete conflict with the state. Across the Atlantic, Mexico provided an example of the Catholic Church in a duel to the death with a secular republic. For many years the bishops and clergy of Mexico had been denounced as the apostles of superstition and oppression; on the other hand, the churches were full, and the clergy controlled most of the schools and hospitals. Governments enacted anti-clerical laws (1874, 1917), and largely failed to enforce them. In 1923 there was ominous anger from the government when the bishops dedicated a huge monument to "Christ, King of Mexico", and the explosion came when Plutarco Calles was elected President of Mexico in 1924. The old laws were now revived, and fresh restrictions added, with the declared intentions of cutting drastically the numbers of clergy (according to the wishes of the local authorities) and of restricting their work to the conduct of religious services. Religion was to be totally excluded from all schools, public and private. In retaliation the bishops forbade their priests to conduct any worship at all. Most of the bishops were exiled, and hundreds of priests and laymen shot. The *Cristeros* fought back, and the next President of Mexico, Obregon, was assassinated by a Catholic. A truce was patched up in 1929, but the anti-clerical

[1] The great novel by Georges Bernanos, *Diary of a Country Priest* (1936), was translated in 1937 and an English version of Henri Godin and Yves Daniel, *France Pagan?*, was edited by Maisie Ward in 1949. The years 1879-1930 were summed up by Adrian Dansette, *Religious History of Modern France* (1948; Eng. trans., London, 1961).

legislation was retained. The government authorised under 200 priests to serve a Catholic population of 17 millions. The 1935-7 anti-clerical campaign under President Cardenas drew from Pius XI the Papacy's first theological exposition of the subject's right to rebel (in the Encyclical *Nos es Muy*). It was only in 1940 that a President of Mexico, Avila Camacho, declared himself a believer. In the next two decades the Catholic Church recovered confidence with missionary help from the United States; but it could scarcely claim that Christ was still visibly King of Mexico, or the Virgin its Queen.[1]

The countries to the south in Latin America, while less violent than Mexico, have become about as secular. Catholicism depends on its priests, but 1950 statistics showed under 25,000 priests to over 154 million people in Latin America. Although it may still be dangerous for a Latin American ruler to fall out with the bishops if he has alienated a great many other people as well (as the Argentinian dictator, Peron, discovered too late in 1955), the twentieth century has thus brought to an end the whole effort to impose Spanish or Portuguese Catholicism on the New World. The twentieth century has also seen in Spain and Portugal themselves an anti-clerical Republicanism which has been checked but which, no doubt, has not been disposed of for ever. The contrast between Spain (or Portugal) and Mexico is instructive. In all three countries political instability went with economic distress. In all three countries the Catholic Church was identified, rightly or wrongly, with the exploiters of the peasant and the worker. In all three countries hostility to the clergy erupted periodically. Spain and Portugal knew violent anti-clericalism in the nineteenth century. In 1931 Church and State were separated in Spain on the model of France in 1905, and under the Loyalist alliance of Liberals, Socialists and Communists mob violence against the personnel and buildings of the Church followed on the model of Mexico. The Spanish bishops, in an appeal to the world, stated that 6,000 priests and 300,000 laity had been murdered. The separation of Church and State and anti-clerical measures in Portugal came earlier (1911). But General Franco's clerically backed revolt in Spain in 1936, and General Carmona's in Portugal ten years previously, imposed a political order and restored a privileged Church (thus lending force to the Pope's

---

[1] Three surveys by United States scholars are: W. H. Callcott, *Liberalism in Mexico, 1857-1929* (Stanford, 1931); J. Lloyd Meecham, *Church and State in Latin America* (Chapel Hill, 1934); K. S. Latourette, *Christianity in a Revolutionary Age*, vol. 4 (New York, 1962), Chapter V. The drama of Catholicism in Mexico was the background to one of Graham Greene's most deeply felt novels, *The Power and the Glory* (London, 1940).

warning to the rulers of Mexico in 1937). The generals had their successes, and were able to establish regimes which have lasted into the 1960s, partly by simple force of arms and by political skill, but also partly because the leadership of the Catholic Church has not been identified with the "enemies of the people" in Spain and Portugal to nearly the same degree as in Mexico. Thus under the Franco or Salazar dictatorship Catholicism has been able to act as a patriotic focus—a role for twentieth-century religion to which we shall return. The bell which tolled for the Spanish Church in the 1930s announced a warning, not a funeral.[1]

So did the sombre bells tolling in Italy and Germany. In the Spanish Civil War, Italian and German military aid was given to Franco and therefore to the defence of the Catholic Church against the "lay" republic with its Communist backing. The Fascist and Nazi regimes in their own countries had working relationships with organised Christianity right up to the end. In Italy one of Mussolini's early achievements was to conclude the Lateran Treaty with Pope Pius XI in 1929, acknowledging the sovereignty of the Vatican City State, providing for a large annual subsidy to the Vatican as an indemnity for the former Papal States which had now been absorbed into Italy, and giving the Church a privileged position in Italy (Catholicism was to be taught in the schools, national laws about marriage and divorce were to be subordinated to the Church's laws, etc.). A Concordat was negotiated between the Vatican and the Nazis soon after Hitler's coming to power in 1933, and, like the 1929 Treaty in Italy, this Concordat has never been revoked. Most Protestants in Germany accepted Hitler, and like the Catholic priests the Protestant ministers drew the bulk of their income from taxes collected by the Nazi government. These happy relationships of Church and State were strained when the Vatican defended against Mussolini the rights of the Catholic Church in youth work which the Fascists sought to monopolise, and in Nazi Germany first censorship and then persecution of the Church deepened into a spiritual crisis recalling Soviet Russia or Mexico; but the claim of the Fascists and Nazis to stand for "positive Christianity" against Bolshevism, and the patriotic support which they received until the end of the war brought national disaster, were enough to confuse the picture even for sensitive Christians.[2] Thus Martin Niemöller,

[1] E. Allison Peers, an English scholar, wrote *Spanish Tragedy, 1930-36* (Oxford, 1937), and *Spain, the Church and the Orders* (London, 1939).
[2] See Daniel A. Binchy, *Church and State in Fascist Italy* (New York, 1941).

whom the whole Christian world rightly honoured for the courage of his opposition to the Nazi interference with Protestant church life, in 1933 congratulated Hitler on withdrawing from the League of Nations, and in 1941 asked to be released from his concentration camp in order to return to active service in the German Navy. We shall consider Germany later in this book for the lessons learned so bitterly under Hitler were crucial in the reshaping of the twentieth-century Church.[1] Meanwhile, we may go to the edge of Europe, to consider an astonishing development.

The Turkish Empire had been ruled by the Ottoman Sultan who was also Caliph or Commander of the Faithful, thus symbolising in his own person the unity of politics and religion in the household of Islam. Turkey had governed its life according to the Prophet's holy book (the *Quran*) supplemented by the decisions taken as questions arose in the early years of Islam (the *Sunna*) and by the elaborate code of law worked out in the Middle Ages (the *Sharia*). Men had worn the brimless *fez* because it was suitable for prayers, to give one example of a religious regulation binding on all; and women had been veiled and separated into *purdah*, subject to divorce at the husband's will and without political rights. Memorising the *Quran* in the original Arabic had been the main task in education. But the modernisation of the young Turks and of Zia Gok Alp (a poet inspired by Auguste Comte) was given feet and fists by the passionate conviction of Kemal Ataturk and others that after its defeat in the world war Turkey must join Western civilisation at whatever cost. The Caliphate was abolished with the Sultanate, and since that historic year (1924) Islam has had no Commander of the Faithful. The *Sharia* was no longer part of the law of the land; instead, civil codes were adapted from Europe and decided such matters as divorce in secular courts. The *fez*, the veil and other time-hallowed customs were denounced in favour of Western dress. Women were given legal safeguards and political votes. No religious instruction was allowed in the new network of schools set up by the State. The greatest mosque in Istanbul, which had been the greatest church of the city when it was the Christian Byzantium, was turned into a museum, and the use of Arabic for the call to prayer was made illegal; the *muezzin*, if he had to call, must call in Turkish. Subsequent Turkish regimes have not kept up Ataturk's secularising zeal, and the Muslim religion has retained much of its hold on the rural masses. The study of Islam has come back to schools and universities, and it is said that

[1] See below, pp. 107, 291–2, 305–6, 315.

five thousand mosques were built in the decade 1950-60. But one reason why the Democratic Party was replaced in the military coup of 1960 was that it was alleged to favour religious reaction, and in its constitution, approved by a referendum in 1961, Turkey has remained a secular state on the French pattern—something undreamed of before Ataturk.[1]

The Dilemma of Islam

No other Islamic country has undergone changes as drastic as these in Turkey, partly because no other country is geographically so suitable for Westernisation (although also because no other country has had to deal with the Sultan-Caliph as the symbol of the old order). But in parts of Islam there already exists an intelligentsia moulded by an education which is Western in its ethos; the development of technology extends Western influences more subtly; and Western popular culture seeps through. It is possible to prophesy that other situations will develop towards an explosion or slow erosion which will do at least as much damage as was done in Turkey to the traditional fabric of Islam, unless Islam can reform itself voluntarily. And "Islam reformed," as Lord Cromer wrote when reporting on Egypt in 1908, "is Islam no longer."[2] Cromer's insult contains this truth: that when the *Quran*, the *Sunna* and the *Sharia* cease to regulate daily life, but instead criteria are applied which derive ultimately from the secularised West, then the unity of Islamic society has been disrupted, and a new chapter must open in Islamic history.[3]

Islam is indeed in a dangerous position under this social impact of secularisation. Islamic society was the personal creation of the prophet Muhammed, who founded a single community, both political and religious, armed with the scimitar as well as with faith, so that a witty French sociologist could aptly describe Communism as the Islam of the twentieth century.[4] As we have seen, Christianity developed such a religious-political society fairly quickly—indeed, at the first available opportunity. But what gives some justification to the argument that Christianity is not wedded to a static view of society is the fact that the founder of Christianity lived in circum-

[1] See Nyazi Berkes, *The Development of Secularism in Turkey* (Toronto, 1964).
[2] *Modern Egypt*, vol. 2, p. 229.
[3] The flood of discussion about "What is Islam?" has been summed up in two outstanding surveys by Western scholars: Cantwell Smith, *Islam in Modern History* (New York, 1957), and Edwin Rosenthal, *Islam in the National State* (Cambridge, 1965).
[4] The comparison was developed by A. van Leeuwen, *Christianity in World History*, pp. 342-8.

stances far different from the circumstances of the founder of Islam. Muhammed entered a social vacuum in Arabia; to the West, his armies met no enduring opposition until they came to Tours and Vienna; to the East, the Caliphs of Baghdad and the Moghul Emperors of India ruled glorious civilisations in the name of Islam. Jesus and his first followers formed a small minority under the Roman empire and under the Hellenistic culture, so that they had no prospect of inaugurating their own society. St. John well understood Christ's rejection of the political hope of Jewish Messianism: "My Kingdom is not of this world." Christendom, when it was a united, sacred society in the European Middle Ages, was a mixture of Roman and Greek with specifically Christian elements; and always in the Christian tradition there remained many traces of the original separation of God and Caesar, religion and politics, Church and State. Now that the compromise called Christendom has disintegrated, the separation of Church and State in the West colours the whole modern world—and destroys the classic concept of Islamic unity.

It is not merely a question of the separation of Church and State in the future of Islam. The regulations governing the religious life of Muslims were largely untouched by the Turkish reforms—which is not surprising, since some of the most important of them have the authority of the Prophet himself. Muhammed, unlike Jesus, was a law-giver, and he set the style for the prolific legislation which has regulated the lives of Muslims.

Among the customs which he created were the Five Pillars of Religion: witness, prayer, almsgiving, fasting and pilgrimage. Each "pillar" has been surrounded by vast discussions by Muslims and their critics during the twentieth century, but the relevance of each, as erected by the Prophet, is dubious if Islamic society is to be modernised. For *witness*, fundamentally a confession of Allah and his Prophet, was militantly aggressive and included the duty of the "holy war" against infidels, understood as the defence of liberty to worship Allah. Can this now be interpreted solely as the duty of war against sin within? *Prayer* was regulated precisely in postures and words, and was to be in Arabic. Can this discipline be relaxed as Christianity has had to relax its equivalent disciplines in the West? (Only a sixth of the world's 300 million Muslims normally speak Arabic.) *Almsgiving* was defined so as to take a high and regular proportion of one's income. Can this be continued as a secular state provides education, social security and welfare services? *Fasting* included abstention from all food and drink during the daylight in the month of Ramadan. Is this possible in an industrial society? *Pilgrimage* was to Mecca, to which the daily prayers were directed. Can this Arabian city retain its sacred centrality when Arabia, under the rule of the puritanical Wahhabi movement since the eighteenth century, has become one of the most backward parts of Islam—despite its oil wells?

Such questions are typical of Islam's modern dilemmas, and it is not surprising that so many of Islam's teachers still give the fundamentalist answer. Islam, they proclaim, is what is laid down in the *Quran*, the *Sunna* and the *Sharia*, and it all stands or falls together. We may call this a totalitarian ideology if we wish, but we should understand that their religious law has been much more than a mere system to past generations of Muslims. It was the will of Allah, expressed without ambiguity or confusion. Muslims in controversy with Christians have constantly said that, despite all the merits of Jesus, Christianity suffers from being an otherworldly idealism; it does not give enough clear instructions for daily life. And now Muslims are being asked to refashion their faith so that it becomes as otherworldly as the Christianity which they saw in action in the crusaders of the Middle Ages, or more recently in the colonialists who seemed to rely more on the whisky bottle than on the Bible.[1]

Yet, even in Islam, many voices today urge that religion must be separated from government; in a free society, it must be renewed as a spiritual faith helping modern people towards the eternal God, in the privacy of their own hearts and consciences. Ali Abd ar-Raziq wrote with this theme on *Islam and the Principles of Government* (Cairo, 1925). The controversy led to his expulsion from his teaching post at the Al Azhar mosque-university, but his modernist principles have been echoed and developed since in Egypt.[2] The courts administering the *Sharia* have been abolished, and Al Azhar has itself been modernised under the Nasser government. Syria, Jordan and Iraq have gone the same way. In the North African states, the Muslim traditionalism of the peasants and wandering *bedouin* was encouraged by the struggle with the French as Catholic colonisers; but Tunisia in 1957 took a momentous step when it prohibited polygamy on the ground that the Prophet had decreed that all a man's wives should be treated impartially—a thing said to be impossible in the circumstances of

[1] Sympathetic Western presentations of Islam's social heritage include W. Montgomery Watt, *Islam and the Integration of Society* (Evanston, 1961), and Reuben Levy, *The Social Structure of Islam* (Cambridge, 1962).

[2] For the history since Muhammed Abduh at the turn of the century, see Charles C. Adams, *Islam and Modernism in Egypt* (Oxford, 1933), and Nadav Safran, *Egypt in Search of Political Community* (Cambridge, Mass., 1961).

modern society. Even in Pakistan, created in 1947 as a national home for Indian Muslims (under the largely agnostic Jinnah), the description of the state as an Islamic Republic was abandoned in the revised constitution after the military coup of 1958, and no attempt has been made to enact for the nation all that the Islamic tradition prescribes.[1] Pakistan's alliance with Red China against India is a fairly striking example of realism in power politics. The Arab League, founded in 1945, was modelled on Western political alliances and has not been thoroughly Islamic in the traditional sense, although it has achieved such identity as it has found possible through its anti-Israeli drive, and although many Arab leaders and conferences have declared that Arab culture depends on Muslim religion. One of the most progressive states in the Near East, Lebanon, offers the spectacle of Arab liberalism in a half-Christian country.[2] Much of the future in the Near East must depend on the impact of a Marxist, or at least of a radically Westernising, Socialism. "Quranic Socialism" is sought by many, and is no more ridiculous in its aspirations than is Christian Socialism or Buddhist Socialism, but the *Quran* does contain much material which is difficult for a modern Socialist, exactly because the Prophet was more interested than the Christ or the Buddha was in the details of social justice in his time. Because of the apparent irrelevance of the regulations in the modern world, only Saudi Arabia, Afghanistan and Yemen survive as states officially placed under Allah and Islamic law. To many millions of Muslims who still live in the Soviet Union, or in the constitutionally secular, largely Hindu, Republic of India, the separation of Church and State is basic to their hope that some form of Islam will survive to guide their children. Already in India some important Muslim thinkers have emerged, interpreting Islam as vision, not law.[3]

Pluralist Societies in Asia and America

Need this separation of Church and State be disastrous to religion? To a large extent it seems to have been in Russia and China, but the evidence from other countries shows that it need not be—so that religion may have a future within the "pluralist" type of society in which various religions and secular bodies co-exist under the more or less neutral benevolence of the state.

[1] See Leonard Binder, *Religion and Politics in Pakistan* (Berkeley, 1961).
[2] See the history of *Arab Thought in the Liberal Age* by a Christian scholar, Albert Hourani (Oxford, 1962).
[3] See Aziz Ahmad, *Studies in Islamic Culture in the Indian Environment* (Oxford, 1964).

We have already noted the religious recovery in secular Turkey. Today Islam makes its fastest progress (mainly through traders and other non-professional evangelists) precisely in an area where it must compete peacefully with paganism and Christianity for the allegiance of individuals or of small groups, and where it must tolerate a great many pagan customs surviving in its adherents' habits. Here Islam gives Muslims a pride in belonging to a great brotherhood, without the burden of attempting to regulate all the details of the life of any one society; it is, in other words, more a private religion than a comprehensive ideology. This area is tropical Africa.[1]

At the other end of the Islamic world, Indonesia may be more typical than Pakistan as showing the trend of our time. Indonesia is overwhelmingly a Muslim country, and the education of its people still relies mainly on Muslim schools. Yet Islam only gradually conquered paganism in this vast archipelago, and never established a monopoly. Moreover, Christian missionaries under the Dutch colonialists succeeded in establishing many schools and churches including the powerful Battak Church, and when the Dutch were forced out this Christian element was sufficiently strong, and sufficiently indigenous, to survive.[2] The result of this history is that in Indonesia Christian and other minorities are recognised in law (as in Pakistan) and definitely encouraged in practice (as they are not in Pakistan) because all available resources are needed for nation-building. This separation of Church and State in Indonesia flies in the face of the history of Islam, and is resented by many Muslims. But religion remains strong. Sukarno's regime had to put belief in God first among the declared principles of the Republic (the *Pantjasila* enunciated in 1945), and Sukarno's downfall amid the massacre of perhaps half a million was due partly to Muslim reaction against his flirtation with the atheist Communists. The murders in the name of Islam gave an added point to the emphasis on "religious socialism" and "consensus" among Muslims and Christians who had accepted Sukarno's "guided democracy" as an alternative to anarchy.[3]

[1] See the Introduction by I. M. Lewis in *Islam in Tropical Africa*, which he edited (London, 1966). W. Spencer Trimingham in *Islam in West Africa* (Oxford, 1964) and *Islam in East Africa* (Oxford, 1959) has traced the emergence of this new form of Islam, comparing it with the fanatical theocracy which Muslims felt obliged to establish in the nineteenth-century Sudan.

[2] See Hendrik Kraemer, *From Missionfield to Independent Church* (London, 1957).

[3] See the pro-Sukarno essay written for the World Council of Churches by P. D. Latuihamalio, in *Responsible Government in a Revolutionary Age*, ed. Z. K. Matthews (New York, 1966), pp. 213-31. For the social background, see *Local, Ethnic and National Loyalties in Village Indonesia*, ed. G. W. Skinner (New Haven, 1959), and a study of two towns by Clifford Geertz, *Peddlers and Princes* (Chicago, 1963).

Although some Asian countries remain unified religiously (Thailand, Cambodia and Laos are examples of a traditional Buddhist monopolies), the separation of Church and State is practised in the different circumstances of other Asian countries without ruining religion.[1] In Japan, for example, the Shinto religion ceased to be the creed of a militant state and the Emperor renounced his divinity in 1946; yet the Japanese have always been interested in a syncretistic mixture drawn from different religions of Chinese origin (specially Confucianism and Buddhism), and in their own local experiments, while being, like the Chinese, most concerned with order and prosperity in the world. And Japan since 1946 has continued to be what the Emperor's brother called it: a "laboratory" for religion.[2]

In the Philippines, where Church and State are separated, the still-flourishing folk religion is a mixture of Catholicism and paganism dating back to the Spanish missionaries in the sixteenth century. This Filipino version of Christianity is prized because it is indigenous, and in contrast both with the non-Christian religions of Asia and with the Protestantism of the United States. Reformers would say that it is too contentedly indigenous, and that it discourages modernisation and economic advance, but our point here is that religion still has a grip on the people, so that even when social change becomes more revolutionary religion may not be abolished easily.[3]

Greater examples of the separation of Church and State in the world today are provided by India and the United States. Those two gigantic countries are officially secular states. Historically, the main motive in choosing this status arose from the fact that both republics were from the beginning federations of states including citizens of many religious persuasions. Their governments are pledged by their constitutions to give no privileges to any religious body. Yet religious bodies of many kinds flourish in both countries; and this fact may indicate the style in which the social roles of religious bodies should be reshaped in the modern world.

Limitations of space and of first-hand experience do not permit a detailed comparison of India and America.[4] Anyway, the future of

---

[1] Essays on the varying national situations were collected in *South Asian Politics and Religion*, ed. Donald E. Smith (Princeton, 1966).

[2] See Raymond Hammer, *Japan's Religious Ferment* (London, 1961).

[3] See Peter Gowing, *Islands under the Cross*, published for the National Council of Churches (Manila, 1967).

[4] As was provided by an American scholar, Donald E. Smith, in his treatise on *India as a Secular State* (Princeton, 1963).

ndia is uncertain. Formed in 1947, the Republic of India prohibited all discrimination on grounds of religion, race or caste in its constitution of 1950 and elected a Muslim President as the head of its secular tate in 1967, yet Hinduism still accounts for more than three-quarters of its population. In the short run, Hinduism may be strong enough o use the machinery of the central government to suppress practices which are offensive to the Hindu conscience, such as "cow-laughter"; after all, it was a Hindu fanatic who in 1948 assassinated Gandhi in revenge on his liberalism. In the long run, Hinduism with ts caste system and other outmoded social customs may not be lexible enough to accept the modernisation of the country, and China's solution may have to be India's. The corruption and inefficiency which spoil India in the 1960s, and the multiplication of wealth in the hands of the capitalists and landlords while the standard of living of the masses remains stationary or falls, are ominously like the defects in the Kuomintang in China in the 1940s— and the moral energy of Hinduism may not be enough to cure these diseases, despite the idealism of Gandhi's heirs.[1] But even if the present Indian Republic fails, the idea of a secular state administering a argely religious society is unlikely to perish during the twentieth century—for that is the strong character of the United States of America, to which we may now at last turn.

An English writer may be permitted to observe that the lessons of American religious history have not yet been taken with anything like adequate seriousness in discussion about the future of religion. Even American thinkers have allowed themselves to be mesmerised by European patterns. For example, European religious history suggested to Max Weber that the National Churches and the small splinter-groups were almost completely different in atmosphere; the "church-type" must be distinguished from the "sect-type". American thinkers copied this approach.[2] Above all, modern European secularisation was interpreted by a host of intellectuals whose influence was large in the United States; if God was dead in Europe, it seemed to follow that he must be in America. But in fact the religious histories of Europe and of the United States have been surprisingly different.[3]

Religious pluralism became the American destiny because when the thirteen colonies federated in the course of their rebellion against

[1] B. E. Meland, *The Secularization of Cultures*, records the warnings which this sympathetic American scholar gave in lectures in India in 1964-5.
[2] The translation of Ernst Troeltsch, *Social Teachings of the Christian Churches* was influential here (2 vols., 1912; Eng. trans., London, 1931).
[3] A careful study has now been provided by a British scholar: E. R. Norman, *The Conscience of the State in North America* (Cambridge, 1968).

George III no single National Church could be contemplated. Many of the American colonies had their own Established Churches (the last to be disestablished was that of Massachusetts in 1833), but amid this variety a federal government could not make a religious option. Anyway, religion was not popular in the American Revolution; scriptures more influential than the Bible were Tom Paine's *Rights of Man* and *The Age of Reason*, and thinkers more influential than any churchman were the sceptical philosophers Benjamin Franklin and Thomas Jefferson. However, it was a largely unexpected consequence of this crisis for American religion that the churches were now exempted from the dilemma of being either "church-type" (i.e. identified with King George III or with some other reactionary force) or "sect-type" (i.e. narrow, ignorant and bitter). So gradually a new type of church emerged: a free church. Most of the early settlers who had crossed the Atlantic in search of religious liberty and material opportunity had thought that their dream of the Kingdom of God in America must involve something like the European pattern of a communal religion, although on a different basis; only so could a godly commonwealth be built in the wilderness. What now remained from the colonial period in American history was the recurrent American dream that the way to Paradise could be reopened by the sweat of Adam's brow; but the godly commonwealth, in so far as it has been built in the history of the New World, has been founded on the basis of real liberty, involving pluralism.

In the infant United States, the number of regularly attending church members seems to have been very low, according to one estimate about five per cent of the population; but surveys suggest that nowadays well over half of the United States goes to church regularly, and the American Institute of Public Opinion reported in 1955 that ninety-seven per cent identified themselves with one of the major religious groups. The "Great Awakenings" of the eighteenth century, with their focus in the theology of Jonathan Edwards, began the rebirth of Protestantism in the life of America, but four great crises may be seen in the subsequent story of the churches. One crisis came at the Frontier: as the American people moved West, the preachers moved with them. In Sunday schools or in revival camps, or during uncountable hours of homely talk, the preachers won the hearts of many of the pioneers.[1] Another crisis was the immigrant flood: as the millions poured in from Ireland or Continental Europe, they found or brought with them the churches which could serve as

---

[1] The classic study was F. J. Turner, *The Frontier in American Life* (New York, 1920).

familiar landmarks in America, preserving their languages and customs.[1] The third crisis came with Americanisation: even when the use of English and pride in being American became dominant in the second and third generation after immigration, the American churches have still been valued as a means of preserving or gaining some identity in this mobile society by recalling ethnic and cultural roots, and by reaffirming the idealism of the American dream. And the fourth crisis came with industrialisation: as the cities grew the churches were weakened, but the weakening seems to have been less in America than in Europe, partly owing to heroic efforts by American churchmen to reach and serve the urban masses.[2] Thus American religion has flourished through identifying itself with the people after the most fruitful crisis for the churches in the whole of their history in the New World—the First Amendment to the Constitution of the United States in 1791, enacting that "Congress shall make no law respecting an establishment of religion, or prohibiting the free exercise thereof."[3]

The Social Reality of American Religion

The peculiarities of the American religious scene are often misrepresented abroad, in the belief that the religious overtones given to the "manifest destiny" of "America the Beautiful" are humbug, for at heart the American is as godless as the European. Thus recent decisions of the Supreme Court, sharply separating Church and State and culminating in the 1962 prohibition of even the simplest of prayers in public schools, have been cited as proof that secularism is the real creed of America. What is not so widely known outside the United States is that the churches enjoy massive concessions under the tax laws. Up to a limit, a benefactor to organised religion may deduct his charitable gift from his income before declaring his tax liability. The churches are not taxed, and only recently have municipalities begun to tax church-owned businesses. Thus it is partly at the state's expense that the American churches maintain their highly impressive network of elaborate buildings, specialist personnel and millions of amateurs for the purpose of "Christian education". A few American children appear to escape all religious

[1] The classic study was H. Richard Niebuhr, *The Social Sources of Denominationalism* (New York, 1929).
[2] See A. I. Abell, *The Urban Impact on American Protestantism* (Hamden, Conn., 1962).
[3] The best introductory narratives are Franklin Littell, *From State Church to Pluralism* (New York, 1962), and Jerald C. Brauer, *Protestantism in America* (revd. edn., Philadelphia, 1965). See also J. T. Ellis, *American Catholicism* (Chicago, 1956).

instruction, but (through Sunday schools and "released time" on normal schooldays) most of them seem to be educated at least as effectively as British children in the elements of Christianity and in the routine of church membership, although in the United States public money is not spent on religious instruction so openly as it is in Britain.[1] Nor is the effective influence of religion in the life of society much less strong in America than it is in Britain, although in the United States there is no equivalent to the Established Churches of England and Scotland. The custom of the Houses of Congress to begin their daily work with prayers (more spontaneous than those offered in the Houses of Parliament at Westminster) symbolises a real, although perhaps somewhat vague, allegiance to religion among American adults—specially since the Chaplain's official prayers are supplemented by prayer breakfasts and other manifestations of "piety along the Potomac". Few American statesmen are indifferent to religion; at least, very few indeed tell their electors that they are.

Confusion in the assessment of American religion as a social phenomenon is often caused by observers whose discussion of it proceeds after an unreasonably narrow definition of the word "religion". Thus we find a British sociologist, Dr. Bryan Wilson, writing that "belonging to a faith in America becomes unconnected with distinctive belief to an extent quite unparalleled in Europe."[2] What he means is that many American Protestants change their denomination because a particular church is more convenient to their home or because a particular congregation includes more of the kind of people they would like to be identified with in friendship or at least in prestige-giving association. But it does not follow that these mobile American Protestants hold *no* "distinctive belief". If we compare them with more thoroughly secularised Europeans, we do not find that their private morals are always superior, but we do find that they are more optimistic and more gregarious—or, to put it less pompously, we find that Americans believe in progress and together-ness. Despite the ethnic mixture, despite the vice and violence, there exists a moral consensus in American public opinion. We also find that these American characteristics are usually connected with a belief that religion is good for an individual and for a nation—any kind of religion. This is a layman's attitude, although shared by many leaders of American religious thought. It can lead to truly dreadful banalities, as in the speeches of Dwight Eisenhower, but it

[1] See Paul Freund and Robert Ulich, *Religion and the Public Schools* (Cambridge, Mass., 1965).
[2] *Religion in Secular Society* (London, 1966), p. 94.

:an also lead to the appeal to God which was the central theme of
he Gettysburg Address—and it is not secularism.

To be sure, the American churches in the cosy atmosphere of their
"suburban captivity" are often fairly remote from the harsher
realities of twentieth-century life.[1] But dilution of earnestness seems
to be absolutely inevitable once churchgoing becomes a large-scale
social phenomenon; and critics are often grossly unfair to the
surviving hard centre of American church life. For what do the
American millions meet, when they escape into their churches?
They meet there the endorsement of their own prejudices and
illusions, to a considerable extent—but unless the preacher has
completely diluted the religion which he has been commissioned to
proclaim, the millions are also liable to meet ideas which are
dangerous. Almost all American churches expose their ministers and
congregations to the reading of the Bible, to the singing of hymns
which embody historic Christianity, and to the practice of worshipping a transcendent God. Much of American religion remains
theologically conservative. American Catholicism, for example, is
dominated by its clergy, and the clergy are dominated by an Irish
respect for religious (although not for social or political) authority.
Among the Protestants, much Fundamentalism survives; great
denominations such as the Southern Baptists and many (especially
"Missouri Synod") Lutheran congregations are solidly conservative;
and even the avowedly liberal churches, even the "community
churches" which do not belong to a particular denomination, are
not without roots in historic Christianity. Although Unitarianism
is more successful in America than in Britain, attempts to found
churches which should be liberal rather than distinctively Christian
have had remarkably little success. What is surprising, in view of the
popularity of American religion, is not how *much* but how *little* its
theological content has been diluted.

It can be said that both the civil religion of contemporary America
(i.e. the watered-down "democratic" faith which pleases the millions
by confirming what they believe already) and the less compromising
and more challenging "old-time" religion in its various forms are
at bottom religions of escape—for, it can be said, none of this religiosity is allowed to argue with the crude materialism which dominates
Americans in real life. This verdict is pronounced by some Americans,
as well as by many foreigners who criticise America's material

[1] A relief from sociological or theological lamentations of this fact was the witty novel
about a People's Liberal Community Church by Peter de Vries, *The Mackerel Plaza*
(Boston, 1958).

prosperity while envying it; and (as we shall see in the next chapter) there are certainly some signs that such a verdict on American religion may be gaining validity as the psychological impact of secularisation increases.[1] Yet at present the verdict seems unnecessarily harsh. The truth in the 1960s seems to be that in the United States the religious communities exercise a considerable influence on the daily lives of their members. The society as a whole is pluralist, and no particular variety of religion dominates it, but the religious life of this pluralist society is *communal*—which, sociologically speaking, means that it is strong. In this respect the United States may be compared again with India.

The caste system has been of the essence of Hinduism, and its power still largely survives although the state has put its legislation and its influence behind some major reforms (the abolition of untouchability, the permission of marriages between members of different castes, etc.). Almost every Hindu born before 1945 has experienced his membership of a caste as an important factor in his psychology, and almost every Hindu has expressed this membership by participation in religious ceremonies presided over by a member of the Brahmin caste. Recently the necessities of "communal" development in independent India have compelled the government and other agencies to classify all citizens of the Republic in neighbourhoods, without regard to their castes. There has been a stream of anti-caste legislation since 1955, and influential spokesmen such as K. M. Panikkar have prophesied that the caste system must, and will, be transformed in the modernisation of India. Already in the cities and industries of India, caste divisions begin to lose their significance for fellow-workers who jostle each other in the crowded public transport or on the factory floor. Many in the younger generation of the elite share Gandhi's contempt for caste. But the overwhelming majority of Indians is still to be found in the villages, engaged in the work of subsistence agriculture and in domestic duties, with a few modern amenities but mainly in a timelessly conservative atmosphere. Here, in the village and the home, lies the strength of Hinduism. Here its rituals are almost always compulsory, indeed almost always unquestioned and beloved, symbols of the identity of the family and its kin (the "extended" family). The future of Hinduism seems to be bound up with the question of the future of this group life at the parched grass roots of Indian society. At present the withering away of the "extended" family in the Indian village is

[1] See below, pp. 129–130.

too remote for its consequences to be foreseen. A more immediate prospect, to the discussion of which we shall return, is that the Hindu stress on kinship will survive, and the Hindu ritual will survive, more strongly than the supernatural element in the Hindu religion.[1]

The communal sense of American Christianity is also strong, for communalism survives in urban America, however different its forms may be from those of rural India. (Indeed, in view of the divisions between White Anglo-Saxon Protestants, Catholics, Jews and Negroes, some observers go so far as to speak of an American caste system.) One great difference between American and Indian communalism is that in the United States the religious bodies to a considerable extent *create* the social communities. Recent studies of Roman Catholic parish life have painted, in the style of academic sociology, a picture of the "nuclear group" at the heart of a parish, around its priests.[2] The influence of this group is extended to a much wider circle of Catholics, mainly through regular pastoral visitation by parish priests. It has often been stated that such parish life depends on the discipline, and also on the relative poverty and educational backwardness, of American Catholics, many of whom are of Irish or Polish stock; and it has been added that the priests' lack of influence on the major worldly concerns of Catholic parishioners—on their family life, politics, attitudes at work, etc.—shows that secularisation is already eroding the authority exercised by the religious group and its representatives. We may agree that as the sophistication of American Catholics increases, their solidarity is likely to decrease. Much will depend on the clergy's handling of the laity's current revolt against the official teaching on birth control. But the social cohesion of American Catholicism is still very strong. It depends in part on the national network of parochial (i.e. denominational) schools built and maintained at enormous cost, and the present rumblings of Catholic critics against this education system as divisive and wasteful do not seem likely to lead to a major reversal of the policy.

Moreover, even if American Catholicism becomes more like American Protestantism, it will still not lose all sense of community.

[1] See K. M. Panikkar, *Hindu Society at the Crossroads* (New Delhi, 1955). Recent sociological studies which stress the enduring divisions in Indian society with their religious expressions include those by Irawati Karve: *Kinship Organization in India* (2nd edn., Bombay, 1965) and *Group Relations in Village Community* (with Y. B. Damle, Poona, 1963). See also below, pp. 215–16.
[2] E.g. J. H. Fichter, *Social Relations in an Urban Parish* (Chicago, 1954). For studies of parishes in Britain, see Conor Ward, *Priests and People* (Liverpool, 1961), and John Hickey, *Urban Catholics* (London, 1967).

The sociologist Gerhard Lenski has investigated the attitudes of Protestants and Jews, as well as of Catholics, in the great urban area of Detroit. He concentrated not on doctrinal problems but on attitudes to work, politics, family life and education—and he found that the religious factor was stronger than he had expected. "From our evidence," he wrote,[1] "it is clear that religion in various ways is constantly influencing the daily lives of the masses of men and women in the modern American metropolis . . . Depending on the socio-religious group to which a person belongs, the probabilities are increased or decreased that he will enjoy his occupation, indulge in installment buying, save to achieve objectives far in the future, believe in the American Dream, vote Republican, favor the welfare state take a liberal view on the issue of freedom of speech, oppose racial integration in the schools, migrate to another community, maintain close ties with his family, develop a commitment to the principle of intellectual autonomy, have a large family, complete a given unit of education, or rise in the class system. These are only a few of the consequences which we have observed to be associated with differences in socio-religious group membership, and the position of individuals in these groups."

The picture here presented is not a simple one of orthodox religion controlling personal and social behaviour; the interaction of religion and life is much more subtle than that. Nor is it a picture likely to give joy to all religious leaders—for many of the attitudes revealed have little to do with the Christian Gospel, and sometimes have not much to do with the leaders' official teaching (on social issues, religious leaders tend to be more liberal than their followers). But it is a picture of religion linked with the whole of the life of a community within Detroit. Since the emphasis of the German sociologist Ferdinand Tonnies on the intimate, organic community (*Gemeinschaft*) as contrasted with the looser, more functional society or organisation (*Gesellschaft*), many analysts of our culture have taught that, for better or for worse, the day of the real community is over in modern society. But in American cities, communalism—and religious communalism at that—survives.

Many Americans see no present signs that the influence of their religious communities is decreasing. "Most of the changes now occurring in the structure of American society," Professor Lenski concluded, "are weakening and reducing in relative size those elements in the

[1] *The Religious Factor* (revd. edn., New York, 1963), p. 320.
[2] On p. 319.

population least involved in the churches (e.g. first-generation immigrants and members of the working class), and strengthening and enlarging those elements most involved in the churches (e.g., third-generation immigrants and members of the middle classes)." The reference to immigrants indicates a development vital to the churches' strength. We have already mentioned that in the past, in the absence of secular agencies, the churches played an important role in the process of integration. They provided communities where the immigrant would feel at home (and often would be able to speak his native language); and these communities gradually and painlessly Americanised themselves (e.g. by adopting the English language for public services). The evidence suggests that this has been a role of diminishing effectiveness, as immigrants—or at least, their children—have become embarrassed with churches which might be reckoned backward-looking, and have turned instead to the more secular institutions of America (schools, trade unions, etc.) where the old European cultures are submerged (through ceremonies honouring the Federal United States flag, etc.). But the *third* generation is often the one which values the churches most, finding in them now convenient places for meeting friends and spouses without embarrassment. The churches are now thoroughly American and thoroughly respectable—but are valued because they are carriers of what seems attractive in a European group's culture which has lost most of its political and secular expressions.

Professor Lenski's reference to the decline of the anti-clerical working class, as capitalism progresses into a general prosperity not expected by Marx, is an even more important sociological observation. In the United States, many of the religious prophecies of Marx seem to have been falsified along with many of his economic predictions. The vast and growing middle classes of America tend to associate churchgoing with respectability, leisure and culture. As the days of struggle by the various ethnic groups have receded into history, the symbol of the American dream has become not the revolutionary barricade, but the "friendly" church—the coffee-stained heart of the long weekend in the affluent suburb. This "friendly" church probably owed much of its appeal in the harder days of the past to the ethnic sources of American denominationalism; but we have also to note that as America's ethnic groups mix and rise in the contemporary melting pot, so the separation of the denominations loses much of its old appeal—yet the "friendly" church survives as the great symbol.

It is important that critics should in fairness acknowledge that the strength of these American religious communities is connected with a moral consensus in the whole nation. In affluent America as in poor India, the religious communities may be valued by society chiefly as means of expressing and increasing that moral consensus. In India, the vitality of Hinduism (and of the minority groups of Muslims, Christians, Jains, Parsis, etc.) is due in part to the widespread Indian agreement that while the economic tasks of nation-building are urgent in order to avert famine, economic advance should not be bought at the price of denying the importance of the individual's spiritual life. In the United States, where economic progress is accorded a far higher priority, there survives a strong belief in certain values which the churches promote—those values of togetherness, helpfulness and enthusiasm for culture which add dignity to "the American way of life". As if to symbolise this moral consensus, most states in the Republic of India prohibit the public sale of alcoholic liquors, as the United States did for fourteen years of this century. Most Indian leaders constantly stress the importance of religion in the life of the country, and it was symbolic of much that Nehru's wish that there should be no religious ceremonies at his funeral was set aside by his heirs in deference to public sentiment. The Supreme Court of the United States, precisely in the years when it was driving religious worship and instruction out of the public educational system, was insisting that that system should be integrated racially. As many voices from the American churches have proclaimed, racial integration is one of the hardest possible ways of saying that America has a moral consensus, expressed in the formula that it is "one nation under God, indivisible, with liberty and justice for all".

It seems clear that in the United States as in the Republic of India, *the "secular" state governs a people which is still profoundly religious.* Thus we find that an eloquent critic of the parochial smugness and "suburban captivity" of the American churches presents this argument on the basis of an essentially religious understanding of that ambiguous term, "secularisation". "The ordering of life," runs this critic's definition of secularisation, "falls to mankind under God and not by delegation from the religious hierarchy."[1] In that self-revealing phrase from an American radical, the intoxication or despair created for the intellectuals of Europe by the death of God has been reduced to the religious democracy which has been at the heart of the American dream since the Pilgrim Fathers. One of the

[1] Gibson Winter, *The New Creation as Metropolis* (New York, 1963), p. 38.

most distinguished of American sociologists has, indeed, described the United States as "the new modern version of the Christian society". "By most of the standards of our dominant tradition of liberal Protestantism," he added, "it is a society that must be said to have advanced far along the road of institutionalising the basic moral precepts of its religious base, however far it falls short of the desired level of perfection."[1] Whether or not we agree with that recent assessment of the American ordering of life, we may certainly conclude with a Victorian Englishman, Lord Bryce: "so far from suffering from want of State support, religion seems in the United States to stand all the firmer because, standing alone, she is seen to stand by her own strength."[2]

Religion in Europe

When we return to the Europe where the modern form of secularisation began, and when we ask what may be the significance for Europeans of the twentieth-century revival of religion in the United States, the correct answer seems to be complicated—for in American religion various elements are fused which cannot be expected to come together in exactly the same way elsewhere. More than any other religious figure, the evangelist Billy Graham has challenged the whole West in the 1950s and 1960s with the self-confidence of godly America—but Europeans, whether impressed or cynical, cannot possibly adopt Dr. Graham's style. The present uncertainty in Europe may be seen by asking briefly *whether the United States or Sweden is likely to provide the best clue to the future of English religion.*

In England during the first half of this century, the figures for weekly church attendance slumped from nearly a quarter of the population to nearly a tenth. York, for example, is the seat of one of

[1] Talcott Parsons in *America and the Future of Theology*, ed. W. A. Beardslee (Philadelphia, 1967), p. 153.
[2] James Bryce, *The American Commonwealth* (London; 2nd. revd. edn., 1891), vol. ii, p. 584. Bryce was echoing a famous remark about the Church by the seventeenth-century Pascal. Apart from Will Herberg, *Catholic, Protestant, Jew* (cited above, p. 49), some recent books on American religion are: Reinhold Niebuhr, *Pious and Secular in America* (New York, 1957; British title, *Essays Godly and Ungodly*); A. Roy Echardt, *The Surge of Piety in America* (New York, 1958); Martin E. Marty, *The New Shape of American Religion* (New York, 1959) and *Varieties of Unbelief* (New York, 1964); Gibson Winter, *The Suburban Captivity of the Churches* (New York, 1961); Peter Berger, *The Precarious Vision* (New York, 1961) and *The Noise of Solemn Assemblies* (New York, 1961). But these were criticisms of conventional piety by radical intellectuals, and it is fair to balance them with comment by a minister with a better historical perspective and a warmer sympathy with the life of an ordinary congregation, such as Ronald E. Osborn, *The Spirit of American Christianity* (New York, 1959). It is also fair to remember that the self-criticism of the American churches has inspired an impressive amount of courage in thought and action: see, e.g., Earl H. Brill, *The Creative Edge of American Protestantism* (New York, 1966).

the Church of England's two archbishops, and is dominate
architecturally by York Minster. But in York on a Sunday in 194
only one citizen in twenty-one attended Anglican worship, whereas i
1901 it had been one in seven.[1] Since a considerable prosperity an
education came to England between 1900 and 1950, such figure
suggest that the "withdrawing roar" of religious faith may hav
been speeded by material and intellectual progress. But the puzzle i
how to interpret this trend.

The York statistics may represent some of the delayed effects c
nineteenth-century alienations between the churches and th
industrial democracy. Trends in religious observance frequentl
register a delay before they reflect trends in social and cultural lif
and it would not be surprising if the English churches in the twentiet
century were paying for the sins of their Victorian fathers. If this i
the correct analysis, future trends may show an upward swing i
religious observance, so that England resembles the United States i
its piety as well as in more mundane matters. On the other hand, th
flourishing American churches may reflect the influence of som
special factors in American social history, and these factors may prov
to be temporary even in America. In that case, the present mora
and religious inspiration of the American way of life will be replace
in actual fact by the anarchy which superficial observers of ethics an
religion already attribute to the American people. Amid the genera
collapse of religion due to the psychological impact of our secula
century, the model for the religious future of England (and of man
other countries) will be Sweden. It may be that England, for all i
agreement about the virtues of tolerance and kindness, will neve
recover the stronger moral consensus of the American way of lif
and its religious celebration; instead, England will come even close
than it now is to the Swedish variety of tolerance, kindness an
moral liberty.[2]

In Stockholm, statistics showing the regularly churchgoing elemer
in the population hover around three per cent. The Director of th
Institute of Religious Sociology in Stockholm has recently reckone
that over the country as a whole, including all denominations, th
figure is about six per cent.[3] Yet more than most countries Swede
was once a religious unity, and this past is recalled by the fact tha
only two per cent of Swedes have exercised their legal right to co

[1] See B. S. Rowntree and B. R. Lavers, *English Life and Leisure* (London, 1951).
[2] A discussion was provided by Alasdair MacIntyre, *Secularization and Moral Chang*
and David Martin, *A Sociology of English Religion* (both London, 1967).
[3] In *The Scandinavian Churches*, ed. L. S. Hunter (London, 1965), p. 50.

tract out of contributing to the upkeep of the (Lutheran) "Folk Church". Not many more refrain from having their children baptised, their daughters married and themselves buried in church; and most Swedes are still solemnly confirmed in order that they may receive Holy Communion. The Swedish Church possesses many beautiful buildings which seem to belong to the landscape; its organisations and finance are directly under the control of the state; and its well-paid clergy act as civil servants, collecting the statistics of births, marriages and deaths. What, then, has ruined the religion of Sweden? The history of the period approximately 1875-1925 records the alienation of the essentially authoritarian and rural Folk Church from the new industrial workers, but since Sweden's brand of Socialism has now secured both social justice and economic prosperity what matters even more than that legacy of working-class bitterness is the alienation of the middle classes. And what matters even more than the anti-Christian character of many of the effective trends in public opinion is the lack of vigour in the Christian response to the secular challenge. Swedish Christians do much good work, of course, but there seems to be a prevailing complacency. Thus we find the Christian sociologist just cited writing about Sweden: "There is no need for concern over a supposed retreat from Christian moral standards; what is happening rather is that the norms of Christian morality are now being accepted, not because they are imposed by society and regarded as authoritative from the first, but because personal experience of life has shown them to be true."[1]

Miss Kathleen Nott, who is known as a contemptuous critic of T. S. Eliot and other Christians,[2] published an account of a stay in Sweden which expressed a good many reservations about that country, "the most comfortable and least cosy in the world". When she went to Sweden her mind was full of its social problems. "The Swedes are so accustomed to being asked about their high suicide rate that officials get it in first . . . The best counter seemed to be, 'Well, no, it's the drunkenness I've called about'—or the divorce rate—or the lunacy—or the homosexuality."[3] She left the country feeling that its human problems have reached their present proportions precisely because Sweden is a society which does not interfere in people's private lives unless people misbehave in such an anti-social way as to demand the attention of the social workers and even

[1] See p. 53. See also *Sweden in the Sixties*, ed. I. Wizelius (Stockholm, 1967).
[2] *The Emperor's Clothes* (London, 1953) was a sustained attack on "the dogma in the manger".
[3] *A Clean, Well-Lighted Place* (London, 1961), p. 26.

of the prisons. Here we have a welfare state which has explicitly left its citizens' morality to their free choices. Here we have, too, "a standardised mass-culture distributed through broadcasting, newspapers, etc., which imposes a superficial uniformity but is basically a-ethical: the image of man is presented without his deeper motivations; themes such as sin, guilt, responsibility, anxiety, aging, sorrow and death are being eliminated; and we are left with a superficial description of happiness and prestige."[1]

This withdrawal of the state from concern for people's morals or motives may be part of what being a secular country means, if secularisation is taken in a more radical sense than in India or the United States; and it contrasts with the strong pressure of public opinion on private behaviour under the regimes of Communism's quasi-religion. On the whole, Miss Nott seems to have thought the prize of individual freedom worth the cost of moral disorder in Sweden—for, as she says, a free society must come to terms with the fact that its citizens will have some anti-social tendencies. Sweden apparently no longer needs a Folk Church, or even a quasi-religion as a substitute for its Lutheran past. Its moral unity is apparently only of pride in being affluent and tolerant. Its religion has apparently been overwhelmed by the impact of our secular century.

The Pluralist Society

In assessing the potential significance of American religion for Europe and for the future of civilisation, we may try to simplify a complex picture by considering first the significance of *the pluralist society under a secular state.*

The example of the United States shows that a society genuinely open to religion as well as to other convictions may be built on the basis of the separation of Church and State. And this may be all that many secularists demand; for example, H. J. Blackham, the Director of the British Humanist Association, urges not the abolition of religion but the end of any pretence that it should have the monopoly. "Religious faith," Mr Blackham writes, "belongs along with all ultimates of interpretation, choice, aim, dedication, aspiration, worship. Because these cannot be required or sanctioned by a society without losing their authenticity, they are not therefore without profound effect upon society."[2] If this is to be the pattern of the

---

[1] H. Aronson of the University of Lund, in *Christian Social Ethics in a Changing World*, ed. J. C. Bennett (New York, 1966), p. 265.
[2] *Religion in a Modern Society* (London, 1966), p. 129.

future, many religious believers will welcome the challenge. They believe that a secular state can leave sufficient opportunity for "religion" in its more limited sense, according to the nineteenth-century ideal of "a free church in a free state", but above all they believe that a secular state can be built on the moral unity given by the general acceptance, by religious believers and agnostics alike, of some "self-evident" truths of Natural Law, or at least of the duty to secure liberty, dignity and justice for all through the tasks of nation-building. Thus for broadly social as well as for narrowly religious reasons we find that a social analyst who is perhaps the shrewdest thinker among Indian Christians, M. M. Thomas, is an advocate—although also a careful definer—of the secular state;[1] as was the leading intellectual among Catholics in the United States, John Courteney Murray.[2]

The debate in modern England has its special interest. J. N. Figgis in *The Churches in the Modern State* (London, 1913) advocated a position not far from the pluralism of Thomas and Murray. But the formal establishment of the Church of England has remained, and during the first quarter of the century Nonconformists resented the privileges involved. In the second quarter their cry for disestablishment diminished, partly because the Established Church's privileges had decreased, but a wish to liberate the Church from the Crown's nomination of the bishops, Parliament's veto over changes in worship, etc., has remained. The probable solution of this problem looks like being the re-establishment of the Church of England (particularly in connection with its reunion with the Methodist Church) according to the pattern provided by the established (and Presbyterian) Church of Scotland. The Church of Scotland is a National Church in the sense that it accepts an obligation to serve the whole nation, and is honoured by the nation as such; but the state has no control over its government. Such an arrangement applied to England might secure many of the advantages of "a free church in a free state" while avoiding the disadvantages for the churches which exist in the American form of the separation of Church and State. The advantages would be that both Church and State would secure their integrity; and the disadvantages which could be avoided would be the difficulties of the American churches in relating religion to government at the national and local levels, and to the state-sponsored schools. The possibility arises of a National Church which

---

[1] *The Christian Response to the Asian Revolution* (London, 1966).
[2] *We Hold These Truths: Catholic Reflections on the American Proposition* (New York, 1960).

may offer the contributions of religion to public life (as symbolised at the coronation of the monarch) without confusing religion with politics.[1]

In recent years the debate in England has shifted away from the more formal aspects of establishing a church to the more substantial question, whether it is right to give religion privileges in the educational, broadcasting and television systems of the nation. When comparatively few Englishmen regularly go to church, such privileges seem anomalies. However, surveys of public opinion show that the privileges are not in fact widely resented. The great majority of English parents seem to want religious worship and instruction in schools, and religious broadcasts have large audiences. It seems probable that improvements in the communicating power of religious broadcasting and education will take place in the context of continuing privileges for religion. Much attention has also been given to the relationship of law and morality. Until recently many British laws attempted to force an old-fashioned version of Christian morality on to a public which rejected the doctrinal basis of that ethic, and a healthy distinction between crime and sin is only beginning to emerge in current legal reforms. But it is unlikely that British (or other) law will ever be entirely without moral content. Some evidence that the British people wishes to observe high standards of decency and compassion comes in its acceptance of the legal prohibition of public prostitution and racial discrimination.[2]

This confused situation has resulted in a contrast between two thoughtful books by distinguished lay members of the Church of England. In *The Idea of a Christian Society* (London, 1939), T. S. Eliot argued that although only the community of believing churchmen could be expected to reach the highest standards, the whole of society could be expected to conform with Christianity to the extent, for example, of accepting public regulation of private morality. In *The Idea of a Secular Society* (Oxford, 1963), D. L. Munby rejected this argument in favour of a society without a common philosophy and without official images, but with a deep respect for the variety of individuals and for the importance of facts. Many in England would probably feel that, while the rejection of T. S. Eliot's nostalgia for the sacred society of Christendom was inevitable, Mr. Munby was unrealistic in his minimising of the role of public opinion with its

[1] See *Church and State in Britain since 1820*, a collection of documents edited by David Nicholls (London, 1967.) A similar discussion has arisen in Sweden.
[2] Good examples of recent British discussion are Michael Keeling, *Morals in a Free Society*, and Basil Mitchell, *Law, Morality and Religion in a Secular Society* (both London, 1967).

images and agencies. The moral pressure exercised by society is still a great reality; and perhaps what Mr. Munby meant to defend was not the "secular society" but the "pluralist" or "open" society. On Mr. Munby's showing the *state*, not the society, needs to be secular. And if the society is genuinely "pluralist" it may not be necessary to enforce a complete separation of the religion in that society from the work of the state. Religious bodies, like general charities, may—and to a certain extent must—have dealings with a secular state. It may be possible to work out an arrangement for safeguarding the freedoms of all citizens in a pluralist society, while relating the agencies of religion to the public agencies.

Popular Churches in the Pluralist Society

We may consider next the relevance of the American pattern of *active churches which depend on popular support, not on state patronage.*

There are some signs of an increased willingness of church members in Britain and Western Europe over recent years to give money to support their churches, whether or not they attend church as often as was the former pattern. When Tom Harrisson revisited the English "Worktown" (it was actually Bolton) after an absence of twenty years, his new survey noted that although attendance at the local churches had declined, their income had increased. This seemed "in part a product of the affluent society; in part a deepening sense of responsibility towards religious institutions by those who remain concerned. This sort of change is difficult to measure . . . It is not the sort of feeling that can be expressed by an ordinary Briton holding it—sometimes only vaguely and far down in private opinion—when asked by a stranger, however subtly questioning."[1]

For the future of the Church of England, for example, the sixty-six per cent of the total population who were in the 1960s baptised members of the Church may matter less than the six per cent who then received Holy Communion at Easter. The fact that the establishment of the Church of England as the National Church has received few formal, legal changes since the return of Charles II to his throne in 1660 may matter less than a development which, although unofficial and often unpopular, has been continuous in the spiritual life of that Church since the middle of the eighteenth century. This internal development has, in successive (and to some extent incompatible) stages, struggled for an integrity of obedience to the

[1] *Britain Revisited* (London, 1961), p. 85.

Bible through the Evangelical movement; for an integrity of Christian fellowship around the Eucharist through the Tractarian movement and the ensuing Catholic revival; and for an integrity of intellectual life and social responsibility through the Broad Church movement, liberalism and modernism.[1] When journalists—clever men who are critical and smart but not too obviously unsympathetic —visit the British churches in the 1960s, they tend to note two things: an obvious bewilderment among churchgoers and church leaders about their minority role as secularisation advances, and a somewhat baffling faithfulness which sustains this minority in their defiance of current trends.[2] Such books by shrewd outsiders explain why books by realistic insiders often still end, after recording all the difficulties, on a note of hope.[3] If a hopeful note is less often struck in the English Free Churches, the (Presbyterian) Church of Scotland remains confident. In Scotland about 1¼ million out of a population of 5 millions are communicant members of their National Church, and it is reckoned that some sixty per cent of the population have connections with this Church, with Roman Catholicism or with one of the smaller religious bodies.[4]

The religious statistics of Scotland disclose a situation not entirely unlike the prosperity of the American churches. The Church of Scotland, and to a lesser extent the Roman Catholic Church there, belong to the people, as do the American denominations. Behind this popularity lies a history almost as arduous as the history of American religion—and, significantly, it includes for a period a close parallel to the American pattern of a number of denominations competing to reach the people.

The Reformation which reached its climax in 1560 pledged the Church of Scotland to pastoral care for every parish in the land. A special consequence was a nation-wide educational effort. During the next three centuries many ministers and congregations rejected the discipline of the National Church, and specially after the Disruption of 1843 the Presbyterian system was duplicated through-

---

[1] The best introduction to the history, with a bibliography, was provided by J. R. H. Moorman, Bishop of Ripon, *The Church in England* (revd. edn., London, 1967).

[2] Examples of this kind of literature are Paul Ferris, *The Church of England* (London, 1962) and George Scott, *The RCs* (London, 1967).

[3] Examples are Kenneth Slack, *The British Churches Today* (London, 1961); Roger Lloyd *The Church of England 1900-1965* (London, 1966); *The English Catholics 1850-1950*, ed G. A. Beck (London, 1950). An African sociologist, Dr. K. A. Busia, has studied congregations in an English industrial city, Birmingham; see his *Churches in Urban Britain* (London, 1966).

[4] Contrast Christopher Driver, *A Future for the Free Churches?* (London, 1962), with John Highet, *The Scottish Churches* (London, 1960).

out the land, with the "Free Kirk" confronting the "Auld Kirk".
But in the twentieth century, in a process which reached its climax
in 1929, most of the Presbyterian dissenters have been reconciled to
a National Church which has adjusted itself to many of their
demands. Without this history of strenuous effort and self-criticism,
conditions would not now be so favourable for the Church of Scotland
today, for what the history amounts to is the absorption of the valid
protests of the Reformation and Disruption into the historic continuity of national religion. We may contrast this history with that
of Scotland's old ally, France. A fundamental fact of modern French
history has been the failure of the French Reformation—a failure
which, although never complete (for French Protestant churches
have survived), was virtually sealed by the intolerances of the
Catholic Louis XIV and of the rationalist French Revolution. The
Catholic Church has been the only possibility for most Frenchmen
who wished to be religious—and the French Catholic Church,
despite bursts of independence, has been effectively controlled either
by the state or, after 1905, by the Vatican. This prolonged attempt
to impose uniformity made it difficult for renewing energy to flow
into French religion from roots in the life of the people. However,
we may reject the ideal of uniformity without abandoning the view
that the most effective church is a great National Church into which
dissenting protests have been absorbed. Dissent for the sake of dissent,
when the protests have lost much of their topicality, is not to be
recommended if what a church seeks is influence in the life of its
nation. Scotland shows that—and not only Scotland. Between 1900
and 1960 Free Church membership declined by about forty per cent
in an English population which increased by about a third. This
decline in the "dissenting" religious bodies in England has been
greater than the decline in the Church of England, which has been
slowly reforming itself in the directions desired by the original
Nonconformists.

Active churches which depend on popular support are, then, still
possible in the modern world—whatever Marx thought. And it does
not seem to be finally disastrous if the support comes mainly from the
middle classes—whatever Marxists now say. Christianity when
domesticated in its "suburban captivity" in the United States is
plainly open to much criticism; but such a Christianity, however
unromantic, may have lessons to teach. We have to ask not whether
American affluence will survive but what will be the cultural consequences of its gradual spread throughout the West. Economic

trends seem likely to falsify Marxist predictions, and make almost all North America and almost all Europe middle class. What will that mean to the churches? At present in England only about twenty per cent of the population identifies itself as middle class, and of the present bulk of the remainder it is true to say that "one aspect of working-class styles especially important for participation in church life is the widespread resistance to *any* kind of major involvement in voluntary associations, trade unions included. With every step up the status scale active participation in voluntary associations of every kind increases."[1] The spread of suburbia over the face of Europe may bring into new prominence that important American phenomenon: the keen support of voluntary associations including the suburban family church.

Religion and National Culture

Finally, we may consider the wider relevance of the role of the American denomination as *the carrier of a national culture* (Lutheranism preserving Swedish memories, etc.), a role which becomes all the more significant when political independence has been lost through confederation or conquest.

The twentieth century has certainly witnessed in Europe a surprising recovery by some churches which have, at least to some extent, overcome their alienation from their own people. This can be seen in France. We noted that the identification of the French Catholic Church with the *ancien régime* of the eighteenth century and with the monarchies of the nineteenth century brought about its downfall early in the twentieth century. A few Christian democrats such as Marc Sagnier, and a few Christian socialists such as Charles Péguy, made lonely protests, but the Church's identification with the enemies of the Republic was effectively questioned only when priests and laymen fought and suffered in the trenches of 1914-18. Over 4,500 priests were among the million French casualties. That suffering by its Church for *la patrie* was repeated under the German occupation, 1940-44, when Catholics and Protestants worked together in the Resistance and Catholic priests went voluntarily to minister among the working people deported to Germany (although it was also true that many Catholics supported the Pétain regime). Frenchmen grew bored with anti-clericalism. Diplomatic relations with the Vatican were resumed in 1921; and both the reactionary bishops and the

[1] David Martin, *A Sociology of English Religion*, p. 105.

anti-clerical politician Edouard Herriot failed to sabotage the Catholic Church's agreement with the Republic. After the second war modest state subsidies to church schools became possible. And so French religion slowly came to have a spiritual integrity which was more than the spirit which had fought to preserve the visible integrity of all Catholic institutions and doctrines; and the new religion was humble, charitable, outgoing. The desire to form specifically Christian fellowships within the secular environment led not to a Catholic Party but to Catholic Action's "apostolate of the laity". Catholic Action applied to France the maxim of Pius XI, the Pope who encouraged it in the 1920s and 1930s: the Christians in a particular group or class must spread their faith among their own companions, much as the Church in Asia or Africa must be rooted in the local life, must become a "native mission". In 1941 the *Mission de France* opened its seminary at Lisieux, to train priests not for the comfortable routine of a *bourgeois* parish but for an unprecedented mission within the dechristianised areas. A map of the religious geography of France, and a crucifix, looked down on the students during their meals. The *Mission de Paris*, founded by Cardinal Suhard in 1944 for the industrial proletariat alienated from the parish churches, led to the experiment of the worker-priests.

The tragic drama of these worker-priests—crushed as they were between Communism and other anti-clericalism in the working-class, and indifference or hostility in the bulk of the Church—emphasised the continuing problem of the Church's alienation from the people.[1] So did the refusal to be baptised, made by one of the century's most brilliant and saintly converts, Simone Weil. She hated the idea of separation from the mass of her fellow-countrymen. That made her refuse to eat extra food in her illness, and brought her to her death in 1943; it also made her refuse to become a member of the Catholic Church. "I love God, Christ and the Catholic faith," she wrote, "but I have not the slightest love for the Church . . . What frightens me is the Church as a social structure."[2]

Yet the inner recovery of French Catholicism could not be crushed. It has been expressed in the vision of intellectuals such as the philosopher Jacques Maritain or the novelist François Mauriac, men of

[1] The best short study of this is by a German scholar: Gregor Siefer, *The Church and Industrial Society* (1960; Eng. trans., London, 1964). The background is given in Adrien Dansette, *Destin du Catholicisme Français 1926-56* (Paris, 1957) and other works cited in Siefer's full bibliography. See also Émile Poulat, *La Naissance des Prêtres Ouvriers* (Paris, 1965).
[2] See her letters and papers, *Waiting on God* (1950; Eng. trans., London, 1951), specially Letters I and II.

integrity concerned to relate the traditional faith to the realities of the twentieth century. The Catholic review *Esprit*, founded by Emmanuel Mounier, has been since 1932 a focus for a "personalism" which has claimed freedom and fulfilment for humanity instead of privilege for the Church. As if anticipating such a movement, the French philosopher Henri Bergson in his last book distinguished between *Two Sources of Religion and Morality*.[1] One source was static; that kind of religion conserved the moral conventions of the group, as Durkheim had said. But there was another source, both more mysterious and more commendable, which produced a dynamic and adventurous religion and an "open" morality of human dignity and growth. To that religion, born in the human spirit, Bergson at the end gave his allegiance.

Of course, philosophy is not enough. What of practical religion? The French worker-priests were disciplined, and some left the Church. At the same time, the leading French theologians with liberal views were exiled from Paris and silenced. There seemed some prospect of a return of the "black terror" of 1907. But when Pius XII died, the French cardinals played a leading part in the election of the more liberal John XXIII, and French churchmen (including theologians disgraced in the 1950s) were among the spiritual masters of the Second Vatican Council. With many of its insights now preserved in that Council's decrees, no Church in the world has done more than the French Catholic Church to embody the spirit of Christian renewal, reaching out to the people in the people's language. (The sociological researches sponsored by the Church have been inspired by this motive.) And in 1965 a symbolic gesture came to mark the new mood: permission came from Rome for the revival of the experiment of priests in full-time industrial work, under slightly different conditions and with no publicity. The working class to which the priests returned was more prosperous, and there was some likelihood that a militant proletariat preferring Communism to Catholicism would be a diminishing factor among the French Church's problems. The dechristianisation of France has, of course, not been reversed, but with its four million regular communicants the Church of the 1960s is in better heart than was the Church of the 1900s.

In France, then, such reconciliation as has been achieved between the clergy and the people has been helped by the Church's patriotism: a patriotism of the trenches and also a patriotism of "open" love.

[1] 1932; Eng. trans., London, 1935.

But Catholic nationalism is a wider phenomenon, for the Catholic Church has been supported in other European countries by peoples who, in a time of a national crisis, have found in the Church the great sanctuary of national memories and hopes. Cardinal Mercier of Malines, who from 1914 to 1918 was with King Albert the symbol of Belgian courage under German occupation, has had an unexpected number of successors. The greatest example of Catholic nationalism is, of course, Irish Catholicism. The Catholic Church virtually *was* Ireland when the country was exploited and Irish culture derided by English Protestants; when political independence was won in 1922 the Catholic Church received no establishment or endowment, but also needed none, in order to be the Church of the Irish people (with a strong and growing membership in the Northern Protestant counties united with Great Britain). The majority of the Irish people is now dispersed outside Ireland—and everywhere gives strength to the Catholic Church.

The national spirit has sustained Catholicism even under Communism. The Catholic Church has been the heart and soul of Poland through the centuries when the country has been poised precariously between Protestant or Nazi Germany and Orthodox or Communist Russia. Independent Poland after 1918 gave a privileged position to Catholicism. Although the German and Russian occupations from 1939 executed or deported thousands of bishops and priests as the leaders of Polish patriotism, the revolt of 1956, while not changing the Communist character of the government, freed Cardinal Wysynski from gaol, instilled a respect for popular religion into the state authorities, and even (for a time) restored religion to the state schools. The Polish Communists organised a mostly abortive movement of "patriotic priests" to work with them, but it was precisely by being the symbols of remembered independence, proudly patriotic in the latest phase of Poland's sufferings, that the Polish priests loyal to their own tradition have achieved and retained their popular following. The failure of the 1956 revolt in Hungary to secure similar concessions was due partly to the Hungarian churches' record of support for Nicholas Horthy's pro-Nazi regime (1920-45); but the partial liberalisation of Hungary since 1956 has included more freedom for the religion which still survives fairly strongly, as the controversial figure of Cardinal Mindszenty recedes into history. In another country under Communist rule, Czechoslovakia, religion, although severely handicapped until the democratisation of 1968, has gained both in internal morale and in the respect of the people, in comparison with the inter-war atmosphere of French-style anti-clericalism. We are not claiming that the future of the Catholic Church in Eastern Europe is assured. Thousands of bishops and priests—perhaps as many as 10,000—were executed or exiled in the decade 1945-55, and the Church which has survived carries many wounds. Control by the Vatican, which to many has belonged to the essence of Catholicism, has become tenuous, although only in China have the links with Rome been broken completely. All that is being claimed is that under Communism the Catholic Church has become a carrier of national culture rather than a supporter of social reaction. Marx could not foresee this social process which has made it possible that the Church will outlive the Communist Party in the hearts of the people.

At the other end of the political spectrum, the Catholic Church in Spain and Portugal has owed much of its hold on the people to the fact that the old religion—the religion which blessed the crusade against the Moors in Spain and the discovery and colonisation of America and the East, the religion which kept its glamour while the country grew old and poor—has remained the symbol of national pride. The Spanish laws of 1938-9, re-establishing religion in the schools and state grants for the clergy, said so very plainly: "Catholicism is the very marrow of the history of Spain." And in many parts of Western Europe since 1945, the leadership of Catholics has been conspicuous among the Christian Democrats who have led national reconstruction; for after the collapse of Hitler and Mussolini, as after the fall of the ancient Roman Empire, the Catholic Church has in the eyes of Europe appeared as the City of God against which "the gates of hell shall not prevail".

We have also to remember the nationalism of Russians and others in the Orthodox Churches. If we ask why the Greek Orthodox Church, despite great problems and scandals, retains such a grip on the affections of the Greek people, we receive a similar answer: it was the Church which was the shelter of the Greek spirit while the country was under Turkish occupation until 1829, and the memories of that past have not perished. The sufferings of the two World Wars brought Church and people still closer together, and an Archbishop of Athens, the great Damaskinos, was called to lead his country as regent when the alternative after the Second World War was Communism.[1] More recently, Europe has seen Archbishop Makarios

[1] Portraits of the Greek Church were provided by Peter Hammond, *The Waters of Marah* (London, 1956), and Mario Rinvolucri, *Anatomy of a Church* (1965; Eng. trans., London, 1967).

acting as the leader of Greek nationalism against the British, and emerging as the President of independent Cyprus. The Rumanian and Bulgarian Churches are other Orthodox Churches with popular followings, although the Communist regimes have been too efficient to allow their bishops to play a role as nationalist "ethnarchs" in the style of Makarios.

Protestantism also has gained from patriotism. Protestants have been involved in many of the religious situations just mentioned. In Norway under German occupation, Bishop Berggrav became the symbol of patriotism—and that was only one part of the toughening of religion in those stern years.[1] In Germany itself the standing temptation of Christians has been to be *too* patriotic, and at more than one point in this book we shall have to observe the tragic compromises involved. But the defiance of the "Confessing" Church against Hitler, symbolised in the great names of Martin Niemöller and Dietrich Bonhoeffer, turned out to be the true patriotism, and since 1945 in West Germany that group has been significant as a source of moral integrity and self-respect. Its survivors have carried a Christian contribution into new questions confronting society; and the memory of its courage has shown that the *Acts of the Apostles* can be continued into our own time. In very few places since 1945 has the relationship between an old religion and a new society been worked out more impressively than it has been by the Protestants of East Germany—Lutheranism's birthplace. Warned and even strengthened by their experience under Hitler, these Christians have maintained much of their integrity under Communism, but equally significant has been the determination of many of them to love their people and to co-operate with their government within the limits of conscience. Such Christians in a Marxist land have avoided an "inner flight" to the capitalist West, and under a barrage of atheist propaganda many East Germans have been surprisingly loyal to the Church remaining in their midst.[2]

Much of the popularity of the Church of Scotland—to turn to a Protestantism which lives in less testing circumstances—rests on its appeal to Scottish nationalism. Since the union of the thrones of

[1] It is illuminating to compare Adolf Keller's *Religion and the European Mind* (London, 1934) with his *Christian Europe Today* (New York, 1942).
[2] The Communist propaganda against religion in East Germany was documented by Hans-Gerhard Koch, *The Abolition of God* (1961; Eng. trans., London, 1963); the unyielding resistence in the autobiography of Bishop Otto Dibelius of Berlin, *In the Service of the Lord* (1963; Eng. trans., London, 1965); and a more flexible response in Johannes Hamel, *A Christian in East Germany* (London, 1960) and in *Pro-Existence*, ed. Elisabeth Adler (London, 1964).

Scotland and England in 1603, the Church has been Scotland's main national pride, and since the abolition of the Scottish Parliament the General Assembly of the Church has been the chief national forum. The social function of the Church of Scotland in the United Kingdom, in the eyes of the Scottish people, therefore has a close resemblance to the social function of a denomination in the United States, in the eyes of immigrants and their descendants; it keeps "auld acquaintance" alive.

The Church of England is, like the Church of Scotland, national and conservative in the main; but it has a much weaker patriotic appeal. Among the many factors which account for this difference between Scotland and England, the bulk of the English people's lack of identification with a great national cause during most of this century must certainly be reckoned significant. The two world wars brought out the patriotism of the English people, and were accompanied by Days of National Prayer and the like, but few other causes have aroused a secular or religious devotion. The end of the British Empire and the country's economic troubles in the 1950s and 1960s caused a crisis of national identity, but not a resurgence of national pride. The vitality of a National Church must be affected by such sluggish trends in public opinion. We may, however, venture the speculations that the Church of England's fortunes might have been different if England had been occupied by an alien power at a date later than 1066, and that its popularity as a carrier of national culture may yet be strengthened when for economic reasons the English people are forced into a political association with continental Europe. As immigrants of English or Scottish descent are to the United States, and as Scotland now is to England, so England may then be to Europe; and as a social institution the English Church may be strengthened by being a carrier of nationalism during the transition from political to cultural self-assertiveness. It would be a modest destiny after the grand old days of the unity of Church and State—but it would not be secularism.

If this is to be the future of organised religion in England, it will illustrate a theme which has run through this chapter: *trends in society may empty churches, but may also fill them.* Religion still expresses a sense of belonging which is real to many. Religion still binds many groups. The social impact of the secular century, while it has cut deep into organised religion, has so far not abolished it.

CHAPTER THREE

The Psychological Impact of the Secular Century

Gods High and Near

Both belief and unbelief are likely to protest if our analysis is confined to describing religion's functions in society. Man's basic religious sense may be interpreted largely through the faith of the surrounding society; yet it is, after all, the individual who makes the interpretation, and—specially when his society is disintegrated—the individual is liable to be concerned with questions which go deeper than his place in society. What about religion's claim to be the means of unifying a personality more precious than many societies? What about religion's claim to confront the soul with God? Does the statement that man's heart is restless until it rests in God indicate man's true destiny, or does it merely indicate a disease which must be cured if a person is to be healthily himself? It is in such questions that the psychological impact of our largely secular century comes home, challenging in a period of much self-consciousness and individualism the interpretations of the religious sense which the old societies decreed.

When we were studying the religious implications of the disintegration of modern society, we compared this with the social unity which was supported by primitive religion; and now that we are to be more personal, we may begin again by taking a brief look at the psychology of primitive religion. Immediately we may note that among primitive peoples there often seem to be two levels of divinity, which exist simultaneously (the one does not arise out of the other, as the evolutionary theorists of religion used to maintain). These two levels in primitive religion have often been pictured as the realms of the Sky Father and the Earth Mother—the God above being sometimes as remotely benevolent as the light of the sun, sometimes as terrifying in his wrath as a sudden storm, and the goddess beneath always the warm, loving provider of life, comfort and food.[1] A religion flourishes when sky and earth, Father and

[1] There are convenient summaries by E. O. James, *The Cult of the Mother Goddess* London, 1959) and *The Worship of the Sky-God* (London, 1963).

Mother, are kept in one vision. Above is the "high God" who created
the world by the exercise of his mysterious will, and who has now
withdrawn into his eternal blessedness, but who remains in some
sense ruler and judge over all. Below are the gods or goddesses or
spirits whose benevolence or anger may be experienced in particular
times and places, and who need the friendship of mortals. Practical
religion concentrates on worship at the lower level, and therefore on
sacrifices and ceremonies likely to please the spirits. It may be
analysed as polytheistic (believing in many gods) and even as
magical. But primitive religion also keeps alive the memory of the
"high God" through the proverbs of the folk, and sometimes also
through the private meditations of the few who are gifted with special
insight. Primitive religion may therefore also be analysed as monotheistic (believing in one God) and spiritual. The truth seems to be
that both these levels, "higher" and "lower", should be remembered
for both belong to the experience of the primitive worshipper, who
feels his religion as a single whole.[1]

The Western religious tradition has also included the two levels,
"high" and "near". It did so in ancient Greece, where the abstract
speculations of the philosophers were accompanied by the friendly
superstitions of the people, and where the "mystery" religions met a
need because, by promising an initiation into the mysteries of life and
death, they offered to fuse the two elements. It did so in Islam, where
the austere obedience of the Prophet to the one God was accompanied
by the enthusiasm of the Sufi movement for the God who dwells
within the human heart—and by the cult of martyrs and mediators
between God and man, among the Sufis or in the Shia sect. And
Catholicism, taking the European civilisation over from Greece and
Rome, continued to operate at both the high and the human levels.
Most of the philosophy of the Middle Ages sought to be rational in
arguments leading from the order in nature to the existence of one
perfect God, and some of the mysticism would enter the eternal
darkness beyond the personality of this God, but most of the real life
of the medieval Church lay in the heartfelt adoration of Christ, the
Virgin and the saints for favours received as part of God's providential
ordering of life. The God of Catholicism was thus both high and
near; the God of the Catholic philosophers was also the God of the
peasants.

But in Africa and India we can already witness the beginnings of

[1] For recent discussions see *African Ideas of God*, ed. E. W. Smith (London, 1959) and
African Systems of Thought, ed. M. Fortes and G. Dieterlen (London, 1965).

the disintegration of this religious world-view, as of the religious society which sustained it; and in Europe the disintegration has gone far. Essentially, what has happened has been that *the "high God" has seemed to get higher and higher*, more and more remote from the lives and thoughts of men, more and more hostile to them; while the stories of Christ, the Virgin and the saints have seemed less and less adequate as descriptions of life as it is or can be. Already this was the psychological crisis in the Reformation and Counter-Reformation of the sixteenth century. Like many in the waning of the Middle Ages and in the Renaissance, Luther and Calvin both regarded God as hostile to most of the human race, the implacable Judge. However, God was real for almost all in the sixteenth century, and the Reformers and Counter-Reformers who regarded him as terrible succeeded in overcoming their sense of estrangement from God because their sense of deliverance from damnation through the mediation of Christ (and for the Catholics, also of the Virgin and the saints) was so strong. It was, in fact, Martin Luther's stupendous achievement to wrest out of his own spiritual crisis an experience of the overwhelming goodness and grace of the near God, in the lovable person of Christ. That experience, more than anything else, awoke Germany, Sweden and other parts of Europe into the new religious vitality of Protestantism—and awoke the Catholic world also. New systems of Protestant or Catholic thought and devotion were then constructed. But neither the Reformation nor the Counter-Reformation looks very flourishing today, 450 years after Luther's great protest. For many in Europe who have a Christian background, the shape of God has become a vague blur in the back of that background, while the religious objects in the foreground—the conventional portrait of Jesus, and churches with their images of saints—although more real are viewed with little interest, because they also do not seem to belong to the everyday world. God, if there is a God, is the unknown God, and the world, which clearly exists, is best described and used in a secular way.

Freud as a Witness to Secularisation

Sigmund Freud, who died a refugee from Hitler in London in 1939, was the greatest witness to the psychological consequences of this collapse of religion in nineteenth-century Europe. He was able to make his witness with extraordinary power partly because of his genius which combined scientific integrity with imaginative and literary capacities of a high order, and partly because of his social background, which was a group which might be expected to register religion's collapse at least as fully as any other group in the world— the intellectual Jews of Vienna. The Vienna where Freud came to his maturity was famous both for the heights of its cultural life and for the depths to which anti-semitism sank among those who resented the outstanding abilities of many of its Jews. This resentment against the Jews in both the top and the bottom sections of society had a Catholic flavour. Until 1918 Vienna was the capital of the Hapsburg empire with its throne-and-altar alliance, and the Austrian Republic which emerged after the fall of the Hapsburgs was controlled by Christian Democrats who looked to the Catholic clergy for inspiration. But the resentful at the bottom of society were also Catholics. Adolf Hitler was brought up in nearby Linz and spent five bitter years as an unemployed "artist" in Vienna; he despised the Catholic Church almost as greatly as he hated the Jews; but he had been baptised and confirmed and that, tragically, meant something—for he was never excommunicated. When Hitler took over Austria in 1938, the Cardinal Archbishop of Vienna had to be rebuked by the Vatican for welcoming the invasion. This Catholic anti-semitism was, of course, not exclusively Austrian. In its 1933 Concordat with Hitler, the Vatican attempted to secure privileges for the Catholic Church in Germany when the Nazis' anti-semitism was already published and demonstrated. And even if the Austrian and German Catholics of the 1930s had been more sensitive to the iniquity which was to lead to the murder of six million Jews, Freud and others of his race would have experienced the terrible legacy of Christian hatred for the Jews who had "killed God"—a hatred continuous for centuries and only made worse by Luther.[1]

In his early years Freud was taken to church services by a Catholic nursemaid (who was old and ugly and was subsequently dismissed for stealing), and as a schoolboy and medical student Freud faced Catholic anti-semitism. He was not given a religious upbringing, for his parents had rejected the orthodox Rabbinic Judaism which seemed the only religious alternative to conversion to the oppressive Catholicism, but he and his family were acutely conscious and proud of being Jewish by race. When after many difficult years as a student and teacher of orthodox medicine, Freud gradually emerged as a hypnotist and psychoanalyst, most of his patients were other Jews

[1] For a summary of the shameful history of "Christian" anti-semitism, and for an indication of a better approach to Judaism which conceivably may not be too late, see Peter Schneider, *Sweeter than Honey* (London, 1966).

who were also without any personal religion. Religion therefore to him meant primarily the authoritarian, corrupt, anti-semitic Catholicism of Vienna. That was what caused him to identify himself with the crusading Protestant, Oliver Cromwell (after whom he named a son), and with the ancient Semite, Hannibal, in his crossing of the Alps in the march on Rome. That was what made Rome a frequent subject of his dreams. That was what aroused the consuming fire of denunciation in his secularist tract of 1927, *The Future of an Illusion*. Only once, in his last book, *Moses and Monotheism* (London, 1939), written while he was dying of cancer, did he make public a major presentation of a higher variety of religion. There he described the religion of Moses, a manly belief in an all-powerful, all-loving God leading worshippers not to fear or to ritual but to strength and purity of intelligence and life. But as if to show that such a religion could not really belong to the real world, Freud indulged himself in the speculation that Moses was an Egyptian who had acquired this faith from Pharaoh Iknhaton, and who for his pains was murdered by the Hebrews in the wilderness. From this early Jewish experience, Freud taught, there survived a guilt about the murder of Moses, accounting for the Jewish feeling of inferiority; but there also survived an integrity in rejecting all idols (as Moses did), accounting in the twentieth century for the courage of those Jews who were open atheists. As Freud in *Moses and Monotheism* described the lush, foolish, degrading religion into which most of the Jews fell after their Law-giver's death, it is not hard to see what he was thinking about: Catholic Vienna. And as he described Moses the heroic prophet of truth, it is not hard to see whom he really had in mind: himself.

In Freud's reaction to Catholic Vienna, we may therefore see the final phase of that nineteenth-century rebellion against Christendom which we watched at an earlier stage in the analysis of the English industrial cities made by Karl Marx. The idea of God was associated with a social order which was hated. God seemed repulsive and frightening, and his hostile character could be seen clearly on those rare occasions when God's nearness was experienced by unhappy people; or God was simply remote, ineffective, unreal. In all this, the God of Catholic Vienna was rather like the Church of industrial England. The symbols of religion meant little or nothing to Freud and his patients, much as the details of the new Gothic churches built in the industrial cities meant little or nothing to Marx and his workers. Society was breaking up around Freud as around Marx, and each thinker used a particular aspect of the disintegrating social system to

describe the disintegrating religious situation. Freud found the key
in the alienation of children from their oppressive parents—as Marx
found it in the alienation of the proletariat from their industrial work
under the capitalists. Here Freud offered a brilliantly imaginative
reconstruction of man's psychological history—just as Marx built a
fascinating interpretation of social history around the theme of the
class war. For both Marx and Freud religion was an illusion which
dangerously prolonged the helplessness of childhood's need for
protection and guidance in face of the difficulties of the external
world. For Freud, what mattered was the childhood of the individual;
for Marx, the childhood of the race. Both men gave their lives in
order that their fellow-men might "come of age".[1]

If we proceed on the principle which Freud himself taught us, we
must trace Freud's doctrines about childhood and its psychic dramas
to his own childhood. The evidence is not as plentiful as we might
wish. Unfortunately Freud was never psychoanalysed. The standard
biography was written by an Englishman, Ernest Jones, who was
Freud's only highly distinguished pupil who did not break away
from the master; and while making some important points to show
that Freud could be analysed in Freudian terms, Jones revealed less
than the irreverently curious would wish about the secret life.[2] But
enough evidence survives for our purposes.

The Interpretation of Dreams, which appeared in 1900 as the first
great work of psychoanalysis, included many of Freud's own dreams
which he decided to analyse after the shock of his father's death in
1896, and something is revealed also in the glimpses of an intense
and neurotic young man provided by surviving letters. What we
know is that, even allowing for the special relationship between
mothers and sons in Jewish homes, Freud's mother was more than
usually devoted to him. She was not twenty years old when he was
born. Her husband had married her when he was aged forty and
already the father of two sons older than she was. Moreover, her only
other son, Sigmund's younger brother, died in infancy, and Sigmund
had been fiercely jealous of this brother. Sigmund's wish that the
little rival should die had been fulfilled, and (although sisters arrived)
"for the rest of his life he felt guilty, for the rest of his life he felt he
deserved to die, and so he wished death to come and dreaded its
possible approach throughout his life."[3] Freud's conscious relationship with his father was less unusual, and superficially we might say

[1] See, e.g., Reuben Osborn, *Marxism and Psycho-analysis* (London, 1965), specially chapter 6.
[2] 3 vols., London, 1953-7, abridged into one vol., New York, 1961.
[3] Gregory Zilboorg, *Freud and Religion* (Boston, 1958), p. 57.

that all was well. Despite the special complexities of the double family and the tensions which belong to all growing up, Freud lived at home until he was aged twenty-six. But it is not claimed that there was the deep understanding between Freud and his father that there was between Freud and his mother. As Ernest Jones notes, Freud's childhood left him with deep needs both to love and to hate. In adulthood Freud passionately turned for help to male friends, and as passionately quarrelled with them; he published for the world to see views about fatherhood, which, on his own showing, must reflect his childish hatred of his own father.

The representation of the "high God" as "Father" is common to many religions, but is specially prominent in Christianity. Basically, it symbolises the strong love which God has for men. Freud came to believe that God was called "Father" because children invented him as the invisible personification of their fathers, whom they basically disliked as being cruelly authoritarian, etc. The event which particularly called forth this dislike and its supernatural projection was the passion of a boy between three and five years old to possess his mother sexually (the Oedipus Complex). The wish was frustrated by a threat of castration believed to come from the father, and the son felt guilty as well as defeated. This guilt was the basis of the formation of the conscience or "super-ego", a kind of internal father exuding disapproval—and it was also the origin in the individual's life of the idea of God the heavenly Father. The origin of the idea in the life of society was traced back by Freud to an actual murder. In guessing about the life of "the primitive horde" soon after the emergence of *homo sapiens*, Freud picked up some remarks made by Darwin and some speculations offered by the early anthropologists. The young men in the primitive horde decided to kill their leader in order to have the young women whom he controlled. They did this, but were overcome by guilt. They then represented their murdered leader or father-substitute in a symbol; this was Frazer's and Durkheim's totem. This totem, a sacred animal normally not to be hunted or touched, could be eaten in a sacrificial feast. Later the totem was believed to be supernatural, and so religion began. The fate of Moses among the Israelites repeated that primitive drama, but even without such repetitions in "history" its influence was passed on through the unconscious mind by which the human race's collective experience was silently taught to each human infant.

Since neither five-year-old boys nor the men of the primitive horde were available to speak clearly about these incestuous and murderous desires, Freud based his theories on his own memories, on what he was told by his patients, and particularly on what his patients told him about their dream-life, that "royal road to the unconscious". For some years, he tells us, Freud listened to his women patients recalling how their fathers had raped them, and to equivalent confessions about their mothers from men—until he came to see that these were the wish-fulfilments of the reality which was the Oedipus Complex in boys and the equivalent Electra Complex in girls. The conclusions which Freud formed as a result of these experiences were applied to the human race in his amateur anthropology, notably in his book on primitive religion, *Totem and Taboo*.[1] In his *Moses and Monotheism*, he was unrepentant in the face of criticisms of *Totem and Taboo* made by professional anthropologists—criticisms which were specially directed against his reliance on the pioneering British anthropologist, Robertson Smith. "I am not an ethnologist but a psychoanalyst," he wrote. "It was my good right to select from ethnological data what would serve me for my analytic work. The writings of the highly gifted Robertson Smith provided me with valuable points of contact with the psychological material of analysis and suggestions for the use of it."[2] Freud liked to present his work as purely scientific, and in reality it was founded on his deeply impressive carefulness in countless hours of listening to patients and of introspection; nor should we forget that he spent nine years in the study of chemistry, zoology and physiology, before turning to neurology (and so, through hypnosis, to psychoanalysis), so that he had good reasons to claim that he understood the scientific attitude and method. But very few, if any, anthropologists can now be found who take seriously Freud's selection from the evidence about primitive religion; and greatly as all are indebted to the many flashes of genius by which his writings have illuminated all subsequent work for mental health, almost as few qualified and experienced practitioners in psychological medicine take literally Freud's descriptions of the child's unconscious mind.

Driven by a passionately experienced unhappiness which we cannot now completely recover, Freud became not primarily a scientist but a poet for the age of science. He was a researcher, but he was also a great maker of myths. As he listened to his memories and to his patients, he drew from their sordid mess of trivialities some grand, unifying ideas. Nothing was in its depths what it seemed to be superficially—apart, to be sure, from the sexual appetites. All human

[1] 1913; Eng. trans., London, 1919.   [2] See p. 207.

behaviour was determined by a few simple origins; even accidents, even slips of the tongue, could be traced to their causes in the *libido*, and mostly to sex. In order to express these ideas about origins and causes Freud turned to the tragic drama of ancient Athens, for the figures of Oedipus and Electra. When the real, public tragedies of 1914-18 made so much fresh psychological material available for study (specially the cases of battle-shocked soldiers), and as his own experience and reflection matured, Freud turned to the Greek language in order to express other unifying, interpretative ideas. *Eros* was now the word for the force of life and love, and *Thanatos* the name of the resisting force of death, for which men secretly longed. When in 1923 he came to present his doctrine systematically, *es, ich* and *uberich* appeared as a mythological trinity, and they could be expressed also in the Latin more familiar to readers of English translations of Freud's work: *id, ego, superego*. These ideas clearly are myths, although (as tends to happen with myths) they may be given a life of their own, so that we are liable to see an Oedipus as the central figure in the story of every man, a battle between *Eros* and *Thanatos* in an everyday decision, and a geographical division into three in every personality. But more subtly influential than such myth-making was the imaginative power of Freud's personal vision of life. This vision, more than any other, has become the corporate myth of twentieth-century intellectuals. Every vital person's attitudes to God and society were summed up for Freud in the son's wish to murder the father. Here in Freud was the vision of the man of life and love, the man of intelligence and integrity, alienated from religion and from society, and pitted against them to the death. While the masses have turned to other myths, the sensitive few have been in a basic sense Freudians. Freud did not cause their vision; it was caused by the rapid change in their society. For a middle-class intellectual, it was the equivalent of the worker's alienation as seen by Marx. Nor did Freud begin this way of looking at life; it has a long history into the nineteenth century and beyond. But Freud was the greatest teacher of this vision to our time.

The Challenge of Freud

In his *Civilisation and its Discontents*,[1] Freud saw civilisation as the enemy of happiness. Public opinion, reinforced if necessary by the police, prevented people from giving free expression to their sexual and agressive instincts or "drives". Freud, who thought that most

[1] 1929; Eng. trans., London, 1930.

people were too stupid for it to be safe to allow them to run their own lives, on the whole approved of this repression of the turbulent masses, but he was preoccupied by the control exercised by a civilised society over the discontents of its more intellectual members—a control not through the policeman but through the superego. This control, forcing down the vital drives, resulted in neurosis. Many symptoms showing the danger of this repression were quoted by Freud, and they included a prevailing sense of guilt. The First World War was interpreted as the explosion of aggressive drives which civilisation had attempted to repress, but even more dangerous was the cost of civilisation in terms of personal happiness. Freud seems to have experienced (either in himself or through the reminiscences of his patients and friends) the disappointments of civilised, *bourgeois* marriage. He had no high opinion of the intellectual capacities of women (although his daughter Anna became an exceptionally able psychoanalyst). He thought that as a sex, they lacked strong person-alities (because having had no fear of castration they could not develop a formidable super-ego, but could only envy men for their superior sexual organs). Even sexual satisfaction was doubtful in marriage; and what restrained a man from seeking it elsewhere was not his love for his wife but his fear of his superego as the forbidding voice of civilisation. It is not surprising that many of Freud's followers have taken his researches to justify a more thorough rebellion than he advocated against the conventions of civilisation.

In assessing this revolt which has taken the name of Freud, we cannot forget that even apart from the menace of anti-semitism Freud and his patients found the moral atmosphere of Vienna stifling. Many marriages had boredom at their heart, and prudery about sex—a prudery which scarcely corresponded with the adults' secret thoughts—menaced the healthy development of young people. Such a society, binding its members by conventions rather than convictions, was already fundamentally disintegrated, and Freud performed a service by digging its grave. Freud continued to analyse hysterical women, when his senior colleague Josef Breuer withdrew because of the sexuality which was being brought to the surface; and that quiet decision of 1894 may be reckoned as one of the decisive turning points in the progress of mankind towards a saner and happier future. But Freud suggested that the whole of civilisation was as sick as these women, and if this was true of the society around him the analysis throws light on that society rather than on all human history. In integrated, healthy groups individuals have drawn much of their happiness, and indeed most of their identity, from their social environment. For all the tensions involved between corporate and individual wishes, society has not seemed the enemy; and so far from society being viewed as *Thanatos*, many people have believed that they have lived most fully as participants in the group-life. The work which they have done in teams, or as individuals working for markets, has meant for them pleasure as well as toil. They have been proud to belong to a village, a tribe, a city or a nation (Freud, an estranged Jew to the end, analysed all this in terms of dependence on mothers and fathers). They have been specially proud of their society's literature, art and religion (to Freud, despite his love of literature and art, these were all at bottom symptoms of neurosis). They have believed that this cultural activity was what lifted man above the animals (and so did Freud, but it was easy for some of his followers to reduce the total content of culture to the psychological factors which Freud had seen at its roots). They have been proud to rear children (Freud, an excellent father, thought that parental love rested on sexual self-love or narcissism). In particular, society has been thanked for making available partners in sexual happiness. Such partners have sometimes been temporary, "for the fun of it", and society has not taken too heavy a view of such fun; but the main source of sexual fulfilment for civilised mankind has been marriage, in a lifelong loyalty based on joy. Although these things are the platitudes of the history of man, it is difficult to remember them if we separate Freud's books from his exemplary style of life. Freud's position has often been misrepresented, but we must observe that many of those who have been most capable of doing justice to the Freudian analysis of man have in the end judged it to be inadequate.

Freud's excessively biological approach to the study of man in society has been the principal cause for the rebellions against his authority by psychologists who are indebted to his genius. Alfred Adler broke with his teacher in 1911 because he put sexual drives in the wider context of "life-cycles". Adler's chief scientific contribution was a study of psychological compensations for physical inferiorities (small men being argumentative, etc.). When he came to present a general philosophy of life, he taught that what most people desired was power or at least significance—a place in society—and he explored the consequences of a child's place in the family as the training-ground for this life-style in society. Adler may have been as unscientific in his general observations as most members of the medical profession now think he was, yet his insistence that life was not all sex was rightly welcomed by the public, was a stimulus to a more subtle analysis by the professionals, and was to some extent accepted by Freud himself.

In the United States, a school of "Neo-Freudian" and semi-Marxist analysts has arisen (H. S. Sullivan, Karen Horney, etc.), developing some of the insights of Adler and stressing both the duties and the delights of "social adjustment". Their analysis of man may seem to be shallow in comparison with Freud's; from the point of view of Christian theology Reinhold Niebuhr has urged that the individual's drives to pleasure as described by Freud present a problem which cannot be cured by happier homes or a better arranged society, for what Freud described was the fact which in theology is termed "original sin".[1] The Neo-Freudians' purpose may even be sinister in comparison with Freud's, for the individual's adjustment to society may easily degenerate into conformity. Voices have been raised to protest that conformity is the plague of American life—the man becomes the "organisation man", bought by a business corporation body and soul, the woman becomes dependent on the approval of her suburban neighbours—and such voices have added that the use of psychology in order to select "integrated" executives, suggest the sexual appeal of an automobile or advertise a breakfast cereal on the basis of motivational research, is a gross betrayal both of Freud the scientist and Freud the prophet. Fortunately it is not our task to adjudicate in such disputes, where many subjective as well as many scientific elements are involved and are as yet imperfectly assessed. What is clear is that, whatever mistakes may have been made by these Neo-Freudians, the progress of psychology since Freud has involved a very widespread recognition of the inadequacy of his understanding of human nature. To give only one example: it is generally agreed that the infant's dependence on the mother for food, comfort and affection is the first great experience through which both boys and girls learn to relate to others, and infant sexuality, while it is not denied, is subordinated. Such a recognition of the social as containing the sexual but not dominated by it may be found in the great majority of contemporary practitioners of psychological medicine.[2]

[1] *Freud and the Twentieth Century*, ed. B. Nelson (New York, 1957), chapter 15. This volume gathered assessments in connection with the 1956 centenary of Freud's birth and included a bibliography.

[2] See J. A. C. Brown, *Freud and the Post-Freudians* (London, 1961). A Freudian understanding of society was outlined by J. C. Fleugel, *Man, Morals and Society* (London, 1945), but the strength of many psychologists' feelings against Freudianism as unscientific may be glimpsed in H. J. Eysenck, *Uses and Abuses of Psychology* (London, 1951), specially chapter 12.

Bound up with this recognition of man as a social animal has come much agreement that man is more deeply religious than Freud granted. Adler, for one, often emphasised religion. C. G. Jung broke with Freud in 1912 largely because Freud so disliked the mystical and psychical phenomena which were becoming Jung's chief interest in life, and Jung's words in his book on *Modern Man in Search of a Soul* have become famous: "Among my patients in the second half of life —that is to say, over 35—there has not been one whose problem in the last resort was not one of finding a religious outlook on life."[1] Jung explored the connections and the roots of the great symbols of the world's religions in the "collective unconscious" of humanity,[2] and his emphasis on the wisdom preserved in the history of the religions has naturally commended him as an ally to religious believers, specially to Roman Catholics.[3] Erich Fromm, a Neo-Freudian writer without Jung's passion for the mystical, has included the more sexually active and generally agressive under-thirty-fives in the religious world, arguing that there is no one without a religious need to have "a frame of orientation and an object of devotion".[4] Philosophical writers such as Jung and Fromm are usually reckoned by medical professionals to have abandoned the scientific method, and they are clearly open to criticism; but they are only the two most prominent examples of the prevailing view that Freud himself was unscientific in his angry dismissal of religion. Religion to Freud was essentially the fear of a hostile authority, and it has not needed much reflection among his followers to see that, although this element is present in religion and can easily lead to neurosis, both history and observation show that religion is a much more richly varied phenomenon, as wide as life.

Some psychiatrists have given to such religion a respect which is more whole-hearted than that of Jung and Fromm. Dr. David Stafford-Clark, for example, has described the popular theory that religion is wish-fulfilment ("believing because it is more comfortable to believe, because such a belief implies a promise of pie in the sky when you die") as "peculiarly superficial". "It entirely ignores the fact that the central idea of religion is not a projection of gratification, but a quest: a quest for the purpose of life, and for the individual's place in this purpose; a quest for a relationship in which men give

[1] *Modern Man in Search of a Soul* (1931; Eng. trans., London, 1933), p. 264.
[2] E.g. in his *Psychology and Religion* (New Haven, 1937.)
[3] See Hans Schaer, *Religion and the Cure of Souls in Jung's Psychology* (1949; Eng. trans., London, 1951), and Victor White, *God and the Unconscious* (London, 1952).
[4] See, e.g., his *Man for Himself* (New York, 1947).

rather than receive. Worship, not reward, is the consistent feature of the great religions of the world."[1] In *The Individual and his Religion*, Professor Gordon Allport agreed with Freud that much religion is infantile or neurotic or fear-ridden or an "escape from freedom"; but examination of actual examples of religions and behaviour (much in the tradition of his predecessor at Harvard University, William James) convinced Allport that much religion is mature. While Freud had left the impression from the examples he used that religion was either primitive or pathological, Allport, the author of a great book on *Personality*, affirmed that "many personalities attain a religious view of life without suffering arrested development and without self-deception. Indeed, it is by virtue of their religious outlook on life—expanding as experience expands—that they are able to build up a mature and well-integrated edifice of personality. The conclusions they reach and the sentiments they hold are various, as unique as is personality itself."[2]

Allport said clearly: "I make no assumptions and no denials regarding the claims of revealed religion. Writing as a scientist, I am not entitled to do either." This limitation of the scope of psychology is crucial, whether or not psychologists reach opinions which favour religion. Even Freud in *The Future of an Illusion* had acknowledged the limitations of science and had explained that he used the word "illusion" in a special sense, without prejudging the question whether or not the religious emotion might be in touch with a supernatural reality—but Freud had been so obviously and so passionately convinced of the basic falsity of religion that he had in practice forgotten this restriction, and had conveyed to the average reader the impression that religion was illusory in the everyday sense of the word. Allport's greater modesty seems more compatible with the scientist's role, for as L. W. Grensted pointed out, "whether the reality inherent in the holy is the reality of God, or the reality of the father, or simply the reality of the experience, is not within the province of psychology to decide." Freudianism cannot give any account, or make any conclusive denial, of "the reality of the God to whom by the process of projection the characters of the father image, together with characters drawn from other sources, come to be transferred. No argument is possible from the reality of the process to the reality of the things, entities or persons concerned in the

[1] *Christian Essays in Psychiatry*, ed. Philip Mairet (London, 1956), p. 15.
[2] (New York, 1951), p. xi. J. B. Pratt, *The Religious Consciousness* (London, 1921), and R. H. Thouless, *An Introduction to the Psychology of Religion* (London, 1923), were earlier British expositions along much the same line as Allport's.

rocess, for the word reality is used in two different senses in the wo halves of any such argument."[1] This limitation on the hilosophical significance of the psychologist's explorations applies qually to non-Freudian descriptions of the mechanism of religion in he "subliminal self" or "collective unconscious". The reality of God or of the Buddhist *Nirvana*), of whom (or which) children, men and vomen conceive more or less satisfactory images, cannot be deternined scientifically; only the images can be studied by psychology, lthough psychology can certainly help us to see which images are nore (or less) healthy, because they correspond (or fail to correspond) vith human mental health, and which images are more (or less) comatible with the results of experience outside religion. Grensted oncluded his survey of *The Psychology of Religion*: "The findings of sychology are of less importance theoretically and of more importance practically than is commonly supposed to be the case. The ltimate interpretations of cult and creed, in terms of their worth nd their correspondence with what is really true of the being and urposes of God and of the being, obligation and destiny of man, are ery little affected by psychological theory and analysis."[2]

After comments such as those just quoted from Stafford-Clark, llport and Grensted, either favouring religion or restricting the sychologist's right to condemn it, many religious writers have umped to the conclusion that the challenge of Freud may now be ismissed. However, the right conclusion seems to be that, while 'reud's attacks on religion were projections from his own psychology ather than the unanswerable verdicts of psychological science, both hey and the reception given to them were very important indications f the temper of our time. The corruption of Viennese Catholicism, nd in particular its virulent anti-semitism, lay behind the whole 'reudian onslaught, and in the 1960s the Roman Catholic Church as begun to confess that these have indeed been its sins. Much in rotestantism, specially its anti-sexual puritanism and its antintellectual fundamentalism, would have given Freud similar material or prophecy, had he experienced it at first hand in his formative ears (he was acquainted with it through reading and travel); and it nay be as well for the composure of Christians that Freud never nalysed Eastern Orthodoxy. The condition of orthodox Judaism nay be assessed from the fact that Freud, for all his Jewishness, never onsidered embracing its faith, and we are entitled to doubt whether

[1] L. W. Grensted, *The Psychology of Religion* (London, 1952), pp. 159, 160.
[2] See p. 162.

other religions would have looked better under the searchlight of that honesty. It seems reasonable to conclude that religion in Freud's day was in need of a radical reformation.

Clear evidence of the inadequacy of organised religion in Freud's world is provided by the influence of his idea that the psychoanalyst would be the new secular priest. Before Freud, doctors cultivated a heartily cheerful, but often also arrogantly impersonal, manner in order to do what they thought best to their patients' bodies. Freud may be said to have discovered the patient. The chief part of the therapy which he offered consisted of listening to his patients, and a single patient might absorb the attention of the analyst for fifty minutes a day on five days a week for two or three years or more. Ideally, Freud thought, an analysis should never be terminated. He wanted to preserve the impersonal dignity of the medical profession as far as possible, but he came to expect his patients to transfer their deepest emotions to him as a substitute-father; on the whole, the men hated him and the women loved him, and each sex presented its problems for him as a fellow-human. He believed that a cure would probably come if only the patient could talk long enough and frankly enough. The memories which festered like wounds in the unconscious, and which poisoned the patient's whole life, would be healed by being remembered and understood. Brought into the open air and the sunshine, these wounds would become scars on a body which could again be active along life's paths. The analyst might help the patient to understand these memories, but his main role was simply to listen.

The obvious disadvantages about this method of healing were its demands on the patient's time and money; only leisured and well-off people were likely to be able to afford a Freudian analysis. But the demands made of the analyst were scarcely less great, and Freud's acceptance of these demands may be regarded as his greatest victory. Only a few thousands of people in the world have been able to claim that they were "cured" by a Freudian analysis, but millions have sensed that this was an approach to their misery by a man who had disciplined his high intelligence to serve in compassion, and the example of Freud has transformed the Western world's understanding of what care means. Even outside the ranks of professional psychiatry many thousands of "medical" and "social" workers have been, as they would put it, "client-centred". This means that they have become pastors whose care of people has followed the example of love, and that their love has again and again been therapeutic.

Outside the ranks of all these pastors, public opinion as a whole in the West has been profoundly influenced. The "child-centred" approach to education, which only a few extreme progressives advocated in the nineteenth century, has become the philosophy of twentieth-century teachers. The child himself, no longer viewed as an angel or a devil, has become the fascinating battleground of the super-ego and the id, and adults, offering respectful sympathy, have learned that they are themselves the child's chief problems. The self-consciousness of modern adults, in this era of rapid change, would have been massive without Freud, but Freud has taught the West that the dramas of the self matter more than the dramas of society in bringing happiness or misery; Freud has taught the West that the self's most important dramas occur in the unconscious, at a level deeper than the reason or the conscience—at an emotional level which is not revealed by public speech, by intimate confidences, or even by a person's habitual self-knowledge, but which may be explored if only man will have the courage and the patience needed for the conquest of his own inner space; and Freud has taught the West that people, who are all driven by dark, irrational forces and wounded to the heart by memories of events they never desired, should learn to be gentle with each other and even with themselves. In the Freudian description of the self we recognise the stuff of the modern novel, of the modern drama, and of much in modern life. Freud has become, in the words of W. H. Auden, a "climate of opinion" rather than a name, because it is Freud who has taught us that, if we are to love one another, love, instead of being blind to realities, must do what another great modern poet saw was necessary:

> Players and painted stage took all my love,
> And not those things that they were emblems of.
>   . . . Now that my ladder's gone,
> I must lie down where all the ladders start,
> In the foul rag-and-bone shop of the heart.[1]

Specially in the United States the Protestant minister has reconceived his role as a pastoral counsellor in this light, and the Roman Catholic priest is now far less inclined than he was when hearing penitents' confessions to regard himself as a judge. But the corruption of religion cannot be expressed more powerfully than it is in the

---

[1] W. B. Yeats, "The Circus-Animals' Desertion", in his *Last Poems, 1936-39* (London, 1939).

answer which follows the question: *why was this love of man, as man actually is, left to the secular Freud?*[1]

The question of the reality of God remains after all that Freud said; but the strength of the welcome given to Freud's attack on religion demonstrated the strength of Freud's case against the God of his disintegrating but still viciously powerful society. Whatever may be the validity of his assessment of religion as an illusion, the God whom Freud described was recognised as their God by many millions, and many millions have been happy to use Freud's authority in the rejection of this God. It may or may not be wise to make sex the chief topic of a civilisation, and to regard any mention of God a bad taste, but the truth about our century is revealed in the strength of the agreement to do so. It may or may not be possible to build a religion without God, but the religious crisis is demonstrated by the popularity of the attempt. It may or may not be the case that belief in God arises from a three-year-old boy's wish to marry his mother and to murder his father, thus repeating the great murder of the father by the primitive horde, but it is a noteworthy comment on our time that so many have believed that such were the origins and essence of man's quest for God.[2]

A Suicidal Defence of Religion

We have noted that many of Freud's successors in the psychological field have taken more trouble than he did to understand religion. But here we must briefly add that many sympathetic discussions of the role of religion in modern society may in the long run prove no less dangerous to religion than was Freud's all-out attack. For many psychologists have basically accepted Freud's essential point that the whole of religion rests on an illusion. Their disagreement has been on the question, how seriously this illusion was to be taken; and the degree of seriousness with which they have taken the religious phenomenon may be closer to Freud's position than the defenders of

[1] For the insights which are central in the British social services, see Paul Halmos, *The Faith of the Counsellors* (London, 1965) and Kathleen Heasman, *Christians and Social Work* (London, 1965). In the literature of American pastoral counselling after Freud, David E Roberts, *Psychotherapy and the Christian View of Man* (New York, 1950), and Albert C Outler, *Psychotherapy and the Christian Message* (New York, 1954), stand out.

[2] In the vast literature about Freud, the most relevant American contribution was by Philip Rieff, *Freud: The Mind of the Moralist* (New York, 1959). The same author's *The Triumph of the Therapeutic* (New York, 1966) was a more personal and less convincing presentation of "the uses of faith after Freud". Contributions by Christian writers in Britain include the favourable R. S. Lee, *Freud and Christianity* (London, 1948), the hostile H. L. Philip, *Freud and Religious Belief* (London, 1956), and the judicious David Stafford-Clark, *What Freud Really Said* (London, 1965).

eligion would wish. Alfred Adler, for example, who often praised
eligion's contribution to a "life-style", was personally unable to
.ccept religious doctrines.[1]

Freud himself acknowledged that many neuroses had been
.bsorbed in most generations by the myths and rituals of religion.
Ie definitely admired the psychological value of the religion of
.ncient Israel, for example, or the confident Catholicism of the
Aiddle Ages. He also came near to the theory which his ex-disciple,
.ung, developed about the "collective unconscious" as the storage
.lace for the great human neuroses and for the great religious symbols
.hich correspond with them. However, Freud noted that even in
.he days of its strength religion was unable to take care of all neuroses.
.ike many others, he drew special attention to the abominable
.ruelty with which medieval Catholics had tormented the wretches
.hom they accused of witchcraft, and of course he had constantly in
.nind the neurotic character of the Christians' hatred of the Jews.
.bove all, Freud emphasised the guilt and fear associated in all
.elievers' minds with the idea of God as pure and powerful, and he
.elieved that even the Egyptian religion of Moses was neurotic in this
.asic sense. He therefore considered that the atheism which he always
.ssumed to be true was in its psychological effects healthier even than
.he best religion. He saw science as the alternative to religion, and
.lthough he appreciated the difficulty of educating the masses in the
.:ientific method, he nursed the hope that, just as the neuroses of an
.ndividual patient could be cured (however painfully) if exposed to
.he truth, so religion, the "universal neurosis" of humanity, could be
.ured by exposure to science over a considerable period of time.

Erich Fromm, despite his teaching that every man needs a religion,
.ollows Freud when he adds that the religious belief in a God who
.ands outside man and outside nature is an escape from man's
.roper responsibility for his own future. It is part of the "fear of
.eedom" which Fromm analyses as the central temptation of
.ventieth-century man; here Fromm apparently sees no essential
.ifference between submission to God and submission to Hitler or
.talin. The religion which Fromm praises therefore resembles the
.eligion which Sir Julian Huxley advocates. Psychologically it is a
.eligion without the celestial father-figure, and philosophically it is
.religion without a transcendent God.[2]

Carl Jung took a much more favourable view than Freud or Fromm

[1] See the studies of *Alfred Adler* by Phyllis Bottome (London, 1939) and Lewis Way
.ondon, 1956).
[2] See his Terry Lectures on *Psychoanalysis and Religion* (New Haven, 1950).

when he assessed the psychological effects of traditional religion, but he was always unwilling to affirm that the religious symbols which he valued corresponded with any supernatural reality. Sometimes he wrote that this was due to a wish to preserve the objectivity of science within the limits of science, but at other times he seemed to indicate that his personal attitude was one of dis-belief in eternity. His posthumously published autobiography showed him as a man with a thoroughly religious outlook on life, and with many religious, or at least psychic, experiences; but the undiscriminating gusto of his religious enthusiasm must raise the question whether, by the standards of the rational tradition of the West, he was interested in religious truth.[1] Such a defence of religion may be accepted for a time as encouraging participation in religious observances when the alternative is more degrading to man (as it was under Hitler or Stalin, or as it often was in the spiritually empty Western Europe where Jung listened to his patients with their religious nostalgia). In the long run, since the religion which Jung defended contained so much which was irrational, those who put a high value on the human reason are likely to renounce religion, and will be encouraged to do so by the availability of an alternative more attractive than Hitler, Stalin or the West of the 1930s. To give one example: the Roman Catholic dogma of the physical assumption of the Virgin Mary into heaven was defended by Jung on the ground that it was a symbol for the glory of womanhood. Jung rightly thought that Western Europe in his time was excessively masculine in the toughness of its industrial, commercial and political life, and he rightly suspected that masculinity was not enough even for a man, since every man had a feminine side to him. But the Vatican itself has often rejected such help for its doctrines from those who view them as only symbolic, and in this the Vatican seems to be shrewd. It may well be the verdict of the future that the feminine element in human life can be recognised in a simpler and more rational way than through the Roman Catholic dogma of the assumption (or Jung's own jargon about the *anima*, etc.). Thus religion, if it adopts Jung's suggestions for its defence, may find that it has blundered into a suicide no less final than the murder which the angry Father suffered at the hands of Freud; and Freud may be proved right when he expressed for the Jungian defence of religion a contempt more profound than his great dislike of faith in God.

There are, indeed, signs that the presentation of religion as natural

[1] Carl Jung, *Memories, Dreams and Reflections* (1964; Eng. trans., 1965).

rather than supernatural, of the Church as attractive rather than persuasive, and of the idea of God as useful rather than true, may be appealing quite widely to religion's professional defenders. While the century was still young, liberal Protestants and modernist Catholics were accused of holding such views ("immanentism"), and in some cases the accusation was just. The (often excessive) reaction of orthodoxy in Protestantism, and above all in Catholicism, was for a time thought to have discredited these views, but as the second half of the century opened it could be seen that "immanentism" as a theological tendency was far from dead. At this stage we may return to our discussion of that major phenomenon in twentieth-century life, the religion of the United States.

Has God Died in the United States?

The vitality of American religion and the presence of authentic faith within it are not denied by the most thoughtful observers, and these elements in an admittedly very complex social phenomenon were cited in the last chapter when we defended American religion against some of its critics. But only a generation ago American religion seemed to have lost the respect of thinking people: that was the age of the journalism of H. L. Mencken and of the portrait of a revivalist in *Elmer Gantry* by Sinclair Lewis (New York, 1927). The haunting question is whether the popularity of American religion since the 1940s is due solely to a psychological crisis in the nation which few expected before 1929, so that when the long crisis is over the earlier trend of a thorough secularisation will be resumed; or whether the religious resurgence carries enough authenticity to endure into the twenty-first century. At present, the situation can be interpreted in either direction. Since we summarised in Chapter 2 the evidence which points to a solid future for American churchgoing as a social phenomenon, and since in Chapter 8 we shall discuss the relevance of American philosophical theology around the great figures of A. N. Whitehead and Paul Tillich, we may confine our attention here to the warning signals arising from the psychological impact of our century.

The psychological crisis behind the boom in religion can be analysed as a failure of nerve amid the dramatically revolutionary early stages of the birth of a new technological civilisation. The twentieth-century American has been confused by successive shocks to his habits as agriculture yields to industry and as industry yields to the computer; he has been shaken by an unexpected slump and

then by an incredible boom; he has been dragged out of his isolatio
to fight Nazism and Communism; he has been involved against h
will in the tumultuous problems of the world; and he seeks a hidin
place. He cannot find it in any contemporary reality (one possib
analysis runs); he must turn to the "old-time" religion, but preferabl
to a version of that religion which is not too obviously in conflict wit
his secular ambitions. He returns to religion, seeking peace, findin
that "Someone up there likes me"—until he finds more solid sati
factions down here. So the analysis goes, and the analysis can dra
evidence from many escapist tendencies in popular American religio
The four books which became best-sellers amid the literary flood
the religious revival were all manifestos of the cult of serenity: *Pea
of Mind*, by the Jewish rabbi, Joshua Loth Liebmann (New Yor
1946); *Peace of Soul* by the Roman Catholic prelate, Fulton J. Shee
(New York, 1949); *The Power of Positive Thinking* by the liber
Protestant, Norman Vincent Peale (New York, 1952); and *Pea
with God* by the Protestant evangelist, Billy Graham (New Yor
1953). These books may be compared with Ralph Waldo Trine's
Tune with the Infinite (New York, 1897), which sold over a millio
copies; but Liebmann, Sheen, Peale and Graham recorded or
immense change in the American mind since Trine's heyday. Trin
in a new Preface to his book in 1921, observed that "increasin
numbers of men and women are walking these common daily wal
of life among us with a firmer tread, with upturned faces written ov
with a deeper trust . . . Conscious, as was taught by Christ, of th
essential oneness of their lives with the Divine, they realise that i
God's life there is only good . . ." But the anxiety of America in th
1930s, 1940s and 1950s prevented an easy reception of this messag
of infinite comfort. American turned to a God "up there" rather tha
to the "Spirit" which could be heard within the glad hearts of Trin
and his generation. When it turned to Jesus, it was to a Christ wh
was rather more powerful than Bruce Barton's *The Man Nobo
Knows* (a best-seller of 1925 which had revealed that the real Jesu
was like a man everyone knew: the American salesman). Someho
the salesman had died in America, perhaps in the slump of 1929. B
Liebmann, Sheen, Peale and Graham represented a sharp declin
both intellectual and spiritual, from the American best-sellers of a
essentially orthodox Christianity in the late 1920s and 1930s (Harr
Emerson Fosdick, E. Sherwood Eddy, etc.), and retribution w
inevitable. Many thoughtful Americans have felt a disgust for th
popular exploitation of the peace of God, and some have expresse

publicly. Here is a psychological challenge to American religion
hich goes deeper than the point that churchgoing as a social
henomenon is inspired by some non-theological factors.[1]

Thus we find that in the 1960s—when the church budgets and even
ie theological seminaries were still full—theologians who have
ished to define the true essence of Christianity, and to preserve
·ligion in some sense, have not hesitated to express a basic agreement
ith atheism. Paul van Buren's *The Secular Meaning of the Gospel* (New
ork, 1963) argued that since assertions about God are meaningless
-a philosophical claim which he assumed had been demonstrated
eyond the possibility of a convincing contradiction—Christianity
ould be expressed afresh as solely a message about the significance
id power of human freedom and love. Professor van Buren's book
as an interesting revival of Kant's plea in the eighteenth century for
religion of freedom and morality "within the limits of reason alone".

was followed by others in America more emotionally charged and
ore confused, which have proclaimed the "death" of God as the fact
ith which a new theology must begin its reconstruction of the
gnificance of Jesus for real life. It was not entirely clear what such
poks meant by picking up Nietzsche's "death of God" and using
 in thought which aimed at being Christian. Believers have been
ple to point out that if God ever existed he is not mortal, so that
hat looks like his death is his apparent eclipse. Sometimes these
poks have seemed to be saying that the reality of God has been
·lipsed in our time by the more obvious reality of technology. At
her times the books protested that many cheap ideas about God
ould never have survived Calvary. So at one level these Christian
poks about the "death" of God would leave a hope that one day
hristians would see more clearly what kind of encounter with God
·mains valid after the crises of the twentieth century—and of the
·st century A.D. But at another level, which might be deeper, these
poks seemed to be saying: the glory of America is to have realised
iat a magnificent civilisation can be built in the new confidence that
·od was never more than a creation of man's fear.[2]

A book which might have been called "The Secular Meaning of
ie Church" has won an enthusiastic reception in the younger
·neration of Christians, for example among the many students who

[1] See L. Schneider and S. M. Dornbusch, *Popular Religion*, a study of inspirational books
hicago, 1958).
[2] See Thomas Altizer, *The Gospel of Christian Atheism* (Philadelphia, 1966); and for
licious assessments, T. W. Ogletree, *The "Death of God" Controversy* (Nashville, 1966)
id John Macquarrie, *God and Secularity* (Philadelphia, 1967).

are in training for the ordained ministry but who are reluctant to give their lives to work in a conventional parish. In this book, *The Secular City* (New York, 1965), Professor Harvey Cox urged that the work of the Church must be replanned on the basis of an acceptance of many elements in that secularisation of American life which ha been influenced largely by its urbanisation. He argued tha "secularisation arises in large measure from the formative influence of biblical faith on the world, an influence mediated first by the Christian church and later by movements deriving partly from it." These arguments were scarcely more convincing than Professor van Buren's. Whereas van Buren had assumed that the collapse of biblical Christianity must follow the decline of the religious world-view, Cox seemed to be saying that the decline had actually been caused by the Bible's triumph; and much more discussion of the subtle issues involved would be needed to convince those not inclined to accept the authoritarian preaching style of these secular theologians. But more important than such arguments was the tone of these books, and of the welcome for them. The tone indicated that the American return to religion—the return to the God of heavenly peace, the return to the little church in the peaceful village or the suburb—might soon be over. American "Culture-Protestantism", where supernatural faith had always been only one element in the diffused religiosity, might be dropping its religion in favour of its culture. Christianity might be losing its nerve.[2]

This latest excitement in Liberal Protestant theology develops with a contemporary honesty, self-consciousness and brashness, an unbelief which runs through twentieth-century American religious thought. We have already mentioned the reverent agnosticism of William James. A wistfully moving presentation of a religion without God is to be found in many writings by George Santayana, notably his *Reason in Religion* (New York, 1905). Theologians of the time such as Shailer Matthews, with less feeling for the tragic, substituted an evolutionary progress for the transcendent God of the Christian tradition. In effect they baptised American optimism. "A God without wrath," wrote H. Richard Niebuhr about such theologians "brought men without sin into a kingdom without judgment through the ministrations of a Christ without a cross."[3] And Santayana, who

[1] See p. 21.
[2] See Robert L. Richard, *Secularization Theology* (New York, 1967). A symposium, *The Secular City Debate*, has been published, ed. D. Callahan (New York, 1966). See also below pp. 332-4.
[3] *The Kingdom of God in America* (New York, 1937), p. 193.

new a God when he saw one, had little patience with such sentimentality.[1] But perhaps another origin in American society may also
be fairly suggested for this theology. In *A Preface to Morals* (New York,
1929), that shrewd journalist, Walter Lippmann, recalled[2] that "the
God of medieval Christianity resembles a great feudal lord, supreme
and yet bound by covenants to treat his vassals on earth according to
a well-established system of reciprocal rights and duties." He added:
"the God of Modernism, who is variously pictured as the *élan vital*
within the evolutionary process, or as the sum total of the laws of
nature, is really a kind of constitutionalism deified." One of the most
influential of modern religious books in America, John Dewey's *A
Common Faith* (New Haven, 1934), went further in the direction which
Lippmann had urged these modernists to take if they were to provide
in honesty a moral foundation for the Republic. Dewey, in his search
for a consensus among men of good will, rejected Santayana's
nostalgia for the supernatural (a "broken-backed naturalism") but
endorsed what he called "the religious"—by which he now meant,
not the sort of soul-stirring experience which William James had
studied, but the encouragement of high moral conduct by noble
ideals through association with religious customs. He begged religious men to abandon their foolish worship of a transcendent, supernatural God. Dewey's "pragmatism" is commonly regarded as the
public philosophy in American education, and in his *Protestant,
Catholic, Jew* Professor Will Herberg maintains that, although there
are many exceptions (he is one himself), something like this is the
stable religion of the American people beneath the turning to the
supernatural God of peace. The real religion of the United States,
according to this observer, is the "religion of democracy", and the
churches are denominations of it. If this is the psychological truth
of the matter, then the social phenomenon of crowded churches may
indeed be temporary.

Secularisation in Robinson and Schweitzer

It has been argued that Dr. John Robinson, the Bishop of Woolwich
who became world-famous as the author of *Honest to God* (London,
1963), was toying with the idea of a Christianity without God—
although in a style more confused than Professor van Buren's.[3] In

[1] See George Santayana, *Winds of Doctrine* (New York, 1913), specially the trenchant
chapter on "Modernism and Christianity".
[2] See p. 55.
[3] See E. L. Mascall, *The Secularisation of Christianity* (London, 1965).

his more recent writings, particularly his *Exploration into God* (London 1967), Dr. Robinson has shown that this was far from his intention but the letters and reviews printed in *The Honest to God Debate* d record the wish of many in Britain, as elsewhere in the Wester world, to develop a creed like John Dewey's godless belief in "th religious". If that is one lesson to be learned from the most widesprea theological debate to be held in twentieth-century England, we ma rest assured that the identification of God with the more beautifu side of nature and with man's own advancing mind is by no mear as dead as orthodox theologians would like it to be. Over half century before *Honest to God*, R. J. Campbell's electrifying *The Ne Theology* (London, 1907) had included amid much enthusiasm fc pure religion and social progress some loose expressions suggestin that "Jesus was and is God, but so are we". Campbell himself ha been warned off heresy by the replies to him,[1] and had died a blam less canon of Chichester Cathedral, but the "new theology" ha remained powerful in that world which theologians do not normal approach. Alasdair MacIntyre may be right in his summary of th creed of the English in the 1960s: "The difficulty lies in the combina tion of atheism in the practice of the life of the vast majority, with th profession of either superstition or theism by that same majorit The creed of the English is that there is no God and that it is wise t pray to him from time to time."[2]

Five years after the publication of *Honest to God* we can see how th chief significance of that little book as a sign of the times lay precise in its ambiguity. (Thus *Honest to God*, like *The New Theology* before i refuted the suggestion that only what is clear, neat and slick ca excite the public.) Dr. Robinson was aware of this ambiguity in h position when in his Preface he confessed that the line between th "lay" world and "the traditional orthodox supernaturalism in whic our Faith has been framed" was a line which "runs right throug the middle of myself". The spectacle which fascinated was, as London newspaper put it, "an agonising and unusual spectacle— bishop groping for truth, admitting that he does not know all th answers." *Honest to God* could, indeed, be read in two different way so as to leave impressions of two radically different books, and so a to supply both sides in the controversy with ammunition.[3]

---

[1] Such as Charles Gore, *The New Theology and the Old Religion* (London, 1907).

[2] *The Honest to God Debate*, ed. D. L. Edwards (London, 1963), p. 228.

[3] If a fragment of autobiography may be forgiven: when I attended the small conferenc on secularisation held under the auspices of the World Council of Churches at Bossey, nea Geneva, in 1959, I never expected that the theological criticisms of metaphysics which

On the one side of the dividing line between the defence of the
gospel and its betrayal was an *Honest to God* which was unconventional
but basically orthodox. The missionary bishop who wrote this book
was descended from a line of distinguished clergymen, could not
remember a time when he had not wished to be ordained, was a
lecturer at Cambridge University in New Testament studies, was
enthusiastic about making the Holy Communion a more corporate
service of worship, was dedicated to pastoral work in the unrewarding
area of South London, normally preached sermons which (he said)
did not get "within remote range" of revolutionary ideas about God,
and had studied the philosophy of religion deeply enough to be
aware that the images of God which seemed inadequate were images
only and need not be taken literally. For this man, the theological
evolution which he had in mind was "a reluctant" revolution. He
was in love with the Christian tradition; and the revolution could
be seen as a turning back to the first source of the Christian tradition,
to the Bible itself. It was not really the end of theism, i.e. of belief in
God, for he insisted that the revolutionary image of God was only a
different "projection" (as on a map) to depict essentially the same
faith as traditional theism. It was an effort to show that true religion
arises out of real life, and in particular that God is met and loved "in
and through" one's neighbour, so that, in Bonhoeffer's phrase, "God
the 'beyond' in our midst". God in *Honest to God* remained
"beyond", for "the eternal *Thou* is not to be equated with the finite
Thou, nor God with man or nature". Christ remained "the bearer of
the final revelation and the embodiment of God's decisive act", for
it is in Jesus, and Jesus alone, that there is nothing of self to be seen,
but solely the ultimate, unconditional love of God". The love

---

heard there (and at a good many Student Christian Movement gatherings of the time)
would echo around the world. Nor, it seems, did such theological remarks win that vast
echo, until four years later the Student Christian Movement Press, which I was serving at
the time, published *Honest to God*; and even then we initially printed 8,000 copies of the
book, instead of the million copies which were in fact sold within four years. Nor when I
used the term "Christian Radicalism" (quoted from a broadcast by the Bishop of
Woolwich) in my Introduction to *The Honest to God Debate* did I expect the phrase to be
picked up quite so widely as it has been (often, it seems, from that book). My failure to
prophesy these developments can, I now think, be attributed to my failure to see how
widespread was the public interest in the question: do the theologians themselves now
admit that it is all up with Christianity? Some theologians who have taken part in the
discussion about secularisation have given neutral spectators the impression that it was
their basic intention to capitulate to secularism, and men who make no secret of their
belief that the God of Christianity is "dead" have claimed the title of "Christian Radical".
I, of course, claim no copyright in the word "radical", which has often been used in
Christian history (e.g. to describe Reinhold Niebuhr's combination of Left Wing politics
and Right Wing theology in the 1930s); and if it is necessary to distinguish a return to
the roots of Christianity from an atheistic rejection of those roots, I should be happy to
settle for such a phrase as "Christian Reformer", on the analogy of Reform Judaism.

embodied in Jesus evoked Dr. Robinson's courageous faith. "The Christian affirmation is not simply that love *ought* to be the last word about life, but that, despite all appearances, it *is* . . . And that takes an almost impossible amount of believing. It is frankly incredible *unless* the love revealed in Jesus is indeed the nature of ultimate reality, unless he is a window through the surface of things into *God*." Thus Bishop John Robinson endorsed the affirmation of St. John, which was not that "love is God" but that "God is love". Another way of expressing this faith was to say that "love is *of* God", so that "our convictions about love and its ultimacy are not projections from human love; but rather, our sense of the sacredness of love derives from the fact that in this relationship as nowhere else there is disclosed and laid bare the divine Ground of all our being."

On the other hand, Dr. Robinson showed that he was deeply sympathetic with atheism, so that in some moods for him "the Ground of our being" could be (but these crude words are not his) not the inexhaustible source and support of human life, but merely the bottom bit of it. He was prepared to question "the thought of God as a personal being, wholly other to man, dwelling in majesty", although R. W. Hepburn, from whom he quoted that phrase, rightly saw that "to sacrifice it seems at once to take one quite outside Christianity".[1] He was prepared to say that when such a theologian as Paul Tillich speaks of God as being experienced in the depths of human life (instead of "up there" or "out there") "he is not speaking of another Being *at all*. He is speaking of 'the infinite and inexhaustible depth and ground of all being', of what we take seriously without reservation." In that comment on Tillich, Dr. Robinson did not emphasise the "infinite and inexhaustible" mystery which Tillich used to call "Being-itself"; instead, he seemed to equate God with anything anyone might take seriously, and to present God as "the ground of *our* being", as in the title of Chapter 3.[2] On this showing theology might well be reduced to anthropology, for "a statement is 'theological' not because it relates to a particular Being called 'God', but because it asks *ultimate* questions about the meaning of existence" and "statements about God are acknowledgments of the transcendent, unconditional element in all our relationships". Transcendence could now be interpreted as simply the experience of meeting a "thou" who is different from "I", and Jesus himself could be seen

---

[1] *Christianity and Paradox* (London, 1958), p. 193. This book was an important exposure of the confusion which many theologians have permitted themselves behind the defence of being paradoxical.
[2] The italics are mine.

not so much as "the man for God" as "the man for others", "the one in whom Love has completely taken over, the one who is utterly open to, and united with, the Ground of his being". What was the significance of those capital letters in Love and Ground? Instead of explaining this philosophically, Dr. Robinson showed himself as at heart a pastor, for he pressed on to interpret holiness as "the depths of the common", prayer as "to open oneself to another *unconditionally* in love", deep love as the one guide in morality, and the service of the world as the charter of the Church. These were all causes which could amount to the dismissal of God from practical Christianity, although they could also encourage the renewal of the sense of the presence of God in daily life.

What was apparent in *Honest to God* was the necessity of some degree of "secularisation" in Christianity, for the biblical message must be stated with fresh power if it is to reach secular man. But *Honest to God* also made clear the danger, for the restatement can easily leave the impression that the three letters G, O and D when combined are no more than an old way of saying "love" or "Love". Here the challenge of our secular century was seized, but its psychological impact seemed on some pages of *Honest to God* likely to overthrow one of the Church of England's most gifted sons.

So we may turn to study the religious psychology of a greater figure: Dr. Albert Schweitzer. In the English-speaking world remarkably little controversy surrounded Schweitzer's theology, after the initial excitement when his *Von Reimarus zu Wrede* (1906) was translated as *The Quest of the Historical Jesus* (London, 1910). His earlier and fuller explanation of his own view, published in German in 1901, did not become available in English until *The Mystery of the Kingdom of God* appeared in 1925, and by then the "jungle doctor" was widely believed to have turned his back on his youthful indiscretions. By the 1920s (the period of his greatest influence), the public was attracted to Schweitzer's discovery of the ethical principle of "reverence for life". The implications of this phrase, which occurred to him in 1915, were worked out in profound books on the problems of civilisation, in public warnings against the suicidal folly of war which continued until his death in 1965, in his most attractive love for music and for animals, and supremely in his heroic work in the hospital at Lambaréné. Many would describe him as the greatest Christian of the century; and sneers at him in his old age, alleging that his approach to the African was out of date, did little more than to show that when he had abandoned his mastery of the culture of Europe in order to establish his hospital in equatorial Africa in 1913, he had been a pioneer.[1]

Schweitzer was, then, a disciple of Jesus. *But who for him was Jesus?* In his brilliant history of German New Testament scholarship up to his day, he demonstrated that almost all accounts of the psychology of Jesus have rested largely on speculation and thus on the scholar's own psychology. The gospels, although our only evidence for the life of Jesus apart from a few fragments elsewhere, are not modern biographies; and detailed reconstructions of the life of Jesus remind us of the man who peered to the bottom of a deep well, and saw his own face reflected. But Schweitzer observed truly that, amid much that is unknowable about Jesus, some things are clear. To Jesus, God is "a dynamic Power for good, a mysterious Will, distinct from the world, and superior to the world. To Him we yield our will; to Him we leave the future of the world." In the thought of Jesus, "the ethical activity of man is only like a powerful prayer to God, that He may cause the Kingdom to appear without delay."[2] This Kingdom of God was an idea which Jesus, being a first-century Jew, expressed in the language of his time, and the "apocalyptic" literature which has survived from that time shows us that many of his contemporaries thought of a Kingdom which would be introduced miraculously, by God sending his angels, raising the dead, etc. Yet the message of Jesus was not completely identical with such crude hopes, which were doomed to disappointment; and the ethic of Jesus was not merely for the "interim". "Jesus spiritualised the conception of the Kingdom of God, in that He brings it into subjection to His ideal and ethic of love. In due time this transforms the conception of the Kingdom."[3] On the basis of our limited but reasonably secure knowledge of the historical Jesus, it would have been possible for Schweitzer to interpret the message of the Kingdom of God for our time as a faith that the ethical activity of man was in harmony with the will and power of God to transform our wills and to improve the world, so that at some future date hidden from us the reality and rule of God would be acknowledged in the love for each other and for him of all the children of God. Such a presentation of the everlasting Gospel of Jesus, reinforced by a personal example of heroic sanctity

[1] Many books have been written about him, of which the best are George Seaver, *Albert Schweitzer: The Man and his Mind* (London, 1947), and Henry Clark, *The Philosoph of Albert Schweitzer* (London, 1964).

[2] *Christianity and the Religions of the World* (London, 1923), pp. 15-17.

[3] This admission, included in his Preface to the 1954 edition of his *Quest*, seems to have been first made clearly by Schweitzer in E. N. Mosley, *The Theology of Albert Schweitze* (London, 1950), p. 105.

night have had a profound influence in the world-wide Church and throughout the world. For as Schweitzer himself wrote: "A religion possesses just so much of an understanding of the historical Jesus as it possesses of a strong, passionate faith in the Kingdom of God . . . The only thing that matters is this: that the significance of the concept of the Kingdom of God for our world-view is the same as it was for Him."[1]

As it was, however, the psychological impact of our secular century almost overwhelmed Schweitzer as it has almost overwhelmed millions of lesser Christians. The weak point in his own psychology seems to have been his pride. This pride, founded on the possession of extraordinary natural gifts, with an extraordinary energy of mind and body, was disciplined by a life of extraordinary self-sacrifice; but it was typical of Western intellectuals in our time. His pride was noticed by his detractors in his latter years when they commented on his patronising attitude towards the "natives", whom he always treated as children, as the "children of nature". But in taking this attitude, Schweitzer only belonged to his period; the key point is that he regarded his own labours and sufferings in Africa as a sacrifice, an atonement, offered in memory of the many sins committed by Europeans against Africans. More significant was his habit, reflected in many books, of regarding as mistaken all his predecessors in the attempt to understand Jesus, with the partial exceptions of St. Paul and Luther. His intellectual self-confidence led him to a psychiatric analysis of Jesus; he wrote at length about this in a book of 1913, which grew out of his study for a medical doctorate before going to Africa.[2] Not surprisingly, the Jesus whom Schweitzer discovered at the end of his quest, was a hero of elemental spiritual power, a rebel against everything which was merely conventional, and a prophet who was determined to bring in the Kingdom of God; but he was a Jesus who had to be defended against the charge of madness (and not all Schweitzer's readers would consider Schweitzer's defence convincing). Since the Kingdom delayed during the single year which was the total extent of Jesus's public ministry "from seed-time to harvest", Jesus grew convinced that his death was necessary to God, as a sacrifice or atonement for the sins of his people, and that his death would immediately result in the harvest of the miraculous Kingdom on earth. Jesus was, therefore, fundamentally mistaken about his mission (although not insane), and our acknowledgment of

---

[1] Quoted in Henry Clark, *The Philosophy of Albert Schweitzer*, p. 201.
[2] *The Psychiatric Study of Jesus* (Eng. trans., Boston, 1948).

his spiritual authority over our wills ought to be accompanied by our rejection of his view of the world. As Schweitzer wrote: "There is silence all around. The Baptist appears, and cries: 'Repent, for the Kingdom of heaven is at hand.' Soon after that comes Jesus, and in the knowledge that He is the coming Son of Man lays hold of the wheel of the world to set it moving on that last revolution, which is to bring all ordinary history to a close. It refuses to turn, and He throws Himself upon it. Then it does turn; and crushes Him . . . The wheel rolls onward, and the mangled body of the one immeasurably great Man, who was strong enough to think of Himself as the spiritual ruler of mankind and to bend history to His purpose, is hanging upon it still. That is His victory, and His reign."[1]

Schweitzer's Jesus, who sought to conquer God's delay by his own courage, was thus close to Nietzsche's Superman, who sought to take over after God's death. And the consequence of this strange inter pretation of the gospels—which on Schweitzer's own admission discarded all those sayings in which Jesus anticipated an interval long or short, between his death and the consummation of the Kingdom—was that, for all the religious heroism of his life Schweitzer's view of the world was essentially secular. Schweitzer did not share the Christian belief that love is "the last word about life". He believed passionately that it ought to be, and he lived passionately so that love was the meaning of his life and his gift to those who suffered around him; but he often expressed his conviction that life as a whole remained an enigma. He, like his Jesus, was a Prometheus, heroic in his defiance; but in the end also a doomed Sisyphus.

Schweitzer taught that "the spirit of Jesus" could lead any man who would follow along the road of love in faith; but he added that knowledge of the objective world was another matter, for knowledge of the world could be reached only through thought, and thinking yielded no light on any ethical purpose existing or emerging in nature Values should be created by men; they could not be discovered in the universe. This tragic view of reality was reinforced by Schweitzer own experience of the pain of Africa and the ruthlessness of the jungle but it is clear from his autobiographical writings that already as a youth in Europe his compassion was based on his pessimism, and as a young theologian he developed the separation of values from reality which is found, although in a less extreme form, in nineteenth century religious thinkers. "My knowledge is pessimistic,

---

[1] *The Quest of the Historical Jesus*, pp. 368-9.

chweitzer wrote, "but my willing and hoping are optimistic. I am
pessimistic in that I experience in its full weight what we conceive
to be the absence of purpose in the course of world-happenings. Only
at quite rare moments have I felt really glad to be alive . . . But
however much concerned I was at the problem of the misery of the
world, I never let myself get lost in broodings over it; I always held
firmly to the thought that each one of us can do a little to bring some
portion of it to an end."[1]

It is also clear that Schweitzer's ethic of reverence for life was not
based on the Jewish and Christian belief that the world was created
essentially good (although not perfect) by the perfect God. On the
contrary, "ethics consists in this, that I experience the necessity of
practising the same reverence of life towards all will-of-life, as towards
my own. It is good to maintain and cherish life; it is evil to destroy
and check life." This was the religion of the Jains in India, who would
not take the life even of an insect; but it is difficult to believe with
Schweitzer that "the ethic of reverence for life is the ethic of Jesus
brought to philosophical expression, extended into cosmical form,
and conceived as intellectually necessary."[2] For Jesus believed in a
God who ruled the world. Schweitzer, on the other hand, with a
moving honesty confessed that he found it necessary to "experience
in its full weight what we conceive to be the absence of purpose in the
course of world happenings. Only at quite rare moments have I felt
really glad to be alive."[3] "Without understanding the meaning of
the world I act from an inner necessity of my being . . . I fulfil the
will of the universal will-to-life which reveals itself in me. I live my
life in God, in the mysterious ethical divine personality which I
cannot discover in the world, but only experience in myself as a
mysterious impulse."[4] Here is the Gethsemane or Calvary part of
Christianity, and it would be impertinent and useless to speculate
about how much of the Christians' God he did experience in himself
—but it is ominous that Schweitzer placed so little emphasis in his
teaching (or, apparently in his own life) on what had been the heart
of the religion of Jesus: petitionary prayer to God as Father. He was

---

[1] *My Life and Thought* (1931; Eng. trans., London, 1933), pp. 279-80. The German
Protestant theologians' reinterpretation of Christianity as a religion of feelings or values
is associated particularly with the great names of Schleiermacher and Ritschl. It was a
response to the breakdown both of dogmatic Lutheran orthodoxy and of a philosophical
tendency to base religion on reason or ethics. This great debate has set both the standard
and the terms of much theology. For an outline, see James Richmond, *Faith and Philosophy*
(London, 1966).
[2] *Civilisation and Ethics* (London, 1923), p. 258.
[3] *Out of My Life and Thought* (1931; Eng. trans., New York, 1933), p. 186.
[4] *Civilisation and Ethics*, p. xvi.

an agnostic about the possibility of eternal life. Indeed, in his las years Schweitzer would agree with inquirers that he had used the word "God" in order to communicate with conventional Christians

The theological ferment around John Robinson or Alber Schweitzer is, we may conclude, the surface agitation of a deep ocean of religious confusion in Britain and Europe. Surveys of public opinion show a people full of doubt or open scepticism about the existence o God or the immortality of man, and many of those who regularly ge to church disclose themselves as unable to endorse the traditiona faith. In one survey, over forty per cent of those attending Anglican services said that they did not believe in a life after death. Similar surveys have yielded similar results in other Western European countries.[2] We must ask where such a society is tending, for it seem clear that its present confusion cannot remain for ever. It is a "post Christian" society, and we must give due emphasis to both the implications of that phrase: it is a society which in much of it morality and philosophy of life lives on the capital of a Christian belief it used to accept but now rejects, and it is also a society which has found no substitute for Christianity. Thus surveys such as those made by Geoffrey Gorer give a picture of a British people which i rather dully respectable and which responds to the crises of birth marriage and death by a rather pathetic attempt to seek some guidance in the discarded myths and strange rituals of the churches.[3] A Gallup poll in 1968 suggested that 77 per cent of the British people believed in God, 54 per cent in heaven, 23 per cent in hell, and 14 per cen that "peace of mind is getting better".[4]

Secularisation in Judaism and Islam

In other religions there has been a roughly similar abandonment o neglect of the supernatural. Reserving Asian religion for Chapter 5 we may refer now to Judaism and Islam. These are two religion whose adherents have been locked in hatred since the creatio of Israel enraged the Arab world, but whose internal problem

[1] This was brought out in a book on *Albert Schweitzer* written with his approval by a Norwegian, Gabriel Langfeldt, who warmly approved his rejection of the traditiona Christian understanding of God (1958; Eng. trans., 1960). But it is to be hoped tha Schweitzer's religious views in his later years may be revealed more fully, if private paper can be published.

[2] See Mass-Observation, *Puzzled People* (London, 1948), the sequel by Tom Harrison *Britain Revisited*, and the surveys cited by Boulard, Carrier and Martin (above, p. 49).

[3] See Geoffrey Gorer, *Exploring English Character* (London, 1955), and *Death, Grief an Mourning in Contemporary Britain* (London, 1965).

[4] *Sunday Telegraph*, London, 21 July, 1968.

rise from essentially similar tensions between medievalism and modernism.

What, we must ask, is the future of Judaism? Many Jews in their Dispersion have been thoroughly assimilated into a secular society, and have abandoned the beliefs and almost all the practices taught by their religion. But perhaps equally significant as evidence of the pervasive secularisation has been the uncertainty of many of those who, although "emancipated", have wished to keep alive their distinctive and beautiful traditions in religion.[1] In the dilemma of these Jews we see the drama of the question whether secularisation must lead to secularism.

From the first Zionist Congress in 1897 to the victory of Israel in 1967, political Zionism has often seemed a solution to the problem of Jewish identity. However, the orthodox Jews who aroused enthusiasm for the return to the land of Israel—Shapira, Gordon, Cook, Bruer—have not been able to persuade the people to return to their ancestral faith. Theodor Herzl, who more than anyone else was the founder of Zionism, was secular like Freud (and also from Vienna). The writer Ahad Ha-am and the statesman Chaim Weizmann also stressed the cultural rather than the religious elements in the Jewish heritage. As a result of these mixed origins of the modern state of Israel, orthodox rabbinic regulations are prominent in the national life, and the Hebrew language has been revived for daily use, but visitors estimate that the overwhelming majority of the Israelis is indifferent to religion, and the secularisation of the state seems inevitable.[2]

Among Jews outside Israel, an orthodoxy scarcely altered since the Middle Ages has similarly invited a response which capitulates to secularisation. The orthodox rabbis are so sharply in conflict with the modern spirit that they insist that the first five books of the Old Testament were dictated by God to Moses and are permanently authoritative. For questioning such beliefs, one of the most learned of the English rabbis, Louis Jacobs, was expelled during 1964.[3] This reactionary spirit is supported, at least nominally, by many Jewish laymen who wish to be loyal to the faith of their fathers in a century which has seen the massacre of six million Jews by nominal Christians

---

[1] For an introduction to the piety of the home and the synagogue, see W. W. Simpson, *Jewish Prayer and Worship* (London, 1965).

[2] The story of the first decade was analysed in Joseph Badi, *Religion in Israel Today* (New York, 1959).

[3] See Louis Jacobs, *Principles of the Jewish Faith* (London, 1964). This exposition is based on the Thirteen Principles of the great medieval theologian, Maimonedes. Anyone accustomed to Christian theology must be astonished that such an orthodox book gave offence to the ecclesiastical authorities.

and which has not yet seen the end of anti-semitic prejudice and worse. It is understandable that the Jews of Soviet Russia (for example) should often see the religious situation in terms of loyalty to the God of Israel *versus* the latest persecution by the godless. But Conservative and Reform movements also exist among the twelve or thirteen million Jews surviving, particularly among the American Jews; and these movements have adjusted Judaism to the challenge of the nineteenth and twentieth centuries.

In another Jewish movement, the adjustment to modernity has gone very far indeed. The "reconstructionism" or "greater Judaism" advocated by Mordecai Kaplan retains most of the traditional observances in "synagogue-centres" for Jewish communities in the United States, but has abandoned all belief in a personal God. "For the Jews there can be no higher purpose than that of exemplifying the art of so living individually and collectively as to contribute to the intellectual, moral and spiritual progress of mankind."[1] Professor Joseph Blau, an authoritative commentator on *Modern Varieties of Judaism*, believes that this open abandonment of the supernatural is, "despite its grounding in a non-rational philosophy, a reasonable faith for reasonable men", with great potentialities for the future.[2] If he is right, then the long dispute about whether the Jews constitute a religion or a race will soon be settled.[3]

These more liberal movements in contemporary Judaism have an optimistic streak in them (reminding us that they have been nourished amid the prosperity of the United States), but Richard Rubenstein, a Conservative rabbi who is chaplain to all Jewish students in the great university of Pittsburgh, has outlined a Jewish philosophy which rejects hope, consciously echoing Albert Camus.[4] Harvey Cox's *Secular City* is denounced as being too hopeful. Rubenstein urges men to give up waiting for the Messiah—even for a secular one. His own reconstruction of Judaism is based on the two greatest events for the Jews in the twentieth century: the destruction of Central European Jewry, and the building of the modern nation of Israel. For Rubenstein, the first event poses the problem: if God had existed as Lord of History, in accordance with the Judaism inherited from the Old Testament, he would not have permitted this evil. The second event provides the answer: the God of the tradition does not exist,

[1] *The Purpose and Meaning of Jewish Existence* (Philadelphia, 1964), p. 294.
[2] (New York, 1964), p. 184.
[3] The background has been studied with great sympathy by a Christian scholar, Dr James Parkes, in, e.g., *A History of the Jewish People* (London, 1962).
[4] *After Auschwitz* (New York, 1966).

but the earth exists, and modern Jews must escape from the tradition
by cultivating the earth as normal human beings. For Rubenstein,
any talk of the Jews as the Chosen People separates the Jews from the
normal human lot, and therefore runs the risk of bringing on them
another Auschwitz—a disaster which might be made worse, if its
horror could be deepened, by the thought that this might be a punishment by God for his People's sins (as Father Panelou interpreted the
plague in the novel by Camus).[1] But it is not right to try to forget that
one was born a Jew; there must be a deliberate, mature, life-affirming
acceptance of the death of the God of Judaism, and apparently this is
the task to which Rubenstein feels called as a rabbi. "What then of
Judaism? It is the way we Jews share our lives in an unfeeling and
silent cosmos . . . Ultimately as with all things, it will pass away, for
omnipotent Nothingness is Lord of All Creation."[2]

So we may turn to *Islam*. Islam has been less exposed than Judaism
to the acids of modernity, but here again the riddle of theological
modernism is whether in the long run it will restore, or ruin, faith in
God. Nothing is more disconcerting in Islam as observed by its
learned friends[3] than the contemporary lack of basic theology. What
Muslims need is an intellectual debate of the quality of that waged
eight hundred years ago by rational philosophers of the stature of
Avicenna and Averros, and by that great philosophical sceptic and
theological mystic, al-Ghazali. The great Sufi movement of saints
and brotherhoods dedicated to the service and enjoyment of God
reconciled that debate between reason and revelation by claiming
that their mystic experience brought the high Allah near, to dwell
in the human heart, thus clothing in vivid emotions a faith which was
essentially the orthodoxy of the *Quran*. But today the old debates are
largely irrelevant to the new challenges, and in many places the Sufi
movement is largely exhausted as a popular enthusiasm based on a
genuine mysticism. Now is, therefore, a time for a fresh theology.

The best book of twentieth-century Muslim theology is Sir
Mohammad Iqbal's *The Reconstruction of Religious Thought in Islam*
(Lahore, 1930). The reconstruction which it attempted was based on
the method taught by another Indian Muslim, Muh Abduh, who had
found the culture which he knew before his death in 1905 already
present, embryonically but authoritatively, in the *Quran*. Iqbal in his

[1] E.g. in Arthur Cohen, *The Natural and the Supernatural Jew* (New York, 1963).
[2] *After Auschwitz*, p. 225. See also *The Condition of Jewish Belief*, a Commentary *symposium*
(New York, 1967).
[3] Such as Sir Humphrey Gibb in his *Modern Trends in Islam* (Oxford, 1947), and Kenneth
Cragg in his *Counsels in Contemporary Islam* (Edinburgh, 1965).

day argued in terms of the evolutionary life-force which great Western names including Henri Bergson had recently propagated, but which has been abandoned by most Western philosophers. The snag was that this life-force had to be reconciled with the *Quran*'s essential insight into the otherness of God. Looking back on Iqbal's attempt, some questions must be asked. Is it true to say with Iqbal that "the birth of Islam is the birth of inductive intellect" and that "in Islam, prophecy reaches its perfection in discovering the need of its own abolition?"[1] Is it true that in physics the *Quran* anticipated the science of the twentieth century, and in politics had "spiritual democracy" as its ultimate aim?[2] What becomes of the great slogan which was so familiar to generations of Muslims and is emblazoned on the uniforms of the Indonesian youth movement Ansar: "There is no law or authority except in Allah"?

A book such as Iqbal's *Reconstruction* cries aloud for sequels, and indeed there have been sequels, but none on the necessary scale; and it is significant that in his poems Iqbal condemned all Muslim theological debates.[3] The nature of Islam has been discussed endlessly by the experts—but not the nature of Allah. There have been some moving testimonies by Muslim laymen to the power which still comes from the Prophet's personality and poetry: a power which makes for personal integrity and social justice on the foundation of belief in the reality and righteousness of God.[4] There have been books of prayers and interpretation showing that Muslim devotion to Allah is still alive in the hearts of millions—that the call of the minaret to prayer is still heard.[5] But are even these things enough, as the expressions of a living religion? It is meaningless to generalise, for Islam is so vast today, and its destiny awaits tomorrow. But many Muslims and others voice a profound disquiet, for as the regulated unity of Islamic society is eroded by Westernisation and pluralism its fundamental faith in God will have to be very strong to act as the basis of a new kind of Islam; and on present evidence it is doubtful what will remain when the foundations have been shaken.[6] As Iqbal

[1] *Reconstruction*, p. 176.　　　　　[2] *Reconstruction*, pp. 110-11, etc.
[3] See Iqbal Singh, *The Ardent Pilgrim* (London, 1951).
[4] The modern classic is Sayyid Ameer Ali, *The Spirit of Islam* (London, 1891); here a Calcutta barrister urged that Western "Unitarianism and Theism are neither more nor less than the Islam of Mohammed, shorn of the disciplinary rules framed for the guidance of the common folk". Recent examples from Muslim statesmen are Muhammed Jamali, *Letters on Islam* to his son from prison (Oxford, 1965), and Abd-al-Rahman Azzam, *The Eternal Message of Muhammed* (New York, 1965).
[5] See C. E. Padwick, *Muslim Devotions* (London, 1966), etc.; and for two superbly sympathetic and well-informed studies of modern Muslim life, Kenneth Cragg, *The Call of the Minaret* (New York, 1956), and *Sandals at the Mosque* (London, 1959).
[6] See Kenneth Cragg, *Counsels in Contemporary Islam*, pp. 182-93.

warned: "During the last five hundred years religious thought in Islam has been practically stationary . . . The most remarkable phenomenon in modern history is the enormous rapidity with which the world of Islam is spiritually moving towards the West."[1]

Dr. Fazlur Rahman, Director of the Islamic Research Institute in Karachi, has recently issued a very grave warning to his fellow-Muslims. His conclusion after a survey of the last seven hundred years is that "it would hardly be an exaggeration to say that the actual force and efficacy of Islam in practical terms (beyond the political sphere) was reduced to a collection of superstitious beliefs and practices generated by the Sufi movement." Dr Rahman sees that the task of integrating the genuine inner life of the heart—the *élan* of Sufism—with the social code of the *Sharia* must be achieved on the basis of a reconstructed orthodoxy, and he says: "If a correct vision is not forthcoming of what is needed—and, judging from the overall performance of both the conservatives and the modernists to date, one cannot help questioning whether this vision has yet fully developed—irreparable damage might be done."[2]

The Survival of Religion

Thus Freud has fellow-witnesses to secularisation even among the theologians. In Christianity, Islam and Judaism, much of the contemporary scene is bleak for those who expect religious leaders to talk convincingly about God; and this failure of nerve among the professionals only reflects the confusion of the public. However, this is by no means the whole truth about religion in the twentieth century. In a pluralist society, *the individual himself is often plural,* believing one thing with one part of his mind and another with another; and in our largely secular society, many individuals do retain an affection for religion. It is this fact, rather than any theoretical refutation of Freud's *The Future of an Illusion,* which compels us to say that the future of religion is still an open question.

There may be a future in the religious sentiment and community-sense—in the mystical experience of "something larger" and in the clan's worship of the totem as its collective conscience. This emotion may be valued for its psychological wisdom as Jung claimed, and it may be freed from its dependence on a supernatural God as Fromm, van Buren, Dewey, Kaplan and many others have suggested. (We

---

[1] *Reconstruction,* p. 9.
[2] Fazlur Rahman, *Islam* (London, 1966), pp. 246, 250-1.

shall examine this possibility further in later chapters.) But the more traditional supernatural religion does survive, in at least part of the mind of the man who may be "coming of age". We have already noted that the passion of faith survives in millions of Muslims, and it would be unfair to conclude our pessimistic view of Islamic theology at the present day without emphasising that most Muslim thinkers— even the most critical of them such as Fazlur Rahman—believe that its difficulties can be overcome. And it is not only faith within Islam that has preserved into our time the sense of the overwhelming power and glory of a transcendent God. Judaism has kept some of its essential heritage of belief, in the midst of this age of Freud.

Will Herberg, who has studied the popularity of American churches and synagogues so ruthlessly in his sociological writings, is a Jew who by no means endorses Kaplan's "reconstructionism" as the best solution to the problems of Judaism in the twentieth century. On the contrary, he was led back to a Bible-based faith (through Reinhold Niebuhr's influence), and he has written his personal testimony to the living significance of his ancestors' worship of God.[1] Even the tragedy of Auschwitz has not signified to all the death of the God of the Jews. A book entitled *The Face of God after Auschwitz* has presented the great tragedy as man-made; in it, the Jews once again suffered because of the sins of the world; and after it, the face of God could again be seen in blessing. The author of this presentation of Auschwitz has also offered an interpretation of the state of Israel. He points out that a medieval orthodoxy is honoured in Israel because the European Jewry which was destroyed in the gas chambers held such a faith; and he hopes that when time has done its healing work a stronger, more personal and more progressive faith will emerge in Israel.[2] And perhaps in other literature one may already see what such a Judaism, traditional but fresh, would look like; for few books contain more personal religion than *God in Search of Man* by the American Jewish rabbi, Abraham Heschel (New York, 1955), or the earlier, smaller and astonishingly seminal *I and Thou* by one of the spiritual fathers of modern Israel, Martin Buber.[3]

Buber distilled the thought of a brilliant generation of German

[1] *Judaism and Modern Man* (New York, 1951).
[2] Ignaz Maybaum, *The Face of God after Auschwitz*, was published for the Reform Synagogues of Great Britain (Amsterdam, 1965). For a Christian meditation, see Ulrich Simon, *The Theology of Auschwitz* (London, 1967).
[3] *I and Thou*, first published in 1923, was translated into English by R. Gregor Smith (Edinburgh, 1937), who also introduced the thought of Bonhoeffer to the English-speaking world. The best survey of Buber's thought is Maurice Friedman, *Martin Buber: The Life of Dialogue* (Chicago, 1955; revd. edn., New York, 1960). Buber died in 1965. See also below, pp. 346–7.

Jews (Franz Rosenweig, etc.) and, behind them, of the Hasidic mystics of Jewish history—although he also liberated himself from the need to observe the Jewish ritual laws. He moved beyond the rootless individualism of the "assimilated" Jews in the Dispersion. He saw that we are social beings, made by our relationships with others, and that a living faith must issue in better relationships (for Buber, after the horrors of the 1940s, specially in the *kibbutzim* of Israel). He saw that all our increased understanding of the subtleties of the person in community is most valuable when it leads us to see what occurs between man and man is a preparation for, and a part of, the relationship which the personal God has chosen to open with us and sustain with us. Although this relationship does not yield information of the kind that is included in scientific knowledge, nevertheless through it we can know about a reality which is greater than all the objects known to science, a reality which is not a dead *It*, but a living, active *Thou*. Buber learned from, but contradicted, Feuerbach's claim in *The Philosophy of the Future* (1841) that "man with man, the unity of *I* and *Thou*, is God". He included, but transcended, the kind of religion of nature which William James had in mind when he wrote: "The universe is no longer a mere *It* to us, but a *Thou*, if we are religious."[1] And so the great German-American Christian philosopher, Paul Tillich, used to say that it was the awareness of the presence of the personal God, conveyed by Martin Buber, that enabled him to preach at all. Knowing that in our time it is not enough to preach to the converted, Tillich added this comment: "God could never become an 'object' in Martin Buber's presence. The certainty of God always preceded the certainty of himself and his world. God, for him, was not an object of doubt, but the presupposition—even of doubt. That is the only way, I believe, which makes a dialogue with those who doubt and even those who deny God, possible."[2]

As the century opened a number of those Christians who were most sensitive to the problems of faith had already turned to study and to teach the central importance of mysticism and other religious experience. In his Bampton Lectures at Oxford in 1899 on *Christian Mysticism*, W. R. Inge, later Dean of St. Paul's, had made this appeal, and he pursued it until his death in 1954.[3] Dean Inge once described

[1] *The Will to Believe* (New York, 1897), p. 27.
[2] *A Reader in Contemporary Theology*, ed. John Bowden and James Richmond (London, 1967), p. 55.
[3] E.g. in his Hulsean Lectures on *The Platonic Tradition in English Religious Thought* (London, 1926), and his *Mysticism in Religion* (London, 1947). See Adam Fox, *Dean Inge* (London, 1960).

the Roman Catholic scholar, Baron Friedrich von Hügel, as "our greatest theologian". Like the Dean, the Baron combined an emphasis on the experience of God with a wide awareness of the intellectual and cultural life of the age; but more than Inge, von Hügel was specifically Christian in his mysticism, and—perhaps in consequence —was a saint. (Inge's great love was for the Greek philosopher Plotinus, and he was reluctant to see differences between Plotinus and Jesus.) Von Hügel's two volumes on *The Mystical Element in Religion* (London, 1908), based on a study of St. Catherine of Genoa who had died four centuries before, enabled him and others to survive the crisis of faith brought about by the Papal condemnation of the Catholic "modernists". The modernists had appealed to the realities of Catholic experience, rather than to the intellectual formulations of Catholic dogma. In a more balanced way, von Hügel sustained that appeal.[1]

However, neither Inge's Greek philosophers nor von Hügel's Catholic mystics have been the most successful group to communicate to the twentieth century the sheer reality and excitement of religious faith. A thread which runs through much of the theology addressed to our time is the influence of a Dane who died a few months before the birth of Freud, Soren Kierkegaard.[2] As a character, Kierkegaard was infinitely less admirable than Inge or von Hügel. He was, indeed, approximately as neurotic as his anti-Christian opposite number in the history of nineteenth-century thought, Nietzsche; and Freud would have made fascinating case-histories out of both men. But this melancholy Dane had one thing to say, and he said it with a haunting eloquence. Kierkegaard's "one thesis" was, he said, that "Christianity does not exist". He did not mean that one could not be a "knight of faith". He meant that one could not be born a Christian, that one could not be enrolled automatically in a Christian society, that one could not drift into faith. Prophetically discerning the break-up of the Christian society of Europe, Kierkegaard with a sharp and ever-memorable passion expressed his conviction that *a man must choose*. Christian faith was not submission to Christendom (represented for him by the doctrines and conventions of the Danish State Church); it was the leap of personal trust into submission to the self-revelation of the Wholly

[1] See Michael de la Bedoyère, *The Life of Baron von Hügel* (London, 1951). In the 1960s Count de la Bedoyère, dismissed from the editorship of the London *Catholic Herald*, founded a newsletter, *Search*, which took up many of the themes debated in the 1900s.
[2] Good introductions are Walter Lowrie, *A Short Life of Kierkegaard* (London, 1943), and Louis Dupré, *Kierkegaard as Theologian* (1958; Eng. trans., New York, 1963).

Other, the mysterious, transcendent, divine Person. For Kierkegaard "truth is subjectivity", not in the sense that since truth is unattainable the subjective experience is what matters, but in the sense that the all-demanding experience of personal religion (rather than impersonal study or routine acceptance of authority) leads the worshipper into the knowledge of the God whose reality has an "infinite qualitative difference" from the worshipper's own anxiety-filled existence and from the existence of the world. Kierkegaard knew a God more actively personal than the God of Plotinus, and even harder to reach than the God of the Catholic mystical tradition. Above all, Kierkegaard knew a God who, instead of claiming to be beyond contradiction (and both Inge and von Hügel did seek to raise mysticism above all philosophical doubts or theological controversies), called on each solitary individual to choose for himself. And here is to be found the central thrust of the European Protestant giant, Karl Barth, of Reinhold Niebuhr in the United States, and of the Roman Catholic thought which in the 1960s has moved to the centre of the theological scene.

For many, therefore, God is still alive, after all the psychological impact of our time. Despite the secularisation of Sweden, one whom many would judge to be the embodiment of what is best in that nation's character, Dag Hammarskjöld, while Secretary-General of the United Nations, found God in a lonely mysticism. His concentration on suffering and death amid great worldly success may be psychoanalysed in terms of unhealthy self-love, self-dramatising, narcissism, masochism, etc., but W. H. Auden, introducing his spiritual notes after his death, has effectively replied to suggestions that this is the only analysis appropriate to such holiness. Hammarskjöld's fascination with the tremendous mystery of God did for long encourage his self-absorption, because he probed himself and the writings of the mystics tirelessly in order that his intellect might come to terms with his religious sense (thus supplementing Albert Schweitzer's ethic, which impressed his boyhood). But the God whom he slowly found in the deep silence was a God who was revealed in every "thou" (he arranged for the translation of Martin Buber into Swedish) and supremely in the active self-sacrifice of Christ (when he died, *The Imitation of Christ* by St. Thomas a Kempis was in his pocket). If Hammarskjöld's sense of impending death was the last self-indulgence of a self-dramatising narcissist or masochist, this was an indulgence which was other than the suicide to which he had been tempted previously. It was self-indulgence of a kind which would fulfil the self's life by rescuing the Congo and the world from disaster. When he spoke about Christ's cross to the World Council of Churches in 1954, he saw in it the symbol of the Christian's stretching out to the world. Instead of suicide, he met death in the course of duty. In Hammarskjöld's own phrase, his road to holiness passed "through" action for the sake of others.[1]

Religion in a Technical Era

How typical was Hammarskjöld? This chapter and the next are concerned mainly with ideas recorded in books, since such ideas are to some extent precise. Fortunately our age (particularly the religious minority in it) has been so self-conscious that ideas arising out of emotional life have been expressed freely and recorded frankly. But let us repeat: we deceive ourselves if we ignore the self-evident facts that ideas are less important than emotions in increasing the prosperity of sizeable human associations such as religious bodies, and that society at large is not bookish. Indeed, we ought at this stage to remind ourselves forcibly that the psychological impact of our secular century on religion can be seen most clearly in a movement at which Freud scarcely glanced—the movement of *materialism* following industrialisation. Materialism breeds suspicion of all large ideas, and not merely of religious ideas, because an industrial society demands from the millions a modest level of technical skill, rewards them with a modest share in the products of the machines, and relaxes them by spectacles which appeal directly to their cruder emotions and particularly to their appetites for sex and violence. Martin Heidegger's phrase was an apt description of at least this part of modern life: here is "inauthentic existence".

When the twentieth century began, Thorstein Veblen had just diagnosed with a cynical eloquence the disease from which religion suffered in the modern world: the disease of being the amusement of the "leisure class". In his pioneering analysis of the "pecuniary stratification of devoutness", he argued that "the town populations engaged in the mechanical industries" were a phenomenon not to be equated with "the handicraftsmen of earlier times"—and therefore not to be expected in the churches. Industrial workers, he argued, were unable to imagine that a person, or a personal God, could control things. "So long as the individual is the chief and typical

---

[1] See his *Markings* (1963; Eng. trans., New York, 1964) and the biography by Henry P. van Dusen (New York, 1967).

prime mover in the process; so long as the obtrusive feature of the industrial process is the dexterity and force of the individual handi-craftsman; so long the habit of interpreting phenomena in terms of personal motive and propensity suffers no such considerable and consistent derangement through facts as to lead to its elimination. But under the later developed industrial processes, when the prime movers and the contrivances through which they work are of an impersonal, non-individual character, the grounds of generalisation habitually present in the workman's mind and the point of view from which he habitually apprehends phenomena is an enforced cog-nizance of matter-of-fact sequence. The result, so far as concerns the workman's life of faith, is a proclivity to undevout scepticism."[1] And many besides Veblen have developed this analysis of the dehuman-ising and therefore secularising consequences of industrialisation. The workman's "matter-of-fact" outlook, brought about by his status as a hand hired to mind a machine, seems to have been as powerful as his suspicion of the church-related bosses in turning him from religion. Indeed, the French religious sociologists, to whom reference was made in the last chapter, tend when they theorise to regard industrialisation as intrinsically hostile to religious belief, whether or not the working class feels that it is oppressed in the name of religion. They draw this conclusion from the evidence of greater decline in observance of the religious customs of the Catholic Church, in those parts of France which contain some industry although the surrounding area is mainly rural. A line of quarries across a map will be accompanied by a line of empty churches. This impresses French sociologists because they are aware that peasants also have their class grievances against the clergy, yet may go to church in larger numbers than industrial workers. Here on the map is represented that "alienation" about which Marx wrote, with the industrial worker alienated from his religious roots—and from the satisfactions which he had enjoyed while he was a "handicraftsman".

A French Protestant thinker, Professor Jacques Ellul, has recently argued in a large book that, as industrialisation continues, men's concentration on technical skills and mass amusements must threaten the whole of moral, cultural and religious life, at least as this has been traditionally understood; for the essence of technique is to compel the qualitative to become the quantitative.[2] Many churchmen have expressed alarm about the psychological impact

[1] Thorstein Veblen, *The Theory of the Leisure Class* (New York, 1899), Mentor Books end., p. 215.
[2] *The Technological Society* (1954; Eng. trans., New York, 1964).

on religion of the industrial city's materialism, one of the most perceptive warnings coming from the future Pope Paul VI as a result of his pastoral experiences while Archbishop of Milan.[1] Muslim, Hindu and Buddhist leaders similarly lament the eclipse of spiritual traditions as industrialisation begins to transform the East. But religious believers, unless they are countryfolk untroubled in their conservatism, scarcely need such warnings, for they know in their own experience how difficult it is to relate the metaphysical idea of eternity or the spiritual discipline of meditation or the imagery of a pre-industrial religion to the atmosphere of a factory, a laboratory, a college, a working team, an office or a city street dominated by the practical application of science to the rapid production of standardised material goods. When the threats of unemployment and starvation were real, when work and worry took all of a man's hours when he was not escaping from his lot through sleep or drink, could a man be expected to take an interest in spiritual refinements? General Booth founded the Salvation Army on the principle that a man's stomach must be quietened before his soul could be saved. And in more prosperous times dedicated to technical progress, the timeless mysteries of God, man and the universe, and the always unsatisfactory attempts of religion to pierce the mysteries by symbols and rituals, do indeed seem luxuries for the leisured.[2]

Why, then, should we not conclude that the psychological impact of the secular century is bound to be complete—that the "matter-of-fact" atmosphere of industrialisation will necessarily lead to the triumph of "undevout scepticism"? Religious believers would be foolish to pin their hopes on dramatic success in the current experiments in "industrial evangelism". These experiments, designed to counteract secularisation in Britain, Western Europe and the United States, have been on a small scale. They have often depended on a particular leader or set of circumstances, and a change here can destroy their effectiveness. Those who understand such experiments best, and who know the missioners and laymen of outstanding quality associated with them, warn us not to expect too much.[3] Nor should too much be

---

[1] *The Christian in the Material World* (1962; Eng. trans., Quebec, 1963).

[2] I experienced the atmosphere most instructively when on the staff of the Student Christian Movement, which had almost everywhere to abandon its struggle to form religious groups for students in British technical colleges.

[3] Richard Taylor presented experiments in Britain in *Christians in an Industrial Society* (London, 1961), but since then the Sheffield Industrial Mission, the leading experiment, has experienced a specially problematic period. See also, from Germany, George Symanowski, *Christian Witness in Industrial Society* (1960; Eng. trans., Philadelphia, 1964); from France, Georges Velten, *Mission in Industrial France* (London, 1968); and from Asia, the East Asia Christian Conference's report on *God's People in Asian Industrial Society* (Kyoto, 1966).

made at present of the work among the economically underprivileged in their residential areas. Such work has called forth some remarkable ministers and ministering communities, particularly in the United States;[1] but the example of Britain shows that such work, however valuable it may be in meeting the crisis of the hour, declines when the economic situation changes. (In Britain, as the century began, the poorer sections of the middle class and some respectable workers were closely allied with the Free Churches, an alliance expressed in the virtual identification of "Nonconformity" with the Liberal Party sweeping to power in 1906, and even the sedate Church of England produced some heroic slum priests in the East End of London and elsewhere, but within a quarter of a century the social and ecclesiastical scene had changed—even in the Welsh mining areas, where the chapels had been real centres.) The realistic hope, from the point of view of religion, is that the mid-century experiments may be caught up in *favourable changes within the industrial society itself*. During and after such changes, the rethinking of religious ideas and methods which industrial evangelism encourages may yield results on a larger scale than has yet been experienced, and the devotion of those who have often, at great cost to themselves, maintained a token presence of Christians in an industrial society may win a visible response in gratitude.

In the previous chapter we have already hinted how the future of an industrial society may be more favourable to religion. All that needs to be stated here is that, as more and more of industrial and clerical work is performed by automated machines, the status of the worker improves (provided that work or its equivalent in satisfaction is available to him). The working class at the beginning of the century was brutalised by the industrial process. As Veblen noted, the "dexterity and force" of the craftsman were no longer needed; nor were the skills of the agricultural labourer, wise in the ways of animals, crops and neighbours. We need not grow sentimental about village life, or about the pre-industrial town, to see that something was lost in industrialisation. Rural conservatism led to paganism, or within Christianity to superstition; in the town also it has never been easy to be a saint—as the Christians in Corinth had reason to know when St. Paul wrote to them; but the physical and spiritual ugliness of the industrial revolution brought a new debasement to the humanity condemned to live under it. The machines were the real heroes of the

[1] One striking record, better than its title, is Paul Moore, *The Church Reclaims the City* (New York, 1964).

new process, and the "hands" who ministered to the machines, or the clerks who toiled on routine tasks in the administrative offices, were a little lower than the machines—as industrialists often demonstrated when they had to make decisions which put efficiency in production above humane considerations. Life at that stage of the industrial revolution was so inhuman that we cannot wonder that, apart from using the churches as allies in the social struggle, the working class saw little relevance in the aspirations and sentiments of religion; for religion, whatever else it may be, is a lofty affirmation of the spiritual dignity of man. But the revolution in cybernetics need not lead to a further reduction in the status of man, reducing him to the functions of a robot and denying him all activities which cannot be measured; on the contrary, this new stage of the industrial revolution, by releasing man from brutalising toil, creates the possibility of a new humanism in an industrial society.

This will not necessarily bring benefits to religion. Those who are thrown out of employment by the latest phase in the industrial revolution may be reduced to a sullen bitterness in which religion will still seem too good to be true. Those who remain in industry, now clearly the masters of their machines, may be too full of pride in man's technical achievements to be willing to trouble their minds with the ancient mysteries. But at this early stage of the transformation of our society it is already clear that men and women will not be able to control the new industrial process if they regard themselves as "hands" or as brutes. The new industrial man must in truth "come of age". His mind must be stretched in new directions in order that it may exercise the new mastery; and the new directions will be wider even than the widening field of technology, for the problems of administration and distribution, which are so often human problems, are replacing the problems of manufacturing as the potential bottle necks in the supply of goods, and the new technical developments will themselves demand imaginative and subtle planning if their consequences for human lives are to be enriching rather than destructive. Educational and cultural advances will not be optional in this society where the limiting factor will be not material poverty but a lack of imagination. Although much in the old types of religious thought will then seem even more out of date than it does now, possibly in this new social climate people's minds will no longer be quite incapable of understanding the concerns and styles of religion.[1] They may be

[1] "Liberal studies", or "the Arts", including some treatment of religious problems, have become an important part of the curriculum in many colleges of advanced technology.

willing to concede at least that man, who has tamed the machines, is a more noble animal than seemed likely amid the grime of an industrial city, when Marx or Veblen wrote.

A humanistic religion may flourish in such a climate, whether or not it involves belief in a transcendent God; for a transcendent man, who through the technical revolution will have recovered more than his old "dexterity and force", may see life in a new light. He may come to believe that the "matter-of-fact" sequence can be overcome by his spiritual faith as well as by his technical intelligence. Nor need believers in the dignity of man merely wait to see this happen; they can be inspired by their faith to make it happen. At the end of a study of the political implications of the technological revolution, a leading French Socialist wrote: "In every instance, the real problem is the role of man in society, his future, his vocation, the ultimate meaning and purpose of human life. The essential function of the Christian Church is to lead men to realize what their vocation is and to translate into the transient techniques of social history the profound insistence on human freedom and human responsibility."[1]

To sum up, then: although we have to recognise that the impact of industrialisation was a major factor in the popularity of Freud's attack on religion, we have to ask whether in the new industrial revolution made possible by cybernetics and other technological advances, other peoples may not copy the people of the United States by using some of their spare energies in religious activities, thus defying Freud's association of religion with savages and infants. In America, it is not only a question of a businessman raising funds for a new church gymnasium or a housewife filling in her morning by coffee in a church group; the religious activity also includes adults taking seriously Bible study, theology and even Hammarskjöld-type mysticism. Professor Arnold Toynbee, for one, has speculated that this American zest for religion will be one of the few possible solutions to the materially rich world's coming problem of profound boredom. "The true end of man," he has written, "is religion", and "we are moving into a period when it will be more difficult to ignore the truth. In this coming age of mechanisation, atomic power, affluence and leisure, religion will surely come into its own as the one boundless field for freedom and for creativity that is open to the unlimited aspirations of human nature."[2]

---

[1] André Philip in *Responsible Government in a Revolutionary Age*, ed. Z. K. Matthews, p. 129.
[2] A. J. Toynbee, *Change and Habit* (London, 1966), p. 226.

CHAPTER FOUR

The Decline and Fall of Christian Dogmatism

The Old Coherence

In previous chapters we have seen that the secularisation of modern society has produced a psychological impact on traditional religion. But our analysis of the religious situation ought not to be *only* sociological or psychological. Obviously enough, education has often been a powerful factor in the communication of a society's beliefs and values, and education has some intellectual content. A more technical society must be a more educated one, so that the number of citizens active intellectually is liable to grow; already modern developments in broadcasting, serious journalism and book publishing have increased the size of the intellectual community and the quantity of its debate on a scale which has created a new cultural (and religious) situation. Already many educated citizens claim that the intellectual objections to religious belief are paramount, whatever may have been the actual causes of their choice of unbelief. Altogether, then, we may say that a considerable intellectual challenge has been presented to the theologians.

We have already discussed, however briefly, the theology of Judaism and Islam in the twentieth century, and in our next chapter we shall turn to Hinduism and Buddhism. In this chapter we can, therefore, spend a little more space on the intellectual challenge to Christian dogmatism—a subject which has given to our century many millions of agitated words.

The *Oxford English Dictionary* reminds us that the meaning of "dogmatism" slides from "positiveness in the assertion of opinion" to "a way of thinking based upon principles which have not been tested by reflection", so that to "dogmatise" can mean to "speak authoritatively or imperiously without reference to argument or evidence". In religion, we may add, the essence of dogmatism is the attitude which regards as obvious something which in fact is received only as a matter of faith. A religious dogma is held to be obviously true, "without reference to argument or evidence", because it forms part of a faith which seems to be obviously true. The system of beliefs to which this dogma belongs is more or less compulsory; for it is a whole society's philosophy.

A society's religion, thus accepted uncritically, has commonly been thought to possess a uniform texture, uniting its moral injunctions (for example) with its myths about the world's creation, and suggesting the dependence of the former on the literal truth of the latter. This is because all (or almost all) of the contents of a religion have apparently been embodied in one revelation, which was to be accepted or rejected as a whole. We can see this in the attitude of most Christians to their traditions—and specially in the attitude of Fundamentalism, where the dogmatism of a society is expressed more imperiously than ever before because that society is challenged by an alien way of life and thought. As a sociologist expresses it: "The less firm the plausability structure becomes, the more acute will be the need for world-maintaining legitimations."[1]

The "Fundamentalists" at the peak of their power in the United States were not ashamed to be so called, because they thought that they were defending the very foundations of the Christian faith. The series of books on *The Fundamentals: A Testimony to the Truth*, launched in 1909, and the World's Christian Fundamentals Association, founded ten years later, prepared the way for attacks on many "liberal" or "modernist" preachers.[2] As a climax in 1925 came the prosecution of a schoolteacher in Dayton, Tennessee, for teaching that man was descended from the lower animals. In this "monkey trial" William Jennings Bryan, a former Secretary of State and Presidential candidate, secured the condemnation of the teacher (and of Charles Darwin) by arguing that all American piety would be in danger if the literal authority of *Genesis* were to be sacrificed. His argument was not entirely ridiculous—after all, his opponent in the court was Clarence Darrow, a well-known agnostic who (honourably) practised law in the Chicago of the gangsters. And Bryan, in the monkey trial, had on his side much support from the Christian Church through the centuries—although before the rise of modern science questions of historical truth in the Bible were seldom posed so sharply as to produce Fundamentalism in reaction.[3]

The popular Catholicism which these Protestant Fundamentalists so hated has been very similar in its absence of intellectual flexibility.

---

[1] Peter Berger, *The Sacred Canopy*, p. 47.
[2] See, e.g., the autobiography of H. E. Fosdick, the great liberal preacher of New York, *The Living of These Days* (New York, 1957).
[3] See Norman J. Furniss, *The Fundamentalist Controversy, 1918-31* (New Haven, 1954).

Among the faithful millions, this absence of flexibility in "the Faith" has, no doubt, been due largely to an absence of thought; but among the intellectuals, great sophistication has been exercised on the development of a rationalism which at every important point has been subordinate to the traditional faith. Probably the most authoritative proclamations of the power of the Christian traditions in this century were the two Papal Encyclicals, *Pascendi Dominici Gregis* from Pius X in 1907 and *Humani Generis* from Pius XII in 1950. Both documents were directed mainly against French Catholic intellectuals who had made concessions to the knowledge and spirit of the day; and both denounced such concessions with a confident dogmatism. Catholicism was a system, these Encyclicals declared; and this system must be defended as an integral whole.

Not only Rome has maintained this conservative view of Catholic Christianity. Charles Gore, the Anglican leader who died in 1932, loved to emphasise what he called the "coherence" of Christian doctrine, founded on the authority of Holy Scripture and the Catholic tradition. He thought that the necessity of bishops was part of this doctrine, and as a bishop he very energetically defended parts of the Church of England's traditional faith and organisation which modernisers were prepared to abandon. He saw this basic conservatism as the only possible answer to the many perils of his time—and already in the first hours of the twentieth century he was warning his congregation in Westminster Abbey of the decay in civilisation and of the evils in store for the Church.[1] Many conservative Lutherans or Calvinists have occupied roughly the same position as Gore, although without his passion for bishops, sacraments and other elements retained by the Church of England from the Catholic tradition.

Conservatives of this kind have not been complete Fundamentalists, for they have been prepared to make some concessions when minor points in the religious traditions were proved wrong by modern knowledge. Pius XII, for example, encouraged biblical scholars to study "the modes of expression of ancient peoples" in his Encyclical *Divino Afflante Spiritu* (1943). Charles Gore alienated his more conservative friends by his acceptance of many of the results of scholarly work on the Bible and by his abandonment of some traditional beliefs such as that Jesus was omniscient. But essentially, the old system was good in the eyes of Pope Pius, Bishop Gore and many thousands of lesser teachers of Christian conservatism. Theirs was a refined version

[1] *The Life of Charles Gore: A Great Englishman* was written by G. L. Prestige (London 1935), and his theology was presented by James Carpenter in *Charles Gore: A Study in Liberal Catholic Thought* (London, 1960).

of the faith of the millions, for what mattered more than their minor concessions to modern knowledge was their burning conviction that the teaching authority of the Bible and the Church could be preserved substantially intact. Whether the Bible was interpreted with a simple Fundamentalism or with a more sophisticated conservatism, whether the Church was thought to be the guardian of the unchanging "deposit of faith" (handed on from the apostles to our time) or was thought to be the teacher of a doctrine which included some developments of the apostolic faith, the Bible or the Church (and preferably both) could be trusted. This meant that when a problem was raised, Christians assumed that the answer to it could be derived authoritatively from teaching which already existed in a sacred book or in a sacred community.

The Authority of the Bible

During the twentieth century this dogmatism is being shattered by the impact of criticism on the material previously regarded as sacrosanct. In the nineteenth century biblical criticism spread from Protestant Germany and proceeded from an analysis of the literary history of the Old Testament (and even of the New) to the higher criticism which expressed and tackled larger questions about the truth of the Bible. The "higher critics" sought to recover the true history of the events which were portrayed in the Bible beneath a thick varnish of comments and legends, and to discern the real authorship and authority of commandments associated by the Bible with Moses, Jesus, Paul, etc. In the twentieth century biblical criticism has widened its popularity, being taught now in schools and even sometimes in pulpits, as well as in universities and the more advanced theological seminaries. Biblical criticism has also made its attack on the authority of the biblical tradition more thorough in our time. Criticism has been bold to assess the early books of the Bible as folk-tales, to discriminate between the Old Testament prophets for their religious and ethical values, to reject miracles including the resurrection of Jesus, to assert that neither of the two spiritual giants of the primitive Church, Paul or John, correctly interpreted Jesus, and even to question freely the authority of the teaching ascribed to Jesus in the synoptic (the first three) gospels. Some of this teaching has been traced by the critics to the editorial or inventive abilities of the early Christians, and some parts were attributed to the limitations or mistakes natural to a first-century Jew such as Jesus.

In particular, the historical Jesus was presented by Albert Schweitze and other critics as being apocalyptic and remote from modern standards of rational thought or ethical behaviour.

Conservative Christians have made some effective counter-attack on biblical criticism, and have caught the critics out in many exaggerations or mistakes. Discoveries in biblical archaeology, for example, have suggested that some biblical narratives reflect the historical circumstances of the relevant time more accurately than some critics supposed; and increased knowledge of the peoples surrounding Palestine has increased appreciation of the uniqueness of the religious ideas with which the Jews interpreted their unique history. The originality of Jesus within this stream of Jewish history has been stressed; Jesus has been contrasted as well as connected with the Essenes who wrote the recently recovered Dead Sea Scrolls, or with the Christians themselves in their second-generation timidity. The destructive atmosphere which made most of the history in the Bible seem mythical, and which attributed most of its theology to Near Eastern or Greek pagans, has therefore been dispelled—at least to some extent, and at least among those who have taken the trouble to study the Bible in depth. But the claims of some theologians that biblical students can now revert to dogmatism in a "post-critical" age are dangerously misleading, for the scholarly counter-attacks on the excesses of the sceptics cannot restore the old authority of the Bible. Criticism has prevented honest and thoughtful students from occupying their fathers' positions on a host of questions. Both among careful students and among the general public it is agreed that, while the extremes of destructive scepticism need not be accepted, the simple appeal to biblical texts to provide an unquestionable authority in support of Christian doctrine cannot be restored. A human element, liable to error, is present everywhere in the Bible.[1]

Indeed, it may be doubted whether the full force of the revolution in biblical studies has even now been experienced by the Christian churches. The teaching of the Orthodox churches has scarcely been touched by the critical spirit. The biblical movement in Roman Catholicism advocates more thorough study among scholars, the laity's access to the Bible in modern translations, and greater prominence for Scripture in worship and preaching. In theology this

[1] Histories of biblical scholarship are provided by *The Old Testament and Modern Study* ed. H. H. Rowley (Oxford, 1951), and Stephen Neill, *The Interpretation of the New Testament 1861-1961* (London, 1964). Examples of recent discussion of the question of biblical authority are James D. Smart, *The Interpretation of Scripture* (Philadelphia, 1961) and *The Church's Use of the Bible*, ed. D. E. Nineham (London, 1963).

biblical movement scored its greatest victory with the movement of the Second Vatican Council towards the belief that Scripture is the sole source of the Church's tradition. But the biblical movement has been acceptable within the Roman Catholic system because it has largely dissociated itself from the "negative" or "modernist" approach of Protestant critical scholarship; it has submitted itself instead in full loyalty to the teaching authority (the *magisterium*) of the Church. Pope Pius XII, while encouraging biblical scholars, reminded them that they must assume that Adam and Eve were actual individuals who "fell", and that the whole human race was descended from these two parents; and this note of caution is typical of a certain ambiguity which remains in the Roman Catholic Church's welcome to modern knowledge. Much sound scholarship has been produced in these circumstances, but also a great flood of pious speculation arising under ecclesiastical inspiration from an uncritical meditation on the text. The intellectual weakness may be seen most plainly in the writings about the Virgin Mary. Only a few hundred words may be found in the Bible about the Virgin, there is no other evidence, and during its first few centuries the Church knew no real Marian doctrine; but in 1959 the published titles relating to this subject by Roman Catholic biblical students were estimated at about 100,000.[1] A few signs have begun to appear that such use of the Bible for such dogmatic purposes no longer satisfies. But the impact of the critical approach on the entire system of Roman Catholic doctrine, and on the whole Roman Catholic understanding of authority, cannot be for ever delayed, and when it comes, it is bound to cause pain and confusion.

Even among Protestants, the regular teaching of the churches will be challenged and shocked as the critical approach makes its full impact. Professor D. E. Nineham has well described the theological heritage: "It has often been thought in the past that being a Christian means holding a certain series of beliefs and behaving, or refraining from behaving, in certain specific ways. Along with this has gone an understanding of the Bible as a source-book from which Christians derive their characteristic beliefs and ways of behaving—a collection of inerrant propositions and irreformable demands and prohibitions, guaranteed by their direct divine origin as timelessly valid and universally binding." "I should like to emphasize," Nineham continued, "how long-lived this attitude was and how

[1] Hans von Campenhausen, *The Virgin Birth in the Theology of the Ancient Church* (1962; Eng. trans., London, 1964), p. 8.

deep-seated it has become . . . Anyone who takes part in the meetings
of the synods of the various Churches as they attempt to lay down the
'biblical norms' of orthodox Christian behaviour must be aware that
such views are very much alive. And is not each one of us aware of
it . . .? When we read of doubt being cast on the accuracy of some
biblical statement, do we not secretly feel that another nail has been
knocked into the coffin of biblical inspiration?" So conservatism
lingers on, even while, as Professor Nineham has noted, scholars today
agree with surprising unanimity that instead of the old view of biblical
authority Christianity should be defined in some such terms as
"putting your whole trust in God for life and for salvation".[1]

If this is the situation among scholars and ecclesiastical leaders, in
the parishes conservatism is still thought to be the only practical
method for pastoral purposes. In many pulpits—perhaps in most—
what "the Bible says" is still quoted in order to clinch an appeal
without further argument. In most pulpits the substantial accuracy
of the passage being preached about is assumed without troubling
the congregation with "scholarly questions". This seems to be true
even in Germany, where the divorce between the universities and
the parishes is long established. Most Protestant preachers in the
twentieth century have, therefore, still to face the problem posed by
the fact that most of the material in the Bible has been filtered
through the preaching or story telling of the community of ancient
Israel or the early Church before assuming its present form.

What we possess in the Bible, according to most of the scholars, is
what was told around the camp fires or when the day's farming was
done or over tables in Jerusalem or in meetings for worship in the
early Christians' homes. It is often possible to pierce through this
form by "form-criticism", and to suggest with a reasonable confidence
what was originally said or what originally happened, and in some
parts of the Bible—as in the court history of King David, or in the
authentic letters of St. Paul—it is possible to have direct access to the
real history. But the bulk of the Bible was shaped by the theology of
the chroniclers or evangelists, whose motives were different from those
of modern historians. The appeal to the Bible today is, therefore, only
in part an appeal to the actual words of Jesus, his forerunners and his
apostles; it is also in large part an appeal to the experience of the
Hebrews and the Christians. The Old Testament, for example,
incorporates many fragments from early days, but the historical
narratives no less than the laws and prophecies in it were edited to

[1] *The Church's Use of the Bible*, pp. 147-8.

strengthen a community's faith. St. John's gospel contains some history, but its main substance seems to be the meditations of its unknown author on what the Church had learned towards the end of the first century A.D. The theology of St. Mark, St. Matthew and St. Luke (in the gospel and in *Acts*) must be considered along with the historical value of the sayings and incidents preserved in the tradition of the local church behind the evangelist. The form in which we have the evidence about Jesus is now seen to be the form given to that evidence by the early Church. This is the reason why in Rudolf Bultmann's *The Theology of the New Testament* the discussion of "The Message of Jesus" occupies less than thirty pages out of almost 600.[1]

If this assessment of the Bible is correct, it follows that preachers will one day have to adopt a new approach. They will have to accept their task of presenting the Bible as a library written by men and by churches for their purposes, not as a book dictated by the Holy Spirit solely for the purposes of God; and when that day comes, popular reaction to the authority of the experiences and convictions of the Hebrews or the first Christians is likely to be a very different matter from the old popular reaction to the Bible as the Word of God. People will be confronted not by the Word of God, but by the Word of God as mediated by the People of God; and unless they ascribe infallibility to ancient Israel or to the early Church, people will be forced to make up their own minds, point by point, about the truth or error of the Scriptures which those Hebrews or Christians wrote. The question must arise: "If the truth about God's revelation . . . be such that those men saw it and wrote of it like that, what must it be for us?"[2] A theology can be built on the Bible thus understood, but the old appeal to the authority of the Bible cannot be sustained among those who are intellectually free.

The Authority of the Church

If biblical criticism has thus questioned the authority of the Bible, the authority of the Church has been eroded in a parallel process which may be called doctrinal criticism.

In the Eastern Orthodox and Roman Catholic Churches, the twentieth century has preserved the image of a teaching Church,

[1] 2 vols., 1948-51 (Eng. trans., New York, 1951-5).
[2] Leonard Hodgson, *For Faith and Freedom*, vol. i (Oxford, 1956), p. 88. In the Pelican Gospel Commentaries, and specially in D. E. Nineham, *The Gospel of St. Mark* (London, 1963), an attempt was made to develop this approach. For a foretaste of the wrath to come in public reaction, see *Vindications*, ed. Anthony Hanson (London, 1966).

infallible on its most solemn occasions and authoritative in the daily guidance of the flock by bishops and priests. As we look more closely at Eastern Orthodoxy, however, we find that, while the liturgy has indeed been preserved with fairly trivial modifications under the control of the hierarchy, the thought of these Churches has usually developed, where it has developed, through laymen such as the theologians in the Greek universities. Among these, the one genius to win wide attention in the West—not in the Orthodox world—was the turbulently eloquent Nicholas Berdyaev, but he was a philosopher in rebellion against most of the prevailing trends in his Church. If the Communist revolution had not exiled him to Berlin and Paris, the ecclesiastical authorities would almost certainly have sent him to Siberia.[1] Eastern Orthodox theology in our time has usually sought to remain loyal to the tradition inherited from ancient days, but its cohesiveness has been expressed in that untranslatable Russian word *sobornost*—a spiritual togetherness in worship and life, resting intellectually on the seven "ecumenical" councils of the Church (of which the last was held in the year 787), by no means identifiable with the argued coherence of Catholic or Protestant doctrine. Whether this kind of conservatism can for ever withstand the impact of our secular century remains to be seen. Partly because the largest Orthodox Church has been forced into a spiritual ghetto by the Russian state, Eastern Orthodoxy has never experienced the Reformation or the scientific movement; and for the most part the Orthodox Churches in the West have been nostalgic exiles in a strange land. But there are some hopeful signs of renewal: in the participation of the Orthodox in the World Council of Churches, in the *Zoe* (or Life) Movement in Greece, and in the slow emergence of religious unity and vigorous theology among the three million immigrants from Orthodox traditions in the United States.[2]

The Roman Catholic Church is, of course, dogmatic. This characteristic can be seen in a lack of theological vitality in the twentieth century—a lack noticeable when one considers that Church's vast resources. Some laymen have been creative theologically—such as Baron von Hügel, or the French philosophers Jacques Maritain, Etienne Gilson and Gabriel Marcel, or Karl Adam and Romano

---

[1] See Donald Lowrie, *Rebellious Prophet* (New York, 1960), and for the background Nicholas Zernov, *The Russian Religious Renaissance* (London, 1965). Summing up his autobiography, *Dream and Reality* (1949; Eng. trans., London, 1950), Berdyaev wrote: "I am above all an heir of the tradition of Dostoevsky and Tolstoy . . ."

[2] The best recent expositions by Orthodox writers in the West are Vladimir Lossky, *The Mystical Theology of the Eastern Church* (1954; Eng. trans., London, 1957) and Timothy Ware, *The Orthodox Church* (London, 1963).

Guardini who exercised a wide and liberal influence in Catholic Germany. There have been some major contributions from priests in the French religious orders (Henri de Lubac, Yves Congar and Teilhard de Chardin) and in the post-war German universities (Bernard Haring, Karl Rahner and Hans Küng). These are intellectual circles which are relatively free from the interference of the Vatican and the bishops—although the three great Frenchmen just mentioned all knew periods of disgrace, and the German professors have not been without their highly placed critics. Many more Roman Catholic scholars could be listed; but the whole of English-speaking Catholicism has not produced a major theologian since Newman's death in 1890, and throughout the Church the half-century after the "modernist" crisis in the 1900s was marked by the crippling effects of the ecclesiastical authorities' censorship and control. Over French theological vitality, the Vatican exercised a close and suspicious watch; towards Latin American superstition its attitude was relaxed. This era culminated in two actions by Pius XII in the second half of 1950. One was his Encyclical *Humani Generis*, already mentioned; the other was his "infallible" proclamation of the dogma that "the Immaculate Mother of God, the ever-Virgin Mary, having completed the course of her earthly life, was assumed body and soul into heavenly glory". This doctrine of the assumption was desired by popular devotion, but was confessedly unsupported by historical evidence, so that its proclamation was the strongest possible illustration of the Roman Catholic hierarchy's dogmatism.

But the evidence seems to show that religious dogmatism has no long future in the modern West—not even when dogmatism is so splendid and triumphant as it has seemed at Rome. Within fifteen years of 1950 the Roman Catholic hierarchy, without changing any doctrine, had modified its rejection of the modern world. The Second Vatican Council made several significant concessions. It acknowledged the Bible as the one source for Christian doctrine, as we have mentioned. In the crucial question how the Bible was to be interpreted, the Council adopted several positions which might lead to a less rigidly dogmatic attitude in the years ahead. The Council stressed the "collegial" (corporate) nature of the teaching authority of the bishops under the Pope; it invited criticism from, through dialogue with, fellow-Christians of other Churches and even total unbelievers; and, while abandoning no doctrine, it pointedly refrained from additions. It now seems improbable that any other dogma will be defined through the exercise of Papal infallibility. Moreover, in the 1960s the

rumblings of the clergy against the law of celibacy, of the laity against
the prohibition of contraceptives and of the left wing against the
political attitudes of reactionary bishops, have developed into open
criticism of the whole authoritarian style and legal structure of
Roman Catholic moral teaching. A new emphasis is emerging on
the primacy of love in ethics and of freedom in the conscience of the
individual. It now seems probable that a severe questioning of the
hierarchy's code of discipline as the content of Catholic morality—
particularly in the intimately emotional matter of birth control—
will lead to doubts being thrown publicly on the hierarchy's past
teaching as the criterion of Catholic doctrine. The Roman Catholic
Church may be on the eve of a period of self-criticism no less
dangerous than the Reformation of the sixteenth century and no less
drastic than the debating which has eroded Protestant orthodoxy
and institutionalism in the nineteenth and twentieth centuries.[1]

In the Protestant world the collapse of dogmatism became evident
during the nineteenth century. The Reformation of the sixteenth
century exalted the Reformers against the Popes, and was in that
strictly limited sense a triumph for individualism, but seldom before
the nineteenth century did the Protestant churches frankly abandon
their struggle for uniformity in their ranks. Over the last hundred
years the view has prevailed widely that Jesus did not entrust his
authority to any Church, except perhaps to the invisible fellowship
of those who obey his moral teachings. Theological fashion has since
the 1920s moved away from the teachers of that low view of the
Church, but such liberal Protestantism has remained the simple
creed of many millions of Protestant laymen. Many of these have,
indeed, maintained that to be a Christian it is not necessary to "go
to church" at all. When the corporate expression of Christianity has
been honoured, the Church has been understood as a fellowship of
laymen trying to live decent lives with help from stories about Jesus
and from such worship as has appealed to individual temperaments

---

[1] The survey by Roger Aubert of *Théologie Catholique au Milieu du XXe Siècle* (Tournai,
1954) was summed up in his contribution to *Twentieth Century Christianity*, ed. Stephen
Neill (London, 1961). A pre-Council survey by an American Lutheran scholar was
Jaroslav Pelikan, *The Riddle of Roman Catholicism* (Nashville, 1959). The most vivid report
on the debates at the Council was by a young American Roman Catholic philosopher,
Michael Novak, *The Open Church* (New York, 1964). For a judicious assessment by an
Anglican bishop, see J. R. H. Moorman, *Vatican Observed* (London, 1967). *The Documents
of Vatican II*, ed. Walter M. Abbott (New York, 1966), was a convenient translation under
Catholic auspices, with Catholic, Protestant and Orthodox comments. For a sketch of
developments since the Council, see Theo Westow, *Introducing Contemporary Catholicism*
(London, 1967). Its leading British theologian, Charles Davis, told why he left the
Roman Catholic Church in *A Question of Conscience* (London, 1967). But the "riddle" of
Roman Catholicism remains.

or congregations. On this liberal, democratic basis an authoritarian teaching could not be successfully erected. Some theologians have attempted to substitute the professor or the preacher for the old-style bishop or priest, but the great Protestant principle has remained: the true Church is essentially not an institution but an event, the event which happens when a Christian obeys Christ.[1]

As a consequence of this low view of the Church's authority, conservative leaders of the Protestant churches have not been allowed to control men's thoughts. The historic doctrinal statements (the Lutheran Augsburg Confession, the Anglican Thirty-nine Articles or the Presbyterian Westminster Confession) are now regarded so ambiguously that it has become virtually impossible to punish preachers who have disagreed with them. An English theologian who died in 1967, J. S. Bezzant, outlined the traditional Christian "scheme of salvation" (based on the verbally inspired Scripture, the rebellion of Satan, the fall of Adam, the substitutionary sacrifice of Jesus to appease God's wrath, the predestination of the elect among the true believers in the Church to the resurrection of their bodies, the endless torment of the rest of mankind in hell, etc.), and added: "This outline has been so shattered that the bare recital of it has the aspect of a malicious travesty."[2] Even the creeds of the ancient Church, while regarded as binding in many theories about the basis of church life, have in practice often not been treated as decisive. The so-called "Athanasian" Creed has become a document of history for theologians, and the Nicene and Apostles' Creeds have been commonly viewed as containing some statements about Christ which need not be taken literally—the descent into Hell or the ascent to the right hand of the Father, and for many also Christ's virginal conception and physical resurrection.

Protestantism from Harnack to Bultmann

It is obvious that great confusion has been caused in modern Protestantism by the debates among the theologians after this collapse

[1] Emil Brunner's *The Misunderstanding of the Church* (1951; Eng. trans., London, 1952) remains a classic statement of the Church's informality. For Brunner the true understanding of the Church depended on the pure fellowship of person with person, and he was interested in the Moral Rearmament movement and also in the Non-Church Movement in Japan. Christian doctrine itself could be best understood as the result of God's personal encounter with man (see his *Truth as Encounter*, revd. edn., 1963; Eng. trans., Philadelphia, 1964). But Brunner's theology was always strongly biblicist. He proclaimed the Gospel much like Karl Barth and other "dialectical" or "crisis" theologians. The power of his proclamation may be experienced best through his short book *Our Faith* (1935; Eng. trans., New York, 1936).
[2] *Objections to Christian Belief*, ed. A. R. Vidler (London, 1963), p. 84.

of ecclesiastical authority. The fear of open confusion inspired many
Roman Catholic boasts that certainty was to be found only in
submission to Rome—until the bishops went to Rome for their
Council, and so moved nearer to joining the debates. A similar fear
made many Protestant churchmen in the English-speaking world
glad that the faithful were not exposed to the theological agitations
in the German universities—until broadcasts and paperbacks placed
radical theology within reach of the millions. Today, an element of
confusion is being accepted by more and more Christians as the only
possible alternative to a dead or doomed dogmatism. But even now the
impossibility of a new dogmatic *system* has probably not been fully
appreciated; for many Christians seem to hope that the faith which
will emerge from the current confusion will be a new kind of dogmatism.

The simplest kind of new dogmatism would be that which was
associated with many of the liberal Protestants in the days of their
battles with the Fundamentalists. By the removal of miracles or of
harsh sayings which were "unworthy" of Jesus and were thought to
be the inventions of the early Christians, the liberals wanted to reduce
drastically the dogmatic element in Christianity, but they still maintained that the original teaching of Jesus was true in a fairly obvious
way, and they were optimistic that modern men of intelligence and
good will would accept it. Adolf von Harnack's eloquent lectures on
"the essence of Christianity", delivered in the University of Berlin
as the century began, presented this reduced Gospel about "God the
Father and the infinite value of the human soul", a Gospel resulting
in "the higher righteousness and the commandment of love".[1]

Here we need not pause to attempt a full criticism of the theology
of Harnack and other "liberals", but we shall simply consider the
claim that this creed was a fairly obvious set of truths, well authenti-
cated by the teaching and life of Jesus. Nor need we deal here with
Albert Schweitzer's point, already mentioned, that the truly historical
Jesus had preached no such message—that (unlike Harnack) the
historical Jesus would not have been a popular professor amid all the
civilisation of pre-war Berlin. The question we must raise is closer to
the criticism offered by Alfred Loisy in his book on *The Gospel and
the Church*,[2] for Loisy argued against Harnack's whole attempt to
define the original essence of Christianity and to condemn the Church
for having added to that pure essence by elaborations which resulted

[1] Translated as *What is Christianity?* (London, 1901). For a collection of extracts with an
Introduction, see *Liberal Protestantism*, ed. B. M. G. Reardon (London, 1968).
[2] 1902 (Eng. trans., London, 1903).

from its own experience. At that stage of his career Loisy was prepared to defend Christianity as developed dogmatically by the Roman Catholic Church. Jesus, having been an apocalyptic dreamer, was (Loisy hinted) not very relevant as the sole arbiter of religion in subsequent centuries, but the Church had been more successful— "Jesus expected the Kingdom, and it is the Church that has come". But here was not the essential point made in the criticism of Harnack. What was most significant for the future of Christian theology was the stress on the *contemporary* essence of Christianity. Christianity, Loisy urged, deserves to be judged as it is today, not as it was in the beginning. No event in the past, however authoritative, —not even the teaching and life of Jesus himself, if that could be recovered in detail—can make sure that the Gospel will be accepted; the hearer must be prepared to open his eyes and ears to the Gospel's strangeness, and to change his life in response to its revolutionary demand. Essentially, this would still be the case even if the Jesus of history was nearer to the Jesus of Harnack than he was to the Jesus of Schweitzer and Loisy. For the Christian critics of Harnack, the Gospel-character of the Gospel depends on the hearer accepting it as good news *for him*, with a personal faith; and this Gospel about God cannot be heard unless the hearer has first faced a profoundly disturbing question about the character and meaning of *his own life*. No doubt this "subjective" element in Christianity has always been present, but in Liberal Protestantism (as in Protestant Fundamentalism and conservative Catholicism) the emphasis had been on the "objective" revelation, and the necessity of a personal choice had been obscured.

In tracing the revolution in Protestant theology since Harnack, we may mention first Karl Barth with his famous attack on the whole notion that the Fatherhood of God is obvious. Barth protested that the God who was obvious was likely to be a false God, for the real God had to reveal himself before he could be known at all. Harnack replied that Barth (his former pupil) was being irrational, and was thus a traitor to the great tradition of German theology. But Barth has continued to prefer the description of the living God given in the atheist Feuerbach's *Essence of Christianity* to Harnack's "essence" some sixty years later. Feuerbach, Barth thinks, got to the heart of the matter; and Barth, taking the great God whom Feuerbach presented and denied, simply said: that God is real.[1] No doubt the

---

[1] See Karl Barth's Introduction to the Harper Torchbooks edition of Feuerbach's *Essence of Christianity* (New York, 1957).

pendulum of living theology would have swung from Harnack position if Barth had never been born; optimism died in the trench of 1914-18, and even in neutral Sweden the urge to take up again the sterner themes of Christian doctrine prevailed.[1] But it was the geni of Karl Barth that gave a storm centre to the new theology of crisis.

As a young pastor in Switzerland from 1909, Barth preached the "Culture-Protestantism" which he had learned in Marburg from h liberal teacher Wilhelm Herrmann (and through him from Albrec Ritschl), and was drawn to the "Religious Socialism" propagated k the Blumhardts from Bad Boll. Thus Barth was the heir to the who nineteenth-century reconciliation of Christianity and culture, an has never abandoned his broad cultural interests (his devotion to the music of Mozart is famous). But he found that this liberal message reform and progress did not wear well in his pulpit at Safenwil, an could scarcely be reconciled with the wartime newspapers. Tw events of 1914 seemed particularly ominous. Ernst Troeltsch, wh studied Christian theology as a department of the scientific stud of the history of religion, resigned as Professor of Theology an became Professor of Philosophy; and ninety-three German intelle tuals, supporting their Kaiser's war in a manifesto, included Barth's horror "the names of nearly all my theological teachers . . I perceived that I should not be able any longer to accept their ethi and dogmatics, their biblical exegesis, their interpretation of histor and that at least for me the theology of the nineteenth century had i future".[2] So Barth turned to an intensive study of St. Paul's Epistle the Romans. In agony of mind he wrote one commentary (1919) an then rewrote it for a second edition (1921). That second edition w the book which burst like a bomb in the playground of the liber theologians.[3]

---

[1] Two well-known books from Swedish Lutheranism, both published in 1930, we *Christus Victor*, in which Gustav Aulen revived the classic doctrine of the cross as t decisive victory over evil, and *Agape and Eros*, in which Anders Nygren contrasted se forgetful Christian love with ordinary, worldly desires (Eng. trans., London: Aulen, 193 Nygren, 2 vols., 1932-9, revd. 1953).

[2] Karl Barth, *God, Grace and Gospel* (1957; Eng. trans., Edinburgh 1959), p. 57.

[3] After a deplorable delay, Barth's *Romans* was translated into English by a Cambrid scholar, Sir Edwyn Hoskyns (Oxford, 1933). But if Barth had studied at Cambridge 1908-9, he might have found some of his own themes of the 1920s anticipated in t Hulsean Lectures of an historian who in revolt against the smugness of Edwardian Engla had become an Anglican monk: J. N. Figgis, *The Gospel and Human Needs* (London, 190 An earlier and greater "Barthian before Barth" in England was the Congregational P. T. Forsyth, who broke with theological liberalism in his address on "The Holy Fathe in 1896, became Principal of New College, London, and poured out a stream of boc until his death in 1921, notably *The Person and Place of Jesus Christ* (London, 1909). Wh the Barthian revolution had made its delayed impact on English-speaking theology, ma of Forsyth's books were re-published.

Barth proclaimed Christian faith as decision after the moment of crisis, in which God miraculously addresses man; and he showed Christian life to be no crown of culture, but a resurrection from the dead. Abandoning the quest for "points of contact" between Christianity and culture, he became a humble pilgrim to the "strange new world" of the Bible. Called unexpectedly into German academic life, Barth continued to develop this stark theology of crisis, making one beginning with *Christian Dogmatics*, only to scrap it and to begin the great *Church Dogmatics*.[1] His booklet *Nein!* (1934) rebuked his fellow-theologian Emil Brunner for continuing to toy with the idea that there might be some revelation of God outside the Bible.[2] Expelled from his professorial chair in Bonn in 1935, Barth moved back to Switzerland to teach (at Basle) and delivered Gifford Lectures in Scotland (at Aberdeen) with a destructive zest. Entitled *The Knowledge of God and the Service of God* (London, 1938), they were based defiantly on the Scottish Confession of John Knox and his fellow-Calvinists of 1560, and they made clear Barth's conviction that, in the twentiety century as in the sixteenth, no genuine knowledge of God is available without obedient faith in the Word of God, who is Jesus Christ. Without the eye of faith, even "Christians" who see Jesus as the Rabbi of Nazareth see only the *incognito* which conceals God.

Barth's negative view of Liberal Protestant dogmatism has largely prevailed. To say this is not to say that the Barth of the 1920s and 1930s was unanswerable; indeed, he has been answered to some extent by the Barth of the 1950s and 1960s, who has confessed that his earlier onslaught against the natural reason was exaggerated. While still denying that "natural" theology is a way from man to God, Barth has been increasingly overwhelmed by the sheer joy of the Gospel which he has served, by the humanism of the God who has chosen to be human for ever in Jesus Christ; and the humanity thus blessed by God has been praised by his servant Karl Barth also. Partly because of this shift of emphasis, Communism has never been denounced by Barth as Nazism was; indeed, he calls on Protestants in Eastern Europe to accept it.[3] Barth's fierce hostility to religion outside Jesus Christ must be understood as part of his prophetic indignation against the "German Christians" who,

---

[1] Eng. trans., Edinburgh, 1935 onwards. The story of Barth to 1931 has been interpreted by T. F. Torrance, *Karl Barth: An Introduction to his Early Theology* (London, 1962).
[2] See *Natural Theology*, ed. John Baillie (London, 1946).
[3] Barth's position here was analysed in the comprehensive study by Charles West, *Communism and the Theologians* (London, 1958).

merging piety with patriotism and worship of evolutionary progress with adoration of the Aryan blonde beast, supported first the Kaiser's war, and then the greater evil of Nazism. His booklet on *Theological Existence Today* was a ringing call for faithfulness to the Gospel in 1933, and in May 1934 he wrote all but one sentence of the Barmen Declaration of the anti-Nazi "Confessing" Church, with its proclamation: "Jesus Christ, as he is attested to us in Holy Scripture, is the one Word of God, whom we have to hear and whom we have to trust and obey in life and in death. We condemn the false doctrine that the Church can and must recognise as God's revelation other events and powers, forms and truths, apart from and alongside this one Word of God."[1] It was Barth's supreme moment, and after it his violent onslaught against the inoffensive Brunner—who shared his Evangelical faith but was more realistic in his assessment of human culture—has come to seem ridiculous, for he was applying to Brunner a passion which would have been better kept for more extreme and dangerous representatives of "Culture-Protestantism". However, when all the exaggerations have been forgotten, fundamentally the negative achievement of those fighting years does stand, and today it is increasingly seen to have brought about a permanent revolution in Christian theology. The Barthian revolution may be seen as the great blight.[2] Or it may be seen as the great purification, according to one's view of the liberal, but still basically dogmatic, "Culture-Protestantism" which it replaced.[3]

Karl Barth's proclamation of Jesus Christ as the Word of God was far less comprehensively dogmatic than the older Protestant orthodoxies; nevertheless it was dogmatic of set purpose, and its imperfect contact with a modern, critical approach to the Bible and to Christian tradition and language explains why Barthianism already belongs to history. If we ask what has effectively replaced the theology of Harnack among reflective Protestants, we must turn to the thought of the Marburg Professor, Rudolf Bultmann. Bultmann regards himself as continuing Barth's work in "dialectical" or "crisis"

[1] For the Declaration and what resulted from it up to 1945, see E. H. Robertson, *Christians against Hitler* (London, 1962).

[2] Such a description of the influence of Barth is a feature of the only survey so far published of *Religion in Britain since 1900*, ed. G. Stephen Spinks (London, 1952). There have been many examples of indignant anti-Barthianism in the United States.

[3] Barth's most forceful statement of his position may be found in lectures delivered amid the ruins of the University of Bonn in 1946 and published as *Dogmatics in Outline* (1947; Eng. trans., New York, 1949). His lectures in the University of Chicago in 1962 on *Evangelical Theology* (New York, 1963) embody his mature reflections on the theologian's task. For introductions to his work as a whole, see Arnold B. Come, *An Introduction to Barth's Dogmatics for Preachers* (Philadelphia, 1963) and H. H. Hartwell, *The Theology of Karl Barth* (London, 1964). See also below, pp. 348–351.

theology. Essentially, what he has done is to show that the ambiguity which Barth found in nature and in history as a whole is present also in the events which to Barth so clearly revealed the Christians' God.

Bultmann's programme for "demythologising" the New Testament was first outlined in an article of 1941.[1] The controversy caused by that short document has been immense, passionate, profound and bitter—partly because so many unsatisfactory elements in traditional Christianity are (somewhat confusingly) joined together by Bultmann under the one word "myth". But as the discussion begins to settle down after a quarter of a century, the effect of the impact of Bultmann's challenge begins to be seen. The "demythologising" programme includes not only an insistence that the spatial imagery of traditional religious talk ("he ascended into heaven", etc.) cannot be taken literally, and not only an emphasis that the traditional symbols in the religious world-view mean little to modern man, and not only a consistent rejection of all anti-natural miracles (the physical resurrection of Jesus, etc.), and not only a drastic criticism of the gospels as history, but also something which we do not find in previous German critics—or in the English-speaking modernists who had for long been voicing roughly similar opinions on those points. Bultmann's "demythologising" programme arises from a great scepticism about whether *any* event can by itself reveal God. For him, even a non-miraculous, solidly historical event does not show God's nature and activity at all obviously. Bultmann advances an interesting reason for this emphasis that God is not revealed through events without a personal response. He maintains that the God who is not mythical cannot be reduced to the level of particular events and made an object among other objects. The real difficulty of the religious language in which Christianity has been expressed since New Testament times has been, for Bultmann, its tendency to present God as a god who appears among men like the gods in the Greek or Hindu myths. This, he thinks, is what has made Christianity incredible in our time, despite the eloquence of theologians such as Barth. Bultmann's solution to this whole problem of the inadequacy of "objective" events to reveal God is to stress the "existential" character of faith. By this he means that Christian faith arises out of the depths of a person's own existence, and declares what an event means to that person. For example, the myth of the physical resurrection of Jesus

[1] Reprinted with a variety of replies in *Kerygma and Myth*, ed. H. W. Bartsch (London, 1953).

176 *Religion and Change*

represents (and may obscure) the fact that the apostles' own faith rose at Easter. This faith involves a new self-understanding, and a new style of personal life ("authentic existence"). The faith is, in part, a response to past events, but the significance of those events is seen in terms of their interpretation which transforms personal existence. This faith is what makes an event "eschatological", i.e. a disclosure of ultimate reality, for that person. In the event its potential "eschatological" significance slumbers until that person's faith can "awaken" it.[1] For example, the apostles' faith rose at Easter as an interpretation of the solidly historical death of Jesus as the "eschatological" event. In a famous sentence, Bultmann laid bare his existentialist view of faith by writing: "The question of God and the question of myself are identical."[2]

We do not have far to look if we ask what influences have contributed to the urgency of this teaching that *faith* must interpret history, and so lead to "authentic existence". Bultmann has told us that his "demythologising" programme was sparked off by a plea for help with their preaching from some of his pupils who were serving as chaplains in Hitler's army. In Bultmann's lifetime Europe was made, smashed and remade by political forces which owed their psychological power to their ability to interpret the whole of European history in the light of a central idea. The textbooks in the schools had to be written and rewritten. Christianity, if it was to survive, could not be understood as a faith with less power over history; yet Christianity was plainly unable to do battle with the political forces on their own ground. The power of Christian faith could be presented only as power over *personal* history; its drama could be read not in the newspapers but in people's hearts. Nor should we wonder why history to Bultmann is usually disastrous and dead (the symbol of this for him is the judgment which the crucifixion of Jesus pronounced in all human hopes)—until the Christian faith, the Easter faith imposes a new interpretation on it (by seeing in one bit of this tragic history, the cross, the place where the glorious future of man is made manifest to faith). For Bultmann and his fellow-Germans, the history of the first half of the twentieth century brought little but disaster and death. Therefore for him, faith, and only faith, is what gives hope to history. "Man," as he once wrote, "can never jump out of time, but

[1] *History and Eschatology* (Edinburgh, 1957), p. 155.
[2] *Jesus Christ and Mythology* (New York, 1958), p. 53. This book remains the best short presentation of Bultmann's thought. A more substantial *Introduction* to his theology is that by Walter Schmithals (1966; Eng. trans., Nashville, 1967). Bultmann discusses his position with critics in *The Theology of Rudolf Bultmann*, ed. C. W. Kegley (New York, 1966).

as only to choose whether his present is to be determined by the past or the future."[1]

In the "demythologising" of Rudolf Bultmann, we witness, therefore, the abandonment of the appeal by Protestant theology to past events or past teachings which of themselves would authenticate an "orthodox", "liberal" or "neo-orthodox" creed. The whole dogmatic attitude is discredited. The society which laid down the dogma has disintegrated. A *personal* faith is seen to be vital. Each man for himself has to decide how his experience is to be interpreted. He must choose one past event which will enable him to escape from the burden of the remainder of the past. He must place his faith on a bit of history which will lead him beyond ordinary, tragic history into authentic existence.

Natural Religion and the Necessity of Faith

Barth and Bultmann in their different ways have shown Christian theologians the absolute necessity of faith. The truth of the Gospel was not so obvious as the happier generation of liberal "Culture-Protestantism" had liked to suppose; on the contrary, Barth in relation to "natural" theology and Bultmann in relation to "revealed" theology repeated the cry of Martin Luther that a Christian could know nothing and could be nothing without a personal, radical faith responding to the "free gift" of the gracious God. Thus both Barth and Bultmann restated for our time the essential insight of the sixteenth-century Reformation, "justification by grace through faith". However, as we trace the decline and fall of Christian dogmatism, we have to move outside the world of theology proper in order to consider the fate of a dogmatism which was vaguer than anything preached by the liberal theologians of "Culture-Protestantism".

Essentially dogmatic because convinced that all men should recognise its truth, "natural" religion has often been thought likely to lead to the universal acceptance of a watered-down version of Christianity. In the eighteenth century the Deists (and many who sympathised with them) abandoned the traditional religion because its authority seemed to depend on an incredible system of miracles and prophecies, and because its central dogma, the Atonement of

[1] R. Gregor Smith, *Secular Christianity*, p. 135. Professor Gregor Smith, who is his most distinguished English-speaking pupil, well sums up Bultmann's view of the past: "The *Geschichte*, the happenedness of the past, is certainly not given existence by our recognition of it; but it is recognized as existing only as it appears in the present as a real event" (p. 85).

God and man through the sacrifice of Christ, repelled their inte
gence and morality. They turned instead to a Christianity "i
mysterious", to a Christianity "as old as the creation". They quie
accepted and taught a calm and clear belief in a Supreme Being
Author of Nature, who had created the universe, who had left it
operate according to rational laws, and who had placed in it, as
masters, rational human beings with a moral law already written
their hearts. In this belief, Jesus became a teacher with a happy ɡ
as a story-teller, illustrating a religious philosophy which almost
men accepted anyway. At the end of the eighteenth century Willi
Wordsworth arose as another teacher, rebelling against the phi
sopher's description of nature as a lifeless machine (as others h
done before him), but still essentially concerned to experience and
communicate the God of nature without reference to the books a
sermons of the specifically Christian appeal to revelation. Here w
the God of many of the enlightened in Britain and Europe, and hɛ
was the God mentioned in the Constitution of the infant Unit
States. Here was, in short, "natural" religion, the religion of
sensible men (even of the mocking Voltaire). Because its doctrir
seemed obvious commonplaces needing only a poetic touch
become the universal religion, such a philosophy was able to un
a whole society; and because its happiness about the divine bei
volence owed much to the Christian joy in the God of love, it w
able to help in a return to a more traditional faith for many (as i
Wordsworth himself).

As the twentieth century has gone its way that acceptance of
well-ordered universe, that praise for Jesus and for other poets of t
obvious, and that appeal to the God of nature as the modestly retiri
author of reason and of happiness, have not been the public phil
sophy. No Karl Barth has been needed to denounce such "natura
religion among non-theologians. On the contrary, Albert Schweitze
presentation of the conclusion of thought about the natural world h
been typical of the general attitude. The malignant power of evil
the human heart and in society has been experienced by our tir
against a background of a disordered nature without purpose
meaning. Religious belief has seemed to be not agreement with t
inevitable but a decision to defy the appearances of nature and
human nature in the name of a God who is mysteriously transcende
over, and victorious over, the evil and disorder. For the thoughtfɛ
worship has increasingly become either an impossibility or a leap
faith, and it has been ever more difficult to study theology in the w

aid down by Lord Gifford when he founded the Gifford Lectures in he Scottish universities: "as a strictly natural science, the greatest of all possible sciences, indeed, in one sense, the only science, that of infinite Being without reference to or reliance upon any supposed special, exceptional or so-called miraculous revelation".

We may be able to express some of the difficulties which many feel with "natural" religion in our time if we consider one or two recent books by religiously minded scientists. The contemplation of nature as known to modern science often produces an attitude of awe in the face of the indescribable greatness, majesty, beauty and order of the universe. Many a scientist reverently ponders the process by which matter, organised in ever greater complexity, gives rise to the life of fish, birds, animals and men. He takes very seriously the "phenomenon of man" (to use the title of Teilhard de Chardin's book which, when published in France in 1955 after its author's death, fascinated so many). He believes that to a considerable extent man can now understand his own place in nature, and can control his future evolution, which will be mainly mental and cultural, with untold glories to come. Thus along the "living stream" of evolution there is carried the "divine flame" in man, to use the titles of the Gifford Lectures which an eminent zoologist, Sir Alister Hardy, delivered in Aberdeen twenty years after Karl Barth.[1]

But the God of the Bible cannot be found clearly in all this evolutionary panorama. Teilhard de Chardin and his many Christian admirers have been reluctant to admit this, but the point was made with admirable clarity by Sir Julian Huxley when he introduced *The Phenomenon of Man* to the English-speaking world (London, 1959). Teilhard's vision of Christ as the fulfilment of evolution, as the incandescent centre of a universe aflame, and of God as the *point Omega* towards which the whole immense process of evolution moves, was described more brutally by another scientist, Sir Peter Medawar, as "tipsy, euphoric prose-poetry".[2] Teilhard's superiors in the Jesuit Order, who decreed that his books could not be published during his lifetime, had for all their tragic clumsiness grasped the truth that the science being described was not necessarily as Christian as Teilhard thought it was.[3]

[1] 2 vols., London, 1965-6.
[2] In a review in *Mind* (1961) reprinted in his *The Art of the Soluble* (London, 1967).
[3] Among the many favourable books, see the study of *Teilhard de Chardin: Scientist and Seer* by Charles Raven (London, 1962); *The Religion of Teilhard de Chardin* by Henri de Lubac (1962; Eng. trans., London, 1967). There are biographies by Claude Cuénot (1959; Eng. trans., London, 1965) and Robert Speaight (London, 1967).

Sir Alister Hardy's *The Divine Flame* may be studied as a learne
honest and clear presentation of a natural theology conceived wi
reference to the latest science. Hardy's chief purpose was to emphas
that science had produced no valid evidence against the transcende
God of theism being true, and to plead for scientific research in
religious experience, in the hope that such research would thr
light on the nature of the divine.[1] But Hardy did offer some sugg
tions of his own, and the negative character of these should be enou
to remind us how unlikely it is that scientific research will ev
positively demonstrate the existence of God. Hardy rejected cru
doctrines of the Atonement ("that the appalling death of Jesus wa
sacrifice in the eyes of God for the sins of the whole world, or th
God, in the shape of his son, tortured himself for our redemption"
ideas which are "among the least attractive in the whole of anthr
pology"[2]), and he also rejected the tendency to take the image of t
Sky Father literally ("the reality must be something very different")
Was he, then, able to accept for himself the transcendent God of t
theists? He wrote as a "theistic humanist", but the understanding
God which he felt able to state in his book was in parts barely co
patible with what the theistic tradition has regarded as the heart
the matter. Thus he quoted the Marxist biologist, J. B. S. Haldar
about what Auguste Comte called the "Great Being" above me
"To my mind the teaching of science is very emphatic that such
Great Being may be a fact as real as the individual human consciou
ness . . . and it seems to me that everywhere ethical experien
testifies to a super-individual reality of some kind." But the sar
quotation showed what the Great Being was to Comte and Haldan
"If the co-operation of some thousands of millions of cells in o
brain can produce our consciousness, the idea becomes vastly mo
plausible that the co-operation of humanity, or of some sections of
may determine the Great Being. Just as, according to the teachin
of physiology, the unity of the body is not due to a soul superadded
the life of the cells, so the superhuman, if it existed, would be nothi
external to man, or even existing apart from human co-operation.
Hardy's suggestions about prayer were such as to crystallise t
uneasiness of most theists.[5] "Instead of supposing that one gre
personal-like Deity is thinking out simultaneously the detailed answ
to millions of different problems of all the individuals in the world,

---

[1] I am indebted to Sir Alister Hardy for his reply to my review of his Gifford Lectures
the Unitarian journal, *The Inquirer* (London, 17 June, 1967).
[2] *The Divine Flame*, p. 218.
[3] See p. 242.   [4] See p. 230.   [5] See p. 23

it not more reasonable to suppose that some action is set in motion by prayer which draws the particular solution for each one of us from our own subconscious minds?"

If the God of the Bible cannot be found clearly through "natural" theology, it is also sadly true that no meaning at all in the total pattern of nature may be demonstrated with scientific certainty. The sheer size of the universe deters most scientists from attributing a meaning to it; the silent immensity of these infinite spaces frightens them, as it did Pascal. Copernicus and Galileo did more damage to the religious world-view than is commonly granted by religious believers, for they began the modern astronomy which has treated this planet as a speck in a universe which is crowded with uncountable galaxies, stars and satellites—and which is growing at a speed faster than the speed of light. We on earth know simply nothing about the purposes of our planet's companions. We do not know if there is life elsewhere in the universe—life which may be far superior to our own. Even on this planet, the facts discovered by science seem larger than the values cherished by men, much as the life on the bed of the Atlantic Ocean is larger than the life on the ships which pass above. *Homo sapiens* knows very little about any purposes fulfilled by any other species thrown up by evolution.

Can man see a purpose behind his own evolution? The answer is far more difficult for science than a "natural" religion finds comfortable. The twentieth century's great advances in biochemistry, molecular biology and genetics have prevented many scientifically minded people from endorsing "natural" religion's sense of the uniqueness and grandeur of human life. That sense remained strong for many even after Darwin's demonstration of man's descent from other animals, and the new scientific revolution has not made nearly so great an impact on public opinion as did the dramatic controversy around Darwin. But in at least two ways the knowledge has placed a question against the idea that evolution led up to man (a natural tendency if not by a divine design).

First, the physical basis of life is now much less of a mystery than it was for all previous human generations. A scientist has defined life as "a partial, continuous, progressive, multiform and conditionally inter-active self-realisation of the potentialities of atomic electron states." At first sight that definition may not seem to have dethroned man or God, but the scientist who offers it assures us that "the study of the origin of life is likely to prove a greater solvent of old ideas and attitudes than any branch of science has been in the past". In particular, old religious beliefs will, Professor Bernal assumes, "become essentially unintelligible if not ridiculous".[1]

Second, recent advances in genetics have shown in astonishing detail how the evolution of every species, including our own, is the result of genetic mutations which occur at random, without reference to the biological needs of the animal. Evolution does, in fact, depend on a vast lottery. These mutations are almost always harmful and recessive—a shorter neck may emerge when the species needs a longer one. Mutations which contribute to evolutionary progress do so because members of the species without them are more liable to perish or to be killed without producing offspring, and therefore over great tracts of time the descendents of the original winners in the lottery survive through their superior adaptation to their environment. It is a way of advance which is wasteful, risky and slow beyond anything we could have planned. Huxley, Hardy, Teilhard de Chardin and many other distinguished scientists emphasise the part played in evolution by the inquisitive, adventuring spirit of many animals, by the formation of habits in a species, by the slow influence of those habits on an animal's physical development, and by the transmission of information and skills by parents and by groups; and these aspects which may be described as purposive, or at least as psychic, do deserve to be pondered by those who would see evolution as a whole. Starvation and death at the hands of rival predators are not the only, and may not be main, instruments of "natural selection". But unless we are to subscribe to the clearly false teaching of Lamark (who died in 1829), revived in our time by the Russian Lysenko, that acquired characters can be inherited genetically, we have always to come back to the random nature of the genetic mutations which are the raw material of evolution. The mechanism of genetic inheritance appears to be completely independent of any effects arising from mental or moral progress, or even from the use or disuse of physical organs. The genes which an organism will pass on are not influenced by its experiences. The result may be progress, but it is progress in which the selection by machine-like laws of material provided by sheer chance plays an alarming part. God may be emerging or even in control, but, if so, he emerges out of, or he allows, a process which few, if any, lesser potentates would have chosen as a method of working.

The possibility of an ultimate absence of meaning in nature, the possibility that nature may be a mere survival-machine which sorts

[1] J.D. Bernal, *The Origin of Life* (London, 1967), pp. 166, 168, 182.

out the genetic lottery, has haunted the scientific conscience in this century—just as the pointlessness of daily existence has haunted the artistic imagination. For many it has amounted to the death of the God of "natural" religion. T. H. Huxley used to tell Victorian England that evolution had no more connection with theism or atheism than geometry had. Sir Alister Hardy himself states clearly that the "natural theology" which he commends contains no hard facts about the divine power which are demonstrable with scientific certainty. "The most important issue for a natural theology" is recognised as the question: "do these forces which play so important a part in man's religious life belong only to his sub-conscious mind or do they indicate some extra-sensory contact with some Power beyond the self?" And although future experiments may help, Hardy states that "natural" theology provides no answer to this question at present. "It would be folly to speculate and pretend at this stage that we have any idea as to the true nature of this power," he writes, adding: "it is for our natural theology of the future to tell us more."[1] In this situation of scientific uncertainty, Hardy recognises that "natural" theology is optional; in other words, that *it is a religious faith*—just as much as Christian orthodoxy is. "Our view of life is no doubt coloured by our temperament," he has written. "One person sees evolution simply as the result of changes brought about by random chemical mutations being selected in different ways by the ever-changing physical environment; another sees it essentially as the manifestation of a living process selecting (unconsciously) the changing chemical units, and pushing itself by creative novelty into every position that will hold it".[2] In 1916, Teilhard de Chardin wrote to a friend about his vocation: "To tear away the mask of atheism from these new currents of thought and expose them as Christian—that is my great hope." But shortly before his death in 1955 he asked himself: "How is it, then, that I find myself in a class alone, as it were? Alone in having *seen*? . . . May I not be, after all, at the mercy of a mirage within me? I often wonder." The conclusion which we draw from the biographies of Tielhard is that he would not have "seen" Christ as the flaming heart of the universe if he had not first accepted Catholic devotions to the "sacred heart" of Jesus and to Jesus in the bread at Mass.[3]

It is only right to add after such criticisms that the religious understanding of the universe chosen by Teilhard and Hardy is clearly a

[1] *The Divine Flame*, pp. 101, 230-1.
[2] In *Biology and Personality*, ed. I. T. Ramsey (Oxford, 1965), p. 78.
[3] The quotations come from the (as yet) untranslated *Ecrits du Temps de la Guerre* and *a Christique*. See Robert Speaight, *Teilhard de Chardin*, pp. 75, 329.

live option for well informed, deeply thoughtful and thoroughly honest scientists, although it cannot be supported with scientific proof. As long as it is presented *as one option* among a number of possibilities, it appears to be intellectually respectable. Indeed, this attitude has had a long and distinguished history in our century.[1] Many philosophers, while wishing to reject any religion which was opposed to science, have hymned the evolutionary process as favouring man's noblest values, and religious believers have found support in that vision. Although it may be difficult for us to imagine it when we read that book after half a century, as a young man Teilhard de Chardin was thrilled by Henri Bergson's *Creative Evolution*.[2] Teilhard's English equivalent, Charles Raven, had his own debt to the *Emergent Evolution* and *Life, Mind and Spirit* of Conwy Lloyd Morgan, who was Professor successively of Zoology and of Philosophy.[3] If a God of order could not be proved from the design of nature, at least a God of goodness (or values which were more or less a substitute for such a God) could be glimpsed emerging in nature's broad tendency British philosophers wrote Gifford Lectures which now survive in large volumes, like granite monuments to that era of cosmic optimism.[4] Statesmen contributed also, such as Field Marshal Smuts, who turned from his leadership of the Union of South Africa and the new British Commonwealth to explain the natural tendency of the universe to greater and greater wholes.[5] Scientists of the eminence of Sir James Jeans interpreted the latest physics to show how "the universe begins to look more like a great thought than like a great machine. Mind no longer appears as an accidental intruder into the realm of matter; we are beginning to suspect that we ought rather to hail it as the creator and governor of the realm of matter—not of course our individual minds but the mind in which the atoms out

---

[1] For a fair-minded presentation of many "natural" theologians—all the more valuable because it is by a philosopher who, after being attracted by the earlier philosophies of idealism, is known primarily as an exponent of Christian existentialism—see John Macquarrie, *Twentieth Century Religious Thought* (London, 1963).

[2] *Creative Evolution* (1907; Eng. trans., London, 1911) did not argue for belief in a transcendent God, but with its emphasis on an instinctive intuition into the dynamic life of the universe, it was one of the first books to counteract the crude materialism of the French anti-clericals. The Catholic philosopher Jacques Maritain was among the other Frenchmen led by Bergson to a more sympathetic and adventurous attitude to religion.

[3] Charles Raven's Hulsean Lectures on *The Creator Spirit* (London, 1927) and his Gifford Lectures on *Science and Religion* and *Experience and Interpretation* (Cambridge, 1953) showed the enduring influence of Lloyd Morgan's Gifford Lectures (London, 1923-6).

[4] Specially notable—although not specially readable—examples are Seth Pringle Pattison, *The Idea of God in the Light of Recent Philosophy* (Oxford, 1917), with its deduction of human immortality from the rational character of nature, and Samuel Alexander, *Space, Time and Deity* (London, 1920), with its interpretation of space-time as the body of the "emergent" God.

[5] *Holism and Evolution* (London, 1926).

of which our individual minds have grown exist as thoughts."[1] Sir Arthur Eddington also taught that "the idea of a universal Mind or *Logos* would be a fairly plausible inference from the present state of scientific theory."[2]

Yet for all the distinction of such philosophers and scientists with their "natural" religion, the tradition represented by them always had its sceptical critics within the philosophy of science.[3] What matters even more to the student of science as a social force is that somehow that kind of philosophy became unfashionable. After the mid-1930s, fewer philosophers and scientists could be found talking about the universe as anything other than a problem to be solved by astronomy. In part, this change of mood among the intellectuals was due to the new coldness in the atmosphere of the society around them, but in part, it was due to a more sophisticated understanding of the nature and limits of scientific knowledge. That the depression in the social climate should contribute to such a notable lowering of philosophers' temperatures shows clearly that the ardour of successive Gifford Lecturers for natural religion always had to compete with a chill at the heart of natural science. To change the metaphor: many in our time, although they have tried to be as sensitive as their predecessors were to the glory of the flower of human genius and love, have found their minds drawn more and more to the sordid roots of the flower, and to the apparently accidental planting.

Martin Heidegger's *Being and Time* (1927; Eng. trans., London, 1962) was a grand metaphysical construction in the high tradition of German philosophy. Heidegger then saw man as thrown into an "inauthentic" existence which serves no external purpose, and which must be dominated by anxiety as the inexorable move to death brings home the threat of nothingness. As an alternative to despair Heidegger for a time sympathised with Nazism; later he retreated to even more obscure philosophical activities instead of completing the projected second volume of the great metaphysical work. Professor W. McNeile Dixon, who more modestly and winsomely wrote one of the most truly existential books of our century as the Gifford Lectures of 1935-7 on *The Human Situation*, declared: "The first and last of all life's complicated circumstances, the presiding fact, utterly astonishing, even stupefying, is that we are utterly in the dark about everything."[4]

---

[1] *The Mysterious Universe* (Cambridge, 1930), p. 148.
[2] *The Nature of the Physical World* (Cambridge, 1928), p. 338.
[3] E.g. J. B. S. Haldane, *The Philosophical Basis of Biology* (London, 1931).
[4] (London, 1937), p. 199. He was eloquent on the inscrutability of nature: see pp. 79–85, 119–131.

This despair—the philosophical equivalent of T. S. Eliot's poet[r]
of the "waste land"—may pass, as the preceding optimism passe[d]
The posthumous popularity of Teilhard de Chardin, or the reviv[al]
in America of the "Process" philosophy of A. N. Whitehead, may [be]
signs that in the mid-1960s a mood of optimism returned and soug[ht]
a basis in "natural" religion; and we shall return to these mysterio[us]
matters in Chapter 8. But what will remain with us for a lor[g]
time is the memory of the chill, teaching us once more that it [is]
dangerous to be dogmatic on the basis of "natural" religion. Th[e]
God of nature is in fact *not* obvious, once "natural" religion is teste[d]
by reflection. A choice is involved; and this choice must be made [by]
the person who is confronted by the mystery.

This is why many recent religious thinkers have confessed that th[e]
twentieth century is truly for them also the age of history in whic[h]
the certainty of God has been eclipsed, or has died—and in whic[h]
the atheist's counter-attack on God, mounted in reply to th[e]
aggression of traditional religion, has ceased to be relevant to life[s]
real experience. Faith, if it is to arise now, must arise on the ruins [of]
certainty, and must always have doubt as one of its ingredient[s]
Here—or so these thinkers claim—is religious adulthood. Childre[n]
see things in black or white: "it is" or "it isn't", "it's true" or "it's [a]
fairy tale". The adult is not so certain. Many an old story, authorit[a]
tive when we were children, may turn out to be like a fairy tale; b[ut]
in the fairy tale may be hidden a vision which is more important tha[n]
all science. So God is not assumed calmly, or denied confidently; th[e]
idea of God has become a mystery, to be grasped by faith—or not [to]
be grasped at all.

"An increasing number of people," a German theologian wro[te]
in 1965, "are so gripped by this experience that they can no longer re[c]
oncile it either with theism or with atheism because these two positio[ns]
alike betray a naïve, undisturbed ideological confidence. No attem[pt]
to relate the new experience to such settled positions does justice to th[e]
reality of the mind's oscillation between them, to its inability eith[er]
to answer or to drop the question concerning the meaning of existen[ce]
and the purpose and goal of history . . . In this continuing reflecti[on]
—a process which is not so much articulated as experienced—th[e]
only constant factor is the uncertainty itself, which it is impossible [to]
ignore since it is felt to be rooted in the conscience. The phrase 'th[e]
death of God' is meant to give theological expression to these change[d]
psychosocial conditions."[1]

[1]Dorothee Solle, *Christ the Representative* (1965; Eng. trans., London, 1967), pp. 11-1[2]

A Transition—to What?

We may now use a slight sketch of some recent tendencies in English religious thought in order to ask the question, where Christianity is ending amid the collapse of its old dogmatism.

The limitations of the appeal by Christians both to revelation and to nature can be seen in the theological work of William Temple, Archbishop of York and of Canterbury. Temple's mind was formed at Oxford University by "idealist" philosophers who taught that "spirit" and "value" were supreme in nature. Among these was the Master of Balliol, Edward Caird, an expounder of Hegel and Kant.[1] Philosophers such as Caird might not be able to accept for themselves the whole of Christian orthodoxy, but most of them came from Christian backgrounds, they preserved Christian ethics even if they had doctrinal doubts, and they made it easy for their pupils to hold that life had a spiritual purpose. In this tradition, Temple believed that the universe could be interpreted around the incarnation of Christ—that it lay under the controlling hand of the God and Father of Christ. He gave expression to this philosophical faith in many articles and addresses, in two theological books,[2] and in his Gifford Lectures on *Nature, Man and God* (London, 1934). Behind such statements was the great impressiveness of Temple's personal serenity. It would be difficult to name any more impressive Christian of the twentieth century.[3]

The son of an archbishop, himself secure in the approval both of the authorities of Church and State and of the Socialist movement to which he gave valuable leadership, William Temple was a beaming sun, warming the hearts of many. But his integrity prevented complacency, so that although much of his theology now seems as dated as the philosophy which sustained it, in at least two respects Temple's theological insight has summed up the problems discussed in this chapter, and has influenced his successors in England, if not elsewhere.

First, Temple renounced the old appeal to an authoritative revela-

[1] When Caird had been a Professor at Glasgow, his philosophy had influenced another future Archbishop of Canterbury, Cosmo Lang, who as a student cried aloud: "The Universe is one and its Unity and Ultimate Reality is God!" J. G. Lockhart, *Cosmo Gordon Lang* (London, 1949), p. 13. Caird had a similar influence on a young man who became a dominant figure in the Church of Scotland: see Augustus Muir, *John White* (London, 1958), p. 7.
[2] *Mens Creatrix* (London, 1916) and *Christus Veritas* (London, 1924).
[3] For an account of his life, see F. A. Iremonger, *William Temple* (London, 1948); and for an American scholar's assessment of his theology, Joseph Fletcher, *William Temple* (New York, 1963). See also below, p. 315.

tion. He was not basically critical of the old tradition; not man
years after his ordination his lingering doubts about the virgin birt
of Jesus were dispelled during a symphony concert, and his be
known devotional writing was based on a conservative view of th
authorship and historicity of St. John's gospel.[1] But Temple's know
ledge of the scholars' criticism of the Bible led him to the conclusio
that God does not "speak" in the sense of uttering propositions whic
are repeated by prophets or church leaders and thus become bindin
on all who would be reckoned as believers. It is in the *event* that God
revelation is discerned, supremely in the events to which Christia
refer when they think of Jesus; and the interpretation comes after th
event, although until the event has been interpreted, the revelatio
is not complete. For Temple, revelation was therefore "the coinc
dence of divinely controlled event and mind divinely illumined
read it aright".[2] St. John's gospel, for example, was for him "vali
history so far as its record of events is concerned", but the discours
attributed to Jesus in it might be partly the interpretation of th
events by St. John. He believed that most of the Bible's witness
events, and almost all the undivided Church's interpretation of then
was correct, but this distinction between event and interpretatio
(which was clearer than Barth's idea of revelation through the Wor
of God) could be used by others taking a more sceptical view of th
ability of the Bible and the Church to record or to interpret even
aright.[3]

Second, Temple renounced the old appeal to "natural" religio
Although he regarded himself as a philosopher, he was fundamenta
a Christian prophet and church leader who owed his self-assuran
to his glad acceptance of almost the whole traditional faith. It
significant that he withdrew quite rapidly from university teachin
to a headmastership and an ecclesiastical career. In his philosophic
books a basic confusion lurks beneath many passages because Temp
repeatedly presented as the conclusion of "philosophy" positio
which he did in fact adopt because he was a Christian; as Emil Brunn
wrote to him, "your natural theology is natural only in appearanc
whilst it is in truth Christian."[4] Already in those books Temple was te
ding to speak of a "general revelation" granted by God outside th
Bible rather than of the "knowledge" alleged to be reached in a pure
"natural" religion, and his sympathy with the younger generation

[1] *Readings in St John's Gospel* (2 vols., London, 1939-40).
[2] *Revelation: A Symposium*, ed. John Baillie and Hugh Martin (London, 1937), p. 107.
[3] See John Baillie, *The Idea of Revelation in Recent Thought* (New York, 1956).
[4] F. A. Iremonger, *William Temple*, pp. 531-2.

theologians arising in Britain after the completion of his *Nature, Man and God* led him to see that man's faith in God, and particularly the Christian's faith in God through Christ, should be distinguished far more sharply from knowledge about nature than had been the custom in the intellectual circles to which he had belonged in his early years.

In 1937, writing the Preface to a Report on *Doctrine in the Church of England,* Temple confessed that as he reviewed "the result of our fourteen years of labour, I am conscious of a certain transition in our minds, as in the minds of theologians all over the world." This was the transition from a "Christocentric metaphysic" to a "theology of Redemption". A theology of Redemption, Temple explained, "tends rather to sound the prophetic note; it is more ready to admit that much in this evil world is irrational and strictly unintelligible; and it looks to the coming of the Kingdom as a necessary preliminary to the comprehension of much that now is." Two years later, when war had broken out, Temple wrote that "our task with this world is not to explain it but to convert it. Its need can be met . . . only by the shattering impact upon its self-sufficiency and arrogance of the Son of God, crucified, risen and ascended, pouring forth that explosive and disruptive energy which is the Holy Ghost."[1]

William Temple then looked to the future: "We must dig the foundations deeper . . . And we must be content with less imposing structures. One day theology will take up again its larger and serener task, and offer to a new Christendom its Christian map of life, its Christocentric metaphysic." Twenty years later his successor as Archbishop of Canterbury, Dr. Michael Ramsey, asked: "Has the day of which he spoke begun to dawn?"[2] Our answer must be: not yet. The 1970s are unlikely to share the mood of the tragic crisis in which the Barthian or semi-Barthian "theology of Redemption" flourished, but the decline and fall of Christian dogmatism has resulted

---

[1] Article in *Theology* (London, November 1939). A transition more violent than Temple's from "philosophical" to "biblical" theology was made by another Anglican theologian, L. S. Thornton. As a young man Thornton tried to relate an orthodox Christology to A. N. Whitehead's Process philosophy, seeing Jesus as the supreme "novelty" in the evolving universe. His *The Incarnate Lord* (London, 1928) thus resembled the speculations of his contemporary, Teilhard de Chardin. Even then, Thornton (like Teilhard) was accused of being inconsistent, by bringing the unique incarnation of God in Christ into the uniformities of the scientific world-view. Thornton later wrote his best book, *The Common Life in the Body of Christ* (London, 1942), a biblically based exposition of the nature of the Church (he was a monk). Finally he rejected all attempts to go beyond the form of revelation chosen by God in the Bible, in his three volumes entitled as a series *The Form of the Servant* (London, 1950-6); and in other writing he propounded some fanciful applications of biblical texts to current ecclesiastical controversies, e.g. on episcopacy.

[2] *From Gore to Temple* (London, 1960), p. 161.

in such a severe shock to theology that it seems probable that tl
rest of the twentieth century will be devoted to digging, not buildin
Christian communities survive and may grow, but a "new Christe
dom" is not on the horizon. Christian faith survives and may reach
clearer understanding of its place in the age of science, but
"Christian map of life" cannot be drawn in a period when—
Dr. John Robinson, Bishop of Woolwich, has remarked—the proble
confronting Christian map-makers is what "projection" to use in tl
attempt to describe God to an age of scepticism.

Many, observing the collapse of the old Christian appeal
authority, have drawn from the spectacle conclusions opposite
Archbishop William Temple's. The rejection of revelation as
redemption as unreal ideas is now taken for granted among mc
Western intellectuals, and it is today inconceivable that a philosoph
of Temple's power would be as impervious as he was to the force
secularist attacks on the basic structure of Christian belief. It
recorded that Temple's flow of eloquence, which normally w
unfailing whether the subject was doctrinal, devotional, ecclesiastic;
social, philosophical or literary, and which shied away neither fro
the problems of the nature of Christ nor from the reform of tl
banking system, did on one occasion falter. It was at a conference
students, and the subject was "Why I Believe in God". Temple's ta
to the students was "almost a complete flop", and afterwards]
explained to a friend: "You see, I have never known what it is
doubt the existence of God."[1] Had William Temple's mind bec
formed in a slightly later epoch of English intellectual histor
there might have been many more occasions when nothing cou
have been said authoritatively in the sphere of religion, even]
him.

The secularised agnosticism of so many educated people in o
time has been expressed philosophically by the linguistic analy;
which has dismissed all religious statements (and all the "idealis
metaphysics which may be regarded as a semi-secularised form
theology) as meaningless apart from any incidental light which su
statements may throw on ethics and psychology. The "empirica
approach in philosophy is primarily British in origin. It is at least
old as David Hume, who died in 1776; it made its most dramat
advances through the work of three philosophers of Cambrid;
University in the twentieth century, G. E. Moore, Bertrand Russ
and Ludwig Wittgenstein; and its most influential form in the prese

[1] F. A. Iremonger, *William Temple*, p. 379.

ay is provided by the philosophy taught in Oxford University. Its
ifluence on Continental Europe has so far been limited, but some
f Freud's contemporaries in Vienna formed a notable circle of
hilosophers dedicated to the analysis of language, and there are
gns in the 1960s that, as Europe's tragedies recede, this calm
pproach will be favoured over the soul-searching of existentialism.
n the United States empiricism, although delayed by the German
ifluences which are strong in American universities, is making rapid
eadway.

The attack on religion from this philosophical movement is
ecorded most eloquently in Professor A. J. Ayer's *Language, Truth
nd Logic* (London, 1936). This was a youthful and passionate, and
ierefore over-simplified, manifesto for "logical positivism" (and its
uthor lived to modify its demands), but it nevertheless expressed a
ery widespread impatience with metaphysical speculations. Apart
om the necessary truths of mathematical logic, the only reliable
ropositions have seemed to be those capable of verification by
zientific experiments. Historical, aesthetic and ethical statements
iight have to be fitted in; room might have to be found on which to
est the validity of philosophical arguments such as this "verification
rinciple" itself. It might be too much to demand that all meaning-
il statements should be capable of verification; a looser test might
e enough, asking what their opposite would mean or how they might
e falsified. A particular statement might be legitimate, although it
efied philosophical analysis, if it was a useful contribution to a
irger proposition which was meaningful; it might be part of the
game" of the language appropriate to a particular approach to
eality. But however subtly the first enthusiasm for logical positivism
iight need to be redefined, the contempt for attempts to interpret
fe in the universe as a whole has remained prominent. Natural
eligion and Heidegger-type metaphysics have been attacked or
;nored, no less than historic theism. Some European philosophers,
ich as Karl Jaspers,[1] have insisted on keeping the metaphysical
adition alive, and in the 1950s and 1960s there has been more
ietaphysical activity in the English-speaking world; but this return
） the old questions (if not to the old answers) does not amount to a
hange, or to the immediate prospect of change, in the general
itellectual climate of the age of science.

In an essay on "Gods",[2] Professor John Wisdom told a parable

[1] See, e.g., his *Philosophical Faith and Revelation* (1962; Eng. trans., New York, 1967).
[2] Reprinted in his *Philosophy and Psychoanalysis* (Oxford, 1953).

about two people returning to their long neglected garden, a
finding that to some extent the garden is still in order. One says th
a gardener has been at work, and he persists in this belief althou
no one has recently seen a gardener, and no tests can prove
activity. The other person says that no gardener comes. In 1g
Professor Wisdom told that parable in order to stress the ambigu
of nature, the impossibility of proving religious belief correct, and
the obstinate endurance of faith's interpretation of the patterns
the facts. Six years later Professor Antony Flew "developed" t
parable. Here the parable has been adjusted, we might almost s
twisted, in order to stress the folly of the person who believes in t
activity of the gardener. Flew argues that the force of a religic
assertion may be dissipated completely by the admission that t
evidence is against it, although the believer continues to make t
assertion; "a fine brash hypothesis may thus be killed by inches, t
death by a thousand qualifications." In Professor Flew's parable
can see what can happen to "liberal" or "natural" religion when t
mind of man no longer feeds in worship on the authority of the Bi
or the Church or on the revelation in the event or the experien
Here is the full intellectual impact of our secular century. For in t
parable the sceptic at last turns on the believer and demands: "J
how does what you call an invisible, intangible, eternally elus
gardener differ from an imaginary gardener or even from no garder
at all?"[1]

The Remaining Faith of Christians

Taking Christianity as the great example, we have recalled t
intellectual impact of our time on religion. The twentieth century I
been a fertile time in theology, perhaps as fertile as any in history. Y
theology's impact on religion has on the whole been negative; it I
been part of the disintegrating impact of our secular century. This
because most thinkers of our time have seen what was wrong in t
authority previously ascribed to the inherited religious tradition, t
have not seen any convincing alternative. The general impression I
on the public has been that the truth of Christianity is very doubtf
If it is true that man is in some sense a perpetually religious anim
the vacuum left will not remain unfilled for long, and in our next t
chapters we shall study attempts to replace Christianity by old fai

[1] Reprinted from *University* in *New Essays in Philosophical Theology*, ed. A. Flew and
MacIntyre (London, 1955), p. 96. For a fuller statement of his scepticism, see Anth
Flew, *God and Philosophy* (1966).

from the East or by new faiths arising within the West. Here we need add only a brief epilogue in order to suggest in outline what kind of response to this very severe challenge may be emerging among thoughtful Christians.

Each part of the decline and fall of Christian dogmatism has seemed for a time like the collapse of Christianity itself. If the infallibility of the Bible is destroyed, if the Church is no longer the divinely guaranteed custodian of faith and morals, if even the "liberal" Christian's appeal to the Bible of nature and to the Church of the pure in heart is made uncertain by reflection, many people draw the conclusion that for the sake of intellectual honesty they must cease to be Christian believers. The old coherence has gone, and faith seems impossible on any other basis. Some Christians, however, have retained their faith in a modified or purified form, and William Temple was not the last to do so.

Such Christians have been impressed by the mood behind Ludwig Wittgenstein's well-known verdict that "the right method of philosophy would be this: to say nothing except what can be said, i.e. the propositions of natural science, i.e. something that has nothing to do with philosophy: and then always, when someone else wished to say something metaphysical, to demonstrate to him that he had given no meaning to certain signs in his propositions." But, in the view of these Christians, theology may still find one foundation for its work in Wittgenstein's immediately preceding sentences: "There is indeed the inexpressible. This *shows* itself: it is the mystical."[1] Once again we must repeat that the religiously minded person has to contribute to this "showing" by *choosing* between the symbols through which "mysticism" seeks expression. The Christians whom we have in mind choose the symbols of, and around, Christ; for if the Bible is no longer the Word of God from cover to cover, it still contains a word which can touch the heart, deliver it from anxiety, and lift it to God. A whole new art of preaching and a whole new practice and literature of devotion need to be developed in order to bring out the significance of the Bible in these terms, but the essence of the matter is already clear and some such preaching and writing have already emerged. If the Church is no longer the infallible institution, it still appeals as "the blessed company of all faithful people", and if the Jesus who is known in the Church is no longer the Christ of the dogmatic centuries, he remains for many the Christ in whose work and words the inexpressible God shows himself. If religious claims are

[1] *Tractatus Logico-Philosophicus* (London, 1922), pp. 187-9.

not verifiable or falsifiable like ordinary propositions, it does not necessarily follow that they are vacuous.[1]

We may add that these Christians believe that the conclusions of biblical scholarship, destructive as they must be for the old style of authority in religion, do not destroy an impact which is greater than the impact of criticism on dogma; namely, the impact of Christ on the Church and the Christian.

The New Testament presents a problem to the scientific historian precisely because it provides little evidence of Jesus outside its witness to this impact; despite the hopes of Adolf von Harnack and of many other liberal scholars, there seems to be little possibility of recovering a "Jesus of history" by discarding the "Christ of faith"—for a reason which Harnack stated but did not emphasise enough. The gospels "were not written with the simple object of giving the facts as they were; they are books composed for the work of evangelisation."[2] St. Mark, in the earliest gospel to have survived, witnesses to a supernatural saviour no less than does St. John in the latest, and the earliest preaching of the apostles, so far as it can be recovered, seems to have had much in common with the Gospel according to St. Paul. The evidence about Jesus comes to us through a Church which already worshipped him, and the four gospels are all sermons rather than objective biographies. But the Jesus Christ who was worshipped was not a featureless cypher, nor a myth created by the Church. On the contrary, he dominated the Church; he was worshipped as the Lord and his unique character was seen as mediating the purity and power of God. Both the discourses of Jesus in St. John's gospel (with his sevenfold "I am . . .") and the letters to the seven churches in St. John the Divine's Revelation spoke to the early Christians in such terms. Moreover, the glorified Christ who was thus worshipped was believed to have this status in eternity mainly because he had appeared on earth as the humiliated Jesus, as a man among men. He lived in heaven; he lived in the Church; he was abroad in the world but he had lived in Palestine. In everyday history, in his flesh, men had first seen his glory. The New Testament accordingly provides much evidence that the early Christians were deeply interested in the life and teaching of this historical Jesus. The New Testament also suggests that these Christians were for the most part incapable of the sublime feats of spiritual vision and aesthetic imagination which would have been required to invent the whole of the story of Jesus

[1] As the mature Wittgenstein granted: see W. D. Hudson, *Ludwig Wittgenstein* (London 1968).
[2] Adolf von Harnack, *What is Christianity?* (1958 British edn.), p. 27.

n the New Testament there is clearly enough some authentic history, lthough in the forms in which it has reached us it is interpreted history. ome of the interpretation put on all the authentic life and teaching f Jesus by the early Christians seems to us ephemeral, fanciful, or ncompatible with the spirit of Jesus himself; but in many places nodern Christian readers of the New Testament rightly recognise in he interpretation a legitimate development of the tradition and a vorthy part of the teaching which Jesus began but did not conclude efore his death. If we approach the New Testament in this way, we re not entitled to avoid awkward questions about whether a parti- ular saying or event attributed to the historical Jesus in the New estament is historically authentic in the form in which it has reached s, but this approach does end up with a portrait of Jesus Christ, umiliated and glorified, historical and eternal—a portrait which is ot a photograph accurate to the last detail, but which is *as a whole* eliable and powerful.[1]

It is instructive to recall some of the conflicts between the "liberals" r "modernists" and the "conservatives" or "neo-orthodox" which nade the interpretation of the New Testament so controversial for heologians in the 1930s and 1940s. At the end of the first quarter of ur century scholars who discarded the "legends" of miracles in the ospels, and who deplored the elements of "superstition", "specula- ion" and "fantasy" which (they believed) had been brought into he rest of the New Testament from the pagan religions of the time, eemed (at least in their own eyes) to have come to represent "modern cholarship". Such modernism (so its supporters assumed) was the onsensus of all free minds in Christianity, and the only force which indered its progress in the churches was the force of an unreasoning onservatism which might be expressed either through the discipline mposed by administrators or through the sentimentality or cruel ysteria of uneducated worshippers.[2] The positive side of this modern- sm was the Liberal Protestantism which we have already seen in the implified creed of Adolf von Harnack; and the "neo-orthodox"

---

[1] The quest of the historical Jesus which scholars have resumed in recent years (but in a nood and with methods different from Harnack's) was well presented in H. Zahrnt, *The listorical Jesus* (1960; Eng. trans., London, 1963). The outcome of the latest scholarship vas brilliantly allied with a concern for the ordinary student of the Bible today in two ecent books with rather different emphases: C. F. D. Moule, *The Phenomenon of the New Testament* (London, 1966), and John Knox, *The Humanity and Divinity of Jesus Christ* (New York, 1967). See further below, pp. 322, 349–356.
[2] Examples of this approach were provided by H. D. A. Major, *English Modernism: Its Origin, Method and Aims* (Cambridge, Mass., 1927), and E. W. Barnes, *The Rise of Christianity* (London, 1947). One of the best devotional expositions was T. R. Glover, *The Jesus of History* (London, 1917).

reaction against it reached its fullest elaboration in the *Chu
Dogmatics* of Karl Barth. But we may mention here the fact that
England "neo-orthodoxy" was, although part of a general retu
within the Christian minority to a deeper consciousness of
Church,[1] also the conclusion which some scholars claimed as
only position consistent with a return to a deeper study of the N
Testament.[2] The apostles' preaching was about the Jesus who h
been glorified through his resurrection, thus fulfilling both
promises in the Old Testament and the promises in his own teachir
and the riddle of the New Testament was, therefore, *not* how
Jesus of history had been so disastrously obscured by the fantas
"Christ of faith", but whether the claims made by Jesus *and*
apostles could be acknowledged by the reader's faith.

Looking back over this controversy, many present-day students
the New Testament would probably agree that these protests
modernists rendered a major service by compelling many in
churches to face up to the incredibility of many of the details in
New Testament's portrait of Jesus and the early Church; yet th
would add that it is not enough for us today to take as the Gospel
simple creed of Liberal Protestantism about the Fatherhood of G
and the brotherhood of man. Under the impact of tragic times,
have come to feel more sympathy with the early Christians than
modernists could ever produce. We have come to see why those ea
Christians needed the Church; why they needed to worship the Lc
Jesus so ardently; and why the centre of the Church's Gospel shif
so soon from the Fatherhood of God as preached by Jesus to
saviourhood of this Jesus who alone could effectively reconcile
penitent believer amid a sinful world, to God the Father now reveal
in his holy love. The apocalyptic fantasies of the Jews of the fi
century about the coming of the Messiah (the Christ) and his golc
age, and the philosophical speculations of the Greek-speaki
Gnostics about initiation into the secret wisdom of a new age
aeon), certainly provided some of the mythical language in wh
the authors of the New Testament proclaimed their faith in Jes
but recently these speculations have been seen not as the contempti
effusions of the uneducated but as the symbols of the "ultim
concern" of an age which in Jerusalem or in Athens, even before

[1] A history written from this point of view is Horton Davies, *Worship and Theolog
England: The Ecumenical Century, 1900-65* (Princeton, 1965).
[2] Historically important books, by scholars of Cambridge University, were: Edv
Hoskyns and Noel Davey, *The Riddle of the New Testament* (London, 1931), and C. H. Dc
The Apostolic Preaching and its Development (London, 1936).

Christian proclamation, knew that its foundations were being shaken. We have reached this better understanding of the Jewish and Greek backgrounds of the New Testament partly because of the progress of scholarly investigation,[1] but also partly because we ourselves live in a time of troubles. We know what it means to need the Gospel *about* Jesus, not merely the Gospel *of* Jesus; to need "a man from heaven". Paul Tillich presented the fruits of twentieth-century experience as well as the fruits of twentieth-century research when he said: "I believe that the whole New Testament is united, including the first three gospels, in the statement that Jesus is the Christ, the bringer of a new *aeon*."[2]

It is also instructive to examine the extended reference made to the four gospels by the Second Vatican Council.[3] At first sight, this seems Fundamentalism. "The Church has always and everywhere held and continues to hold that the four gospels are of apostolic origin . . . Holy Mother Church has firmly and with absolute constancy held, and continues to hold, that the four gospels just named, whose historical character the Church unhesitatingly asserts, faithfully hand on what Jesus Christ, while living among men, really did and taught . . ." But a closer examination shows that the Council did not assert that the gospels were like tape-recordings of the teaching of the Lord. "The sacred authors wrote the four gospels, selecting some things from the many which were handed on by word of mouth or in writing, reducing some of them to a synthesis, explicating some things in view of the situation of their churches, and preserving the form of proclamation . . ." Thus the most authoritative gathering of church leaders in this century has recognised that an element of human interpretation was already present in the most holy of the Scriptures. The possibility opens that thoughtful Roman Catholics may in the future join with Protestants in recognising that the Lord Jesus Christ may make himself known in this element of interpretation, as well as in the accurate history, for the Christ with whom Christians deal is not a Jesus who has ceased to "do and teach": he has inspired some in every generation after the first apostles. This understanding of the continuity of Christ through the Christian centuries is already prominent in the Roman Catholic Church through the great reverence given to "tradition"; unfortunately,

[1] Convenient summaries may be found in D. S. Russell, *The Method and Message of Jewish Apocalyptic* (London, 1964) and Hans Jonas, *Gnostic Religion* (Boston, 1958).
[2] *Perspectives on 19th and 20th Century Protestant Theology* (New York, 1967), p. 223, in the course of a shrewd criticism of Harnack.
[3] In Chapter V of the Dogmatic Constitution on Divine Revelation.

however, the tradition of the Church has been held to be competent to add to the historical evidence of the Bible, which is precisely the sphere where tradition cannot be treated as authoritative, except on a prior basis of dogma.

It is also instructive to examine more closely the position of Rudolf Bultmann. This great scholar has been (many would hold) unreasonably sceptical in his assessment of the interest of the primitive Christian community in what Jesus did as a matter of fact "teach and do" before his crucifixion. But Bultmann's close study of the Christ of the New Testament seems likely to stand where it emphasises the transforming impact of this Christ on the early Christians; and at the end of his notoriously brief discussion of "The Message of Jesus", Bultmann showed that the teaching, as well as the achievement, of the Jesus before his crucifixion did contribute to this impact. "For Jesus, God became a *God at hand*. He is the power, here and now, who as Lord and Father enfolds every man—limiting and commanding him . . . For Jesus, man is de-secularized by God's direct pronouncement to him, which tears him out of all security of any kind and places him at the brink of the End."[1] Such a Gospel, however brief, is not vague; and Bultmann does regard it as the task of the Christian Church in each generation to repeat and interpret this message of Jesus. Asked what was the Gospel for an industrial society as represented by the steel workers of Sheffield, Bultmann wrote in a private letter: "The basic sin is man's self-will and his intention of trying to live by his own wisdom and power . . . The grace of God release him . . . The surrender of self-will to God occurs in actual life through loving one's neighbour . . . To such surrender to the grace of God and to the neighbour, the Gospel promises freedom, power and life . . . We hand everything over to the grace of God, who gives us what is to come."[2]

Bultmann has explicitly rejected the charge that his insistence on faith's existential character reduces Christianity to an existentialist philosophy, i.e. to an understanding of man's predicament without a Gospel of God. On the contrary, Bultmann says the silence of most existentialist philosophers about God is what reveals that they are not Christians; *but he is*. "I cannot speak of God as my God by looking into myself. My personal relation with God can be made real by God only, by the acting God who meets me in his Word."[3] Again: "From the statement that to speak of God is to speak about myself, it by no

[1] *The Theology of the New Testament*, vol. i, pp. 23-5.
[2] *The Honest to God Debate*, ed. D. L. Edwards, p. 138.
[3] *Jesus Christ and Mythology*, p. 59.

means follows that God is not outside the believer."[1] Again: "The fact that God cannot be seen or apprehended apart from faith does not mean that he does not exist apart from faith."[2] If to retain this Gospel of God is to remain essentially mythological, as some of Bultmann's critics (for example, Fritz Buri, whose position resembles Albert Schweitzer's) have alleged, then Bultmann tells us that he is unashamed of the Gospel. And a man such as he has earned his right to this faith. Acutely aware of all the historical problems involved in traditional Christianity, and no less aware of the secularisation of Nazi Germany (and of industrial England), Bultmann proclaims this Gospel of a "God at hand" because of his own experiences. No doubt Bultmann, like others, has had many experiences which suggest that personal despair is the valid reaction to human perplexity and tragedy. That is why he stresses so greatly that only *some* moments are "eschatological", revealing ultimate reality, and why he lays such emphasis on the crucifixion of Jesus as the most powerful of such moments.[3] But it is grossly unfair to deny the right of a man such as Bultmann to trust these "eschatological" moments rather than the others. Difficult as it is for Bultmann or anyone else to speak about such moments of "eschatological" vision, they are real enough; they remain real amid our century's progress and catastrophe; and no law of "modern thought" can be allowed to prohibit all reference to them. And, following Bultmann even if at a lower level of intellectual life and integrity, many other Christians still feel entitled to say: "We, too, have had our moments of light as well as our long periods of darkness, and we, too, have chosen to live by that light in faith." A deeply personal choice is here acknowledged as necessary, and all dogmatism is avoided; but the choice is made, and made for faith. *Here the appeal is not to dogma, but to personal experience interpreted by faith.*

Does a faith such as Bultmann's, interpreting personal experience, leave history and nature in darkness? It has often been alleged by critical fellow-theologians that this is the inevitable effect of Bultmann's concentration on faith through the individual's experi-

[1] See p. 70.
[2] See p. 72.
[3] In the thought of Bultmann, what a depth has been added by our century's tragedies to the way in which Harnack expressed the existential character of the Gospel, lecturing to his Berlin students before Christmas 1899! "No doubt it is true that the view of the world and history with which the Gospel is connected is quite different from ours, and that view we cannot recall to life, and would not if we could; but 'indissoluble' the connexion is not . . . The man to whom the Gospel addresses itself is 'timeless', that is, it addresses tself to *man*, who in spite of all progress and development, never changes in his inmost constitution and in his fundamental relations with the external world." Adolf von Harnack, *What is Christianity?*, p. 112. See also Bultmann's introductory essay in the Harper Torchbooks edition.

ence of the Word of the "God at hand". But the personal basis of thi existentialist Gospel does not rule out the possibility of insights int the whole life of the earth and the universe. For although accordin₁ to this theological movement nature is no longer a clear proof of God' already completed design, yet the world can still be the "theatre o God's glory", an environment suitable for the people to whom th₁ glory of God is being revealed; and the order, progress and beaut₁ which are present in the world (making its evolution a drama rathe: than a lifeless theatre) can still be seen as reflections of the divin₁ glory. The only point on which the new approach must insist is tha all this is known only as a result of a choice made by a faith whic₁ grows out of personal experience.[1] But this personal basis of faith i₁ God's control over nature and history is not a weakness; it ca₁ support a courageously persistent clinging to faith in God throug₁ much anguish. A personal faith may fully acknowledge the evil i₁ the world, yet through its own power such a faith may place this ev₁ in the context of good, or at least may overcome the evil's power t₁ crush the spirit of the person concerned. In a reply to Professor Flew' parable about the "invisible, intangible, eternally elusive" gardener an Oxford philosopher, Professor Basil Mitchell, told another parabl₁ —this time about a leader of the resistance in German occupie₁ Europe. This leader warned his patriotic followers that, in order t₁ deceive the Germans while he lived under their power, he woul₁ pretend to collaborate with them. He did so collaborate, and th patriots' faith in him was strained almost to breaking point, but th patriots remembered what he had told them, and they trusted tha when their country was liberated the truth about their leader woul₁ be made known to all.[2] The message of this parable was, of course that under great strain the Christian believer may continue in hi *essential* faith because he has had experiences which he has interprete₁ as experiences of God, and these experiences have given him a hop for the future. Here again the appeal is not to dogma, but to experi ence—to the Christian experience which is presented by St. John' story of Mary of Magdala meeting the eternal Lord of Easter an₁ supposing him to be the gardener.

But many would say that the light which the West now needs i not the Easter light.

---

[1] See, e.g., W. A. Whitehouse, *Order, Goodness, Glory* (London, 1960).
[2] Also in *New Essays in Philosophical Theology* (cited above, p. 192).

CHAPTER FIVE

Light from the East?

The Challenge to Christianity

One of the most striking paradoxes in our time is that Western society is so powerful economically and culturally that its influence covers the face of the earth, yet it finds its own inherited religion so hard to believe that it is poor—many would say bankrupt—in the things of the spirit which are still held in deep respect by Africa and the East.

Outside the United States Western society is, in comparison with others in history or around the contemporary globe, spiritually disintegrated. This is largely because of the secularising impact of our century on the social, psychological and intellectual life of the West. The religions of other contemporary societies have to some extent been subjected to the same influences, but outside China they are as yet relatively stable. Inevitably in this situation, many suggestions have come from East and West alike to the effect that secularisation is a just punishment on the arrogance of the Christian Churches. Christianity's best policy is, it is said, to learn humbly from other religions, so that the spiritual resources of the West may be renewed. Here, it is claimed, could be the new Reformation or the new Pentecost needed by an exhausted Christianity. The small numbers of missionaries from the East to the West, and of Western converts to Eastern faiths, by no means exhaust the significance of this challenge or offer.

The modern Western interest in Eastern religion can be traced back into the nineteenth century. Sir Edwin Arnold's long poem *The Light of Asia* popularised Gautama the Buddha; and Orientalists such as the Oxford scholar, Max Müller, translated the sacred books of Hinduism and Buddhism, incidentally giving to the East the benefit of chronologically ordered scriptures. A World Parliament of Religions was held in connection with the Chicago World Fair in 1893, and the young Hindu, Swami Vivekananda, there spoke with electrifying force about India's spiritual gifts now on offer to the West. The World Congress of Faiths has sponsored a dialogue

between the religions since 1936, and during this period the centre c
discussion has shifted from the intellectually disreputable "theosophy
(founded in 1875 and dominated by collectors of religious curiositie
such as Madame Blavatsky and Mrs. Besant) to a more thoroug
study of the historic theologies and spiritualities.

Many of these communings between West and East, like man
other good things, were encouraged by the imperial connection, bu
the end of empire in two revolutionary decades, 1947-67, has full
released the bitterness of the East and the guilt of the West. This wa
symbolised by the popularity of K. M. Panikkar's book on *Asia an
Western Dominance* (London, 1953) with its triumphant announce
ments that the Vasco da Gama epoch in Asian history had ende
and that the Christian missionary effort had failed. All over Asia
and now all over Africa also, the anti-colonialist revolt has had i
religious implications.[1]

The branding of Christianity as colonialist was partly unfair to th
subtle relationships between missionaries and governments; mo
missionaries had purely religious motives, and few governmen
welcomed their potentially trouble-making initiatives and criticisms
Yet in practice missionary pioneering had often stimulated bot
Western commerce, with its tendency to exploit, and the extensio
of Western political rule. Missionaries had whipped up domesti
interest in Asia and Africa; missionaries in difficulties had been give
the protection of Western consuls and soldiers, specially in China
and missionaries in educational and medical work, or their assistan
such as teacher-catechists and hospital staff, had received subsidie
from colonial governments. Westerners abroad for commercia
political or military purposes had been regarded as Christians b
people whose religious and social identities were still unified, and th
Christian religion had been judged wherever there had been objec
tionable behaviour. Both missionaries and lay Westerners had in fac
entangled Christianity with colonialism, and it was too much to hop
that the separation of these ideas—although vital if the indigenou
Church was to flourish in days of national independence—coul
proceed smoothly.

Although national independence has been secured, the legacy c
colonialism in Christian history is still not exhausted. All over Asi
and Africa Christianity is now seen as the white man's religion, an

[1] Buddhism's anti-colonialist role in one corner of the British Empire was shown
D. C. Vijayavardhana, *The Revolt in the Temple* (Colombo, 1953).
[2] A judicious survey was provided by Stephen Neill, *Colonialism and Christian Missic*
(London, 1966).

many in the non-Christian world link this with their fears of American and European economic and cultural imperialism. Although the white man's military interventions have grown more spasmodic, Algeria in the 1950s and Vietnam in the 1960s have remained symbols of what the white man can still do. "Quiet" Americans have promoted "Coca-colonisation"; and gentlemanly British and civilised Europeans, without leaving their own shores, have inflicted terrible damage on young nations by refusing to pay good prices for the raw materials which they have imported from Asia and Africa. Much of the Afro-Asian anger may be unfair to the good intentions behind interventions or aid from the United States, Britain and Europe, but it is foolish for Westerners ever to forget the fact of the continuing bitterness of many Asians and Africans (to say nothing of the bitterness of Latin Americans against North American capitalists).

This identification with colonialism or neo-colonialism has been one of the greatest obstacles to the spread of Christianity in the contemporary world. Many Latin Americans have rejected both the Catholicism which looks to the Spanish or Portuguese past and the Protestantism which looks to North America, and they have turned instead to a home-grown Spiritualism, to more intoxicating local religions or—more commonly—to secularism. In his book on *The Religions of the Oppressed*[1] Vittoro Lanternari has studied the spiritual revolt which has come where the "natives" replied to the white man's exploitation by reviving a primitive paganism and combining it with a messianic expectation derived from Christianity itself. Dr. Lanternari presents examples from Latin America and the Carribbean islands, from the South Sea islands of Melanesia and Polynesia, and from the Red Indian tribes within the United States. Similar patterns may be found in the thousands of Christian or semi-Christian "independent" churches in Africa, united only in their dislike of missionaries[2]—or in the many new religions which have arisen in Japan since Christians dropped the atomic bombs.[3] The same revolt against the spiritual dominance of the West largely explains why Islam makes greater progress than Christianity in Africa—and why some American Negroes have become Black Muslims. The revival of Hinduism in the 1940s and 1950s was an anti-Western, anti-Christian baptism for the newly born independent nation of India. When B. R. Ambedkar led the Indian "untouchables" into Buddhism in the

[1] 1960; Eng. trans., New York, 1963.
[2] See *African Independent Church Movements*, ed. V. E. Hayward (London, 1963).
[3] See Harry Thomsen, *The New Religions of Japan* (Tokyo, 1963).

1950s, he not only restored Buddhism to its native India; because tl Christian Church was still identified with power and privilege, l also ended the missionaries' hope of an imminent mass-movemei into Christianity. When U Nu built his World Peace Pagoda ne: Rangoon in the 1950s, it did not seem to be a move likely to repla< St. Peter's, Rome, as the centre of the world's religious hopes f peace; yet the world in the 1960s has depended on the Buddhi tranquillity and compassion of another Burmese statesman, U Thai Hammarskjöld's successor as Secretary-General of the Unit< Nations. Those nations whose past has included both Christiani and colonialism have often seemed morally inferior to such Eastei peace-makers. And in many parts of Asia the continuing power Buddhism in the life of the people is shown by the continuing partit pation of its monks in national politics.[1]

So the rejection of Christianity as colonialist dominates mai discussions about religion in our time. But some specifically religio criticisms of Christian arrogance have been made widely in Asia ai Africa—and find a ready echo in Christianity's homelands. Tl Eastern counter-attack, so little expected in the flood tide of tl West's civilising mission, now often. looks like winning.[2] One of tl current objections is that Christianity has been organised hierarcl cally, and its priests and preachers have dominated society with thoroughness unknown to non-Christians. Judaism and Islam, ar to a slightly lesser extent other religions such as Hinduism in i regulations for its different castes, have had elaborate codes conduct based on religious law. It has been a very serious, and almc unheard-of, step for an individual to defy the code. Yet for all tl strength of their codes and their castes, none of these religions h developed a tyranny over the individual as thorough as the Inqui: tion in Catholic Europe or the Puritan theocracies in Geneva < Scotland or New England. The basic reason seems to be that on Christianity has given such prominence to its clergy, separating the into a full-time profession, making their ministry of the Word ar Sacraments some kind of essential mediation of the Divine grac entrusting them with disciplinary powers and matching their wo with the divisions of civil society so that in each parish the priest

---

[1] In *The New Face of Buddha* (New York, 1967), an American reporter, Jerrold Schec\ has paid tribute to the vitality. of Buddhism—sometimes resulting in an alm "Christian" use of violence.

[2] As is shown by a book such as Geoffrey Parrinder, *The Christian Debate: Light from East* (London, 1964). An imaginary meeting between adherents of three world religic and two Buddhists was constructed by Ninian Smart in his *A Dialogue of Religions* (Lond< 1960).

preacher might be a judge, and in each diocese the bishop might be
a lord. The clergy of other religions may have been honoured as being
uncanny or wise or powerful, but they have seldom enjoyed such
power as these envoys of the Carpenter of Nazareth.

It is, therefore, not surprising that there exists a widespread revolt
in the West against the fussy, domineering officials of the Church, and
a widespread sympathy with the East's alternative ideal for the
religious leader: the *guru*, the holy man who is holy not because he
has been appointed and paid by an institution and trained to preach
that institution's doctrines, but because he has peace in his heart, the
peace of his vision of eternity. And it is also no accident that the
psychological and intellectual impact of our time has made specially
fierce attacks on Christian doctrine.

More than any other religion, Christianity has attempted to system-
atise and to enforce the use of images and ideas expressing the divine.
Christianity has not been the most monolithic of the great religions;
Islam has been that, but Islam has been united by its elaborate law,
the *Sharia*, while its theology, for all its sophistication in medieval
times, has been based on only a few ideas about the transcendence
of Allah and on the one image of the Prophet and his Book.
Christianity has not been the most fertile of the religions in its
teachings; Hinduism has been that, followed by the Northern or
Mahayana Buddhism, but these other religions have proliferated their
mythologies in order to suit devotional needs or tastes without
attempting to reconcile one myth with another (as we have noted,
their very scriptures were in confusion until Western scholars set
them in order). What has been unique to Christianity has been the
zeal with which its hierarchy has used its powers of discipline in the
attempt to impose a single, vast system of beliefs and values on all
who wished to be saved. No other religion has a record of theology
reducing the greatest metaphysical mysteries about God, about man
and about the unique "God-manhood" of Jesus Christ to simple-
seeming sentences which could be adopted by a council or other
authoritative body and made compulsory on all believers by
anathematising the slightest disagreement as heresy most foul; and
in no other religion has intellectual discipline been accompanied by
such a strenuous effort to make worship elaborate yet also uniform.
Christianity has produced a wealth of symbols, in stones or glass,
statues or icons, sermons or hymns, and has often regarded one set of
these symbols as essential to the portrayal of the divine. Admittedly,
Christianity has been divided in its theologies and its symbolisms, yet

within each tradition—Catholic, Orthodox or Protestant—there ha
been much the same attempt at uniformity. Admittedly, Christianit
has nurtured mystics and moralists who in their different ways hav
discounted doctrine and organisation, yet the doctrine and th
organisation have been the forces which have meant religion to th
common people. Since the fourth century A.D. the history c
Christianity has been dominated by the combination of Roman lav
with Greek philosophy, improbable as such a future would hav
seemed in Nazareth or Jerusalem; and the discipline which conquere
the Roman empire and the intellectual confidence which closed th
schools of Athens have largely accounted for the power of Christianit
in Europe and the world. It has been the power of a system. Too mucl
of the history of Christianity has been a history of uniformity
achieved or attempted.

This fateful legacy from Rome and Greece may now prove to b
Christianity's undoing, for almost the whole world—East and Wes
alike—now rejects this idea of religion as uniformity. When we as
why some aspects of the life of an impoverished country such as Indi
have appealed so deeply to many sensitive spirits in the affluen
West in our time, we have to answer that the West acknowledges th
wisdom of the Hindu insistence that the ultimate is "not that, nc
that" (*neti, neti*). Here, too, is one secret of the popular appeal c
Zen Buddhism, in its origins a military (or at least aristocratic) cul
in China and Japan: Zen does not intellectualise. Professor Arnol
Toynbee speaks for many of his contemporaries when, in the con
cluding pages of his great *Study of History* and in other books, he use
the continuing yet gentle power of Eastern religion to hammer hom
the truth of the anti-Christian protest of the Roman pagan, Q
Aurelius Symmachus, that "the heart of so great a mystery cannot b
reached by one road only".[1]

God in East and West

Many of these criticisms of Christianity would be echoed by man
Christians. Since Dostoevsky depicted the Grand Inquisitor in *Tl
Brothers Karamazov*, many Christians have known who is the re:
enemy of Christ: the disciplinarian who crushes human freedom i

---

[1] The position of Arnold Toynbee is summarised in his Gifford Lectures on *A
Historian's Approach to Religion* (London, 1956), and in his *Christianity among the Religio
of the World* (London, 1957). For Asian reactions, see Thomas Ohm, *Asia Looks at Weste
Christianity* (New York, 1959), and the more intellectual *Christianity: Some Non-Christi
Appraisals*, ed. David W. McKain (New York, 1964).

the name of Christ. The Inquisition is now over. A new humility
leading to a new flexibility is seen to be indispensable to a new shape
for the Christian Church, and to a new statement of Christian belief,
without which Christianity seems unlikely to survive on any large
scale. But the heart of the religious debate is, of course, *the question of
God*. We must turn now to the onslaughts which have been delivered
in the name of Eastern religion against the West's identification of
religion with the worship of one supernatural God.

This Eastern attack on the Western idea of God is not so simple as
we might wish for the purposes of exposition, since Eastern religion
is itself a very large and complex phenomenon, giving rise to a
bewildering variety of beliefs and to an equally great variety of
Western reactions to those beliefs.[1] A religion in the East is not
so much a road (a Westerner cannot help feeling) as a traffic
junction without a policeman. Indeed, many in East and West
alike have refused to agree that Eastern religion can be summed
up so as to suggest a radical contrast between the Eastern and
Western conceptions of God. Under the influence of Judaism
and Christianity, the West—it is acknowledged—does mean by
the word "God" the eternal and holy Other; but the East also—
or so it is claimed—worships the same God, although in many
different ways.

While Director of the Centre for the Study of World Religions at
Harvard, R. L. Slater sought to counteract the prevailing sense of a
deep contrast between the Eastern and Western religious worlds.
He quoted Dr. Friedrich Heiler's address to the Ninth International
Congress for the History of Religions in Tokyo in 1958, in which that
eminent scholar saw seven principal areas of unity manifested by all
the higher religions: (1) the reality of the transcendent, the holy, the
divine; (2) the immanence of this transcendent reality in human
hearts; (3) the identification of this reality with "the highest good"
for man; (4) its identification with "ultimate love"; (5) the way of
man to God as a way of sacrifice, renunciation, resignation, prayer;
(6) the way of love, uniting man to man; (7) the way of love as "a
most superior way to God".[2]

Such a synthesis of the higher religions would clearly be relevant to
the religious problems of the West, for it would represent much in the

---

[1] Convenient introductions to the vast literature on reactions in the West may be had
through F. A. Dewick's Hulsean Lectures on *The Christian Attitude to Other Religions*
(Cambridge, 1953), or through the essays and bibliography in the symposium on *The
Theology of the Christian Mission*, ed. G. H. Anderson (New York, 1961).
[2] R. L. Slater, *World Religions and World Community* (New York, 1963), p. 38.

West's own vision of God, with the way of love substituted for the Inquisition. *But does such a synthesis really do justice to the religion of the East?* Here we must set aside the religion of Islam; Islam, of course, belongs to the Afro-Asian world geographically, but it belongs to the same spiritual family as the Christianity and Judaism of the West— and it has been discussed, however unsatisfactorily, earlier in this book.[1] Hinduism and Buddhism will be sufficient varieties of Eastern religion for us to consider at this stage.

In Hinduism, *bhakti* or devotion to a personal God has been taught by a succession of philosophers, of whom the greatest was Ramanuja (in the eleventh and twelfth centuries A.D.). This religion of human love responding to the divine grace has produced many noble lives, remembered particularly in the tradition of devotional hymns. Kabir, the Punjabi hymnologist, and Nanak, the first of the Sikh *gurus*, bridged the gulf between Hindu and Muslim by the purity of their love of God. And it is not only this *bhakti* version of Hinduism that has affinities with the Western idea of God. In the descriptions of ultimate reality by many Hindu philosophers we find a tone which is near to the tone which theists adopt when they state their belief in God. In the philosophy of the ninth-century Sankara, for example, the unity or "non-dualism" between the ultimate reality (*Brahman*) and the self (*Atman*) is stressed—yet the *Brahman* enjoys Being, Consciousness and Bliss (*Sat, Chit, Ananda*), and from it all existence, awareness and happiness derive; and the Self which is one with it is somehow a deeper, purer self than is the "I" of everyday personal experience (the "empirical ego" of Western philosophy). Thus the Hindu idea of the identity of the *Brahman* and the *Atman* can be presented as resembling the Western idea of the identity of God in the universe with God in the soul (in Dr. Heiler's words, "the immanence of this transcendent reality in human hearts"). Holding such a view of Ramanuja's *bhakti* Hinduism and even of Sankara's more wide-spread "non-dualism", many Western observers of Hinduism have been glad to welcome India's closeness to the West in a sense of "the reality of the transcendent, the holy, the divine". Thus it was possible for a Protestant missionary such as J. N. Farquhar to argue that Christ fulfils the highest aspirations of Hinduism.[2] C. F. Andrews, the friend of Ghandi and probably the greatest of twentieth-century missionaries in India, could declare that he saw the light of Christ in the eyes of Hindus, and the same generous assessment of Indian religion has

[1] See above, pp. 77-80, 145-7.
[2] *The Crown of Hinduism* (London, 1912).

been expressed more philosophically in a recent book by a Roman Catholic theologian with a Hindu father.[1]

Buddhism, like Hinduism, can be assessed by Westerners as a religion continuous with the type of religion which has prevailed in the West. Thus Gautama the Buddha can be understood as the One who reveals ultimate reality—as a prophet, but also as more than a prophet, as the incomparable man who attaches to himself the kind of worship which Christians give to Jesus. Gautama the Buddha taught that man would be absorbed into *Nirvana*, and at first sight this revelation seems to have little to do with the claims about God made by the prophets of Israel, by Jesus and by Muhammed. But what is *Nirvana*? The *Mayahana* variety of Buddhism finds a positive glory in *Nirvana*, and the conception of *Nirvana* as a mere Nothingness is rejected passionately. The most popular sect of *Mayahana* Buddhism teaches about a "Pure Land" which is like the Christian's heaven; and it believes that entry can be secured by faith in the name of Amitabha, a saviour or *bodhisattva* who made a vow to liberate all sentient beings before he would himself enter the supreme bliss, and who in his infinite compassion is willing to suffer for their sakes. *Mahayana* Buddhism prays to the Eternal Buddha in deep devotion, but it believes that the Buddha-nature can be found in many people and animals, on the path to liberation. Its doctrine of the "three bodies" of the Buddha—eternal, incarnate in a person, and generalised—sounds very like the Christian's belief in God as Father, Son and Holy Spirit. Kyan-yin, a female *bodhisattva*, has played a role in Chinese Buddhism approximately similar to the role of the Blessed Virgin Mary in Roman Catholicism. It is not surprising that some Christian thinkers have found some of the teaching of Christ foreshadowed in the teaching of Gautama, who had compassion on all who were ignorant of their eternal destiny.[2] Nor is it surprising that Professor Arnold Toynbee, for example, has often argued that *Mahayana* Buddhism should be regarded as Christianity's greatest ally in the modern world.

But there is, of course, another tradition at work in religious contacts between East and West. This is a far more controversial tradition. It declares that *Judaism, Christianity and Islam are basically incompatible with Hinduism and Buddhism, so that the religion of the East*

[1] See B. Chaturvedi and M. Sykes, *Charles Freer Andrews* (London, 1949), and Raymond Panikkar, *The Unknown Christ of Hinduism* (London, 1964).
[2] For two sympathetic Christians' assessments of Buddhism, see George Appleton, *On the Eightfold Path* (London, 1961), and W. L. King, *Christianity and Buddhism* (Philadelphia, 1962).

is not likely to purify the religion of the West. Instead, the spiritual triumph of the East would mean the end of the faith of the West. This insistence on a radical difference can itself take two forms. First, it can take the form of a denunciation of the "polytheism" (worship of many gods) of Asia. The average Muslim's contempt for the average Hindu's piety has had this justification. When Christians first went to the East from Europe, most of them were horrified by the "pagans" who sacrificed to "devils". Sacrifices in Hindu temples can seem to visitors a very squalid and evil debasement of humanity in front of repulsive idols, into our own day, and many modern Hindus would agree with such Western critics in wishing to cleanse the temples, to change the caste system drastically, to abolish the untouchability of the lower castes in practice as well as in law (as the burning of widows at funerals was abolished by the British a century ago), and to reform Hinduism in other ways. Buddhism has seldom aroused this moral repulsion, but in practice it does incorporate a great deal of primitive religion or "animism", and in our own time the Westernisation of China has involved a fierce attack on Buddhist "superstition".

Probably this contrast between polytheism and monotheism should not be considered the major religious issue now at stake. Every religion, when it has to cater for great numbers of people, in practice has to tolerate (however uneasily) local superstitions about the powers of local spirits. We may be reminded of this by the Roman Catholic Church's hospitality to the cults of local Virgins and saints, or by the worship at tombs or the rites to placate the spirits or *Djin* in Islam. But "higher" religion always sees these images of God as images only —rather like the national flags to be found in the sanctuaries of liberal Protestantism. They are to be used, and perhaps to be worshipped, if that helps the popular mind, but they are not to be regarded by the thoughtful as in themselves ultimate. For higher religion, the ultimate remains the One—the "One without a second". If the divine exists, it must be basically unified: that seems to be demanded once men think strenuously and clearly. This is taught in the first of the Hindu Upanishads, and very few Eastern philosophers dispute the point. Polytheism is not the real issue. The real issue is this: *in the last analysis, does the divine exist in distinction from the human?*

Religion in the West has been so heavily influenced by monotheism that since the end of Caesar-worship in the Roman empire the confusion of the human and the divine has been inconceivable for almost all religious thinkers—apart from the unique case of Jesus (where, indeed, it was one purpose of the official Chalcedonian

Christology to teach that the divine and human natures were *not* confused). The God of Western religion stands distinct from, and above, all nature, including human nature. Man is regarded as sinful and mortal. The God who of his own will choose to bestow the gift of life on a man may choose to bestow on that man the further gift of eternal glory; but even in eternal glory a man will always be in an important sense distinct from God, like a fish swimming in the ocean of God. Such is the legacy of the prophets of Israel, among whom the prophet from Nazareth should be reckoned; and Christianity, for all its Trinitarianism and Mariology, has remained monotheistic except in its corruptions. And ever since the wrath of the prophet Muhammed against the idols of Arabia and against the blasphemies which he saw, or thought he saw, in a corrupt Christianity, *shirk* (the association of any creature with God) has been the supreme sin in Islam. Moreover, Judaism, Christianity and Islam have shared a suspicion of mysticism (although also an ability to breed mystics)—because the distinction between the Creator and the creature can be blurred so easily when interpreting the mystical experience of unity. But the religion of the East has not been dominated by the austerity of this worship of the One God. The classical philosophy of Hinduism and Buddhism is clear about the ultimate identity of man with ultimate reality. Moreover, it is clear that man has both the duty and the capacity to see this identity through meditating about himself. Once man sees this, he is liberated from the limitations of human life and from the sufferings which come with these limitations. "That art thou" *(tat tuam asi)*—the words with which Uddalaka taught his son Svetaketu that he was one with the true Being, the Cosmic Power, as salt was one with water in salt water—are deeply sacred words in Hinduism, and their refusal to admit any ultimate duality between the *Atman* and the *Brahman* has coloured the whole of Indian thought.[1] And these words are developed by Gautama's teaching that the one salvation lies in *Nirvana*, which is compared with the blowing out of the flame of a candle. The original teaching of Gautama has been recovered by Western scholars over the last hundred years, and on the whole it justifies the Southern Buddhist school of *Theravada* (the Doctrine of the Elders) against the *Mahayana* Buddhism of the North. Gautama did not regard himself as in any sense divine, he did not offer any help except his teaching, he did not express any belief in God or gods, and the essence of his message was the impermanence of the self.

[1] See Ninian Smart, *Doctrine and Argument in Indian Philosophy* (London, 1964).

Individuality was at present held together by a temporary combination of elements in those doomed to live; but in *Nirvana* all traces of it would disappear. The *Nirvana* of Gautama certainly seems closer to the Western idea of Nothingness than it does to the Western idea of heaven. Gautama taught, as Uddalaka did, that the salt must merge with the water—that man must merge with the ultimate; but, unlike Uddalaka, Gautama refused to say anything positive about the ultimate, the salt water.

If in its main emphasis Eastern religion does deny that there is any reality higher than man, then it cannot complain if many Westerners regard it as incompatible with the worship of God. Among the most recent and best informed Western students of Hinduism and Buddhism, we therefore find a tendency to say that the East's basic theme is not the "prophetic" insistence on the otherness of the transcendent, the holy, the divine, but is the "mystical" identification of the human heart with the ultimate reality in the universe. The contrast between "prophetic" and "mystic" forms of prayer has been emphasised,[1] and the Swedish scholar, Archbishop Nathan Söderblom, made this the theme of his Gifford Lectures on the "basal" forms of personal religion in West and East.[2]

This strong contrast between the "prophetic" and the "mystical" was put with tremendous emphasis and prolonged effect by Dr. Hendrik Kraemer in his *The Christian Message in a Non-Christian World* (London, 1938). Kraemer wrote that book for the Tambaram Conference of the International Missionary Council, and in it he stressed that the Christian message was the proclamation of the Word of God in the Bible—a message for which there was little or no preparation in non-Christian religions. The realisation of the identity of man with the ultimate reality of the universe was the goal of religion in Asia, this Dutch scholar declared; *but precisely this was the supreme blasphemy to Christians, for it put man in God's place.* Here was the application of Karl Barth's theological revolution to the world-wide missionary strategy of the Christian Church; and Dr. Kraemer always insisted on its truth—although he lived to modify some details of his polemical presentation of 1938, and to witness an ever-growing resistance to this clear division between the Christian and the non-Christian.[3] Our own analysis would suggest that Kraemer, by a

[1] Especially in Friedrich Heiler, *Prayer* (1918; Eng. trans., New York, 1932).
[2] *The Living God* (London, 1933).
[3] His later writings afforded impressive evidence of the width and continuing liveliness of his mind. See his *Religion and the Christian Faith* (London, 1956), and *World Cultures and World Religions: The Coming Dialogue* (London, 1960).

process not unknown elsewhere in the history of thought, was correct in what he affirmed, and mistaken in what he denied. He was correct to describe Christianity as unique; he was also correct to say that a religion usually works, and usually deserves to be judged, as a whole; but he was mistaken in his denial of a substantial continuity between many elements in Christianity and many elements in other religions. This unwillingness led him to adopt an unsympathetic attitude to every non-Christian religion as a whole. The kind of "no" which Christians have rightly given to degrading superstitions in Western or Eastern paganism—for example, Nazism— was wrongly extended by Kraemer and his circle to include elements in the religions of the East which Christians ought to welcome and revere.[1]

A more balanced presentation of the continuity and discontinuity is found in the writings of the Oxford scholar, R. C. Zaehner. While deeply versed in the scriptures of the Eastern religions, and while sympathetically aware of the similarities between some of their teachings and monotheism, Professor Zaehner does not hesitate to stress the radical contrast between their "wisdom", exalting man, and the monotheistic "prophecy" about God, the prophecy which has become the religious heritage of the West.[2]

Western scholars such as Kraemer, or even Söderblom or Zaehner, may be thought prejudiced in such an assessment of the significance of Eastern religion. But we should note that the rejection of a transcendent God is a common theme in the missionary literature of Hinduism, for example in the California-based "Vedanta for the West" movement of Aldous Huxley, Christopher Isherwood, Alan Watts, etc.[3] In the earlier writings of Alan Watts, the "supreme identity" among the world's mystics turned out to be the Supreme Identity between the Self and Ultimate Reality, but more recently Mr. Watts has recognised an obstinate incompatibility between Christian (and other) faith in God and this Supreme Identity which he wishes to commend. "If the Christian view of the world is true," he now says, "the Hindu cannot be true. On the other hand, if the Hindu view is true, the Christian can also be true—in the sense that the situation of seeming to be a soul other than God and in peril of damnation could be one of the most extreme and adventurous roles

[1] See, e.g., *No Other Name*, an attack on syncretism by W. A. Visser 't Hooft, the former General Secretary of the World Council of Churches whose courage did so much to rally Christians against the evils of the 1930s, 1940s and 1950s (London, 1965).
[2] Specially in his *At Sundry Times* (London, 1958) and in the *Concise Encyclopaedia of Living Faiths*, which he edited with an Introduction and Conclusion (London, 1959).
[3] See *Vedanta for the Western World*, ed. C. Isherwood (New York, 1948).

of the Self.''[1] An even more clearly non-theistic philosophy (rather than the *Mahayana* religion of salvation) has been stressed by D. T. Suzuki and by many other Buddhist evangelists in the West.[2]

Since Eastern religion is so vast and so ambiguous, it is impossible to prophesy accurately what will be its future development. Hinduism and Buddhism could develop internally in the direction of a stronger, simpler and purer belief in "the reality of the transcendent, the holy, the divine". In that case, a religious alliance based on Dr. Heiler's seven areas of unity might well become the dominating factor in the religious situation of the world; and many worshippers of God, in East and West, now long to see that day. On the other hand, Hinduism and Buddhism could develop in such a way that the secular humanists of the West would greet the emergence of a common consensus *on the basis of atheism*; and already in some Western reactions to the spirituality of the East there are some signs showing how a universal atheism might look. When meditation is recommended by Eastern religious philosophy as the way of attaining such knowledge, Western man may be willing to hear the call from the many distractions of getting and spending to the contemplation of a deeper level of existence through the love of nature, through art, through music and through silence. When Eastern mysticism discards all images, Western man may feel vindicated in his sense that the symbols of religion have failed. And—here comes the crunch— when the "non-dualist" Hindu says that the *Atman* is the *Brahman* (Uddalaka's salt water), Western man may be willing to translate it into his own language as "Glory to man in the highest". When Gautama teaches about *Nirvana*, Western man may be willing to see here the brave and glad acceptance of the loftiest destiny which is compatible with the truth that everyone must die, never to rise again.[3]

How will the choice be made between these two possible impacts of Eastern religion on the West, for or against belief in God? Here we must revert to a point previously made in this book. In religion, a choice for belief or unbelief is not likely to be primarily a result of a coldly rational examination of all relevant arguments; in religion, a choice is much more likely to reflect a whole person's involvement in

[1] *Beyond Theology* (New York, 1964), p. 205. Compare his earlier book, *Supreme Identity* (New York, 1950).
[2] Examples of the teaching given to British inquirers may be found in Christmas Humphreys, *Zen Comes West* (London, 1960).
[3] The idea of the meeting of Eastern and Western religions in repudiation of the supernatural has attracted a number of recent writers. Its fullest statement was perhaps F. S. C. Northrop, *The Meeting of East and West* (New York, 1946).

a whole situation in a whole society. Social and psychological factors will powerfully influence the West's future attitude to the spirituality of the East. An equally important, and connected, point is that while the West changes the East will not remain a static society. Eastern religion should not be assessed primarily as an affair recorded in libraries. It is a living reality—and to live is to change.

Western thought presses remorselessly on Eastern religion as on every other area of Eastern life, through the East's need to import science and technology. Even if the East never develops as an industrial society comparable with the nineteenth- and twentieth-century West, its style of life and thought must change profoundly. Even if the political and cultural influence of the West in Asia decreases, the multiplying population of Asia will make the avoidance of famine the central concern of Asian politics. The East will demand, and will be ready to pay any price for, efficiency in the government and progress in the economy. This crisis, already grave enough, seems likely to deepen, and with it will grow the prospects of a social revolution on something like the Chinese pattern, seeking to modernise every corner of the national life. Eastern religion has too often been considered in isolation from this social context. We cannot be sure what will be the fate of religion in the Asia of the future, but the examples of China and Japan offer grim warnings to those who foretell the wider and wider adoption of the kind of synthesis for which Dr. Heiler spoke in Tokyo.

China, Tibet and Japan, traditionally the heartlands of the *Mahayana* Buddhism, have been modernised in a systematic attempt to bring them into the same category as post-Christian Europe; and so far Buddhism does not seem to have displayed anything like the resilience under attack to be found in European Christianity. In China (and perhaps in Tibet also) the millions have found enlightenment—or have obediently echoed slogans proclaiming that they have —in dialectical materialism, not in the Buddhist renunciation of all desire. In post-war Japan, Buddhism has indeed survived, but amid the astonishing economic boom it has not been nearly so active as the "new religions" which are concerned more about progress in this life than about ultimate reality.

Secularisation may come even in India. It is ominous for the future that Gandhi, who embodied so much of theistic Hinduism that the masses believed him to be an *avatar* or incarnation of God, consistently opposed industrialisation and many other aspects of the modernisation of India—and that his successor Nehru felt compelled

to reject Gandhi's religion as well as his social conservatism. It may
be that M. N. Roy, the atheist who used to argue that Nehru's
compromises with Hinduism, although limited, were a tragic betrayal
of the social revolution, will be proved right in the march of history.
Devotional Hinduism has a very deep appeal for the Indian soul at
present, but the drama of the evolution of Indian society is by no
means concluded.[1] The twenty-first century may see India a secular
state in social reality as well as in constitutional law, thus giving a new
force to something which Dr. Radhakrishnan wrote in 1927: "Hinduism is more a way of life than a form of thought. While it gives
absolute liberty in the world of thought it enjoins a strict code of
practice. The theist and the atheist, the sceptic and the agnostic may
all be Hindus if they accept the Hindu culture and life. Hinduism
insists not on religious conformity, but on a spiritual and ethical
outlook on life."[2] The examples of India's neighbours, Ceylon and
Burma, are relevant. The struggle against British colonialism was
accompanied by a high enthusiasm for "Buddhist Socialism"—which
was the attempt to build a just social order on the specifically
Buddhist alternative to selfishness. But the early enthusiasm in
independent Ceylon and Burma has not lasted, any more than the
early idea of an Islamic Republic lasted in Pakistan. All over Asia
the coming pattern may be shaped by regimes which pay little more
than lip service to a supernatural religion.[3]

Some religion there is sure to be in the East of the near future, for
the masses cannot be expected to accept a quick and complete
abandonment of the religious traditions which have given them some
sense of identity and purpose through thousands of years. Even in
China the anti-religious bias of the Communist regime may have to
be modified before the regime achieves stability, and of all Eastern
countries China has for many centuries been regarded as the least
other-worldly. In pluralist societies elsewhere in Asia, many of the
familiar rituals and myths may be continued to form the religion of
the people. After all, few nationalist leaders have yet had the courage
to break with the religious past, for they know too well how the masses
still feel. But beneath the continuity of ritual and myth in popular

[1] For a Christian assessment, see William Stewart, *India's Religious Frontier* (London,
1964). The best biography is Geoffrey Ashe, *Gandhi* (London, 1968).
[2] *The Hindu View of Life* (London, 1927), p. 77.
[3] An experiment of "Buddhist Socialism" was studied by Donald E. Smith in *Religion
and Politics in Burma* (Princeton, 1965). A sensitive English visitor to Burma, Dr. Trevor
Ling, recorded his impressions in *Buddha, Marx and God* (London, 1966). For Burma, see
also W. L. King, *A Thousand Lives Away* (Cambridge, Mass., 1964), and Ernst Benz,
Buddhism or Communism? (1963; Eng. trans., New York, 1965). For Ceylon, see W. H.
Wriggens, *Ceylon: Dilemmas of a New Nation* (Princeton, 1960).

religion, the doctrinal content of the East's future religion may well be based on the ultimacy of man rather than on belief in the supernatural.

If this is likely to be the future of Eastern religion, then its message for the West must become more problematic than Hindu or Buddhist evangelists now like to admit. *For if the ultimacy of man is to be the final conclusion of religion in a secular society, why should the West learn this from the East?* The West's home-grown atheism, post-Jewish, post-Christian or post-Islamic, seems to be a tradition which is vigorous enough to need no strengthening from the secularisation of the Hindu *Brahman* or the Buddhist *Nirvana*; and there are advantages to be preserved by the West in keeping to its own tradition, as we shall now see.

Religion and the Dynamism of the West

The real objection to the West's adoption of the Eastern world-view lies in the static character of the East which gave rise to that world-view. The West is dynamic, and for it to adopt a static philosophy would be for it to turn its back on all that has made modern Western society. For all the errors of the West, its dynamic energy has thrust towards the transformation of the world; and despite the defeat of colonialism, the nineteenth and twentieth centuries have been the period when this thrust has awakened the East. And Western religion has been a key factor in this energy. The very faults of the Western churches bear witness to this. The churches are rightly criticised as being too talkative, too highly organised, too authoritarian, not meditative or mystical enough. Yet religion as "the flight of the alone to the Alone"—the kind of religion which was desired by the Buddha, by Sankara and by many other great teachers of India—has, as a matter of history, often left history behind, condemning it as unimportant. "Neither Hinduism nor Buddhism, in its classical formulation," writes R. C. Zaehner, "pays the slightest attention to what goes on in this world."[1] We need not ignore the great charitable and cultural achievements which are a glory of Eastern religion to reach the conclusion that Eastern religion, when regarded as essentially an escape from the miseries of this earth, has been more harmful to man's progress on earth than all the dogmatism of Western religion. The Christian Church's aggressive entanglement with colonialism, and its arrogant dismissal of the "heathen" East, are scandals; yet the

[1] *The Convergent Spirit*, p. 36.

Church has at least been vigorous. By the cohesiveness of its theological and liturgical life, and by its network of officials and congregations, the Church has developed and safeguarded a remarkable
energy, whatever vices it may have displayed in the process. This
vigorous energy has made Christianity the first world-wide religion
in history. In the world today, although in many nations the Church
is a small minority, in some its representation is minimal and in some
(e.g. Tibet) no Christian congregation is known to exist, members of
every race are to be found among the Christians.[1]

There must, it seems, be far-reaching consequences for the spiritual
future of mankind in the historical fact that the scientific revolution
which has created modern civilisation, Western and Eastern, occurred
in the West, not in the East; in the society whose Chosen People was
Israel, not in the far larger society whose Chosen People was India.
We need scarcely emphasise the obvious point that this fact of history
does not by itself prove that the traditional religion of the West is
destined to overthrow the traditional religion of the East. The traditional religion of the West may be overthrown and replaced within
the West. What is suggested by history is only this: that the dynamic
character of Western religion is likely to be preserved in whatever
may come in the West, and is likely to influence the East in coming
centuries. The more static religion of the East—despite its many
merits and despite its great contemporary appeal in East and West
—is unlikely to have such a strong future as the scientific revolution
takes its course.

Much turns on the question: *why did Christendom give birth to modern
science?* Both India and China were civilised while Europe was
barbaric, and China in particular has a magnificent record of scientific inventions. But it was Europe that was the birthplace of the
scientific revolution, and Europe at that time was a continent saturat-
ed by centuries of Christian teaching. Recent studies may perhaps
now be summarised so as to suggest an honest (although very
sketchy) account of the rise of Western science in relation to its
religious background.[2]

Too much should not be claimed by religious believers. The
explosion of science in the West seems to have resulted from a

[1] Some Tibetans, Afghans, etc., have become Christians outside their home countries,
where Christian missions have been prohibited.
[2] See A. N. Whitehead, *Science and the Modern World* (Cambridge, 1926); Herbert
Butterfield, *The Origins of Modern Science 1300-1800* (London, 1949); E. A. Burtt, *The
Metaphysical Foundations of Modern Physical Science* (London, 1951); John Dillenberger,
Protestant Thought and Natural Science (New York, 1960); C. F. von Weizsäcker, *The
Relevance of Science* (London, 1964); and below, pp. 323–330.

complicated combination of factors including a fusion of its religious tradition with a rationalism derived from the philosophy of pagan Greece. Just as rationalism by itself was not enough, as we are reminded by the failure of Ancient Greece to exploit the experimental method, so religion by itself was not enough to produce a scientific civilisation, as we are reminded by the technological incompetence of the men of the Old Testament. And if religion did encourage science, Christianity did not have a monopoly here. Jews have played a large role in the advancement of knowledge and in the application of science to life, while Islamic culture by reviving the mathematical and philosophical legacy of the Greeks gave birth to its own brilliant period of intellectual life and was the teacher of medieval Christendom. The religious tradition of Europe was, of course, dominated by the figure of Jesus, the prophet of God's love for the world, the poet who saw reflections of that divine love in the processes of nature and in the lives of men; yet Jesus and the early Christians were consumed by their love of God more than by their love of the world, and their vision was of God speedily bringing in his Kingdom to replace the present age of the world. This might be interpreted (as by Rudolf Bultmann) as a warning against the subjection of the authentically human by the merely material—or it might lead to a withdrawal into otherworldliness. Thus Max Weber, as if warning us in advance against much shallow talk about the secular Jesus, summed up his impression as a sociologist studying the origins of the Christian religion: "Jesus held in general that what is most decisive for salvation is an absolute indifference to the world and its concerns."[1] It is evident that the contribution we are looking for was not absolutely unique to Christianity, and took some time to make itself clear in that religion.

A. N. Whitehead believed that the modern scientific spirit had its origin in the medieval Christian insistence on the *orderliness* of the Creator. The vision of God in St. Thomas Aquinas, "conceived as with the personal energy of Jehovah and with the rationality of a Greek philosopher", was contrasted by Whitehead with the Asian conceptions of a God who was "either too arbitrary or too impersonal".[2] Another English philosopher, Michael Foster, put the emphasis on the freedom of the Creator in the thought of the Middle Ages (as compared with, for example, Plato). God with his energy and rationality was free to create this, that or the next universe *ex*

[1] *Sociology of Religion*, p. 273.
[2] *Science and the Modern World*, p. 14.

nihilo ("out of nothing"); only a close observation of "the wisdom of God in creation" could tell what had been his choice. The book of nature, as well as the book of Scripture, must be studied reverently.[1] But perhaps these philosophers did not sufficiently bring out the historical complexity of this unique phenomenon, the rise of science in Christendom. In the Middle Ages there were men who in various ways anticipated the seventeenth century's enthusiasm for scientific experiments, but the prevailing tendency was one of reliance on the authorities of the ancient world, specially Aristotle.[2] Indeed, an extremely important characteristic of the rise of modern science was its willingness and ability to ignore, and if need be to defy, the pronouncements on scientific matters of the official custodians of the philosophical traditions, so that the names of Galileo and Darwin must stand for ever as reminders of the warfare of science with theology, of experiment with dogma, of progress with reaction.[3]

We must observe also that the personal religion of scientists and of philosophers of science has sometimes encouraged them to adopt attitudes which subsequent researchers and thinkers have had to abandon in the name of truth. An example may be found in that brilliant company of Christians who led the scientific revolution in seventeenth-century Europe—men whose faith went deep, although often it did not coincide with that of the ecclesiastical leadership. Names such as those of Galileo himself, Copernicus, Kepler, Pascal, Descartes, Boyle, Locke and Newton are rightly held in honour wherever science is honoured, and many (if not all) of them were devout believers, but running through much of their thought was the philosophy of "mechanism". This had two essential themes. First, nature was like a machine. God was needed to construct the machine, to start it working and to correct its mistakes, but otherwise he did not come into the picture. Second, the mind of man was like a ghost in this machine. It was essentially different from the matter which constituted the bulk of the universe, partly because it was by his mind that man could know the God of nature. Both these ideas in the philosophy of "mechanism" were remnants of the Christian philosophy of the Middle Ages, and they remind us of how the pioneers of the modern scientific movement were also partly

[1] Michael Foster's three articles with this theme appeared in the journal *Mind* (London, 1934-6).
[2] The history of medieval science was outlined by A. C. Crombie, *Augustine to Galileo* (London, 1952).
[3] The most influential exposition of the twentieth century's heritage in this field has probably been Andrew D. White, *A History of the Warfare of Science and Theology* (New York, 1896).

dogmatists, sleep-walking into their new world.[1] Such ideas have had to be abandoned, as scientists and philosophers have pressed on to examine all nature as a continuous whole without reference to a Creator and without any complete discontinuity between the inorganic and the organic, between matter and mind.[2]

We must, therefore, express the Christian contribution to the rise of modern science in a quite complicated and guarded way. But after recognising the complications, we may reasonably attribute to the Christian Bible, which was recovered for the Protestant laity in the sixteenth century, two ideas which have been crucially significant for the scientific civilisation, as this civilisation has spread from the seventeenth-century West to dominate the twentieth-century world. We may fairly interpret the two key ideas of "mechanism", which we have just outlined and rejected, as debased versions of the two ideas now to be expounded; and we may fairly claim that when the influence of these ideas on the modern West is contrasted with the religious philosophy most characteristic of the East, the scientific civilisation is seen to be post-biblical rather than anti-biblical.[3]

Nature and History

The first of these ideas concerns *nature*. For the Bible, nature from beginning to end is the creation of God. Its existence derives from his will. This means that nature itself is not divine, nor does it contain gods. Nature is a mere creation, and therefore men can investigate nature without fear, even without an inhibiting reverence. Men have been created superior to the rest of nature; in them, rather than in stars or mountains or waters or groves or cows, is the "image of God". Men have been given the dominion over nature; in the *Genesis* myth, Adam names the animals and cultivates the earth with a power which is not taken away from him after his sin. On the other hand, nature, while not divine, is sacred, because the God who created it made it "very good", in the words of *Genesis*. God has given to his whole creation much of the beauty and order which belong in their perfect purity to his own nature and which can be seen specially in God's noblest work, man. Despite some appearances to the contrary,

[1] See Arthur Koestler, *The Sleep-Walkers* (London, 1959).
[2] The force of modern rejection of "mechanism" may be felt in Gilbert Ryle, *The Concept of Mind* (London, 1949) which is already a classic of philosophy; or, from a different origin, in L. Charles Birch, *Nature and God* (London, 1965), a summary of much other literature by a biologist who is a Christian.
[3] This exposition owes much to the regrettably short book by the late H. Richard Niebuhr, *Radical Monotheism and Western Culture* (New York, 1960).

the God of Western monotheism is fundamentally reasonable and responsible, and the goodness of his creation is demonstrated by the fact that normally he rules according to his law in nature, not by extraordinary miracles. Everything he did, God did on purpose; and with the help which comes from his inspiration, men may detect this purpose by using their minds on his work. Scientists humbly studying the handiwork of God therefore find themselves "thinking God's thoughts after him". Wherever they look in nature, through the telescope or down the microscope, they can expect to find an order existing or emerging; an order which ultimately they will understand. This is the presupposition of modern science, but it arises before science, in religion.

The second religious idea behind the rise of Western science concerns *history*. Here again there has been an extensive recent discussion.[1] To Western monotheism, history from beginning to end is under the control of God, for the divine will which initiated and sustains the whole of creation is being worked out with a special energy through the doings of men. Every event can therefore be traced to the will of God, or at least no event occurs without the permission of God. This belief can inhibit the scientific method, when events are ascribed to God and the study of secondary causes is dismissed as trivial. The Hebrew scriptures, Christian medieval chronicles and the history of Islam are full of examples of this. But the belief in God's control over history is in the long run of crucial significance for modern intellectual activity because it leads to the belief that events hold an important meaning which should be extracted from them. They are not in the last analysis either accidental or illusory. Within the general revelation of God's purpose in history, a special revelation is received through particular events. Reading the "signs of the times", and discerning in current events urgent proclamations of God's will, has been the most prominent activity of religious prophets, from Moses (or earlier) to the present day. Key events have been linked together by the prophetic tradition as conveying a disclosure of God sufficient to arouse a saving faith in men; here in these sacred events is the history of our salvation, for here in a unique sense the Creator has acted. All history should be interpreted in the light which shines through these events, and what we see here, announced and effectively inaugurated, is the purpose of God to establish his kingdom on earth as in heaven, ultimately

[1] See Alan Richardson, *History, Sacred and Profane* (London, 1964), for a discussion and a comprehensive bibliography.

bringing all events entirely under his sovereignty. The whole of history is thus progressive, for the clue to all history is the coming of the Kingdom of God in history, to embrace all history. Even Albert Schweitzer, who emphasised (and exaggerated) the supernatural, apocalyptic elements in Jesus's understanding of the Kingdom of God, had to admit that Jesus's denunciation of life as it is before the Kingdom comes does *not* lead to a withdrawal from the world. "It is characteristic of the unique type of the world and life negation of Jesus," he wrote, "that his ethics are not confined within the bounds of that conception. He does not preach the inactive ethic of perfecting the self alone, but active, enthusiastic love of one's neighbour. It is because his ethic contains the principle of activity that it has affinity with world and life affirmation."[1] Great cultural consequences have flowed from the significance attached by Jews to the Exodus of Israel from Egypt, or by Muslims to the conquest of Medina and Mecca; but the most important result of the historical nature of Western mono-theism has naturally been connected with Christianity, which is the faith most deeply involved in particular events. The dating of years from the birth of Christ was the beginning of modern chronology, and mod-ern historical scholarship as it flowered in nineteenth-century Germany had its roots in critical methods first used in biblical studies.

Such ideas have influenced far more than the intellectual life of the West. Since Max Weber's *Protestant Ethic and the Spirit of Capitalism*[2] drew the attention of historians and sociologists to the role which religion had played in the rise of the modern Western economy, there has been a prolonged debate which has modified Weber's argument in details. But the main contention stands: Christianity, which already in medieval Europe had consecrated the growing prosperity of the towns (through guilds, etc.), has since the sixteenth century placed an increasing emphasis on the duty of the individual to improve himself and the world in this life, on the sacredness of daily work, and on the virtues of industry and thrift. This emphasis on the commercial virtues, so frequent among Protestants, has recently come under challenge, as theology has to adjust itself to the prospect of an affluent leisured West whose wealth will be produced largely by automation not by manufacturing; in these rich societies Protestants have to be told to relax and enjoy it.[3] But in the main, the

[1] Albert Schweitzer, *Indian Thought and its Development* (London, 1936), p. 4.

[2] 1920; Eng. trans., London, 1930. See R. H. Tawney, *Religion and the Rise of Capitalism* (London, 1936). The ensuing controversy was presented in *Protestantism and Capitalism*, ed. R. W. Green (New York, 1959).

[3] See Robert Theobald in *Economic Growth in World Perspective*, ed. Denys Munby (New York, 1966), pp. 155-72.

Christian emphasis on work is unlikely to be superseded as a necessity of the modern age. Indeed, one of the best informed recent discussions of *Religion and Progress in Modern Asia* points out that "today's Asia shares with the age of the Protestant Reformation the problems of the first emergence of historic society and historic religion into the modern world", and that, mainly for this reason, "Christianity, through missionaries and local convents, has had an influence on cultural modernisation in Asia out of all proportion to the small number of people involved . . . Although there is great variability from country to country, Christianity and Christian institutions, especially schools, have been important catalysts for change."[1]

The same scholar faces the challenge to the religions of the East. "Let us consider . . . what a religion of historic type must do if it is to contribute maximally to modernization. It must be able to rephrase its religious symbol system to give meaning to cultural creativity in worldly pursuits. It must be able to channel motivation disciplined through religious obligation into worldly occupations. It must contribute to the development of a solidary and integrated national community, which it seeks neither to dominate nor to divide . . . It must give positive meaning to the long-term process of social development . . . It must be able to accept its own role as a private voluntary association and recognise that this role is not incompatible with its role as bearer of the society's ultimate values."[1] We saw in Chapter 2 that no historic religion has yet completely transformed itself in this way (Filipino Catholicism, the deepest-rooted large Christian community in Asia, is scarcely modern on this showing); and we must emphasise that it is not impossible for any religion to undergo "modernisation". But it has in fact been Christianity that has come nearest to playing such a role, and some of the most constructive comment on the role of religion in contemporary Asia has come out of the East Asia Christian Conference and the Institutes on Religion and Society which are linked with it.[3]

We must add that in Christianity lie many of the origins of the modern democratic idea, for all the influence of the secularising French Revolution. Ancient Israel was plainly not a modern democracy, for its God, Yahweh, ruled through judges or prophets or kings; essentially, it was a theocracy. Yet Israel was closer to

[1] Robert N. Bellah in the symposium which he edited on *Religion and Progress in Modern Asia*, based on a 1963 conference of Asian intellectuals (New York, 1965), pp. 198, 203.

[2] *Ibid.*, p. 202.

[3] The most able presentation of the Christian attitude to economic growth which is known to me is the concluding essay by Charles Elliott in *Economic Growth in World Perspective*, cited on the previous page. See also below, p. 223.

equality than was Ancient Athens, for while the religion of Israel was a religion extolling brotherhood under Yahweh the civilisation of Greece rested on a mass of slavery. The early Church had no clear theory about society, and the medieval Church reflected the inequalities of feudal society (to the extent that bishops and monasteries owned serfs), but even then Christians taught that a person's relations with the personal God were the most important thing in life, and that Christ had died for all; and the thrust towards human equality which marked the seventeenth century did receive a powerful impetus from Protestant Christianity. For all its endorsement of the medieval picture of an ordered, hierarchical society, mainstream Protestantism, through the active life of its local congregations, trained countless numbers of the lower middle classes in the democratic arts of free speech and corporate decision making, and so equipped them to rise in society. About the elect in these congregations, if not yet about the broad mass of humanity, Protestantism declared: their consciences are inviolable, for God speaks to their consciences in secrecy and silence, and their souls are invaluable, for God sent his Son to die for them. A sense of the sacredness of the individual was thus one of the great contributions of Protestantism to the world, and it appealed to biblical authority. In the nineteenth and twentieth centuries Protestantism, a more democratic Catholicism, and a non-theological Protestant ethic have all been forces making for the social progress of the masses; and all these forces— while owing much to economic and political factors—have appealed to the Christian Bible as a manifesto of man's dignity and fundamental equality.[1] Through the missionary movement, and through the wider dissemination of Christian and post-Christian values in the whole impact of the West on other societies, these values have contributed greatly to the recent awakening of Asia and Africa. The charitable works of the missionaries, serving those whom the other societies despised and rejected, have conveyed, more effectively than many words, what it is that Christianity believes about every individual. The Hindu imitation of these acts of charity is perhaps the highest tribute which the East has ever paid to the West. But the whole modern rise of democracy is indebted to European Christianity's estimate of the individual.

These ideas about nature and history, and about the dignity of man at work and in politics, can be paralleled roughly in parts of

[1] I contributed an essay on "Equality as Part of Our Heritage" to Daniel Jenkins, *Equality and Excellence* (London, 1961).

Eastern religion. But they are not so basically characteristic there as they are in Western monotheism; and they have not been so widely influential in society. On the contrary, the basic attitude to nature in the East has been one of awe, whether this be the fear which the villager has for the spirits dwelling in local objects, or the desire of the philosopher to devote his whole being to the contemplation of nature so as to be absorbed into harmony with it. In the East men have not *used* nature as they have in the West, for while desiring to escape from many of its manifestations they have given to its essence the worship which is reserved in the West for God alone. This seems to be the fundamental reason why the many inventions which came earlier in China or India than in Europe did not lead to the thorough application of technology as the means of taming nature. One of the most curious facts in cultural history is that the law of *karma*, stressing that rewards or punishments inevitably follow thoughts and actions, did not lead to a development of an understanding of scientific causality (despite the efforts of some recent Hindu and Buddhist apologists to claim this), whereas in history the Jewish-Christian view of nature, shot through as it was with the miraculous, did produce the ideas of natural law and natural science. The explanation seems to be that the Jewish-Christian view interpreted the occasional miracle as the revelation of the permanently true nature of things—and was convinced that the true nature of things included the mastery of man over nature, symbolised in the Israelites' miraculous crossing of the Red Sea and in Christ's miraculous resurrection from the dead.

If the East has not used nature as nature has been used in the West, neither has the East valued history as history has been valued in the West. At its centre, Eastern religious philosophy concerns not the interpretation of history nor its transformation, but its abolition in timelessness. Mythologically, history may be described as *lila*, the play of the gods; more philosophically, as *maya* or cloudiness.[1] History consists of one life after another, one cycle of events after another, and does not move towards a goal. The *Bhagavad Gita* has in India become "the scripture of the new age, the main foundation on which its ethic, its social doctrines and even its political action depend. Its message is carried daily to the common man in a thousand new popular versions". So K. M. Panikkar points out, explaining that the basic contribution to the "Hindu Reformation" of two of India's greatest spiritual teachers, Bal Gangadhar and Tilakard Sri Aurobindo, was to exalt the ideal of the person of equable mind,

[1] For a Christian assessment, see P. D. Devanandan, *The Concept of Maya* (London, 1950).

without selfish desire, working for the welfare of the world. To this noble ideal Gandhi added the doctrine of *ahimsa* or non-violence.[1] We can well understand how the beautiful *Bhagavad Gita* has come to be so deeply loved, and why so many have been inspired by it towards an activism suited to India's present needs but calmly spiritual and truly civilised. Yet we cannot help asking whether this will be the final scripture of India's new age. For when we read the *Bhagavad Gita* without a modern commentary, what do we find is its story? The divine Krishna, incarnate in a charioteer, tells the prince Arjuna to take part in a civil war, for that is his destiny as a warrior— and it does not really matter who will die in the battle, for all will be reborn anyway. Another relevant point is that although the incarnation of Krishna in the *Bhagavad Gita* is a beautiful story, like so much else in Eastern religion this revelation of the insignificance of human life is expressed with a revealing absence of reference to real history. It does not matter to Indian spirituality whether or not an actual charioteer ever spoke to an actual prince before an actual battle.

All interpretations of existence use some mythical language, but whereas the mythological elements in Western monotheism have grown around the historical events (for example, the crucifixion of Jesus), which are believed to hold the key to the riddle of life, in Hinduism and Buddhism mythologies flourish without any anchorage in events. Incarnations of the divine such as the Hindu *avatar*, or perfections of human nature such as the Buddhist *bodhisattva*, arouse the devotion of the masses but not the assent of historians. Legends have clustered around the story of Jesus—but if the quest of the historical Jesus is difficult, the quest of the historical Rama, Krishna or Amitabha is impossible. It is no accident that vast tracts of Eastern history are, in comparison with the care of Western chronology, dateless. Oscar Cullmann has written of the "linear time" of Christians, in contrast with the "eternal recurrence" in the East's "cyclical" time. In other words, all time in the Christian West had a centre in Christ and moved towards an end, the victory of Christ, but time in the East had no general meaning, the only pattern being one made by events repeating each other.[2] The widespread beliefs of the West that history had been short, and that the future would be shorter still, did handicap acceptance of the nineteenth-century discoveries of the immense vistas of evolutionary time, and it is interesting that Hinduism and Buddhism presented no obstacles to

---

[1] K. M. Panikkar, *The Foundations of New India* (London, 1963), pp. 36-46.
[2] See Oscar Cullmann, *Christ and Time* (1946; Eng. trans., Philadelphia, 1951).

the scientific world-view on that score; but if we ask whether the Western or the Eastern vision of time is more harmonious with the scientific world-view, only one answer is possible. As Dr. Joseph Needham points out, in the West "the Enlightenment secularised Judaeo-Christian time in the interests of the belief in progress which is still with us, so that although today when 'humanists' or Marxists dispute with theologians they wear coats of different colours, the coats (to an Indian spectator, at least) are actually the same coats, worn inside out."[1]

Of course the attitude towards nature and history which we have just attributed to Eastern religion is very far from the whole truth about the many thousands of millions of human beings who have lived in the vast area thus vaguely described. In particular, the high culture of the great Chinese Empire was closer than India was to the West (as Dr. Joseph Needham has shown). Taoism did lead to an intense interest in nature, and Confucianism revered the history of the family and the state. In Buddhism itself, there has been some glorious art to tell the Buddha's story, and culture has arisen on the basis of Buddhist compassion for the transitory life of men and animals, as in the empire of Asoka in India. In Hinduism there has been much healthy emphasis on the duties of the lover and the householder before the stage of life comes when one should wander off in poverty to seek peace of soul; and the erotic sculptures which adorn some Hindu temples exceed Western railway station book-stalls in their delighted portrayals of the lusts of the human animal. But we need not indulge in Christian propaganda about the "escapism" of Eastern religion, or in the ignorance of Western contempt for the "timeless Orient", if we repeat that, taking the society concerned as a whole over a long period, there has been a basic difference between the destinies of East and West. In its broad outline, the contrast in their histories, as these histories have been inherited by our own time, is clear. China, for all its past glories, was so backward when the twentieth century began that heroic surgery was needed if the disease was not to be fatal, and the surgery has eventually taken the form of a wholesale rejection of the ancient culture. Although India has not yet been desperate enough to seek Westernisation at that price, many modern Indians experience a growing alienation from their past, and the same tension—apparently inescapable once modernity has been experienced—may be seen in

[1] *Time and Eastern Man* (London, 1964), p. 50. Dr. Needham may be reckoned the world's leading authority on the history of science in Asia.

the literature of Western disillusionment with Indian spirituality. Rejecting both the religion and the materialism of their own civilisation, sensitive Westerners have been attracted by books about the wisdom of India, and have found themselves against their own wishes disgusted by the sights which they have found at the end of their pilgrimage.[1] Such literature could be paralleled by many Asian (and African) records of disillusionment with the "Christian" West, but other literature by Indians themselves, written precisely in order to preserve and to present their spiritual heritage, drives home the contrast between East and West.

These Indians warn the West about the consequences of a doctrine of God. At first sight the West would be inclined to shrug off such talk as metaphysical and meaningless. Some reflection might persuade the West to welcome the warning, because as we have seen the intolerant dogmatism of the West's religious past is now a source of shame. But if the West goes deeper still into the warning from India, it will see that what is at stake is nothing less than the question whether personality is a mere "appearance". The scientists of the West have increasingly revealed to the wonder of men a universe infinitely more mysterious than "common sense" sees, and superficially the latest Western physics resembles the East's ancient doctrine that "all our differentiations merge into a unified cosmic Oneness",[2] but the main appeal of science to the West has been its differentiation of personality from nature and its subjection of nature to personality. And the theologians of the West have always known that the personal must be transcended in the eternal if "the eternal" is real, but they have almost always believed that personal power and personal love, the keys to the improvement of man's earthly circumstances, are also the best categories by means of which man may begin to understand and obey the ultimate reality.

India's warning against the personal was put clearly in a recent book by the head of the Vedanta Society of Southern California. "Devotion to the *Ishwara*, the personal God, may lead a man very far along the path of spirituality; it may even make him into a saint. But by itself it does not give the ultimate knowledge. To be completely enlightened is to go beyond the *Ishwara*, to know the impersonal Reality behind the personal divine Appearance. We become *Brahman*,

---

[1] The classic example was Katherine Mayo, *Mother India* (New York, 1927), which Gandhi described as "the report of an inspector of drains". A powerful recent account was Arthur Koestler, *The Lotus and the Robot* (London, 1960), which also covered Japan. See also Stark Murray, *India—Which Century?* (London, 1967).
[2] As is argued in, e.g., Ruth Reyna, *The Concept of Maya* (London, 1962).

since *Brahman* is present in us always. But we can never become *Ishwara*, because *Ishwara* is above and distinct from our human personalities. It follows, therefore, that we can never become rulers of the universe. To rule it is *Ishwara*'s function, and the desire to rule it is the ultimate madness of the ego."[1] Yet to rule the world has become the desire of man "come of age" in the West, and he learned this desire when he believed that his Father was the personal God.

Religion and Suffering

Sarvapelli Radhakrishnan, the philosopher who became President of India, has painted a noble and deeply attractive picture of India's religious tradition. "This figure of Siva, the great Yogi," Dr. Radhakrishnan wrote in a typical passage, "has been here for five or six millennia dominating the spiritual landscape of India, indicating that perfection can be achieved only through self-conquest, through courage and austerity, through unity and brotherhood in life. This ideal is to be met with in the seer of the Upanishads rapt in communion with the Eternal, in the calm and compassion of the Buddha victorious over ignorance and ill-will, in the ecstasy of the saint who, through his heart's surrender, becomes one with Universal love, and in the servant of God, who, lifted above selfish desire, carries out on earth the will of the Transcendent Supreme."[2] But such a picture is the equivalent of writing a history of Christianity with no realism about its psychological and social roots. We need not deny the splendour of the ideal, if we ask what have been the deep roots of Eastern religion in Eastern society. And if we ask that question, we discover the one fact which dominates all others in religion's significance for the East: *the fact of suffering*. We discover also that Eastern religion does not transform suffering; it seeks detachment from it.

In Hinduism and Buddhism alike, an estimate of man which seems superbly optimistic has in fact arisen from a bleak pessimism, and what looks like humanism turns out to be the annihilation of man. For the basic teaching of these religions is that to be a man is to be miserable, and that a man cannot enter bliss and remain human. If he is to escape from his misery, an individual must be *absorbed* into the divine, or into nature, or into nothingness. Only a tiny minority in any one generation attains the enlightenment which leads to this

[1] Swami Prabhavananda, *The Spiritual Heritage of India* (New York, 1962), pp. 289-90.
[2] *East and West: Some Reflections* (London, 1955), p. 20. See *The Philosophy of S. Radhakrishnan*, ed. P. A. Schipp (New York, 1952).

absorption; and in the lives of this minority, only a few moments are ecstatic because enlightened. This is why Hinduism has placed so much emphasis on the Brahmin caste as the only full recognised status group; and why Buddhism—where a spiritual genius who belonged to the *kshatriya* or warrior caste led a revolt against the caste system—has taught that for an aspirant really to "take refuge in the *Dharma*" (Buddha's Doctrine) he must also "take refuge in the *Sangha*" (the Buddhist Order of contemplative, mendicant monks). If we ask why Buddhism virtually disappeared in its native India, the answer is simple: its monasteries were destroyed by Muslim conquerors. The superior status of the Brahmin caste or the Buddhist *Sangha* is the Eastern equivalent of Christianity's clericalism; although the Hindu pundits and the Buddhist monks do not have the disciplinary powers of Christian priests or ministers, in fact their status represents a more severe verdict on the common people than has been characteristic of Christianity. Traditionally Hinduism has taught that one's place in the caste system indicates one's moral and spiritual worth, for it shows what was one's behaviour in previous incarnations. For both Hinduism and Buddhism, ordinary people's lives are significant only in so far as the virtue in them accumulates into merit which is rewarded by enlightenment in another incarnation (for Hinduism, in another caste); and since an inconceivably vast number of reincarnations in animal or human lives will be necessary before all who are capable of enlightenment attain it, the significance of an individual existence is small. Human life, which has so little meaning bestowed on it by these religions, consists largely of suffering. The "Four Noble Truths", which were the original essence of Buddhism, state clearly that to live is to suffer, and that therefore the supreme problem for man is to avoid being reborn by eliminating the desire to live. The common way of accounting for the presence of so much evil in the world is to say that it is a punishment for misdeeds in previous incarnations, according to the iron law of *karma*. We need not deny the humanitarianism of many Hindus and Buddhists in the past and present if we observe that the main impression left by these religions is that most of the evil in the world cannot be reformed away, and probably ought not to be, for without it the justice of *karma* could not operate. Thus fatalism has been encouraged, whatever the modernisers of these religions may say. Indian religion has been based on the negation of life, as Albert Schweitzer saw so clearly— Schweitzer, who saw also that the message of Jesus was not the simple, cheerful life-affirmation of liberal Culture-Protestantism. And

Schweitzer, who was so critical of Western civilisation's decay, saw that essentially what was missing in Indian religion, at least until the renewal of Hinduism under the impact of the message of Jesus, was a unifying principle teaching the active love of the neighbour based on obedience to the mysterious God who as "ethical Will" is greater than all the world's forces. Compassion was taught by the Buddha, but it was not a compassion which drove Buddhists to attempt to heal mankind's sores; it was the compassion which interpreted all life as suffering, and which therefore bestowed as its greatest blessing the secret of escape from life.[1]

The history of deviations from the official religions shows the contrast between the forms taken by protest in the West and in the East. In the West, the religious sects, protesting against the established churches and social customs of the time, have sometimes abandoned hope for this life, but for the most part they have sustained themselves by the faith that the God to whom they turned would bring in his kingdom of justice and love. Until this kingdom came, the sects have done their best to improve their lot on earth. But in the East, the sects have sought escape through the absorption of the individual into the object of worship, with few consequences for everyday life. Max Weber put it with his formidable jargon: "The Occidental sects of the religious virtuosos have fermented the methodical rationalisation of conduct, including economic conduct. These sects have not constituted values for the longing to escape from the senselessness of work in this world, as did the Asiatic communities of the ecstatics: contemplative, orgiastic or apathetic."[2]

The Hindu and Buddhist world-view arises from a profound and prolonged human experience of suffering. Suffering, it says, cannot be ended except by the end of man. In the conditions of life which we know, such a view can never be completely falsified, for the burden and mystery of evil can never be completely removed. But in the West, and increasingly in the East, a more optimistic view is taken of the capacity of the human intellect to lessen human suffering by active love and by the application of the natural and social sciences. The humanity which holds this hope and faith is, in its own eyes, sharply distinguished from the animals, many of which it tames or eats, and from the rest of nature, which it confidently uses. It accepts the gift of life with joy. In this humanism lies the challenge to religion of "man's coming of age", and it is clear that the religious pessimism

---

[1] See Albert Schweitzer, *Christianity and the Religions of the World* (London, 1923).
[2] *From Max Weber*, p. 291.

which has dominated Hinduism and Buddhism cannot for long survive the challenge. This is clear not only as a point of philosophy; it is being demonstrated day by day in the transformation of Eastern society and its religion under the impact of the West.

Dr. M. M. Thomas, the Director of the Christian Institute for the Study of Religion and Society at Bangalore, has recently pointed out that the newly independent nations of Asia are searching for new spiritual foundations in order to prosper in the modern world. Their technology demands that nature should be taken seriously. Their democracy demands that the person acting in history should be taken with an equal seriousness. Their religious traditions do not view nature or the person in this way, and therefore their religious traditions are on trial. Dr. Thomas writes: "The recognition of the reality of nature and the manipulation and conquest of nature by man have been very necessary for Asia to develop the concept of man as distinctly standing out of nature. In this sense science and technology have contributed to Asia's spiritual awakening of the personal."[1]

Dr. Thomas quotes from a recent booklet called *The Christ We Adore* by Swami Ranganathanandan of the Ramakrishna Mission, which calls for the "detribilisation" of Christianity. He comments: "What the Swami calls dogmas of Semitic tribalism are those of the prophetic tradition which saw God acting in history for the judgment and salvation of mankind, and made the drama of historic existence a movement of ultimate spiritual significance. There is no doubt that Jesus himself shared this framework and saw his messianic vocation within that setting. Furthermore, it is this prophetic spirituality which has made its impact through Western secularism and Christianity on Asian peoples and cultures in modern times and awakened them to what I have called the personal dimension of human existence. Therefore any rejection of the prophetic tradition as tribalism is a denial of the fact of Jesus as he is presented in the gospels, and is also detrimental to the spiritual quest behind the new Asian awakening."[2]

As an Indian Christian, Dr. Thomas believes that Israel's prophetic tradition, summed up by Jesus, will eventually be acknowledged as the answer to Asia's spiritual quest. This may well be the future in the long term, but it seems likely that before Christianity can be acknowledged as the light of Asia many decades, and even centuries, must pass during which it will still be branded as colonialist—and during which Eastern religion will be transformed internally by

[1] *The Christian Response to the Asian Revolution*, p. 68.
[2] *Ibid.*, p. 119.

pressures in its own evolution, pressures which may take it further
from belief in the God of monotheistic prophecy. If the suffering of
Asia through famine increases tragically, and if Asia does not accept
this with its traditional fatalism, it is probable that the political and
economic way of escape will be thought to involve not Christianity
but a Marxist or other version of Christianity's secularised child,
Socialism. Meanwhile we may leave the matter with the modest and
clear words of the English secular humanist, H. J. Blackham: "In
Europe it has reasonably been said that Christianity made a major
contribution to the development of both science and democracy, and
is therefore at home in modern culture. In the East modern culture is
an import or an imposition and may therefore be harder to reconcile
with traditional religion. In both cases the open society offers the best
way and the best hope."[1]

Since the impact of the West on the East is not likely to diminish
(even if Western *religion* continues to be rejected by the East), much
of the future of the whole world will depend on what the West makes
of its own religious heritage. It is ominous that the mechanistic view
of God's relation to nature, which we saw to be characteristic of
Christian scientists in seventeenth-century Europe, lapsed before long
into open Deism (the belief that God is so remote from nature and
man that for practical purposes he does not matter); for Deism turned
out to be the road to agnosticism and scepticism. We must discuss the
relations of religion and science in the West further (in Chapter 8),
but we can see now that the move from Deism to agnosticism may be
typical of a wider process in the life of the post-Christian West. The
historian traces modern civilisation to its origins in European
Christendom, and, contrasting post-Christian lands with others, he
may conclude that secularisation is in some sense the fruit of the
Christian Gospel. But that does not prevent secularisation from
developing its own drive, whatever its origins may have been; nor
does it prevent secularisation from acting as the enemy of the Gospel
now that the help which Christianity provided is no longer needed.
As a Christian historian has put it, in a discussion of religious liberty:
"A Christian civilisation by its very nature has to develop towards
what its most faithful servants feel to be its own undoing. Once
civilisation has so far advanced, freedom of conscience becomes the
first requisite for a Christian order of things, even if the result is a
kind of world in which it is harder to be a Christian."[2] Another

[1] *Religion in a Modern Society*, p. 169.
[2] Herbert Butterfield, *Christianity in European History* (London, 1951), p. 35.

historian has made this simple comment on the complicated truth about the origins of modern science: "The sixteenth and seventeenth centuries were Christian in orientation and conception . . . The great scientists were consciously Christian, and they were certainly unaware that they stood on philosophical grounds which were destined to threaten and, for some, to undermine Christian thought . . . Hence, they could not understand why churchmen should be at all opposed to their discoveries . . . The theologians were only too afraid that the direction taken by the new science would destroy Christianity, and promote atheism as they understood it. They were remarkably right."[1]

What we have so far suggested may be summed up like this. *Any religion dominating the West is likely to be dynamic, unless its society ceases to be dynamic. In the past, this energy came mainly from the religious belief of monotheism; the spiritual legacy of Christianity, Judaism and Islam did much to inspire the scientific civilisation; and it is difficult to imagine that the dynamism will be inspired in the future by the religion of the East.* But we must turn now to examine suggestions that Western man in the age of science should worship neither his traditional God nor himself, but some external force which is a secular substitute for the God of Christianity.

[1] John Dillenberger, *Protestant Thought and Natural Science*, British edn., pp. 186-7.

CHAPTER SIX

A New Religion for the Secular West?

"Modern man appears to suffer acutely from his loss of emotional reassurance," a sociologist, Dr. Bryan Wilson, reminds us, in a study of the consequences of secularisation.[1] This anxiety-making result of the "death" of God, so familiar in the West, has led to many attempts to fill the vacuum by a religion similar in some ways to historic Christianity but substantially new. These new religions or quasi-religions have differed in the elements which they have adopted from the old faith, and corresponding with these differences of theological content have been differences of social appeal. All such substitutes for Christianity are worth considering with respect and sympathy. Certainly the orthodox Christian churches are in no position to sneer at them, for had it not been for the churches' failure these new religions or quasi-religions would not have been necessary. But as the last quarter of the twentieth century approaches, we observe the failure of the new movements to replace Christianity in the hearts of the Western millions.

Aware of this failure, secular humanism is increasingly taking the line that there is no need to replace Christianity by any substitute on terms dictated by the religious tradition, for (it is suggested) modernisation gradually results in the disappearance of the need for "emotional reassurance", the need to which the old religions ministered; Dr. Bryan Wilson is among the humanists who offer speculations to this effect. Some evidence supports this conclusion, for Western man now seems to have less need of religion than he had before, as science has taken over many of the productive or medical jobs which were traditionally allocated to God or the gods. That is why theologians such as Bonhoeffer have joined in the chorus affirming that man who is "coming of age" may be becoming "religionless". That is why it was possible and necessary to write the first chapter of this book. But a total dismissal of the religious quest

[1] *Religion in Secular Society*, p. xviii.

must rest on the speculation that at some date in the future man's basic religious sense, hitherto one of the most obvious facts about human nature, will be found to have disappeared. When and if that phenomenon arises, it will call for consideration. All that is certain in the 1960s is that Christianity has not been replaced so far in the mind of the West. Western man is still shopping for a religion, and all the philosophies about the human condition need to be brought into relation with this fact.

The Religion of the Life Force

While Aldous Huxley brilliantly promoted Western appreciation of the timeless ecstasy in Eastern mysticism, his brother Julian was campaigning for a new religion based on the dynamism of evolution.[1] In an article evoked by the Bishop of Woolwich's *Honest to God*, he repeated his conviction that "religion in some form is a universal function of man in society, the organ for dealing with the problems of destiny, the destiny of individual men and women, of societies and nations, and of the human species as a whole . . . A humanist, evolution-centred religion too needs divinity, but divinity without God. It must strip the divine of the theistic qualities which man has anthropomorphically projected into it, search for its habitations in every aspect of existence, elicit it, and establish fruitful contact with its manifestations. Divinity is the chief raw material out of which gods have been fashioned. Today we must melt down the gods and refashion the material into new and effective organs of religion."[2]

Sir Julian Huxley's suggestion clearly deserves a careful hearing, for it deals with psychological and social problems to which many other humanists are curiously insensitive. These other humanists put forward a system of values as an alternative to moral anarchy after the collapse of religion. Free thought, free speech, freedom for physical and cultural pleasure, enjoyable friendships—these are usually found high among the values propounded as "humanism". Such values, if more widely held sacred, would indeed make the world a happier place; yet the vision and style of life urged by many modern humanists often seem luxuriously unrelated to the real priorities of actual existence in the world as most people experience this. This gentle humanism reckons too little both with the grandeur and with the misery of man; with the passions, despairs, loves, self-sacrifice and

[1] Notably in his *Religion without Revelation* (London, 1927) and *Evolution in Action* (London, 1953).
[2] Julian Huxley, *Essays of a Humanist* (London, 1964), Pelican edn., pp. 224-7.

dutifulness of the millions. European atheists, after the tragic experience of their continent, often know better than Anglo-American humanists what is the size of the task confronting a movement which would replace the Christian vision of human destiny.[1]

Sir Julian Huxley's quasi-religion of evolution is connected with the Gospel of the "Life Force" preached by George Bernard Shaw.[2] Huxley takes up the theme that science demands new attitudes in ethics and politics—another theme with a long history in our time, illustrated by the immensely influential works of H. G. Wells.[3] Evolution is clearly an idea whose time has come, and the divinity in it— the creative mystery which is the setting of the destiny of the individual and the race—may well be revered as almost God-sized. The stream of life can be pictured as flowing from sources fantastically improbable and remote into a future which will be as superior to our own time as our time is to these origins. *Homo sapiens* has, we are told, eight thousand years of civilisation behind him, but he emerged about a hundred thousand years ago. *Homo erectus* may have emerged a million years ago; life, three thousand million; the earth, four to five thousand million. Another two thousand million years may pass before the earth becomes uninhabitable; and in the history of the immeasurable universe, what will that matter? The stream of life on which man voyages is inseparable from the rest of nature, however unique life and mind may be reckoned. For mind itself is but matter organised in an astounding complexity, and all matter can be

[1] Secular humanism in the United States led to the foundation of the American Humanist Association in 1941 and was expressed in C. F. Potter, *Humanism: A New Religion* (New York, 1930); Corliss Lamont, *Humanism as a Philosophy* (New York, 1949); Walter Kaufmann, *Faith of a Heretic* (New York, 1961); etc. Sir Julian Huxley is cited here partly because in recent years the lead in this philosophy seems to have passed from American to British intellectuals. Examples of British attempts to work out an ethical code backed by a world-view are J. B. Coates, *A Challenge to Christianity: The Task of Humanism in Contemporary Society* (London, 1958); Reuben Osborn, *Humanism and Moral Theory* (London, 1959); Robert Robinson, *An Atheist's Values* (Oxford, 1964); H. J. Blackham, *Humanism* (London, 1968); *The Humanist Outlook*, ed. A. J. Ayer (London, 1968). Gerhard Szczesny, *The Future of Unbelief* (1958; Eng. trans., New York, 1961), reflected the situation in West Germany, where "after the failure of recent substitute religions, Christianity again seems like the unassailable treasure house of all human values" (p. 11). Szczesny opposed Christian dogma, but was none too hopeful about the acceptability of his fellow-atheists' values as the public philosophy for Europe, and he lamented that "as long as public opinion in the West insists that the world can be saved only by accepting Christian postulates as true, the period of unbelief will be greatly prolonged and ever new generations will be driven to cynicism, superficiality and stupidity."

[2] In *Back to Methusaleh* (London, 1921), etc., Shaw popularised ideas going back at least to the *élan vital* of Henri Bergson. See *Shaw and Religion*, an anthology ed. W. S. Smith (London, 1966); and for the background, W. S. Smith, *The London Heretics* (London, 1967).

[3] During the First World War Wells was so moved by current tragedies that he wrote two popular presentations of the religion of evolution, *God the Invisible King* and *Mr Britling Sees It Through*; but the Second World War so added to the depressions of his old age that he wrote one of a tragic century's unhappiest books, *Mind at the End of its Tether*. See Vincent Brome, *H. G. Wells: A Biography* (London, 1951).

studied as one stream of energy, with its source in the dance of its elementary particles. The stream of energy and the stream of life seem to be rivers more sacred than Ganges or Jordan.

Moreover, Sir Julian Huxley and other evolutionists are able to preach that a great purpose may now be seen in evolution. This purpose may be compared in some respects with the will of the traditional God, although in fact it has emerged out of the educational and cultural transmission of human values and skills, the basis of evolution being for Huxley the natural selection of random mutations. This purpose (if we may express it with an unscientific crudity) is the survival and progress of *homo sapiens* by the overcoming of the aggressive instincts which man has inherited from the animals. An individual who instead of either resting or fighting tries out a bold, new attempt to wrest a better life out of nature is, whether he be a bird or a scientist, progressive; a family which rears its infants well contributes to the progress of the species; and a nation which sub-ordinates its selfish interests to the interests of the human race is building up the peaceful world order which becomes essential to the survival of civilisation in the age of expanding, hungry populations and of nuclear armaments. In man's history evolution begins to be "conscious of itself", and man can to a large extent control his own evolution now—whether or not he becomes able to determine his future by the manipulation of the genes transmitted in the creation of new human life, thus entering the paradise of eugenics.[1]

However, when all that can be said in favour of evolutionary ethics has been said (and it may be a great deal more than many sceptical philosophers grant), there remains a basic difference between "is" and "ought", as the philosopher G. E. Moore emphasised in his exposure of the "naturalistic fallacy" at the beginning of this century.[2] This difficulty damages Sir Julian Huxley's evolutionary ethics, for it is impossible to be sure that the evolutionary process ("is") does in fact encourage all the forms of ethical behaviour which we admire ("ought"). Although the feeling that we ought to do what is right may be regarded as an instinct planted in us originally by the individual's or the group's urge to survive, and although many forms of ethical behaviour are clearly advantageous in an evolutionary perspective, this is not a complete account of ethics. Some acts of self-sacrifice which we admire as highly ethical are only remotely

[1] See C. H. Waddington, *The Ethical Animal* (London, 1960); W. H. Thorpe, *Science, Man and Morals* (London, 1965); Konrad Lorenz, *On Aggression* (London, 1966); Alex Comfort, *Nature and Human Nature* (London, 1966).
[2] G. E. Moore, *Principia Ethica* (Cambridge, 1903).

advantageous to either the individual or the group, and many less heroic choices which we have to make in everyday ethical decisions are hard to relate to what seems to be evolution's sole criterion: survival through fitness in adaptation to environment. Indeed, T. H. Huxley (Sir Julian's grandfather, who coined the word "agnostic") in his Romanes Lecture of 1893 declared that "the ethical progress of society depends not on imitating the cosmic process, still less in running away from it, but in combating it."[1]

What T. H. Huxley had in mind when he called on the moral Victorians to "combat" evolution was an ethical evolutionism very different from Sir Julian's. T. H. Huxley was attacking the ethics of Herbert Spencer, according to whom the science of evolution taught a gladiatorial view of life, in which free competition must weed out the unfit. Spencer, on this basis, opposed welfare or education for the poor. The harsh vigour of American capitalism was justified on the same "scientific" basis.[2] "Competition is a law of nature," cried the influential Professor Sumner of Yale.[3] Yet Karl Marx seriously thought of dedicating *Das Kapital* to Darwin, and Engels wrote much about the material basis of life as revealed by Victorian biology. Evolution has, in fact, meant many things to many people in the emotional life of society in the first century after Darwin;[4] and evolutionary ethics is an idea which is so ambiguous that we can see why, with very few exceptions, contemporary philosophers either ignore it or denounce it. Thus A. M. Quinton writes of Sir Julian's attempts in this direction: "Huxley realises that there are many possible lines of future evolutionary development . . . Huxley makes his selection by reference to higher values of a wholly extra-biological kind. An ethical theory that requires this sort of reinforcement, however much evolutionary material it makes use of, is not really an evolutionary ethic at all."[5]

We can see why many hold that it is far more useful to the causes both of science and of religion to be more or less sceptical about evolutionary ethics. Dr. David Lack, for example, writes that "natural selection is amoral, so cannot have produced man's moral

---

[1] See T. H. and Julian Huxley, *Evolution and Ethics* (Oxford, 1947), for a fascinating comparison.
[2] See Richard Hofstader, *Social Darwinism in American Thought* (Philadelphia, 1944).
[3] W. G. Sumner, *The Challenge of Facts and Other Essays* (New Haven, 1914).
[4] See J. W. Burrow, *Evolution and Society* (Cambridge, 1960).
[5] *Biology and Personality*, ed. I. T. Ramsey, p. 119. The essays in this volume by Dr. David Lack and Professor John Maynard Smith concur in this rejection of evolutionary ethics. The rejection was also made vigorously by a philosopher of science, Stephen Toulmin, in *Metaphysical Beliefs* (London, 1957), chapter 1.

or spiritual characteristics." About the origin of some of the most important of moral or spiritual characteristics, all men are, in Dr. Lack's words, "in the dark"; and they will remain in the dark unless the darkness is illuminated by religious faith. Only religious faith dares to suggest that man has these moral or spiritual characteristics because, while descended from other animals, while analysable by biology, physics and chemistry, man is also the child of God and in these characteristics is Godlike. Without religious faith, much of the moral and spiritual life of man must remain a puzzling episode, so that we repeat McNeile Dixon: "we are utterly in the dark . . ."[1]

However, the shakiness of its intellectual foundations may be of concern only to a minority of those to whom the evolutionists address their new religion. What concerns us more here is the question whether the new religion based on evolution is likely to give enough satisfaction to enough people psychologically. Here a large doubt must be expressed. The evolutionary process is magnificent, but the divinity in it is not God, and if human nature continues to want an object at all like the God of traditional religion, then evolution as the object of worship will not give an emotional reassurance at all like traditional religion at its greatest. At first sight the size of evolution may not seem to handicap it religiously. After all, Western mono-theism has insisted that God is infinite. But whereas the infinite God, being purely spiritual, had to be expressed for men in a definite symbolism, law, revelation or incarnation—in some object to which people could give their worship—evolution is a theory about a very great number of objects; and it is difficult for a worshipper to relate himself to a process which is as long as time and as large as the universe. The spectacle of evolution does not in fact easily arouse *worship*; wonder and fear are common reactions to it, but not religious worship. This is the equivalent in psychology of the philosophical objection that no amount of scientific facts, arranged by the theory of evolution, can produce *ethics*. The science of evolution is too complicated to be the basis of a new religion, if the religion is to serve even approximately the purposes which Sir Julian Huxley sees fulfilled in the old religions.

Indeed, it is very doubtful whether the quasi-religion prophesied by Huxley will allow room for any worship. In the essay already cited he grants that "what precise form these new agencies of religious thought will take it is impossible to say in this period of violent

[1] David Lack, *Evolutionary Theory and Christian Belief: The Unresolved Conflict* (London, 1957), p. 108. See above, p. 185.

transition", but he does exclude from his picture much of what man has usually thought essential to religious worship. "In place of eternity we shall have to think in terms of enduring process; in place of salvation in terms of attaining the satisfying states of inner being which combine energy and peace. There will be no room for petitionary prayer, but much value in prayer involving aspiration and self-exploration." Huxley further grants that "Christianity is a universalist and monotheist religion of salvation. Its consolidation and explosive spread, achieved through a long period of discussion and zealous ferment, released vast human forces which have largely shaped the Western world as we know it." But he believes that "an evolutionary and humanist religion of fulfilment could be more truly universal and could release even vaster spiritual forces."[1] We need not doubt that if more people agreed with Huxley's evolutionist philosophy mankind would be more co-operative and happier than it is now. However, we must be clear that, as a quasi-religion, evolutionism is no substitute for old belief in God. It gives us no reality which is really ultimate, despite Huxley's brave talk about an "enduring" process, for in evolution everything changes and everything in the end decays to death. Evolution cannot be trusted as the eternal God has been trusted. Evolutionism also gives us no purpose which really cares for us, despite Huxley's talk about a "satisfying" peace of mind, for in evolution no human life is significant except through its contribution to the progress of the species, in a vast time-scale. Tennyson's poem *In Memoriam*, published nine years before Darwin's *Origin of Species*, cannot after all be faulted as a vision of the ruthless cruelty of nature to the individual according to evolutionary theory. Evolution cannot be loved as the saving God has been loved. That is why H. G. Wells found no help from the religion of evolution when he came to the place where the old religion was at its strongest, where man's mind is at the "end of its tether". And that is why the religion of evolution has so far not caught on widely as a "religion without revelation". It is precisely the revelation of ultimate reality, of almighty grace, that is desired in the West's traditional religion; and no major artist, sensitive to the human condition in our time and serious in utter integrity (Bernard Shaw cannot be included in such a category), has found in evolutionism the answer to the anxiety of man now that this desire for revelation is thought to be a desire for an illusion. The only divinity that really matters to man's religious sense remains "dead" even if evolution is highly impressive, and the

[1] *Essays of a Humanist*, Pelican edn., pp. 227-9.

xistence of the individual—which is what matters supremely to
:very individual—remains, as Sartre and Camus said, "absurd".
Iere are severe handicaps in the struggle to create a new religion
:entred on evolution—which may explain why the quasi-church of
his quasi-religion has faced problems in attracting adequate popular
upport. The evangelistic problems of American secularism have
.lready been indicated. In 1968 the national membership of the British
Iumanist Association, after a membership drive, was under 4,000.[1]

The Religion of Nature

"It is not enough to formulate honest and high ideals," one British
atheist confessed recently. "We must also create the ceremonies and
:he atmosphere that will hold them before us at all times. I have no
:onception how to do this; but I believe it will be done if we try."[2]
Many people in our time also have "no conception" about how to
:reate a new religion—but they also have no belief that they could
do it if they did try. They feel that a "Catholicism without
Christianity" (T. H. Huxley's description of Auguste Comte's
"religion of humanity") needs something more than earnest trying
if it is to replace Christianity. There are, however, many people of
the highest intelligence and sensitivity who, while avoiding these
artificial attempts to create a new religion without God, still seek to
meet the needs of human nature's surviving religious sense within the
categories of secularism. It is the hope of such people that *nature may
be able to take the place of God*. Several things may be meant by the
serious cry for a religious return to nature, and a few aids to reflection
—maddeningly superficial as they must be—may not be irrelevant.

For a few, the religious value of nature may be mediated through
natural science. Clearly, there is an element reminiscent of traditional
religion at its best in science's laboriously truthful observation of the
world, in the comradeship of scientists who are thus pledged to truth,
in the dismissal of prejudices and passions, and in the moments of
ecstatic discovery. Science can certainly teach and sustain honest and
high ideals. But as a quasi-religion, science has this important
disadvantage: the public profoundly devoted to its cause is a minority
composed of intellectuals.

It is significant that Dr. Jacob Bronowski's widely read exposition of

[1] This figure does not include the total membership of local groups, but the Association's
failure to recruit a larger national membership must be a serious handicap in its efforts to
apply political pressure at the national level.
[2] Robert Robinson, *An Atheist's Values*, p. 157.

Science and Human Values (New York, 1958) never got round to answer
ing the question with which it began: was the atomic bomb of 194
the "baby" of modern science? The destruction of Hiroshima an
Nagasaki was, of course, a monstrous misuse of the physics of the ag
of Einstein, Rutherford and Bohr; and of course if the spirit of th
laboratory could spread into the world we should no longer be in th
position we at present occupy—when, in Bronowski's words, "th
body of technical science burdens and threatens us because we ar
trying to employ the body without the spirit." But the problem o
how to employ modern science is caused by the fact that most peopl
are not motivated by purely intellectual passions. Unless a totall
new society arises, the passions to which people are in fact subject wi
not be tamed by making them pure intellectuals; they will be tame
only by a wisdom which is relevant to them. Traditionally it has bee
the task of religion to nourish this wisdom, and it is a measure of th
corruption of contemporary religion that Dr. Bronowski in his boo
nowhere envisaged a role for religion in a scientific society as anythin
but the enemy of truth. "All science," he wrote, "is the search fo
unity in hidden likenesses," and that is a fine description of th
creative scientific mind as it contemplates and penetrates the surfac
of things; but all the religious vision is also a search for unity
Religion seeks the integration of the person in union with the tru
sum of all things. In the light of Hiroshima and Nagasaki, and of th
years since their horror, we may say—as so many, from Alber
Einstein downwards, have already said—that unless the wisdom o
religion can be reborn for the age of science the possibility of misusing
science on a catastrophic scale will remain.[1]

For some, *the use of science* in technical advance can provide th
fascination. At earlier times in this book we have reminded ourselves
of this fascination, and of the welcome which can be given to it by a
mature religion. What we have to mention now is that technology
itself can be a quasi-religion. "Technology has sacred overtones in the
minds of many," one sociologist observes. "To contravene the values
of technology in favor of, say, nationalism or economic profits can
seem as impious to a scientist today as contravention of religious ends,
in the name of economic gain, did to a medieval theologian."[2] In the

[1] The quotations are from pp. 78, 23 of the Pelican edition of Jacob Bronowski, *Science
and Human Values* (London, 1964). It is only fair to add that in his 1964 Preface Dr.
Bronowski wrote: "I would, were I beginning again, give some space also to a discussion
of those values which are not generated by the practice of science—the values of tenderness,
of kindliness, of human intimacy and love."
[2] Robert A. Nisbet in *Religion and Social Conflict*, ed. R. Lee and M. E. Marty (New York,
1964), p. 12.

960s this quasi-religious veneration for the conspicuous use of cience has, indeed, encouraged the diversion of fantastic proportions of the total resources of the Soviet Union and the United States in the race to be the first to land a man on the moon. Here—in a modern version of the moon-worship against which the prophets of Israel's God thundered—is epitomised the belief that technological advance hould take precedence over such causes as consumer-goods for the masses, or food for the children of the underdeveloped world. But we may wonder how many of our contemporaries would actually vote for that allocation of resources; or, at least, we may wonder how many would vote to reach the moon at all costs, were it not for the motivation in the moon-race of a greater quasi-religion, which goes by the name of patriotic pride. We may suspect that even in this age of triumphant technology, not many manage to sustain a devotion to applied science as the central enthusiasm of a lifetime. Technology is valued because it "delivers the goods", to feed and heal and comfort people; but many people fear that technology, if worshipped by itself, would produce a waist-high culture. So the contemporary cry goes up: to learn the wisdom of the heart, neither science nor the application of science is enough.

The clergy preach to more or less empty pews while the people, leaving their household gadgets behind, seek the God of the open air in considerable discomfort; and if the countryside cannot be reached, gardening may be more successful than theology in teaching the citizen on what he depends. And temperaments which are not in love with raw nature can find profound satisfactions through the contemplation of *nature interpreted through art*. The vast increase in popular enjoyment of the arts, so evident in the American enthusiasm for 'culture", cannot be due only to the spread of television, broadcasting, tourism, public libraries, paperback publishing and schools; part of the explanation of this enrichment of contemporary life seems to be that art speaks to depths of the personality where the old religion once spoke. Supremely through its growing love of serious music has our time been enabled to commune with the suffering and beauty, the order and grace in the world. Music struggles with mystery and music delights in goodness, as the sacred scriptures did for previous generations. So the art of man can interpret the world—can console and celebrate; and this is for many an effective (because not a self-conscious or artificial) substitute for the ceremonies and atmosphere of the old religion.

Estimates of nature or of art—especially estimates from a religious

point of view—should, of course, be made with due caution, bu
fortunately we need not plumb the philosophical depths here. If b
"religion" we mean a creed of the kind which Sir Julian Huxle
advocates—if we mean a quasi-religion of nature, or of man in nature
with no transcendent God—then of course a mountain-top or
picture-gallery or a concert-hall is the most likely cathedral of thi
religious atheism; and it is obvious that the interpretation of man'
basic religious sense according to the categories of a godless humanisn
by concentrating on the worship of nature or of art has attractec
many of the finest spirits of our time. But if we are asked to believ
that an atheist's love of nature or of art can be an adequate substitut
for the traditional worship of the transcendent God, then som
reasons for hesitation must be offered.

The love of nature, the love of art and the love of God can flourisl
together. A close and loving observation of nature is evident in th
psalms of the Bible and in the teaching of Jesus. While the art of th
Hebrews and of the early Christians was far from great, it is a matte
of history that Western painting and music—to say nothing o
Western drama and prose—were nurtured in the very churches wher
architecture rose to the heights of beauty, and no story in the worlc
has inspired so much, or such good, art as the story of Jesus. Th
recent breakdown of the Church's patronage of the arts has robbec
worshippers of a major source of inspiration, and has been a factor in
the feeling which many artists have that their society does not car
what they do. Some of the most important movements in modern
Christianity have been those which have sought to reconcile the
churches and the arts in integrity, as media through which the great
truth about the world may be celebrated.[1] In various ways, therefore,
it may be said that Christianity is so deeply in love with the world
that it is a religion of beauty.[2]

On the other hand, history forbids us to assume an *identity* between
the love of nature, the love of art and the love of God. Aesthetic
response and religious response are so intimately related that it is
not easy to be precise about the distinction between the two, but the
importance of seeing a distinction may be learned in the tragic history
of the distortion of artistic integrity to fit the demands of religious

---

[1] The best short book in this field is Roger Hazelton, *A Theological Approach to Art* (New
York, 1967).

[2] So Robert Bridges taught in his long philosophical poem, *The Testament of Beauty*
(London, 1928). Most later Christian poets, under the mighty influence of Eliot, seem to
have found that teaching too philosophical and also too romantically "beautiful", but
Christianity has been unable to divest itself of its own inherited beauties in stone and song,
which were in the background of the testament by Bridges.

sentiment or ecclesiastical censorship. The debasement of art by religion is a familiar enough story, and it is clear that such prostitution is avoided only when mutual respect, freedom and integrity mark the marriage of religious insight and aesthetic vision to make religious art. Now that art has escaped so widely from the tutelage of religion, we need to remember from the history of art that art has good reason to be suspicious of religion's arrogance.

But another reason for emphasising the distinction between the aesthetic and the religious is that neither nature nor art can happily perform all the tasks which traditional religion has allocated to God. The strict prohibition of artistic images of God in Judaism or Islam, and a long history of "iconoclasm" (image-breaking) and Puritanism in Christianity, bear witness to religion's suspicion of art. An individual may indeed regard the enjoyment of nature and art as a substitute for religious faith, and at least for a time this substitute may seem satisfactory or superior. But the limitations of art are liable to manifest themselves in an individual's character by producing a superficial aestheticism, which is the debasement of the artistic sense just as pietism is the debasement of the religious sense. These limitations also appear in the inadequacy of secular art to integrate a whole society, taking over the job done by traditional religion.

The first of these crucial defects is the remoteness of nature or art from the field of *personal relations*—from the field which remains the primary concern of human nature. Modern psychology confirms what common observation suggests: that almost all men and women derive almost all their deepest energies and satisfactions from their relations with their fellows. The pure nature-lover or artist, with little or no need of such fulfilment through society, is, like the pure scientist, in a small minority. The contemplation of nature or of art can calm troubled breasts and ennoble mean hearts, but it is not a real alternative to the speaking of heart to heart. Traditional religion has in fact offered a vast stimulus to human fellowship and a detailed and urgent commentary on personal relations, and if it is to be effective, a new religion must show similar warmth towards the personal. And how intolerably banal that sounds! It would be better to think about those great if sad last days of Leo Tolstoy, who gave up his art for Christ and the peasants.[1]

The second crucial defect in the aesthetic as an alternative to the traditionally religious has appeared in the failure of nature and of art to give *a satisfactory significance to personal lives*. For what is the purpose

[1] See, e.g., the biography by Henri Troyat (New York, 1967). Tolstoy died in 1910.

of human life? It has often been answered: to contemplate nature or art. But the human spirit in every age, including our own, is often left dissatisfied even by those natural glories. This dissatisfaction may come as the life of the senses ebbs away in old age—but also when a person is in the prime of strength. It may come in a bitter loneliness —but also as a search for the ultimate meaning of experienced love. Man in his obstinate belief may seek to enter the most fascinating of all relationships—the worship of the eternal God who, while perfect in his beauty, is also personal in his capacity to respond to love. Such belief may be dying out under the impact of secularisation, but we can recall from the past how many of the greatest artists, musicians, etc., have confessed that for them, in their celebration of the glory which they saw, the natural glories have not been enough. They have said that only God, with nature as his temporary garment and with art as the dim mirror of his beauty, can satisfy the human spirit. In our own time some great artists, musicians and writers have shared in that religious confession; and the alternative has been shown plainly enough, for many novelists and dramatists by their pictures of the desolation of life and death under atheism (and even by their own miseries and suicides) have told the true story of man's restless heart.[1]

Even this superficial discussion may be enough to suggest that nature has its limits as the basis of a new religion, for the worship of it does not mean so much to so many as the worship of the eternal God meant in the old religion. These limits of nature may come to be accepted as the limits of man's useful concern, but meanwhile the religious quest of the secular century continues.

Secular Social Gospels

If nature is dissatisfying because impersonal, where can we find a substitute for the "dead" God of Western religion? Many in our time have tried to reassure themselves emotionally through the ceremonies and the atmosphere of political movements which, while rejecting God, have developed the conviction of Jews and Christians that a glorious Kingdom is to come on earth. The Jews have paid very dearly in Europe during our savage time for giving birth to that Messianic hope, and no theme in the church history of the twentieth century looms larger than Christianity's rivalry with political totalitarianism.

[1] A useful survey of contemporary "images of man" was provided by Maurice Friedman *To Deny Our Nothingness* (New York, 1967). For further discussions see, e.g., Mircea Eliade *The Sacred and the Profane* (New York, 1961).

In Chapter 2 we considered briefly why *Communism* has been the most militant of these political quasi-religions. It has often been pointed out that the atheist Marx never entirely escaped the influence of his Jewish ancestry, and of Protestant theology mainly as communicated through the philosophical idealism of Hegel. History for Marx had a purpose, a purpose which people must serve if their lives were to have meaning. This purpose was opposed by many forces, but its triumph in the end was inevitable, and to speed that triumph men must join actively in the work of the one fellowship which is aware of the secret of history. The doctrines and scriptures of that fellowship must be kept clean as weapons in the fight. A day would come when the patient waiting of the oppressed would be rewarded. It would be a day of plenty, a day both of freedom and of justice for all, when the fulfilment for which men at present sought in vain through work would be granted to them in a perfect society. The class system would wither away. The state itself would wither away. Since each individual would receive from the community according to his needs, there would be no room for envy. Since each people could live in affluence, there would be no cause to provoke war or to encourage colonialism. All these are religious themes, going back to the Old Testament prophets (and to Zoroaster in Persia). These were the themes of the triumph of Light over Darkness, and these were some of the ancient details of the menu at the Messianic Feast. Marx gave these themes a secular twist, but he believed in them passionately, and the history of the twentieth century shows that it has been the religious intensity of Marxist faith, rather than the accuracy of its analysis of the future development of capitalism (which has turned out to be incorrect in almost every respect), that has filled the religious vacuum left by the spiritual bankruptcy of the ecclesiastical institutions of Russia and China and by the despair of the secularised intelligentsia in the West.

But we have only to recall the apocalyptic hopes of Karl Marx as the world moves towards the centenary of his death to realise that Schweitzer's Jesus was not more mistaken than he. Marxism has brought economic progress by its ruthless industrialisation, but when it has approached plenty, freedom and justice for all it has ceased to be Marxist. What has withered away has been Marxist dogmatism, through the development within the "Socialist" country of a more liberal and *bourgeois* atmosphere, with prosperity leading to private property and to private ideas. The power of dogmatic Marxism has been seen to rest to a large extent on the power of a police more efficient than the capitalistic police whom Marx denounced. Th weapon in its hand in the fight for social progress was the dictatorshi of the proletariat, but that weapon turned out in practice to be th dictatorship of the Party over the whole community including th proletariat, ruling by terror; and the Party's rule of terror is no openly criticised and abandoned (outside China). Marxism has als been seen to depend on an indoctrination of the people through th control of schools and of all means of publicity, and through th suppression of free speech—all of which has seemed a good deal mor formidable, and a good deal more repugnant, than the preaching the clergymen whom Marx attacked as the allies of the nineteenth century police.[1]

Marxism as a quasi-religion is now in the midst of the Chines chapter in its astonishing story (perhaps with the Indian and Lati American chapters to come). In Russia, and to some extent i Eastern Europe also, it is viewed much as the Christian tradition i viewed by most Western Europeans: as an impressive relic from th past, which few can now accept literally but which even fewer kno how to replace. In Western Europe, dogmatic Marxism is a spen force. The poor of France and Italy may still vote Communist as th best available means of protest against an unjust society, bu Democratic Socialism seems the clear victor in its long struggle wit Communism on Europe's political Left. In Britain and Nort America, Communism stands no chance at all in the electorat The enthusiasm of Western European or Anglo-Saxon intellectua for Soviet Russia as a "new civilisation" has not survived the succe sive shocks of the age of Stalin and its aftermath in the blood suppression of the Hungarian rebellion.[2]

Western intellectuals have therefore sought other consolations fc the emptiness which they have found in modern life, and thei approach to social problems has become more realistic, mor empirical. Instead of Karl Marx's Newer Testament, we get such

[1] Nicolas Berdyaev, a Christian prophet who was a Marxist as a young man but who w sickened by the Communist Party's brutalities, often drew attention to the eschatologic element in the Russian Revolution, and linked this with the frustrated idealism of Russia Christians. On the day of his death he completed his last presentation of this theme: *T Realm of the Spirit and the Realm of Caesar* (1949; Eng. trans., London, 1952). For a Con munist's welcome to an open attitude among churchmen, and willingness to listen to son Christian criticisms, see Roger Garaudy, *From Anathema to Dialogue* (1965; Eng. tran London, 1967). Donald Evans, *Communist Faith and Christian Faith* (London, 1965), summe up a vast literature in the growing dialogue.
[2] A well-known book of essays by ex-Communists was *The God that Failed*, ed. R. H. Crossman (London, 1950); and the indignation of a leader of American workers at t dangerous illusions of Communism and other quasi-religions of the twentieth century w voiced by Eric Hoffer in *The True Believer* (New York, 1951).

ook as Baroness Wootton's plea for more research in her *Testament r Social Science* (London, 1950). The development of the social iences to something like the status and usefulness of the natural iences is indeed urgent in our civilisation, and already immense enefits have come to mankind from such research and from its ear-headed application to modern social problems. But research is ot religion, nor is it an effective substitute for religion's power; and hen it comes to asking by what vision of destiny men shall live, the aroness joins the British Humanist Association, which we have seen) be faced by problems as a quasi-church for the secular West. 1eanwhile the Western masses, rightly or wrongly desiring a strong 1bstitute for the old faith, have turned to other quasi-religions.

Among these movements, the most powerful has been *nationalism,* 1ce described (by Edward Shillito) as "man's other religion". "By ationalism," writes Dr. Max Warren in a useful recent discussion, "I 1ean that deep inner attitude of mind which distinguishes one group f people, large or small, calling for an exclusive loyalty, which in the 1st analysis limits humanity to that group, and which tends all too 1sily to treat inhumanly those outside this group."[1] The examples of 'onfucianist China and Shintoist Japan are enough to remind us that 1is attitude has not been exclusively Western, but Western national- m has certainly flourished as a quasi-religion in our time. Com- 1unism itself has made most progress where it has run with the 1ighty wind of nationalism (as in Russia or China, countries which ave always been intensely patriotic) rather than against it (as in ussian-occupied Eastern Europe). When Marxist dogmatism has 1lly withered away, the Russian and Chinese nationalisms may be ft as its (bitterly quarrelling) heirs.

When the twentieth century began, very few intellectuals rophesied that the coming age would include the spectacle of eoples sacrificing their personal freedom and reason on the altar ` the state. Yet millions in this century have been glad to do so. urope in 1914 was a continent itching for war, because the 1triotism of the European powers, of the British and of the Irish, 1d reached fever pitch. "National self-determination" was the .cred principle in the peacemaking of 1918-20. When peace did not ring prosperity or dignity men turned to Communist, Socialist or 1scist nationalism because it claimed the power to end the exploita- on of the people by putting the key instruments of production and 1stribution, and the mass media of publicity, into the hands of the

[1] *The Missionary Movement from Britain in Modern History* (1966), p. 120.

state's nominees. "Nothing outside the state, nothing above the state or against the state; everything in the state and for the state" was the motto of Mussolini's Fascists, and the Fascist march on Rome in 192 inaugurated a Right-wing totalitarianism with which was a quasi religion of "blood and soil" no less militant than the atheisti Communism to which it was so loudly opposed. Here was if we may use in an unintended sense the title of the classic expression of Naz neopaganism "the myth of the twentieth century".[1] The rulers c the totalitarian states got their way by violence, trickery and tyranny but at the time millions agreed to this because their souls as well a their bellies were empty; they needed pride as well as food. In th 1940s, 1950s and 1960s a type of nationalism arose which was a fierce as anything in Europe's history: this was the nationalism of th peoples who had won independence from the European empires, bu were determined to advance out of primitive tribalism by a basi Westernisation. They used nationalism as the West's most poten export.

Nationalism has not been a religion according to the *Oxford Englis Dictionary*'s definition of religion as the "recognition on the part c man of some higher unseen power as having control of his destiny and as being entitled to obedience, reverence and worship". Bu nationalism, whether European or ex-colonial, is a quasi-religion because it provides visible powers as substitutes for the divine leaders who are acclaimed as fathers, saviours, prophets, philosopher and magicians, the architects of a country's wealth and virtue. Thi Messianic nationalism has used many methods reminiscent of religion initiation ceremonies at birth and coming-of-age, youth movement adult cells, public rallies such as those at Nuremberg under Hitle scriptural slogans such as the thoughts of Mao Tse-tung, sacre songs such as *Lead, Kindly Light* as the anthem of the Conventio People's Party during its dictatorial rule of Ghana, temples such a the lavish Congress Halls built in many capitals, statues to be focus for worship such as the representations of Stalin in colossa concrete, or of Nkrumah with the text inscribed beneath for th instruction of Ghana: "Seek ye first the political Kingdom. Nationalism has been sternly puritanical in advocating the practic of those virtues which do not conflict with the interests of a totali tarian state or of its rulers. Firm faith and hard work have bee demanded from every citizen, and, apart from the fate of the minorit who are unteachable and damned, citizens have been promised

[1] Alfred Rosenberg's notorious book was published in Munich in 1930.

lory which will come to their society, if not to themselves.
Nationalism has not hesitated to offer a glowing vision of Utopia,
ompensating for all the struggles of the liberation necessary to
leliver the country from an evil regime—and compensating also for
he natural, accidental or planned shortages of consumer goods and
or the heroic labours necessary to build the new society. Nationalism,
voking the idealistic spirit of self-sacrifice, has made a religious
mpact on our time, and it is not too much to detect in its appeal the
host of God sitting crowned on the grave of supernatural religion.[1]

Some Western countries have escaped, or have outgrown, the
onspicuous hysteria of nationalism, but that does not mean that they
ave no public philosophy. It simply means that their public
hilosophy is harder to define—and may be harder to maintain as a
alid long-term alternative to the religious faith which survives in
heir midst. This vaguer public philosophy does make for human
appiness; its problem is that, in the absence of a vital public faith,
finds itself called to do duty as a quasi-religion, where "gracious
ving" is believed to depend on the acquisition of a large number of
oods.

Many people in the West rebel against this cult of goods. One
eneration of the young therefore likes to think of itself as "beat",
nvying the beatitude which is claimed by those who "opt out" of
odern life. The protest of the next generation of youth can take
ore exciting forms. Marijuana, heroin and LSD have been widely
eddled in recent years as a means of obtaining the ecstasies of
ligious mysticism without the need to discipline oneself in prayer.
ldous Huxley suggested (or seemed to suggest) that Westerners in
hurry, unwilling to spend time on all the processes of the Eastern
ligion which he commended, might take a dose in order to see
od;[2] and since Aldous Huxley a thousand lesser prophets have
romoted the drug cult as a means of instant beatitude. It is arguable
hether this hippy cult is, or is not, less dangerous than the cult of
iolence which currently appeals as an alternative outlet for youth's
volt.

Those who disapprove of such habits in the young may find a
urpose in life in the lodges of Freemasonry and of the other Orders
hich bring middle-aged men together. Freemasonry, with its
orld-wide membership of six millions, clearly meets a need. Its

[1] Some relevant studies are S. W. Baron, *Modern Nationalism and Religion* (New York,
47); C. J. Hayes, *Nationalism: A Religion* (New York, 1960); Hans Kohn, *The Age of
ationalism* (New York, 1962); Ernest B. Koenter, *Secular Salvations* (Philadelphia, 1965).
[2] See his *The Doors of Perception* (New York, 1954).

European and Latin American branches ("the Grand Orient
tradition) have played an important part in the history of the centur
as a focus of militant opposition to the Roman Catholic Church
English-speaking Freemasonry has no such anti-clerical basis; indeed
it insists on belief in God. But all these Orders do seem to be fairl
described as substitutes for the churches. If only a social need wa
being met, bodies such as the Rotary Clubs, without ritual an
secrecy, would be enough; but what exists is a religious need. Bot
the younger generation and the middle-aged are—as many popula
songs affirm—looking for something.

   If secular people discover that neither drugs nor rituals will do a
substitutes for religion, but still desire a cause with which they ca
identify themselves, they can watch a sports team. If they need
myth of the good defeating the bad, they can watch a Western. I
they need more individual heroes, they can adore the stars c
entertainment. If they still need a cosmic vision to surround thei
lives, they can study "what the stars foretell" in many magazines o
journals which find no space for religious sermons. For astrolog
flourishes in the West as in the East, "luck" and "fate" are take
seriously, and a substantial proportion of the public appears to hol
magical views of reality.

   Indeed, Western society, as observed in daily experience or a
analysed by those few sociologists who have had the courage to mak
an accurate study of the real opinions of advanced peoples, i
scarcely "secular" in the style which is attributed to it by philosopher
(and even theologians) who hail the triumph of reason and experi
mental science. In fact, Western society is dominated by passin
fashions in which people find some identity and security—and thes
are fashions of opinion as much as of dress.[1] "In many respects,"
sociologist observes about contemporary England, "the doctrines c
the Church are much more sophisticated than average thinking, an
the problem is too little education and not too much. It would b
absurd to suppose that a population widely nurtured on the *Dail*
Express and *Old Moore's Almanack* finds the New Testament a
intellectual insult or Thomism not compatible with modern logic.
On the scepticism of the English intelligentsia he remarks: "Thes
prejudices are not genuinely understood so much as simply imbibe
with the *New Statesman* as the appropriate atmosphere for those wh
aspire to be intellectual." He concludes: "Technically sophisticate

---

[1] The classic analysis of the United States in this connection was David Riesman, *Th
Lonely Crowd* (New Haven, 1951).

cieties are capable of living by belief systems emotionally and
telectually crass to the point of nausea."[1]

And we have still not mentioned sex. That part of evolution which
considered by the Western belief system as most suitable for
orship is the distinction between male and female, as leading to the
production of the species. The rather elevated literature of the
umanist Associations may not fully emphasise this, but the truth
ay be that it is only through sex that the creative thrust of evolution
able to excite human nature deeply. We can worship the mystery
f sex, and an expression of our worship can be the physical or mental
njoyment of the sexual act. Here is the quasi-religion of modern
rophets so diverse as D. H. Lawrence, Havelock Ellis and Mr.
Iefner, the pundit of *Playboy*.

This new awareness of sex is indeed a powerful formulation of the
Life Force", and it has on the whole brought a clear benefit to
umanity, for it has rolled away a great burden of ignorance, shame,
uilt and misery produced by the Puritanical denial of the centrality
f sex in human life. But even sex as a symbol of the evolutionary
rocess is (over the years) often less satisfying than the traditional
mbolism of God the Creator—for the creative power of nature in
x, however impressive, glorious and delightful, involves men and
omen in emotions which can gradually turn out to be destructive
nd even tedious. Sex if placed not only at the centre but also at the
rown of life, sex if regarded as the object not only of honour and joy
ut also of a cult, sex if welcomed not only as grace and as fun but
lso as the one purpose in an aimless life, sex if worshipped can
amage many other activities which men and women tend to think
re valuable; and when it has satiated men and women, sex loses
ven its fascination. There may be signs of a new Puritanism arising
mong us. Often enough in the history of religion eroticism has served
s a substitute for supernaturalism, and has in the end been discarded,
sually in a wave of hatred for the flesh. Much human experience
ggests that sexual energy, while it enters powerfully and inextri-
bly into many activities which are not openly sexual (any realistic
icture of man must now be post-Freudian), can be disciplined and
blimated outside marriage—and experience suggests also that
arriage is itself not a purely sexual arrangement. History, we may
asonably (if tritely) conclude, teaches that sex should be enjoyed
nd used, not worshipped.

[1] David Martin, *A Sociology of English Religion*, pp. 114-15. For the information of
merican readers: the *Daily Express* is a sensationalist, the *Almanack* an astrological, and the
ew Statesman a Leftist, publication.

So it is that we find a London psychiatrist reminding us that "se
can become a god, and often does so; and a great deal of psych
therapeutic work with people of middle age is concerned with th
withdrawal of the projection of the god image from sexuality."[1] An
so it is that we find that the American Harvey Cox, who is normall
an enthusiast for secularisation, remarks that the secular world als
has its idols. When he surveys the pageant of Miss America (or Mi
Universe) on his television set, Professor Cox remembers that he is
theologian in the prophetic tradition. "After all," he writes, "it
God—not the Girl—who is God. He is the centre and source of valu
... As his gift, sex is freed from both fertility cults and commercia
exploitation to become the thoroughly human thing he intended.
And when Harvey Cox reads *Playboy*, where men use girls as play
things, he concludes: "It is precisely because these magazines ar
antisexual that they deserve the most searching kind of theologica
criticism."[2]

Certainly those who thoughtfully adhere to supernatural religio
may join the independently reflective secular humanists in hopin
that the spread of education will erode the power of these soft sub
stitutes for God. Most of the pleasures just described are, of cours
harmless enough in their proper places, and they or their equivalen
flourished in the epochs when traditional religion integrated society
The point of the criticism which is often made of them by dissatisfie
Westerners is that their place should not be God's place, in a cul
These things (many feel) should not be the things for which ma
lives. For if these things turn out to be the principal competitors wit
Judaism and Christianity as giving significance to human life, it wi
indeed be hard to attach much importance to the idea of huma
progress.

That has, of course, been repeated by many moralists. What is n
so often stressed is the degree to which the younger generation in th
West in the 1960s is itself actively idealistic in rejecting these gloss
prisons of the soul. The older generation may prefer to concentrate o
the small minority of the Western young which relies on drugs
enjoys violence in the course of political protest or is promiscuous i
its enjoyment of sexual intercourse; here, the older generation ca
play a moralising role while at the same time gratifying its curiosit
about (and envy of) the physical appetites of the young—a posture
old as history. But the serious point to be made is that youth seems t

[1] Anthony Storr in *Christian Essays in Psychiatry*, p. 80.
[2] *The Secular City*, p. 199. But Professor Cox subsequently became a contributor
theology to *Playboy*.

e as idealistic today as it ever was, even if drugs to supplement (or
place) alcohol and tobacco are more freely available, and even if
ontraceptives remove some of the obstacles to youth's traditionally
ot sexual desires. Personal relations—including the relations between
en and women, whites and coloureds, the middle classes and the
orkers—are often taken with a deep seriousness. The word "love"
pounded out with as much intensity of meaning as ever in the past.
Iarriage comes early, and great hopes surround it. The crude
ompetitiveness, the triviality, the artificiality and the emptiness of
eace, and the horror and futility of war, arouse as great a disgust
ith adult society as similar characteristics did when past societies
alled forth young reformers.

Since the collapse of Communism in the West the slogans of
olitical protest have been generally felt to be unable to absorb,
arry and justify this great mass of youthful idealism and energy; yet
ie religious vacuum of our time in the West is shown by the fact
aat it does not occur to most of the young that they, these splendid
ebels against materialism, are a generation seeking a religion—a
rusade in search of a cross. Religion to the bulk of this generation
eans a blind or hypocritical conservatism, and above all it means an
Iusion. Most of the young do not take seriously the gimmicks by
hich some clergymen seek to be relevant to teen-age fashions; and
ost of the young know little and care less about the churches from
hich these clergymen come. They would ask: "What are the
iurches now, if they are not the tombs and monuments of God?"[1]

New Spiritualisms

1 our time in the West, one of the substitutes for religion has been
piritualism. At first sight, this seems simply the opposite of materi-
lism. On closer inspection, however, spiritualism can be seen as a
ipplement to materialism, for it claims that death itself is powerless
o destroy the humanity whose glory is celebrated by secular
umanism, and it interprets eternity in the language of material
rosperity.

In the Spiritualist movement, the great problem to be addressed by
eligion has been seen not as the creation of material plenty but as the
irvival of physical death. The age-old attempt to pierce the mystery
f the grave has been organised afresh in characteristically twentieth-
entury ways: at the intellectual level through psychical research

[1] Friedrich Nietzsche, *The Joyful Wisdom*, p. 169.

using scientific methods as fully as possible; in the organisation efficiency of the Spiritualist Churches through the distribution literature, the convening of rallies, the formation of groups and tl support of expert leaders; and, finally, through a warmly compassio ate approach to the griefs of individuals mourning the loss of lov ones. It is typical of the religious inadequacy of the West that in many contacts with the dead as described by Spiritualists the majes of God's heaven, or the bliss of the nothingness of the Buddhis *Nirvana*, has been replaced by a profusion of trivialities—as the de express, or are made to express, their continued concern for tl details of earthly existence and for the domestic side of the after-li where these details are reproduced.

The new Spiritualism is thus to a large extent the old materialis projected beyond death. G. N. M. Tyrrell, in one of the mc thoughtful presentations of the lessons to be learned from psychic research,[1] declared: "When speaking of a future life, the finite ty of existence which psychical research appears to point to, must l clearly distinguished from the immortality which is the goal of tl mystic and which consists in attainment of union with the divine . It has been frequently stressed that telepathy and precognition gi us glimpses of an extended realm of *nature*. Why should not a futu life be another type of natural finite existence? . . . The idea th dying does not launch us into a religious sphere is quite simple on we have grasped the idea that 'nature' need not come to an end whe it ceases to be visible." Tyrrell urged that the Christian church should welcome these ideas, since "the traditional conception of tl supernatural has now become a stumbling block in the way of a reconciliation between science and religion."

Since the churches have on the whole clung to the old orthodox it is symptomatic of the religious need of our time that with fe external aids Spiritualism has established itself as, in some sense, underground church, and has sometimes been a setting for a spiritu life which the saints of the old faiths would have recognised. He sensitive spirits have been able to exercise the wonderful hum powers which the old faiths called mystical and miraculous—ar have done so in the context of a ministry of healing and teachin Here intellectuals have been able to contemplate "para-norma powers in human nature which at present lie beyond the reach the sciences and outside the scope of the usual philosophical attemp to explain man's mind—as witness the keen interest taken

[1] *The Personality of Man* (London, 1945), chapter 30.

sychical research by British philosophers as distinguished as C. D.
road[1] and H. H. Price,[2] and by some psychologists.[3] Here ordinary
.ortals have found reassurance about their places in the universe,
.d a fellowship with the living as well as with the departed. Their
·ief for a dead God, as well as for husbands or children or friends,
.s been calmed if not cured. To many thousands, and perhaps to
.illions, the most important achievement of the modern age has been
s proof that at least some people, for at least some time, can trans-
·nd their material limitations and can even survive death.

Not only death has preoccupied Westerners as a challenge to their
.aterial prosperity. No religious history of our time would be
)mplete without some mention of the general fascination with
.edical problems, which has included widespread interest in "para-
)rmal" healing. Our age in the West has been the first period in
:story to try to make medical care available to all, although the
:tempt has not yet fully succeeded. This massive programme of
·cial welfare has been accompanied by spectacular advances in
.edical science, extending its power to the diseases of the mind and
·scuing uncountable numbers of children and adults from the death
hich would have been their sure fate in any previous century. But
. the eyes of many thousands, and perhaps of millions, all this glory
· orthodox medicine has been dimmed by the religious impressive-
:ss of various medical heresies. Our time has been as interested as
.rlier periods were in the possibility that a man of faith (or at least
· "positive thinking") may order his emotional life better than the
nbeliever, may gain a strange mastery over his body and its ills, and
.ay even bring health to others.

From Rasputin at the Imperial Russian court to a faith-healer in
.e back streets of Chicago, many a strange personality has been found
nong those who have ministered to the Western desire to be cured
ithout the doctors. But this movement has not depended entirely
. personal magnetism. The modern literature of unorthodox
.edicine is enormous. In Christian Science, Mrs. Mary Baker Eddy
unded a religious body which is in many ways exactly what we
.ould expect as a replacement of the historic churches, and despite
s founder's death in 1910 this body has greatly prospered. The First
hurch of Christ, Scientist, Boston, or more precisely its Board of
rustees, wields an executive authority which the Vatican might

[1] *Religion, Philosophy and Psychical Research* (London, 1953); *Lectures on Psychical Research*
.ondon, 1962).
[2] *Some Aspects of the Conflict between Science and Religion* (Cambridge, 1953).
[3] See D. J. West, *Psychical Research Today* (2nd edn., London, 1962), and *Science and*
·P, ed. J. R. Smythies (London, 1967).

important, are as nothing compared with the soul's eternal destin
envy, and the *Osservatore Romano* is as a newspaper less respected tha
the *Christian Science Monitor*. The Christian Science Reading Roon
found in many places in the English-speaking, middle-class world c
much to ensure that Mrs. Eddy's book *Science and Health* is revere
and used as the indispensable key and supplement to the Christia
Bible. But for all its efficiency, this movement seems to owe its sprea
largely to the testimonies of people who have found light, health an
happiness through Christian Science. We cannot wonder that th
agnostic historian H. A. L. Fisher entitled the book which he wro
about it in 1929: *Our New Religion*.[1] Basically its teaching is th
matter is unreal beside spirit, and that diseases of the body a
illusions produced by mental sickness; thus if the mind is 'made an
kept healthy in accordance with Mrs. Eddy's teaching, the body wi
also be healthy. For 'this belief some Christian Scientists have lai
down their lives, refusing medical treatment when gravely ill.

We have here, argued and institutionalised, what William Jam
at the beginning of the century called "the religion of health
mindedness". The interest in "para-normal" approaches to deat
and disease, resulting in the churches of Spiritualism and Christia
Science, springs from the feeling that the churches have abdicate
from their proper concerns. Here is an apparently spiritual Gospe
a Gospel of personal survival and health, and the churches a
criticised for capitulating to the climate of the secular century l
their concentration on the social Gospel. However, this Gospel is l
itself no more adequate to sustain a new religion than is the soci
Gospel's baptism of a current philosophy of nationalism or inte
nationalism, individualism or socialism.[2]

What is lacking in the spiritual and the social Gospels, in compar
son with the great religions of the past, is a vision of reality compr
hensive enough, and profound enough, to be the truth which conver
great numbers of people, or which seems to them the very basis of
truthful and integrated account of the world. Through this enthus
astic acceptance such a vision unites, disciplines and energises
definite fellowship of adherents; and through this fellowship it ca
change or build a whole society. The Spiritualists are right to say tha
the social Gospel is not such a vision, for it deals with the temporar
It neglects that essential strain in religion which is "other-worldly
—which teaches that political and economic arrangements, howeve

[1] A more recent study is by C. S. Braden, *Christian Science Today* (Dallas, 1958).
[2] For some theological discussion of the "Social Gospel" movement among Americ
Christians, see below, pp. 308–315.

Caesar, however excellent a ruler he may be, however useful and honourable, cannot cover everything, and is not entitled to the complete self-surrender of immortal spirits. This applies even to the Caesar of the welfare state. On the other hand, the spiritual Gospel provides only a trivial commentary on life apart from the overcoming of disease and death. Thus we find G. N. M. Tyrrell complaining about Christianity's involvement in this world: "Would it not have been natural to insist that the Kingdom of Heaven is a spiritual state and not a state of society to be some day achieved in this world; that Christianity never promised that the world will be any better than it is today and, although we may hope it will be, that religion would be no whit perturbed if it were not?"[1] The spiritual Gospel neglects that strain in religion which teaches that the vision of ultimate reality heals not only the individual but also society as a whole, beginning with the Church, and conquers not only physical death and disease but also that vast state of man's alienation from the true source of blessedness which is usually called sin. Above all, the spiritual Gospel can easily become a Gospel about the powers inherent in man during his life on earth and after it (for a limited time?). God need not come into it. H. H. Price sensibly concludes that "religious people are compelled to postulate the existence, in some human beings at least, of what may be called super-sensory cognitive capacities," but that this telepathy between people is not at all the same as the sense of the divine. Psychical research, he points out, does nothing at all to establish the existence of God. "It only weakens the powerful intellectual inhibitions which at present prevent the question from being investigated."[2]

To sum up: neither the social nor the spiritual Gospel ends in the old vision of earth and heaven united in the eternal joy of the Communion of Saints, the City of God. Neither Gospel evokes more than a fraction of those intellectual, aesthetic and moral energies, those emotional and corporate forces, which have built up worship in the traditional religions.

New Religious Movements

In this situation, many in the West have reached the conclusion that there can be no substitute for religion, and they have interpreted

[1] *The Personality of Man* (Penguin edn., London, 1954), p. 283. In some expert students, "intellectual inhibitions" have not been weakened by psychical research. See, e.g., C.E.M. Hansel, *ESP: A Scientific Evaluation* (New York, 1966).
[2] *Some Aspects of the Conflict between Science and Religion*, pp. 47-9.

"religion" in the old sense as the attempt of the human spirit t
commune with a reality greater than it and greater even than natur
as a whole. This definitely religious interest, continuing in our society
accounts for the appeal of the new spiritual movements which deviat
from the traditional churches but retain many characteristics o
Christianity. New movements have flourished in the twentieth
century West because their religion seems to be rooted in Wester:
soil, either as a religion of the oppressed or more comfortably.[1]

An example of indigenous Western religion is Mormonism with it
new scriptures revealing the ancient history of America, tracing th
Red Indians to Hebrews who crossed the Atlantic after the fall of th
Kingdom of Judah, and recounting how the risen Christ planted th
Gospel and the Church in that continent. This teaching, which bega
in the 1820s, has become largely respectable after the admission of th
State of Utah to the United States in 1895, and its evangelism i
many places in our century may be seen from its present statistics
this Church of Jesus Christ of the Latter-Day Saints numbers almos
two million full members.[2]

Another American religious movement which has evangelise
around the world began in the 1840s: the Seventh Day Adventist
Another, exhibiting an even greater energy, began in the 1870s: th
Jehovah's Witnesses. These two sects differ in some beliefs, but bot
are obsessed by the Second Advent of Christ and teach that onl
144,000 persons will then be saved out of the human race. In man
ways their vigour preserves into our time something of the origina
deep protest-escapist or revolutionary—against the appalling con
ditions of the poor on "the Frontier" and in the industrial towns o
nineteenth-century America; they are churches for the disinherited
The revival of such a harsh Gospel was understandable in th
economic depression of the 1930s—a period when the poor whit
"Holy Rollers" in the countryside, or Father Divine's Negr
"Heavens" in the cities, also flourished. But it is symptomatic of th
spiritual need of the West that in an age of greater affluence so man
should accept teachings so bizarre.

Two million adherents are claimed by a less aggressively organised
more middle-class, movement of more recent origin: British Israe
which teaches that the white citizens of Great Britain and its forme

[1] For recent discussions with suggestions for further reading, see Horton Davie
Christian Deviations: The Challenge of the New Spiritual Movements (1954; revd. edn., Londo:
1965); Richard Mathieson, *Faiths, Cults and Sects of America* (New York, 1960); and Willia:
McLoughlin, "Is There a Third Force in Christendom?" in *Daedalus*, Winter 196
(Boston, 1967), pp. 43-68.
[2] See Thomas O'Dea, *The Mormons* (Chicago, 1957).

mpire (including the United States) are descended from the ten
lost" tribes of Israel and are the legitimate heirs of the political
romises made by God to Abraham. Larger numbers appear to have
een influenced by a movement also largely middle-class in its ethos:
Moral Rearmament. Originally known as "a First Century
Christian Fellowship", this movement had by the time of the death
f its founder, Frank Buchman, in 1961, ceased to be distinctively
Christian, but its religious basis may be seen in some continuing
haracteristics. It has waged its campaigns to counteract the West's
oss of morale during the economic depression of the 1920s and 1930s
nd more recently to influence the international conflict between the
American or Western ideology and Communism. It has taught the
Four Absolutes"—truth, honesty, unselfishness and love—and also
he need to turn to God for guidance in daily life; but in its enthusi-
sm it has used a mythology scarcely less improbable than that of
ritish Israel, for it has spread stories of miraculous changes in
ndividuals and in extremely difficult political or industrial situations
rought about by the conferences and plays which are its chief means
f propaganda.[1]

We have just mentioned five movements which have attempted to
eplace historic Christianity. Many more "Holiness Churches", etc.,
ave arisen, particularly in the United States, around prophets of
horter-lived effectiveness. Whether they originate among the
ppressed or among the comfortable, whether they look for the
oming of the Kingdom or say that it is among us if only we will
ead between the lines of our newspapers, such movements have in
ommon a falsity which is obvious to almost all whose minds have
een trained to think, and their incompatibility with education
eems to rule them out as faiths for the future. It may be that if the
West moves further from its Christian past, more successful religious
movements will arise to interpret Western man's new spiritual
ilgrimage. Such a movement would need a new prophet, even a
ew Christ. A number of writers have speculated about the possibility.
ome, like Nevil Shute in his novel *Round the Bend* (London, 1951),
ave suggested that the new incarnation of God will come out of
sia to relate Eastern wisdom to the civilisation symbolised by the
eroplane. Other writers, like Pierre Berton in his Canadian best-
eller, have speculated about a Western Christ to come: "some
piritual genius . . . who will take all the incredible laws, postures

[1] See A. W. Eister, *Drawing Room Conversion: A Sociological Account of the Oxford Group
Movement* (Durham, N.C., 1950); Tom Driberg, *The Mystery of M.R.A.* (London, 1964).

and myths of today's Church and turn them inside out . . . Such a
man would by sacrifice and commitment work his modern miracles.
He would have to be a man of vigour, humour, passion, concern,
guts, and, above all, action . . . It is axiomatic that he would be
reviled as the most dangerous of heretics . . . And it is in the cards
that society would find some modern means of crucifying him . .
Yet there would be one or two who, at the moment of his death
would be moved to the point that they would commit their own lives
to his ideals."[1] But in the history of the world only two men, Gautama
and Muhammad, have established their rivalry with Jesus over
centuries and for millions as the revealer and bearer of ultimate
reality among men;[2] and new Messiahs are liable to be judged by a
somewhat alarming standard in the post-Christian West, as may be
seen by the limited success which has come to the Bahai faith since its
announcement that Christ had returned to West Asia in 1863, in the
person of Bahaullah.[3] However unfairly, Europe and America are
liable to insist not only that a new Messiah must be crucified, but also
that on the third day he must rise again.

In his brilliantly written book of 1929, *A Preface to Morals*, Walter
Lippmann referred[4] to "the gifts of a vital religion which can bring
the whole of a man into adjustment with the whole of his relevant
experience." He commented: "Our forefathers had such a religion.
They quarrelled a good deal about the details, but they had no
doubt that there was an order in the universe which justified their
lives because they were a part of it. The acids of modernity have
dissolved that order for many of us, and there are some in consequence who think that the needs which religion fulfilled have also
been dissolved. But however self-sufficient the eugenic and perfectly
educated man of the distant future may be, our present experience
is that the needs remain. In failing to meet them, it is plain that we
have succeeded only in substituting trivial illusions for majestic
faiths. For while the modern emancipated man may wonder how
anyone ever believed that in this universe of stars and atoms and
multitudinous life, there is a drama in progress of which the principal
event was enacted in Palestine nineteen hundred years ago, it is not
really a stranger fable than many which he so readily accepts." And
many who recall the social and religious tumult which has come since
Walter Lippmann wrote those words, and which he has chronicled

[1] Pierre Berton, *The Comfortable Pew* (Toronto, 1965; British edn., 1966), pp. 143-4.
[2] See F. H. Hilliard, *The Buddha, the Prophet and the Christ* (London, 1956).
[3] See John Ferraby, *All Things Made New* (London, 1957).
[4] See p. 8.

with distinction, would say that as a diagnosis of the mind of the West those words still stand.

Not even Mr. Lippmann's own sketch of a humanist morality has filled the vacuum, for it presented as "maturity" a rejection of man's ultimate hope. "A man may take you into the open at night and show you the stars, but unless he feels the vast indifference of the universe to his own fate, and has placed himself in the perspective of cold and illimitable space, he has not looked maturely on the heavens."[1] Here the Mr. Lippmann of 1929 echoed Bertrand Russell's despair as the foundation of "A Free Man's Worship".[2]

Mr. Lippmann suggested "that the function of high religion is to reveal to men the quality of mature experience, that high religion is a prophecy and anticipation of what life is like when desire is in perfect harmony with reality."[3] In effect, this definition makes religion the grand debunker of desire. Reality is grim; religion has to adjust men to it. This is a twentieth-century revival of the Stoic philosophy of the ancient Roman empire, as we see when *A Preface to Morals* gives a highly Stoic definition of the "mature" man. Such a man "would take the world as it comes, and within himself remain quite unperturbed. . . . Since nothing gnawed at his vitals, neither doubt nor ambition, nor frustration, nor fear, he would move easily through life."[4] But the history of Stoicism gives the answer to this kind of hope. Stoicism was outlived by the very Christians whom its favourite philosopher, the Emperor Marcus Aurelius, despised and persecuted, because Christianity had what Stoicism lacked and what human nature wanted. It had *joy*. This joy was based on the conviction that, ultimately, "reality" is not indifferent to the fate of a sparrow, still less of a person. "High religion" which contains this joy teaches that mortal men desire too little, not too much. As a maturer Walter Lippmann has come to acknowledge in subsequent writings, for better or for worse it is a religion of joy, of "peace with

[1] See p. 187.
[2] Bertrand Russell, *Mysticism and Logic*, chapter 3. That famous essay of 1902, however, displayed the fervour of a Victorian preacher, rather than the ice-cold neutrality of a modern logician. On the one hand, the "firm foundation of unyielding despair" must be laid by accepting the truth that man's "origin, his growth, his hopes and fears, his loves and his beliefs, are but the outcome of accidental collocations of atoms" and are all destined to extinction". On the other hand, the "free man's worship" is "to burn with passion for eternal things" and to treat others so that "wherever a spark of the divine fire kindled in their hearts, we were ready with encouragement, with sympathy, with brave words in which high courage glowed." This attitude—like Russell's willingness to allow his life, even in old age, to be agitated by a passionate involvement in public affairs—shows a despair touched by faith, hope and love. It is a typically Victorian combination: see, e.g., A. O. J. Cockshutt, *The Unbelievers*, a study of English agnostic thought 1840–90 (London, 1964).
[3] See p. 193.
[4] See pp. 329–30.

God", that the American people insists on having in our time. An
in recent writings Mr. Lippmann has indicated his growing sympath
with the churches which repeat the Christian Gospel's offer of joy.

We may add that not only the American churchgoer is left dis
satisfied by a modern Stoicism. A British "humanist" such a
Professor R. W. Hepburn states that "given flaws of logic or evidence
much needs to be abandoned" in Christianity; but at the same tim
he gives a nostalgic sigh which is, if anything, louder than Walte
Lippmann's. "There may survive, however, moral concepts of
richness that shows up the meagreness of the humanist's own. An
there may survive ways of seeing humanity, transfiguration of th
supposedly familiar world, which—even when we are quite unab
to assimilate or domesticate them—can haunt and trouble and goa
the imagination."[1]

Here, it seems, is the real reason why the replacement c
Christianity is so hard to achieve. Many observers, while sharin
much of the conviction of Lippmann or Hepburn about the need t
abandon the old, *see no real alternative to the renewal of the Jewish
Christian tradition*, if "high religion" is to come alive for the moder
West. History teaches them how massive is the passion of heroisn
and saintliness which builds a religion, and how vast is the mechanisn
of tradition which sustains it across the centuries; and their knowledg
of the world as it is teaches them that if other faiths are to be com
pared with Christianity in this context, *no alternative to Christian belief ca
make good its claim.* Such observers are often oppressed by the odour c
decay given off by the contemporary churches, and their hearts ar
liable to break when they consider the plight of Christianity; but the
these observers may turn to contemplate Christianity's rivals, an
once again it becomes clear to them where the hope lies.[2]

Can a revival come after an almost complete abandonment of th
old churches? The longing to recover the primitive vitality of th
ancestral faith while discarding most of its traditional organisatio
has inspired a widespread movement of new churches, sects an

---

[1] R. W. Hepburn in *Objections to Humanism*, ed. H. S. Blackham (London, 1963), p. 54
[2] Mr. Leslie Paul, who in his autobiography first popularised the phrase "angry youn
man" and then bravely immersed himself in a prolonged study of the finance an
administration of the Church of England, might be understood from his writings in th
ecclesiastical field as a prophet of doom on the institutional Church. But in his philosophic
work, e.g. in his *Alternatives to Christian Belief* (New York, 1967), he analyses the failure c
these alternatives to answer the meaninglessness and misery which (on the evidence of th
serious secular literature of our time) he finds to be characteristic of the human situatior
It may be that in this assessment Mr. Paul relies too much on written evidence, which ofte
tends to be more dramatic and less complicated than everyday life with its small joys an
duties, but his analysis of the consequences of the West's loss of faith is more profound tha
that offered by many secular humanists.

'assemblies" in the West. These bodies are very varied in their beliefs
nd backgrounds, but many of the strongest accept the label
'Pentecostalism". Conservative—indeed, usually fundamentalist—
n its attitude to the Bible, Pentecostalism holds that the ardour of
'enuine Christianity, as presented in the Bible, is accompanied by
)henomena such as "speaking with tongues" and "faith healing".
['hus every Christian ought to know from his own experience the
:cstasies and extraordinary powers which came to the apostles at
'entecost. This modern "Baptism of the Holy Spirit" was experi-
:nced first in Los Angeles in 1907, but belief in it now unites a world-
vide movement whose evangelism has had special success in the
'acuum left by the corruption of Roman Catholicism in Latin
\merica.[1] At present the movement is largely working-class and
ectarian, and it often represents a protest against degrading social
.nd economic circumstances; but (as with many previous religious
novements) the sense of inner confidence, the Puritan moral progress
.nd the ability to co-operate in a cause—qualities which result from
he success of the sect—are already tending to bring consequences
vhich the early apostles did not expect. The sect's members rise to a
uperior social class; the sect itself is gradually transformed into a
espectable, organised and educated denomination. This process has
)een expounded in Dr. Bryan Wilson's two books, *Sects and Society*
London, 1961) and the more recent *Religion in Society*. Dr. Wilson,
vho so thoroughly investigated the life of the Elim "Holiness" sect,
he Christadelphians and the Christian Scientists, shows himself in
he latter book to be astonishingly ignorant about the traditional
hurches, which he constantly compares to their disadvantage with
he sects. Yet the future of Christianity does seem to depend on the
hurches more than on the sects—not only because the churches
till have an overwhelming numerical advantage over the sects (this
pplies even in Latin America), but also because, as Dr. Wilson
imself shows, the sects are becoming respectable denominations.[2]

When we glanced at religion in the United States in Chapter 2, we
oncluded that the over-simple distinction between the rebellious
itality of the sect and the established vagueness of the National
:hurch must be refined to take account of the denomination, a body
vhich is vigorous and self-aware without being sectarian in the sense
f being fanatically exclusive. It is significant that most reformers of

[1] See Donald Gee, *The Pentecostal Movement* (London, 1949) and Douglas Webster,
entecostalism and Speaking with Tongues (London, 1965).
[2] For an American sociologist's assessment of the sects and the churches, see J. M.
'inger, *Religion in the Struggle for Power* (Durham, N.C., 1946).

the denominations in the twentieth century have chosen to work from within these semi-established churches; there have been remarkably few serious attempts to found new bodies. Indeed, many of these reformers have emphasised the importance of reunion between the denominations. This ecumenical movement of Christian reunion has been the antithesis of sectarianism, yet it has probably been more effective than the sects as a focus for Christian renewal—and now there are prospects of many Pentecostalists joining the ecumenical movement's chief agency, the World Council of Churches. It may be that the future of the Christian community, and therefore the main future of "high religion" at least in the West, will lie in a process which looks very small amid the great dramas of our time, and very tame amid the exciting novelties: the renewal of the denominations.

Our survey of these new quasi-religions and religious sects suggests in brief, that Matthew Arnold's famous saying is as true in the twentieth century as it was in the nineteenth: "Two things about the Christian religion must surely be clear to anybody with eyes in his head. One is, that men cannot do without it; the other, that they cannot do with it as it is."[1] An American sociologist, E. A. Shils, has redently written a penetrating survey of the limitations of secularisation.[2] He concludes: "The need for order, and for meaning in order is too fundamental in man for the human race as a whole to allow itself to be bereft of the rich and elaborate scheme of metaphorical interpretation of existence which is made available by the great world religions. The spread of education and of scientific knowledge as well as the improved level of material well-being, will not eradicate them unless those who have these religions in their charge lose their self-confidence because of the distrust the highly educated hold toward the inherited mataphors." We may now draw one conclusion. *A renewed Christianity would still have a chance.* And so, in Part Two of this book, we may turn to see what is going on today inside the Christian religion. How is its fellowship being reshaped? How is its faith being restated? How do contemporary Christians struggle to receive "more truth"—which is their only hope if their religion is ever again to be the living faith of the Western millions? To these difficult questions, all of which have been very widely and thoroughly discussed, we may—with an impertinence made necessary by the need to be brief—suggest some tentative answers.

[1] Matthew Arnold, *God and the Bible* (London, 1875), p. xiv.
[2] In *The Religious Situation: 1968*, ed. D. R. Cutler (Boston, 1968), pp. 733-748.

PART TWO

CHAPTER SEVEN

A New Shape for the Christian Church

Reunion and Renewal

Many people who would call themselves Christians would say that Christianity needs no separate fellowship at all. "You can be a Christian without going to church" is a very popular slogan. And many practising members of the churches would say that Christianity now needs a fellowship with a shape different from any church's present shape. Throughout the century discontent with the churches has been voiced by Christians. It came to one climax after the First World War, when it seemed possible to remake the churches as well as the nations in order to serve democracy; and in the 1960s the second climax is still at its peak, when the inadequacy of the reforms of the 1920s is announced by hundreds of books and is expressed by despondent clergymen as well as by disgruntled laymen.[1]

The fact that Christianity is divided has contributed significantly to this prevailing sense that the churches need renewal. For one thing, there has been no united front in conservative Christianity. When it has been proclaimed authoritatively that "the Church teaches . . .", the inevitable question has arisen: *which church?* Catholic leaders have often been to the fore in attacks on Protestantism—just as Protestant leaders have often evangelised among Catholics and, in politics, have endorsed a secular approach to current problems (as in education) rather than risk the extension of Popery; and the 1960s, although they have witnessed a practising Roman Catholic in the White House and a saint in the Vatican, have not entirely cleared up all difficulties in this field. The most orthodox among the Christians

[1] In order not to burden this chapter with footnotes referring to a literature which is very large but mostly concerned with detailed problems or passing events, I may confess at once that much of the background of this chapter lies in my membership of the Editorial Boards of the three London periodicals *Frontier*, *Prism* and *New Christian* in the period 1955-66. At the SCM Press I had the privilege of publishing some of the reports connected with the British and World Councils of Churches, and I edited the popular reports on the historic conferences at Nottingham (*Unity Begins at Home*, London, 1964) and Geneva (*Christians in New World*, London, 1966).

have also been those most prone to fight each other, rather than t
work out a joint approach to the modern world.

Many have drawn the conclusions that something has disintegrate
at the very centre of a religion which is so deeply divided, and tha
the reunion of Christians, so far from being mainly a task for diplo
macy and administration, should be accompanied by far-reachin
changes. Among those who have seen Christian disunity as
challenge to a radical renewal have been many leaders of th
churches. This emphasis has been prominent in the work of th
World Council of Churches, which chose as the theme of its Fourtl
Assembly in Uppsala in 1968 the declaration attributed to Christ i
the Revelation of St. John the Divine: "Behold, I make all thing
new."[1] More strikingly still, Pope John XXIII and a clear majorit
of the two thousand prelates who assembled for the Second Vatica
Council in 1962 saw that the Roman Catholic Church must ope
itself to the criticisms of others, and must commit itself to *aggiorna
mento* (renewal). The gatherings of the World Council of Churche
and of the Roman Catholic bishops might easily have become occa
sions for self-congratulation, like most meetings of political move
ments. Instead, they have publicly and irrevocably expressed th
conviction that the disunity of Christians points to many othe
scandals now afflicting institutional Christianity; and they hav
confessed their own sins as well as the sins of fellow-Christians. Th
road to unity has thus drawn the churches out of their isolate
securities into a pilgrimage where the way is tough, the compan
strange and the destination scarcely known.

Millions of words of modern Christian self-criticism have bee
spoken or printed, but it is not easy to trace a strong thread runnin
through the debates. Clearly we need a new Reformation.[2] Few, i
any, of the major theologians of the twentieth century have avoide
comparisons with Luther and Calvin. But wanting does not make
Reformation, and it is difficult to find in these debates a realisti
hope of a renewal on a scale sufficient to create a new religiou
situation. An official of the World Council of Churches has voice
the despair of so many reformers: "If somebody has sufficient courag
to make a study of cynicism, he should buy the reports of all majo
ecumenical gatherings, read them, and see what the churches sai
together. Then he should go to the balcony of his house and loo
over his city at the churches that are standing there, from whic

[1] The most convenient introduction is provided by Norman Goodall, *The Ecumenica
Movement* (London, 1961).
[2] See, e.g., John Robinson, *The New Reformation?* (London, 1965).

teeples have risen to heaven since the Middle Ages, and see how
nothing has happened to them."[1] But the smallness of the change
achieved in comparison with the eloquence of the reformers is not
only the fault of the leaders of the churches; it also brings home to us
the difficulty which has been experienced by many interested
members of churches in gaining from the debates a clear and practical
programme of reform. So much of the prophecy has seemed either
vaguely idealistic or cruelly destructive. Conferences have come, and
conferences have gone; books have exploded, and books have been
forgotten; and the local churches, sullenly resentful or cheerfully
ignorant, have remained much as they were before the prophets
arose. The world has remained largely indifferent to the churches'
internal debates, except when these could provide material for a
brief melodrama of modern progress *versus* clerical reaction, or when
they seemed to touch on public questionings about political or sexual
morality. The humiliation of the Christian Church is the great fact
which stands out, and it often seems that the only solid achievement
by Christians in our age has been their acquisition of a spirit of
penitent humility.

However, even that modest achievement is something significant.
What needs most to be remembered against the background of
history is the rapidity with which the tree of new life has begun to
grow in this humble soil; and we can remember this when we contrast
our time with the nineteenth century.

The nineteenth century saw great activity in the churches of
Europe and America, and in comparison with the lethargy prevailing
over much of the previous century it might be described as the time
of the Christian counter-attack. It was a "century of hope" in
theological as well as in secular terms. Many new religious activities
were made possible by the secular advances. Missionaries could
travel the globe in the new steamers; preachers could stir evening
congregations thanks to gas-light; new churches could be built and
new societies could be organised. But the religion of the West in the
nineteenth century was essentially conservative. In its most self-
revealing intimacies it was nostalgic. It built many thousands of
churches, but most of them copied the architecture of the Middle
Ages. And in many ways that era of hope and expansion, with its
conservative basis, is today a burden on Christian consciences. Their
muscular confidence—all the righteousness and all the energy which
we sum up by the word Victorian—must often seem superior to our

[1] Albert van den Heuvel, *The Humiliation of the Church* (Philadelphia, 1966), p. 51.

own age of general anxiety, of intellectual confusion and of religious failure. In particular, the prosperity of the churches in the nineteenth century is now apt to arouse the envy of hard-pressed clergymen and doubtful laymen.

Yet there was an inherent weakness in nineteenth-century religion. Essentially, what happened then was the application of modern methods to old patterns of belief and behaviour; and these patterns were already doomed by the very modernity which gave them a temporary revival. In ethics, the old patterns of behaviour traditionally derived from Christian belief were still widely respected (often by hypocrisy, "the tribute which vice pays to virtue"), but they were being undermined by the shift in the social forces and by the questioning of the intellectual foundations of belief. The replacement of an Emerson or a Ruskin by a Lippmann or a Camus was inevitable, and those who adhered to some form of Christian belief could not expect to be spared all consequences of the growing revolution in morals. The modern insistence on education and amusement was satisfied partially and temporarily through the activities of the churches, with impressive results for the statistics of organised religion, but the steady growth of truly modern forms of education and amusement was bound to take the crowds from the churches in the long run. Many of the middle class went to church in order to demonstrate their respectability; but a secular life in a suburb would do this better. Many of the working-class, struggling to rise above degradation, used their local churches as means of relief and self-improvement; but their esteem for the churches depended on their own poverty, not on much conviction about the churches' teaching. Their sons and daughters, often housed in characterless but comfortable new areas, would inevitably turn for material welfare to the machinery of the democratic state, and would seldom feel any need for the churches as allies in the social struggle.

This insecure, even artificial, character of much nineteenth-century churchgoing can now be seen to have been associated with another basic defect: its quarrelsomeness. Often basically uncertain about what in the old religious tradition was really appropriate to a rapidly changing world, nineteenth-century Christians seem to have felt obliged to shout all the louder in order to cry up their rival wares. Their religion was often truculently controversial. It spent much energy in fighting atheism or moral ungodliness, and was seldom too selective in its choice of weapons for those fights; but it spent even more passion on controversies between Christians, even between

Christians of the same denomination. The Roman Catholic Church was the most militant, to its gain and loss; but the same spirit resulted in naked competition among the Protestants of America, and in England the spirit of controversy flared up in disputes between the Established Church and the Nonconformists (over the control of religious education, over the compulsory payment of agricultural tithes to the parish priests and even over the right to be buried in the parish churchyards). These competitions and controversies were still fierce enough to blacken at least the first decade of the twentieth century.

Half a century later, there is far less nostalgia and far less truculence in all the denominations. In a sense the churches, too, have "come of age"; they are sadder but wiser, less hearty, less brash, less self-confident, but perhaps no less effective in the mature religion of the spirit. The rise of a maturer charity may be attributed in part to a decline of interest in the religious positions taken up by past generations. The feeling grows that a new age is here. The old answers are, many think, irrelevant—because the old questions are not being asked. In the Roman Catholic Church, for example, the theological freeze which set in with the condemnation of modernism in the first decade of this century was thawed in the dialogue with Protestantism, and even with secularism, which began in the 1950s and 1960s; and already we can see that Roman Catholics learn, to the great profit of themselves and of the world, when they begin to listen before teaching. Within the non-Roman churches the hatchets have been buried for a longer time, and more deeply. A trend which is the central theme of their twentieth-century history slowly moves all the churches towards a reconciliation and a reunion which must jeopardise all their cherished institutions, and the costliness of this change explains its slowness.

The coming together of almost all the Presbyterians into a united Church of Scotland (1929) and of the different Wesleyan traditions into the Methodist Church (1932) were no small achievements in Britain. The union of Presbyterians, Methodists and Congregationalists to form the United Church of Canada (1925), and of these three traditions with the Anglicans to form the United Church of South India (1947), made history even more decisively. In 1968 it seems that in England the next few years will see the union of Congregationalists and Presbyterians to form the Reformed Church, and also the reconciliation of Anglicans and Methodists in "Stage One" of their progress to a full reunion. In the United States there have been significant unions of Protestants who were already heirs of one "confessional" tradition (for example, they were all Lutherans) but who were divided into separate churches because of differences in ethnic origins (for example, they were of German or Swedish stock), in colour of skin or in theological convictions (they were liberal or conservative). Inter-confessional conversations in the United States have been stirred up at various points in this century, but in the late 1960s they may be producing some action as a result of the challenge to full reunion thrown down in 1961 by Dr. Eugene Carson Blake, the Presbyterian leader who later became General Secretary of the World Council of Churches.

All these unions may seem trivial in comparison with the size of the century's challenge to institutional Christianity, but it needs to be remembered that the unions would have been inconceivable if there had not been a humble spirit of self-criticism within the institutions. Ever since the Lausanne Conference on Faith and Order in 1927, it has been clear that a United Church could not emerge without the acceptance of the unfamiliar, and the forty subsequent years in ecumenical history could be summed up as the progress of this unpalatable idea. Presbyterians have recognised that not all questions can be answered by referring back to the Scottish Reformation of 1560; Methodists, have broken away from loyalty to the local chapel and to the memory of John Wesley in order to ask how Methodism might best serve the Gospel in the twentieth century; Congregationalists have forsaken the cherished principle of the independence of the local congregation in order that Christians might combine for their contemporary tasks; and Anglicans have been willing to rethink and reshape institutions so venerable as episcopacy or (in England) the privileged establishment of the Church by the state. Baptists, while more conservative and usually standing apart from full reunion (specially the Southern Baptists of the United States), have not entirely lacked the ecumenical vision.

The search for Christian unity has, indeed, so far been the chief way by which the twentieth century has advanced towards Christian renewal. This is not to say that reunion will automatically result in renewal. On the contrary, the coming together of denominations into a Church apparently big and successful can increase any complacency and remoteness already existing in their leadership, and can result in institutional rigidity. The problem of how to achieve the desirable unity without sacrificing the desirable variety is specially acute in the United States, where very large numbers and physical assets would be involved in any major reunion such as Dr. Blake has envisaged. When a skyscraper is already needed to house the offices of the National Council of Churches in New York, there is evidently some substance in the fear among many Protestants that a Vatican-type organisation, consulting computers instead of consciences, might try to impose uniformity on the United Church of the United States. It has been said again and again that no such intention is, or should be, in the minds of those who promote the cause of Christian reunion, and on the basis of some historical evidence it can be argued that a Church which is large in numbers can also be rich in the diversity of the attitudes to be found in its membership. (The Church of England, for example, is established as the National Church, theoretically on the basis of the Act of Uniformity of 1662—but the Church of England in the nineteenth and twentieth centuries has been nearer to anarchy than to uniformity.) Yet the danger of uniformity is certainly present in any scheme for merging religious institutions and deserves more attention than it generally receives in the flush of ecumenical enthusiasm.[1]

The World Council of Churches in its Assembly at New Delhi in 1961 accepted as a definition of "the unity we seek" the idea that in each place all Christians should be brought together into one fellowship "joining in common prayer and having a corporate life". This definition may have been influenced unduly by the example of South India, where as a result of the comity agreements between the missionary societies the Protestants in a district tended to come from one denominational tradition. For the planning of Christian strategy in a Western city the New Delhi definition leaves all the crucial questions unanswered, except that it rightly implies that congregations should recognise each other, occasionally worship and witness together, and continuously co-operate for certain specialised tasks. Fewer congregations would be needed in a united Church, but many studies in religious sociology suggest that at the local level it is best not to merge *all* worshippers into a monolithic association, for a variety of religious communities can appeal to different neighbourhoods, to different temperaments and to different classes.

This kind of question illustrates another danger: that the reunion negotiations between the churches, with all the theological, pastoral, liturgical and administrative problems involved, will absorb over a long period energies which might have been devoted to relating the

[1] For a study of the American Baptists see Paul Harrison, *Power and Authority in the Free Church Tradition* (Princeton, 1959); and for an ecumenical symposium, see *Institutionalism and Church Unity*, ed. N. Ehrenstrom and W. G. Muelder (New York, 1963).

churches to the society around them. The introspection may continue when the formal reunion has been achieved. Although the Church of South India, for example, has made some progress in its contribution to the total life of India since it achieved unity in 1947, this outreach in service and evangelism has been less than many of its friends had hoped, and the basic explanation seems to be its continuing preoccupation with reunion problems—with problems, that is, which arise out of a Western theology and style of life rather than out of the living faith and culture of its Hindu neighbours. Since the Church of South India has often been used as the chief exhibit in the cause of Christian reunion, it is important that this sobering epilogue to the drama should be pondered.[1] We have to take strongly the warning that Christian reunion is not a panacea for all the diseases which afflict institutional Christianity.

But it must be repeated that reunion will often be the spearhead of renewal in the churches. Two reasons can be given for this.

First, the very sobriety of the discussions involved as denominations come together should remind us that, in order to make progress, *churches like individuals must start where they are and move one step at a time.* The habits of a church, as of an individual, grow into a mass of inertia. Radical pressures can thrust forward dramatically if instead of trying to alter these habits they try to create the ecclesiastical equivalent of Utopia: a Church new and pure. Many articles or books have been written in our time to voice the impatience of Christians with the Church as it is. Some actual communities have been founded to embody a radical group's vision of a purified Christianity. These utterances and experiments have had a great value in disturbing complacency. Yet much of all this brave adventure has got nowhere, for the whole experience of the century cries aloud that, in religion as in politics, Utopia never comes to this earth. No Christian body is ever totally renewed and purified, so that the Christian who waits for that event before committing himself to any church has to wait until he joins the celestial choir. Even the prophets of reform have their own limitations and weaknesses, their own conceits and follies which time reveals all too painfully, so that many in our time have become disillusioned on personal grounds with the prophetic call to purity. Even experiments in twentieth-century

---

[1] The classic statement of a biblical theologian's vision of the ecumenical movement as the rebirth of the Church as the Body of Christ and the Community of the Holy Spirit came out of the South India experience: Lesslie Newbiggin, *The Household of God* (London, 1953). Brave self-criticism was offered in the 1964 report *Renewal and Advance* by a committee under Mr. Rajaiah Paul.

discipleship lose their freshness, and need institutional structures if they are to continue their work; and those structures lead to fresh complaints that the happy pioneering days are over and the Spirit has again been quenched. And during all the impatience and experimentation of the radical minority, the great bulk of the people who are interested in religion does not come into close contact with these experiments, but forms its impressions of Christianity from what is routine and dull, particularly from the everyday behaviour of parents, teachers, clergy and lay friends or colleagues. If the impact of Christianity on the life of the total community is to be strengthened, it is therefore necessary to pay attention to possibly tedious problems raised by the ordinary life of the churches. If the present pattern of life in those churches is unsatisfactory, a preliminary impact is necessary, with a force large enough to disturb the pattern. The experience of the century has shown that, in religion as elsewhere in social life, no challenge to entrenched institutionalism is sufficiently powerful except the challenge of a definite plan to unite the existing institutions with each other. Only this apparently dull, administrative proposal brings about the necessary self-examination in churches from top to bottom, as leaders and led alike are driven to ask: what is essential?

Moreover, it is highly desirable that the problem of Christian disunity should be one of the first of the practical problems to be tackled, for *their lack of unity erects many obstacles for the churches in their approach to the people.* When the tide is flowing strongly in favour of churchgoing (at least in the middle classes), these obstacles are scarcely noticeable. The denominations of Victorian England or of the contemporary United States seemed to flourish because of their competitiveness. (At least, this applies to the towns; the division of a village by the building of several houses of worship has seldom been other than tragic.) But when the tide of fashionable religion recedes, or before it begins to flow, we see clearly that competition is on the whole bad for the churches. The need of a denomination to maintain a network of buildings and officials covering the country, when in any one area supporters are few, absorbs almost all that denomination's energy. It causes an introversion which is none the less real because it is thought to be inevitable, and which is greater than the danger of absorption in reunion negotiations. Complacent self-absorption is the disease; reunion is the beginning of the cure.

Despite many problems which would demand attention, it is probable that a United Church is better able than any of the divided denominations to plan a reasonable strategy and to make a reasonable use of its resources. The hope for the Church of South India, for example, is that greater strength will come if it has the patience to maintain through the problems of union the evangelistic vision in which its union was conceived.[1] It seems beyond question that, if the actual performance of the Church of South India has to some extent been a disappointment, the prospects would have been far worse if Indian nationalism in recent years had been able to say that Christianity consisted of small, divisive sects, each looking to the West for guidance and support. The fate of the Christian mission in China is a vivid warning. But the matter scarcely needs arguing. The need of Christian unity has for too long been recognised as urgent in Asia and Africa—which was why the modern ecumenical movement began in the "comity" agreements between Protestant missionary societies, in conferences of Protestant missionaries, and in co-operation over education, literature, etc.

Even in the prosperous denominations of the United States, where apparently competition seems good for religion, there are aspects of disunity which many Christians consider scandalous. One such aspect is the very appearance of adjacent churches competing for custom. Such rivalry seems remote from the New Testament's description of the fellowship of the Church as the Body of Christ, and devout Americans for whom that description is significant have their consciences burdened. The dependence of each local church on local popularity, while it has kept American religion in touch with the needs of the people, has contributed to the spiritual and intellectual debasement of popular religion to which Americans are increasingly sensitive.[1] The question coming to the fore in the United States, as the movement for Christian unity slowly gathers strength, is how this movement can increase the practical effectiveness of the Christian mission. One consideration which is being stressed is that, as the movement for "inter-faith" co-operation has already enabled the American religious bodies to speak and act together to a limited extent, so a further unity would enable a fuller witness and service, reaching out to the whole society of the United States. A crucial defect in the denominational pattern of American religion has resulted from the pressure on the churches to think primarily of the needs of their own members (with the largely unspoken fear that dissatisfied customers would transfer their membership to a rival),

[1] See A. M. Hollis, *The Significance of South India* (London, 1966).
[2] As we saw above, pp. 86-8, 93, 129-33.

instead of considering the religious task within the whole local community and the whole state. There has been a contrast between the lavish provision made for the internal life of their congregations in the churches of the United States, and the relative poverty of attempts to influence the national life in secular spheres.

In secularised Europe, particularly in Britain, religious worship and instruction through television, sound radio and the state's schools are the chief links connecting the Christian Gospel with the bulk of the people, and it is usually recognised that the use of these public media should be shared by members of different denominations. But special, often insuperable, problems have arisen in Catholic-Protestant co-operation, and even when the worship and instruction are interdenominational there remains the great problem of linking children or adults influenced through these media to actual congregations in which their faith might deepen and grow. The last mentioned problem may have been as significant as any other factor in ensuring that the vast amount of religious instruction put out by Britain's radios and schools has brought few recruits into the churches, although it has checked the general process of secularisation. Historians may well judge that the decisive defeat of Christianity in England was the failure of the English churches to agree about religious instruction in the nation's schools. Not until 1870 was it fully recognised that the Church of England could not educate the people in schools under its own control. Not until 1944 did the Church of England and the Free Churches agree on arrangements for the religious life of the state schools, and even then the syllabus of religious instruction, by concentrating on the Bible as the common bond of the denominations, was dangerously remote from the real interests of the children. In a country such as England, where religion tends to be a diffused and vague consensus rather than loyalty to the life of a particular church as in the United States, the ineffectiveness of religion in the schools has been almost fatal to the place of Christianity in the national life. It is not practical for churchmen to seek a remedy through the widespread expansion of church-controlled schools, although the Church of England and the Roman Catholic Church both still conduct large and valuable educational efforts; and the main hope of a more vital role for religion in the schools seems to lie in adventurous co-operation between Christians prepared to sink denominational differences.

Roughly similar lessons about the importance of Christian co-operation leading to unity are drawn by Christians familiar with the situations within other European countries, particularly West Germany and the Netherlands. Summing up, we may say that the boredom with the ecumenical movement which has been noticeable among Christian intellectuals in the 1960s (in the period when the ecumenical movement has for the first time made a major impact on the Christian public) is a betrayal of realistic hope for Christian renewal. The future of Christianity as a body, and therefore as a force, in the modern world seems to depend on the transforming influence which is being exerted on the churches by the World Council of Churches and by the Second Vatican Council.

The Emerging Church

Although it is difficult to see a continuous thread and a realistic hope in the century's ecumenical and other debates about the nature of the Christian Church, it is not impossible. On the contrary, enough agreement is emerging to enable us to glimpse what a Church may look like if, while remaining imperfect, it is substantially renewed and reunited—and to persuade us that the prospect may be more real at the end of the twentieth century than it was at the beginning.[1]

"The vision that arises," ran the famous Lambeth Appeal from the Anglican bishops in 1920, "is one of a Church genuinely Catholic, loyal to all Truth . . ." But that appeal for Christian unity, brave and moving as it was, did not begin far enough back, and this largely accounts for its failure to secure solid results after initial enthusiasm. Too much of this century's debate about the Church has been dominated by the question of institutional Catholicity, regarded as continuity with the early and medieval Church, *versus* institutional modernity; or by the question of the intellectual tradition, whether Scriptural or ecclesiastical, *versus* other parts of intellectual truth. Too much effort has been put too soon into the attempt to reconcile these elements. The more profitable vision that arises in the debate is of *a Church genuinely Christian*.

Such a Church would approximate, as closely as is possible for sinful mortals, to the singlemindedness implied in Dietrich Bonhoeffer's arresting phrase for the Church: "Christ existing as a community". In some sense it would be an "extension of the Incarnation", to use another bold phrase popular in some of the

---

[1] A more detailed discussion of recent signs of radicalism among churchmen will appear in my chapter in the *History of the Ecumenical Movement, 1948-68*, to be published for the World Council of Churches (London, 1969).

century's Anglican theology. It would recover for the life of Christians, as scholarship has recovered in theology, the New Testament's sense that the Lord who speaks to the churches is continuous with the Lord who spoke in Galilee. But this centrality of Christ in the Church, this dependence of the Church on the continuing life of Christ at its heart, would be experienced and interpreted like the life of Christ in the flesh and like the first disciples' reaction to their Lord. That is, the presence would be personal: it would be communicated through personal friendship of the Lord for the disciples, of the disciples for each other, and of the disciples for those who would turn to them; it would evoke a personal response, changing with circumstances, liable to misunderstandings and to failures of love, prevailing only because the personal appeal of the Lord Jesus and his saints was so attractive that it was able to persuade into discipleship without destroying the freedom of personal response.

The "extension of the Incarnation"—if that is at all an appropriate way of speaking of the Christian Church—must, it now seems, involve the abolition of legislative categories to describe the authority found in the Church, the abolition of the emphasis on discipline in the work of the Church's officers, and the abolition of mechanical ways of talking about the grace to be tasted in the Church's worship and life. Many modern Christians have been profoundly dissatisfied both with the rigorous and formal emphasis in Roman Catholicism, and also with Protestantism—whether Protestantism is "orthodox", emphasising the "wholly other" remoteness of the biblical God, or "liberal", emphasising the practical duties of daily life. Such Christians have sought a more spiritual religion, emphasising the contemplation of the eternal glory as every man's right. Such a search has often been accompanied by a recovered respect for the Eastern Orthodox tradition, but a very powerful statement of the cause of spiritual religion can come from Christians who remain entirely within the Western Church's devotional heritage. A personal, devotional and pastoral interpretation of the Church's role—a vision of the Church as servant rather than lord—probably represents the attitude of most churchmen today, but it runs up against centuries of legalism.[1]

The influence of Latin law on Christendom has, we may recall, produced in Christianity much of the rigour which Jesus attacked

[1] See, e.g., Kenneth Kirk, *The Vision of God* (London, 1931), a learned, eloquent and serene statement of spiritual religion. But its Anglican author, while Bishop of Oxford, later showed that he was not unaware of the usefulness of the rigorism and formalism of the hierarchical discipline in Christianity.

fiercely when he saw it in the corruptions of his native Judaism. Although Jesus never laid down a clear administrative pattern for the disciples whom he called to follow him and to be his "apostles" or envoys, Roman Catholics, and Catholic-minded people elsewhere, have insisted that his voice must continue legislating through the authorised succession of Popes and bishops and that all Christians must obey these judges; and the Calvinist tradition has affirmed that the Reformed, Presbyterian organisation of the Church is clearly laid down in the Bible. Although Jesus never hesitated to reinterpret the Old Testament boldly and never wrote a book himself, although he taught in short stories and in vivid exaggerations (that is, in Semitic hyperboles), and although the early Christians seem to have had few scruples in adding to or changing these words of the historical Jesus in order to express what they believed was the teaching of the Divine Spirit in the Church, Christianity has become a code.

The key question is now: *can Christianity be a community, but not a code?* The neo-orthodox reaction of the 1930s against Liberal Protestant individualism now belongs to history.[1] What has survived from it has not been an insistence on a particular organisation, such as may be found in countless volumes of Catholic polemic from that period.[2] We do not observe in many now the mood which made Dietrich Bonhoeffer defend the "Confessing" Church against the "German" Christians who compromised with Hitler: "Whoever knowingly cuts himself off from the Confessing Church in Germany cuts himself off from salvation."[3] Even in Roman Catholicism there has been a profound change of tone between the defiant wartime Encyclical on the Church of Pius XII, *Corpus Christi Mysticum* (1943), and the Pastoral Constitution on the Church which was the central achievement of the Second Vatican Council. The Encyclical called Catholics to their own discipline amid far worse terrors, and it called the world to a sanity which could be restored only by embracing the true Church; the Constitution, while abandoning no Roman Catholic claim, saw the Church as the fraternity of the faithful, almost all lay and including (in an ill-defined sense) even Christians who had not submitted to the Pope. The Constitution saw Christians, including

[1] An outstanding exposition was *The Gospel and the Catholic Church* by A. M. Ramsey, later Archbishop of Canterbury (London, 1936).

[2] For an Anglican example of insistence on bishops as essential, see *The Apostolic Ministry*, ed. K. E. Kirk (London, 1946).

[3] For Bonhoeffer then "the known God is our God"; God might have mercy on others, but the promise of God rested on the visible Church, and there the faithful should celebrate the uniqueness and wonder of the revelation. Bonhoeffer's article of 1936 on "The Question of the Boundaries of the Church and Church Union" was translated in *The Way to Freedom*, ed. E. H. Robertson (London, 1966), pp. 75-96.

ecclesiastical officers, as "holy" in the sense that they had been accepted by God; but they were sinners needing constant forgiveness and renewal. It saw the Church as "apostolic", for the whole Church was sent into the whole world to demonstrate the Gospel of love. What has survived the rebirth of the corporate emphasis has been the conviction that the Church is more than a voluntary association, for in its Spirit-empowered fellowship it was intended by Jesus as the prolongation of his work. The Church which wrote the New Testament felt the power of its living Lord in its own life—and if Christianity is not to be reduced to rootless, shapeless democracy, the Lordship of Christ over the Church must be recovered for our time. Many are coming to the conclusion that one way of bearing witness to this Lordship is to recover the leadership of the ministers of the Church—but it must be a leadership with a difference.[1]

In traditional theology, the ordained "ministry" has been interpreted as embodying Christ's three-fold "office" or role as prophet, priest and king—yet the word "minister" comes from the Latin meaning "servant". In the Roman Catholic Church and elsewhere, the "order" of deacons has been regarded as a mere preparation for the priesthood—yet the word "deacon" comes from the Greek meaning "servant". It is clear that the domineering clericalism which has afflicted almost all the churches has been a betrayal of the very idea of the Christian minister, and it is not surprising that a revolt has resulted.

Many young men who might have been ordained in a previous generation have preferred to serve the community, and therefore God, by a ministry or diaconate as school teachers or social workers. They have believed that even in a business career there will be more opportunities of giving effective service than would be likely to come their way if they were in the full-time service of a local church, preoccupied with worship or "services". There is an obvious truth in this emphasis on the role of the layman as a servant of the world for Christ's sake, and increasingly the more profound and creative thinking of Christians about the jobs of the Church's full-time employees is being set in the context of a theology of the laity. Other lines of argument which appeal to the younger generation are those which conclude that, if a man does decide to be ordained, it should be either as a "part-time priest" or as a specialist working outside the local church. It is ominous for the future of the American local

[1] I offered some thoughts about the ministry in *Not Angels but Anglicans* (London, 1958) and *This Church of England* (London, 1962), and edited two collections of essays, *Priests and Workers* (London, 1961) and *Preparing for the Ministry of the 1970s* (London, 1964).

church that such arguments are so often heard in the seminaries where the ministers of tomorrow are trained, but there is obvious truth in this insistence on the Church's need of a flexible strategy in a rapidly changing world.

If the isolation of the institutional Church from the everyday life of laymen is the major challenge, it follows that the acceptance of *honorary clergy*, who earn their livings in secular jobs, can be more than a device for getting "services" taken during a shortage of professionals; it can be a deliberate step to render a service both to the Church and to the world by recognising some men who have volunteered to carry in their own persons the tensions which come with an allegiance to both. Within the institutional Church, such men can make the voice of the world heard; within the secular world, they can have the thought-provoking strangeness of men set apart for God. Within the Church, they can help to break down the isolation of the professional clergy and can bring laymen out of lonely puzzlement and ineffectiveness into groups concerned with the realities of the world; and within the world they may be able to bring many through friendship to a know-ledge of Christ and the Church.

If such are possible roles for large numbers of honorary clergy, the need of *specialist professionals* in the ordained ministry, but not primarily in local churches, is even more apparent. In previous centuries—when parochial clergy were often themselves farmers and identified with the daily work of their parishioners—those few institutions which separated laymen from the routine of the village or town often had their own clergy. Such institutions were schools, colleges, hospitals and the armed forces. It is logical that in a much more complex, more education-conscious and more industry-shaped society more clergymen should feel called to work outside the old routine.[1] Perhaps the most healthy, although also the most painful, experiments in the twentieth-century Church have been those which have taken dedicated men into factories either as "worker-priests", identified with their mates in the labour movement, or as the professional members of an industrial mission. If the Church is to be vital in an industrial society, there must be many future experiments in new forms of "ministry". Among these experiments must be work reaching the controllers of industrial society—careful, humble work, in which theology is combined with a knowledge of economic and social problems.

But realism suggests that *a professional clergy serving a neighbourhood*

[1] See the World Council of Churches report, *The Church for Others* (Geneva, 1967).

through its local church remains indispensable. Despite all the attention which has rightly been given to the worker-priests and to the industrial missions, probably the most effective service given to the working class in the twentieth century has been given by the Christians who have staffed many thousands of unromantic churches in artisan housing areas. A literature has grown about the "down town" churches of America, but equally good work has been done by Christians who have no memorial. Writing by American Christians tends to play down the suburban church in contrast with the "down town" church, but here again we have to be on our guard against inverted snobbery: suburbanites also have souls, and it is not irrelevant to mention that the comfortable suburb may have a longer future than the industrial slum. The work involved in reaching, befriending and caring pastorally for thousands of people, whether in an artisan or in a middle-class area, does justify the full-time dedication of a man who is educated, trained and equipped. As automation reduces the physical labour needed in manufacturing, the "service industries" will absorb more and more manpower; and it would be ironical if in this situation a Church professing to love people as individuals were to be left without a corps of efficient professionals willing and able to give their energies to pastoral care. The tasks confronting Christian theology in a secular world are enough in themselves to justify the separation of many thousands of teachers who will give themselves to study and who will have the time and the experience needed to advise laymen in their own quest for religious truth. As the intellectual status of religion becomes increasingly open to question, and as society becomes more educated, it would be tragic if the Church were to be unable to supply for work of education anyone who had more than an amateur's experience in this field. And as the ordained "ministry", called to these pastoral and intellectual tasks, suffers under inevitable strains, it is surely right that there should be a few men set apart as pastors of the pastors and as teachers of the teachers, whether these men be called professors, chairmen, secretaries or bishops.

Against the idea of the priesthood as a separate caste, mediating between God and men and removed from the normal experience of men by a special training and dress and by the enforcement of celibacy, Protestantism insisted on the priesthood of all believers; and against the idea of the bishop as a feudal lord or as a civil servant, Protestantism healthily reasserted the equality of all ordained ministers. Presbyterianism in particular worked out an alternative to the Catholic structure of the ordained ministry. The minister in his parish would be surrounded, and it was hoped supported, by "elders", each of whom would have a definite role in the running of the church and a special responsibility for a part of the parish. He would also have the company, and it was hoped the inspiration, of neighbouring ministers in a group of parishes formed into a "presbytery". This presbytery would be represented in a provincial or national Assembly, the highest court of the Church. This system lessened the dangers inherent in the individualism of the Catholic priest or bishop, who was the monarch of his petty kingdom but might not be able to turn to any other human being for friendship and help in intimate equality. After many abstract arguments and practical controversies, the Protestant and Presbyterian view of the ministry has begun to prevail among most Christians. There is a growing awareness of the spiritual value of a group of priests, ministers or (the most ancient and useful word) "presbyters", with "deacons" or "elders" or other assistants, as a team at the heart of the work of a parish. More and more experiments are also being tried out which combine the clergy of a neighbourhood in a larger team, whether in a city or town whose social unity cuts across the divisions of parishes or in the thinly populated countryside. A vision of the whole city or of the whole rural district, a grasp of its urgent social problems, a recruitment of a task-force of Christians to help in these problems: all these things may be possible for the team but seldom for the individual. In the larger team, the main responsibility for the normal service of a parish remains with its own clergy, but in addition specialists can be appointed to serve the whole area in education, youth work, hospital or industrial chaplaincies, etc., and both the normal and the specialist work can be undergirded by worship, by common study and discussion of the Bible and by the useful or pleasant exchanges of friendship. In the French Catholic Church, the spearhead of mission is seen to be the *équipe*, or team of priests; for if the priests' fellowship is outgoing it can help to communicate the joy of love.

It is in such a setting that the work of a bishop comes alive: no longer as a lord but as a leader who is "first among equals". A bishop can play a vital part in keeping the specialist experiments of the Church in touch with each other and with the routine of the local churches; and a bishop who serves the clergy of the local churches by being the chief co-ordinator of their work, by being available for advice out of his experience in detailed problems, and by taking trouble to strengthen worship and study, shows why neither a committee nor an executive on a temporary appointment can be so effective as a bishop in the practical tasks of a pastor of the pastors and a teacher of the teachers.[1]

Much more could be said about the ordained "ministry" on its mysteriously spiritual side, but what matters most now is that the ordained, instead of talking about themselves, should *serve* more effectively. In some such ways as those which have just been hinted at, an understanding of the Servant-Lord may be recovered through the "ministry" of the ordained and lay leaders of the Servant Church.

Worship and Education

Among both Catholics and Protestants, one of the dynamic thrusts of the Spirit in the Church of our time has been through the "liturgical" movement, to renew worship. This movement can be understood as a retreat into an unreal, ecclesiastical world, or as a return to the primitive days of the Church for archaeological reasons, and this it often has been; but it need not be, for its essence is *an understanding of the worship of the Church as a drama in which all who take part renew their faith in the Lordship of Christ.*

This was the attitude of the primitive Christian community, but for many in the twentieth century it has become an interpretation authentically their own. The recovery of ancient usages has been only a symbol of this deeper recovery. The liturgical movement understands worship as a corporate activity, and so breaks down the separation of the Catholic priesthood or of the Protestant preaching ministry as a caste holier than the rest. The liturgical movement understands the whole of an act of worship as one drama, and so avoids claiming that the worship is valid only if the priest (or preacher) utters some semi-magical formula. The words which the congregation speaks or sings express a deep involvement in the action. The presence of the Lord Jesus can be felt in response to this strongly corporate, articulately expressed faith: the mechanism can be explained psychologically without it being necessary for us to dismiss a faith so deeply rooted in history, so closely involved in the problems of daily life, as neurotic or hallucinatory. Thus Baptism is honoured

[1] It is regrettable that the report *Relations between Anglican and Presbyterian Churches* (London, 1957), with its suggestion of bishops-in-presbyteries, was wrecked on the rocks of English indifference and Scottish nationalism. But it must be confessed that outside the overseas "mission field", an improved model of leadership by bishops has not been demonstrated clearly in practice.

in the liturgical movement by being rescued from its semi-magical status as something "done" to babies like an innoculation, and by being understood primarily as the reception of adults or children into the fellowship of the Christian community which is represented both in the Baptism and in the subsequent education of the baptised. The "Eucharist" (from the Greek for "Thanksgiving") is restored as the principal act of worship, but as a Holy Communion in which all jointly recall and re-enact the death-and-resurrection climax of the life of Jesus in the flesh, so that through the symbolism of the bread, dedicated and broken, and the wine, dedicated and outpoured, all may together receive the spiritual presence of the eternally living Christ. Babies, and bread and wine which are manufactured— nothing could be more obviously of the earth, yet through the sacramental drama they are made the vehicles of Christ's presence on earth. The sacramentalism which has grown in many parts of the Christian Church during this century has largely escaped from the superstitions which could fairly be attributed to much popular Catholicism in older days; and under strong pressures from secularisation it has demonstrated its ability to sustain many in the Christian fellowship which is incorporated by Baptism and fed by the Eucharist.

In the first days of Christianity, the celebration of the Eucharist took place in the course of a meal (the *Agape* or "love-feast") and before or after a normal day's work (this was, of course, before the Lord's Day, the weekly commemoration of his resurrection, had become the new Sabbath, the day of rest, in Christendom). These two facts about the primitive Church have helped to inspire twentieth-century efforts to rescue sacramental worship from an excessively religious atmosphere of unreality. First, the Eucharist has been followed by a breakfast or other social gathering when the communicants may meet each other as friends, so that the complaint "no one ever spoke to me" may be less justified. It is possible that bolder experiments may be needed, returning to that primitive custom by which the bread was blessed and broken, and the wine blessed and poured, as a "grace" at a meal, making clear the holiness of all food, drink and friendship in God's world. The old rules about fasting before Holy Communion have already been relaxed in the Roman Catholic Church and elsewhere, partly because (outside the North American pattern of Sunday morning at church) Sunday evening may be a convenient time for worship. Second, in many local churches ways are being tested to follow the congregation's service in church by service to the community outside. A church or group of churches may provide a Sunday school for the neighbourhood's children, a youth club with regular and tactful leadership, a coffee bar for teenagers and for others who wander our towns "looking for something", a housing association to help people towards better homes, a group where young mothers can help each other, some social stimulus for women whose husbands are away at work, a system for visiting the lonely and a club to which they are welcomed, a centre for psychological advice (specially over marriage problems), or a simple organisation to supplement the social services by helping the old, the sick and the housebound. When the Eucharist inspires such activities, it can be seen to be what it always has been in theory: a strengthening of effective love, an equipment for Christ's soldiers.

Here again, much more could be said on the mysteriously spiritual side; but here again, too much has already been said—and too little has been done, to show the Eucharist as the people's food.[1]

A radical personalism when applied to the Church's organisation and worship thus removes the over-heavy emphasis on the institutional and intellectual elements in the Christian religion. But this is not to deny that it is good for the disciples of Jesus to come together in order to think about their faith. On the contrary: it is to say that recent history shows how urgently Christians need new educational methods. For centuries Christian education has been confined almost entirely to the duty of listening as a child to a teacher, and as an adult to a preacher; and the nineteenth century was the great age of the Sunday school and the sermon. Our time, however, has seen in many places a decline in the amateur Sunday schools, and has found that religious instruction, even when given by qualified teachers in school hours, usually does not persuade most of the pupils of the truth of the religion being taught. During the twentieth century there have been some great and many good preachers, but both the world and the Church have taken less and less interest in pulpit oratory. These generalisations apply more to Britain and Continental Europe than to the United States, but the level of concern about "Christian education" in the American churches indicates a sense that, despite the immense expenditure of human talent and of money, all is not well. The search for more effective forms of education is for the most

[1] For summaries and reading lists, see J. D. Benoit, *Liturgical Renewal: Catholic and Protestant Developments on the Continent* (London, 1958); Alfred R. Shands, *The Liturgical Movement and the Local Church*, mainly British and American (1959; revd. edn., London, 1965); and J. G. Davies, *Worship and Mission*, mainly theological (London, 1966). But in many ways the charter of this movement is now the Constitution on the Sacred Liturgy, adopted by the Second Vatican Council in 1963.

part still at the experimental stage, but a consensus does begin to emerge that education, like worship, is meant to be a drama shared by the whole group—and is meant to be rooted in that group's ordinary life. Thus in a school, memorisation of the Bible is only a fraction of the educational task. Plays for young children and discussions among older pupils can do far more to enable the teacher to contribute relevantly to the class in terms relevant to the children's own abilities to imagine and conceptualise their intellectual questions and their psychological needs.[1]

A new look at adult education is equally important, for if it ever was possible for a Christian to go through the wilderness and storms of life like a camel, on the strength of an education acquired as a child and haphazardly supplemented by nibbling at sermons, that is a plain impossibility in a world changing so rapidly. The churches have given to adult education a very low status among their priorities and the alienation of so much adult thought from the world of the sermon has been the penalty paid. Only slowly and spasmodically are methods being worked out which involve laymen in a sustained and systematic course of training. For adults as for children, work in a group with freedom to question and contribute is normally essential if the teaching is to be relevant, but this presents a greater rather than smaller challenge to the teacher, and it requires the retraining of those clergymen who are familiar only with the authoritarian monologue of the pulpit.

It is often pointed out that laymen also are to blame: they are not willing to give time and energy to a deeper study of religion. The answer emerging to this objection is that the churches must rethink their priorities, sacrificing other activities in order to encourage adult education. Each local church needs rooms where arm-chairs face each other, instead of pews facing a pulpit. There laymen, respected as thinking adults, may come to terms with some theological and ethical teaching and may be able to absorb the truths in such teaching through an open and free discussion. Many (although not all) sermons in church can be sacrificed in order to make room for such education.

Each local church needs also to meet outside its own premises, in the homes of its members and their neighbours. At times Holy Communion may be celebrated on the kitchen table, or the Bible

---

[1] The American literature is far more voluminous, but I wish to record my debt to the two books by Harold Loukes, *Teenage Religion* (London, 1961) and *New Ground in Christian Education* (London, 1965), and my happy association with him in publishing the journal *Learning for Living*.

studied in the living room, but the pattern need not be formal. It is in such intimately small meetings that strangers can be welcomed and friends made, and it is out of the discussion, fellowship and prayer of such "house-churches" that a spontaneous wish may come to enter the Church's larger congregations. More and more churchmen in our time are coming to see that such groups are an essential part of the Christian's education at the deeply personal level, and that a congregation without them can be tragically impersonal. That is one of the lessons taught by the East Harlem Protestant Parish in New York, which since 1948 has brought some of the underprivileged people of that notorious slum together in a deeply impressive strength of Christian fellowship.[1]

But increasingly modern Christians are recognising also the importance of occupational groups and problems. The world of the local church is usually the world of the suburban home; whether on its own premises or in "house churches" its discussions may be remote from the work to which the men (and many of the women) give so much of their lives, partly because each job has its own problems— or at least its own expressions of the basic human problems. It is particularly in the discussion of the ethical and other tensions arising in a job away from home that the "lay colleges" are vital. In these "lay colleges" laymen—not only churchgoers—can feel quite free to speak just what is in their minds. Often this is nothing specifically theological or religious but it may reveal their frustrations in living, and the Church as an independent agency can have a useful role in sponsoring such probes into embarrassments. What is the purpose in my work for society and myself? What are the injustices, dishonesties and inefficiencies in the organisation which thwart the most satisfying human behaviour? How can relationships with colleagues and the public be improved? Such are some of the questions which arise. An answer may come slowly, both through the group's own discussions and through the contributions made by those who are more expert than the average layman in theology, psychology and ethics. Many new houses for lay conferences and training courses, adequately equipped with staffs, libraries, etc., are needed, and some have already been founded. The churches of the United States have a long tradition of "conference centers", and have strengthened that tradition since the Second World War. From the ruins of that war, there dramatically arose in Germany a serious and increasingly

[1] See George W. Webber, *God's Colony in Man's World* (Nashville, 1960), and Bruce Kenrick, *Come out the Wilderness* (New York, 1964).

elaborate attempt to bring laymen together in Evangelical Academies; and in the Netherlands and other parts of Europe, this German initiative has been taken up by Protestants and Catholics. But elsewhere in the world, lay colleges exist more precariously.[1]

A more educated, leisured and richer society may support such methods of Christian training, and a more united Church may be able to provide for them out of the economies elsewhere; but at the present stage of the twentieth century, it is impossible for the honest observer to do more than to record that there seems no alternative to a massive expansion of adult education if the churches are not to abdicate from the intellectual life of the modern world. The most hopeful signs that this challenge is being taken seriously come from the United States, but the American style of "lay training" is acknowledged to contain many defects, while apart from occasional "missions" or "campaigns"—which all too easily are unrelated to local realities and to the deepest problems of laymen—pathetically little is done in this field by the churches of, for example, Britain.

So we return to worship, as religion must always return. For if new houses for study and discussion are needed, so also are new centres for the deepening of the life of prayer. The Roman Catholic, Orthodox and Anglican churches have a long tradition of monastic houses and "retreat" houses where lay people are welcome to take part in the spiritual life of the resident community and to give time to private prayer, under guidance or alone. In recent years it has been seen that such houses need to welcome experimental methods in a definitely lay atmosphere, without forcing the monastic pattern on to lay people whose minds may be full of harsh problems thrown at them by contemporary experience. Some new patterns of monastic or semi-monastic life have been worked out by communities which are convinced that the medieval style of discipline is basically relevant to our disintegrated age, but must be adjusted in modern conditions. Few recent developments in Protestantism have attracted so much spontaneous interest and loyalty as the Taizé Community in France and the Iona Community in the (Presbyterian) Church of Scotland.[2]

It is in this context that the future of the great houses of prayer should perhaps be seen. In Europe many of these cathedrals or large

[1] The story of the renewal of German Protestantism after 1945, greatly helped by these Academies, has been told by an American scholar, Franklin H. Littell, *The German Phoenix* (New York, 1960). When Dr. Hendrik Kraemer, who crowned his career by service as Director of the Ecumenical Institute at Bossey, delivered the Hulsean Lectures, he produced Protestantism's first treatise on *A Theology of the Laity* (London, 1958).

[2] An introduction to these centres of renewal was provided by Olive Wyon, *Living Springs* (London, 1963).

churches have been inherited from the pious or proud church-builders of the Middle Ages; tourists flock to them in ever-increasing numbers, but tourism is not accepted as their sole purpose. In America, and to some extent in Europe also, massive new churches have been built within this century, and the future will have to face the question, what cause they can serve apart from being examples of architectural skill. It is often said that such cathedrals are follies now that Christendom is over, and clearly new building projects deserve to be scrutinised. But a time when new houses are clearly needed for lay conferences and for private prayer, a role may be discerned for some buildings which teach worship by their own majesty. Aesthetic standards are being raised in the whole population. and these great churches can make a relevant contribution precisely by aiming at excellence—in their beauty as buildings, in the art old or new which they house, in choral or instrumental music, in the regular offering of the praise of God and in special acts of worship, where the aspirations of the community may be dramatised.[1]

The current mood of contempt for the local church must pass if Christianity is to have a strong future, but from the "house church" to the cathedral new structures of the Church need to be developed, supplementing the local church. What has just been written may seem visionary, but every sentence has behind it a substantial body of discussion and of experiment somewhere in the world.

Catholic Substance and Protestant Principle

Paul Tillich spoke about modern history as essentially "the Protestant era" because it is based on the questioning of inherited traditions. The key idea in the work of the Royal Society in seventeenth-century London, for example, was experimentation. Instead of consulting authorities such as Aristotle or Galen, the scientists would examine nature for themselves; and Thomas Sprat, the Bishop of Rochester who wrote the history of the Royal Society, explicitly compared this appeal to nature with the Protestant appeal to Scripture, behind and if necessary against all ecclesiastical traditions. But Tillich also saw that Scripture was too remote and ambiguous to provide the sole basis of a living religion. The message of the Bible must be conveyed to our time by generation after generation whose experience was in

---

[1] The ideals and work of the new Coventry Cathedral are described by H. C. N. Williams, *Twentieth Century Cathedral* (London, 1964).

294   *Religion and Change*

its essence identical with the experience of the prophets and apostles; and it must be expressed in our time through the living voice of a teacher and, above all, through the life and worship of a religious community. Tillich, for all his insistence on a Protestantism based on the psychological drama and "ultimate concern" of each individual, never forgot his Lutheran childhood—or the debt of Martin Luther to the Church of the Middle Ages. He therefore spoke also about the importance of "Catholic substance". By this phrase he meant that tradition of people and buildings, myths and rituals, dogmas and customs, which nurtured the Protestant individual, which spoke to him at a level deeper than everyday reasoning, and which by its own depth encouraged him to interpret the meaning of its symbolism of the ultimate for his own concern and for his own existence.[1]

Tillich was by no means isolated among modern Protestants in his guarded respect for "Catholic substance". The adoption of many traditional customs of worship (prominence for the altar, candles, surplices, etc.) and of ancient prayers and hymns such as *Te Deum Laudamus* in the churches of the Free Church tradition has coincided with an emphasis in Catholic circles that the ardour of devotion, the dignity of ordered worship and the beauty of disciplined holiness constitute the true spirit and splendour of Catholicism—not any institutional or doctrinal rigidity or any frigidly "correct" copying of the past. This increase of traditionalism in the atmosphere of worship has been accompanied by a breakdown of individualism in matters of belief. For the triumph of criticism is only one fact about the twentieth century; another is the triumph of collectivism. The days of the lonely Protestant getting instruction from his Bible without help from priests or commentators seem to be drawing to a close, despite the remaining power of Fundamentalism; and the appeal to tested experience instead of the sacred book, the new essence of Protestantism, seems to result in practice in a willingness by laymen to learn from each other in discussion and from the experts, whether this learning process is conducted mainly through the local churches (as in the United States) or through broadcasting and television (as in Britain).[2] The community is needed if the message of the Bible is to be heard as relevant. The twentieth-century Christian community is needed—for other laymen can speak convincingly about what the message of the Bible has meant to them in their lives, and the ordained

[1] See the essays by Paul Tillich, *The Protestant Era* (Chicago, 1948) and his dialogue with students, *Ultimate Concern* (New York, 1965).
[2] See, e.g., the reflections on the growing sophistication of American Christians offered by the pastor-sociologist, Anton Boisen, in his *Religion in Crisis and Custom* (New York, 1955).

leaders of the Church can attempt to bring all these diversities into a living whole. But the community of the other Christian centuries is also needed in the background, and here theologians can be useful. Thus within non-fundamentalist Protestantism the tendency has been to abandon the battle-cry of the sixteenth-century Reformation, *sola scriptura* ("test all doctrines by Scripture alone"), and to substitute for it a more subtle appeal to a more comprehensive tradition embodying the total fact of the Christian community of all times and places (*sola traditione*).[1] But the question remains: what is the significance of the tradition now? *What is Catholicism for us today?*

"It is not of Catholicism in the grip of the exploiter, but of Catholicism as a living and lived religion, as a school of souls, that modernists are thinking . . . It is the spirit of Christ that has again and again saved the Church from the hands of her worldly oppressors within and without . . . It is easy to quench a glimmering light caught by the eyes of a few; but not the light of the noonday sun— of knowledge that has become objective and valid for all. It is through knowledge of this kind that God has inaugurated a new epoch in man's intellectual life . . . Shall He do less for man's spiritual life when the times are ripe? And are they not ripening?" So in the 1900s George Tyrrell voiced a hope which, at the time, he seemed to take to a tragic grave.[2]

In the 1960s we seem to be witnessing the partial fulfilment of that hope of a new day; but the new day has not dawned in the way that Tyrrell expected. Catholicism in the age of the Second Vatican Council is, in Tyrrell's words, "saved" by "the spirit of Christ"; but the Spirit of Christ saves the Church not through a new theology "valid for all" but through the mostly gradual and mostly hidden renewal of the fellowship which may at a later stage make the theology which is needed. So in the 1960s we can say only that the times may be *almost* ripe for the inauguration of the new epoch in man's spiritual life, for a Catholicism greater than anything yet seen in the history of the Christian Church.

Before the 1960s the question "What is Catholicism?" might have been answered in one of three ways. Catholicism might have been defined as that which has been believed everywhere and always by all Christians. However, in Christian history few propositions have enjoyed popularity on that scale, and a solid institution could not be

---

[1] The latter slogan came near to being adopted by the World Conference on Faith and Order sponsored by the World Council of Churches at Montreal in 1963.
[2] *Christianity at the Crossroads* (London, 1909), pp. 280-2.

built on the basis of them. Secondly, Catholicism might have been defined as the reproduction of at least the most important elements in the Church of the first few centuries, particularly its doctrinal councils (although the authorities might have disagreed about the dates of the period to be imitated); this was the appeal to antiquity. Thirdly, Catholicism might have been defined as the devotional and doctrinal system developed by the Papacy and its obedient sons in the Counter-Reformation of the sixteenth century and in the Catholic Revival of the nineteenth.

But the Second Vatican Council and the debates around it have introduced the possibility of a more comprehensive understanding of Catholicism. It was not that the Council, or more than a few Roman Catholic theologians commenting on it, clearly envisaged the possibility that the full-orbed Faith might not have been delivered to the primitive saints and transmitted from them through all the Christian generations. No disagreement between the early Church and the modern Church of Rome was stated, and any intention of changing doctrine was always explicitly renounced. The infallibility of the Pope when teaching faith or morals *ex cathedra* was assumed. Nevertheless, the Church was no longer immobile. The Church, instead, seemed to be a mystery not fully disclosed: a company of sinners on pilgrimage, "human, all-too-human", as well as the holy People of God whose redemption has already been purchased. No period, ancient or modern, was held up as perfect. Instead, with penitence for any errors (a penitence voiced by Popes John and Paul), the Roman Catholic Church turned in humility to the tasks of the future. In the great words of the Pastoral Constitution on the Church in the Modern World: "Inspired by no earthly ambition, the Church seeks but one solitary goal: to carry forward the work of Christ himself under the lead of the befriending Spirit. And Christ entered this world to give witness to the truth, to rescue and not to sit in judgment, to serve and not to be served." The concessions made by Vatican II to the good will of non-Christians and to the Christianity of non-Catholics were vital to progress, but in the long run are likely to count for less than this overall emphasis on hope as well as memory.

In making these concessions to present realities and in turning to the future, Catholicism has begun to recognise that it is incomplete. Neither the Church around the Mediterranean in the fourth century nor the Church of the Middle Ages in Western Europe (as reorganised in the Counter-Reformation) is now seen as a model to be copied everywhere and always. On the contrary, reunion with the Eastern

Orthodox or Western Protestant churches has been seen as more than a matter of their absorption into Rome; the existence of a North American activism has been recognised (partly by the sheer fact of international gatherings financed largely in American dollars); and the possibility has been envisaged of a genuinely African or Asian or Latin American spirituality, abandoning many of the European or North American patterns of life and thought and re-clothing the Gospel. The Second Vatican Council talked in Latin, but the diversity of peoples represented among the bishops at the Council made it unlikely that Catholicism would for long preserve the place of Latin, or much other uniformity, in its fast developing life. The Council met in subjection to the Pope, but the theory was made clear that the Church is governed by the bishops together with the Pope, in an indivisible college, and the practice of decentralisation in authority, with a regularly meeting Episcopal Synod as the cabinet in Rome, seems likely to follow. The Papacy may be emerging as a fatherhood encouraging the unity of the spirit in a richly diverse world-wide Church—as the global equivalent of the bishop who locally will be "first among equals". The pilgrimages of Paul VI to Jersualem, Bombay, New York and Istanbul and the reforms of 1967 in the Church's central administration have perhaps been hints of a new Papacy, and that vision may survive Pope Paul's reactionary decrees of 1968 on faith and morals.

The revolution in the understanding of Catholicism may be summed up by emphasising that the word "Catholic" means basically the same as "ecumenical"; that is, it means "universal" (the two words derive from Greek). And the modern history of the word "ecumenical" enables us to state the revolution in the total understanding of the Church's task in the world. For many years "ecumenical" was used to describe the world-wide body of Christians; thus the Second Vatican Council was summoned as an Ecumenical Council. Then it was applied to the special aspect of Christian reunion. In recent years, however, it has been expanded to cover the whole inhabited earth, the Greek *oikoumene*. The essence of Catholicism may thus be defined as the belief that as Christians hasten to the ends of the earth and to the ends of time, they will meet there more and more of Christ, until an ecumenical wholeness is given. As Dr. Hans-Reudi Weber has written: "On this way to the centre and to the frontiers Christians and churches discover that unity which is both God's will and his gift. The ecumenical concern for unity sees church unity as the first fruit of the promised unity of all. It commits us to the struggle for manifesting this unity among Christians and in the whole of humanity. It aims not at conservative reunion or static uniformity, but at the growth into the wholeness of God's rich economy of grace."[1]

The Church in the World

The main contribution of the Church to the twentieth-century world will, it seems, lie in the quality of its own fellowship and thinking. The Church will remain a minority, but it may be a creative minority if its own members can give evidence that they have found here relationships between loving people, and quests of free minds, superior to those normal in the world. "The Christian Community," as Emil Brunner once wrote, "is the great miracle of history, and history is the proof that the gates of hell shall not prevail against it. There can hardly be a more overwhelming personal experience of this miracle than when it is granted to one to greet brothers in Christ in the far east and far west and in many lands inhabited by men of other races, tongues and cultures, and to strengthen one's faith by uniting with them in common prayer to the one Lord. The institutions which we call churches . . . have built up the shell in which this precious kernel has been contained and preserved"—although also, as Brunner went on to say, concealed.[2] The World Conference on Church, Community and State, which met at Oxford in 1937 on the eve of war, with Martin Niemöller who was to have been a chief speaker already in prison, was one of these "overwhelming" experiences, and it was remembered most for its message that "the first duty of the Church, and its greatest service to the world, is that it be in very deed *the Church*—confessing the true faith, committed to the fulfilment of the will of Christ, its only Lord, and united in him in a fellowship of love and service." The message of the conference added: "We do not call the world to be like ourselves, for we are already too like the world." It is therefore neither surprising nor entirely regrettable that so much of the energy of Christians in our time has been given to what seem to be the internal affairs of the churches—to their reunion and renewal. Various factors are involved here. Placed as it is among many other communities or associations in a pluralist society, and having to adjust to the end of a monolithic Christendom, the Church must be more self-conscious than it was in many past centuries. And the self-consciousness which is inevitable may turn out to be bene-

[1] *Asia and the Ecumenical Movement* (London, 1966), p. 44.
[2] *The Misunderstanding of the Church*, p. 116.

ficial. Many voices are still heard, in the 1960s as in the early years of
the century, protesting that the Church is not needed nowadays—
that it is enough for a modern follower of Jesus to make his own
prayer (or vaguer meditation) in secret and to live his own life,
answerable only to his conscience. Such voices do not take the ethos
of secularisation with sufficient seriousness. The "secular" civilisation
which is built on modern science is in some ways the heir of
Christianity, as we have seen; and if it is free of the ideologies which
can be more narrow than the religions which they replace—if it is
really *pluralist*, really open to all the truths glimpsed by its members
—it will not wish to persecute the Church. But if Christianity is to
make its own characteristic contribution to this pluralist society, it
must (it seems) do so after a certain amount of spiritual reflection and
human fellowship in circumstances which are shaped by itself—
otherwise the salt of the earth loses its savour, as Jesus himself warned.
And if the individual Christian is to play in modern society a role
which is related responsibly both to his fellow-men and to his God, the
need of a definitely Christian preparation for the tasks of the world, a
preparation which is renewed in forgiveness after successive failures,
becomes a personal necessity for him—otherwise he will for practical
purposes cease to be a disciple, his spirituality choked by the cares of
the world or withered by the long noonday sun like the growing crop
in the parable of Jesus. In the modern world, more and more
Christians are coming to see that taking the secular seriously means
re-thinking, not abandoning, what belongs distinctively to the Church
of Jesus Christ.

Few, if any, churches in the modern world have been more effective
as national churches than the Church of Scotland, and it is worth
recalling the noble words of the Articles Declaratory of the Constitution of the Church of Scotland in Matters Spiritual, as accepted by
Act of Parliament in 1921. In these Articles, "the Lord Jesus Christ"
is declared to be "King and Head of His Church". Therefore the
Articles continue: "The Church of Scotland, while acknowledging
the Divine appointment and authority of the civil magistrate within
his own sphere, and holding that the nation acting in its corporate
capacity ought to render homage to God and promote in all appropriate ways the interests of His Kingdom, declares that it receives
from its Head and from him alone the right and power subject to no
civil authority to legislate, and to adjudicate finally, in all matters
of doctrine, worship, government and discipline in the Church,
including the right to determine all questions concerning membership

and office in the Church." It is clear that in other countries a satisfactory adjustment of the relations of Church and State cannot be reached on any other foundation, although the precise details of the Scottish settlement may not be reproduced. And it seems probable that both Church and State would benefit greatly in many countries from such an establishment of a free National Church.

Indeed, it is precisely through its own distinctive fellowship that the Church can make a much needed contribution to contemporary society, and it is only on the basis of a measure of success in establishing such a fellowship that the Church may reasonably expect to be listened to when it pronounces on the affairs of the world. The need of the world to become one world has been emphasised by so many prophets that the cry has become a platitude, but in a divided world the growing unity of Christians from many nations is one of the few efforts to reach a global community which have solid and tested achievements to show. If not the "great new fact of our era", as Archbishop William Temple fulsomely called it in 1942, it is still deeply significant. The fellowship expressed in the World Council of Churches, and the internationalism of the Roman Catholic Church, by their sheer existence and continuance under strain are modern miracles of faith.

Nor is the unity of the Church instructive and useful to the world only at the level of international politics. Locally a small and unglamorous congregation of Christians can bring into a real unity representatives of deeply divided classes, races and generations; it can hold together people from very different cultural and intellectual backgrounds; it can even hold together people with clashing personal temperaments. Similar things are done in secular organisations and in non-Christian religions, and the Church often fails to do them: but the fact remains that very few other bodies, if any, have attempted to build unity on the same scale as the Christian Churches—out of many millions of ordinary people, not merely combining them for speeches or prayers but making them an active fellowship where individuals co-operate over a long period of time, in a deeply personal encounter without ceasing to be themselves. In such congregations of the Church we learn why Professor Herbert Butterfield surveyed the Christian contribution to the civilisation of Europe in these terms: "It was by bringing society in general from the lower to the higher level of religious experience that the Church most promoted the cause of civilisation itself, and most affected the character of our western world. Those who preached the Gospel for the sake of the

Gospel, leaving the further consequences of their action to Providence, have always served the world better than they knew, better than those who worked with mundane purposes in mind—sometimes they served the world better than they desired or intended to do . . . Those who . . . nurse the pieties, spread New Testament love and affirm the spiritual nature of man are . . . guarding the very fountain."[1]

In the double schools of discipleship in the Church and apostleship in the world, the individual Christian is gradually trained into maturity. All religion, including the Christian religion, can be used as an escape from reality into fantasy; but we saw in earlier chapters that we are not compelled to conclude that a wish for fantasy was the origin of all religion, and as we observe many religious believers living and working in the modern world we may incline to the conclusion that, whatever may be the truth of their beliefs, their religion has strengthened them as human beings. Religious believers have a special stimulus to co-operate with others and to give themselves to the worthwhile duties of the moment, for they believe that their companions are also the sons and daughters of God—and they believe also that their work, however unromantic or unrewarding, is also the work of God. Being human themselves, they seek satisfactions from their life and work, and from the admiration of others, but when these are not forthcoming they do not entirely despair, for the secret springs of their lives are their desires (however feeble and intermittent) to live and work for God's sake. When they are helpless through sickness or age, religious believers can stabilise their anxieties on the faith that "man's extremity is God's opportunity"; but the "coming of age" of man as the son of God means also that man's strength—the delightful fulness of his powers of body and mind—is also God's opportunity for the accomplishment of great purposes for mankind. And what is true of the maturing effects of all real faith in God seems to be specially true of the faith which can find its special inspiration through the embodiment of God in the man Jesus.

When the purpose of the Church is seen as the maturing of disciples into apostles, and as the service rather than the conquest of the world, then the true character of the Church's contribution to social progress may be seen more clearly.

Catholic Action in Modern Society

The reluctance to accept the world as having its own dignity in its

---

[1] *Christianity in European History*, pp. 25, 55.

creation by God, and the desire to impose the Church's own notions on all the world, have died hard in our century. We think most readily of the pretence in much Roman Catholic teaching that the world must return to the Church for the cure of all its troubles Paradoxically enough, the Second Vatican Council's decree on Modern Communications was a typical example of that failure to communicate the Gospel by a failure to take seriously the persons and structures to whom the Gospel was addressed. Through much Roman Catholic thinking there has been a tendency to say that a movement could serve God only if it wore a Christian, and preferably a Roman Catholic, label, and was controlled by faithful Catholics and preferably by bishops.

This tendency can be seen in the twentieth-century movement known as Catholic Action. The progress of this movement was perhaps the Church's greatest achievement in the late 1920s and early 1930s, and in the 1960s we can see in it some great strengths. Its vision is that the whole of Christianity should be taken into the whole of life, and its realism is that this cannot be done unless youth workers, businessmen, farmers, intellectuals, etc., come together into groups which supplement the devotional groups of a parish church. Both the vision and the realism are superior to Liberal Protestantism' naïve reliance on the Christian conscience of the individual. However the position of the clergy has been a major problem for Catholic Action. Often this movement has encouraged lay initiatives, as in the "see, judge, act" procedure by which the small "sections" of the *Jeunesse Ouvrière Chrétienne* have since the 1920s trained young Belgian and French workers into mature responsibility and militant faith. But the "Jocists" have been only one side of Catholic Action. Another side is suggested by *Opus Dei*, which began in Spain. *Opus Dei* is probably for the most part blameless enough, but it comes under suspicion because its members, many of whom hold high positions in Spanish life, are held to be a secret society under clerical control, a Catholic equivalent of Freemasonry. One of the reasons for insisting that "Catholic Action is the property of the hierarchy"[1] was to lessen the danger of laymen giving a Catholic label to party politics (as in the *Action Française* movement); and another danger in mind was that social action might lead to indifference to religious truths (which was why Cardinal Hinsley in England in 1941 had to abandon his idea of making the *Sword of the Spirit* movement interdenominational). But

---

[1] A description which was a theme of Charles Murphy, *The Spirit of Catholic Action* (London, 1943).

Pius XI, who defined Catholic Action as the participation of the laity in the apostolic mission of the Pope and bishops, cannot be said to have grasped fully the independence of the twentieth-century layman. (He was himself a scholarly official of the ecclesiastical libraries in Milan and Rome, until at the age of sixty-one he was sent as Papal representative in war-torn Poland, becoming Pope only four years later; and as Pope—he made a courageous Pope—he was preoccupied by the need for Catholic discipline in response to political totalitarianism.[1]) The suspicion of clericalism interfering in lay life probably accounts for the fact that Catholic Action has disappointed the high hopes of its founders, and the clergy's authority over these lay groups may be reconsidered in the period into which the Roman Catholic Church is moving after the Second Vatican Council (although, to be sure, no layman voted in that Council).

Connected with Catholic Action has been the network of Christian Democratic political parties and labour movements. Before 1919 there were Centre Parties in many European states, for the most part small and concerned for the political defence of the Church and its schools, and other groups sought an understanding between the Church and the working-class. Amid the problems of post-war reconstruction a socially concerned and progressive lay Catholicism became a stronger political force through the Popular Party of Italy inspired by Guiseppe Toniolo, and through the Centre Party in Germany—only to be abandoned as the Vatican and the bishops made their peace with Mussolini and Hitler.[2] In 1945 "Christian Democracy" was resurrected in order to lead the reconstruction of Europe with Di Gasperi in Italy, Adenauer in Germany, etc. But even in this triumph the movement was ambiguous. On the one hand, uninhibited Catholic lay leadership was necessary in order to fill the vacuum left by the collapse of Nazi and Fascist governments, in the face of the threat of Communism. On the other hand, the gift of a Christian label to short-term, partisan objectives, and the interference by the clergy in political intrigues and elections, were standing invitations to an anti-clerical reaction. Most Protestants, specially in the English-speaking world, would regard this type of Christian activity as justified only in an emergency of the kind which certainly

---

[1] For a contemporary appreciation, see Philip Hughes, *Pope Pius the Eleventh* (London, 1937).
[2] Luigo Sturzo, *Church and State* (1938; Eng. trans., London, 1939), written after this brilliant priest's exclusion from political life, remains the best historical treatment of the problem from a Catholic angle.

existed in post-1945 Europe (as in the Italian general election of 1948, when it took a Pope to defeat the Communists), but which has now largely passed outside the Communist world.[1] The National Catholic Welfare Conference in the United States supervises the largest Catholic Action programme in the world (with over four million pupils in its schools), and has not failed to arouse Protestant and secularist suspicions. But, growing out of the patriotic work of American Catholics in 1917, the Conference has almost always avoided political involvements, and has concentrated on its declared priorities of social welfare, medical care, education and evangelism. When we remember the Catholic following of Father Coughlin the fanatical anti-semite of the 1930s, and Senator McCarthy the fanatical anti-Communist of the 1950s, we see how cautious the Catholic leadership has been in its social comment; and it is of major significance that very popular Catholic lay movements such as the Knights of St. Columbus or the Legion of Mary have avoided almost all entanglement in politics (unless pressure to support the Catholic Church's teaching on moral questions is regarded as political). Even so, President Truman was forced to withdraw a proposal to appoint an American ambassador to the Vatican, and John F. Kennedy would not have been elected to the world's most powerful office in 1960 if he had not repeated during his campaign the pledge that, although a Catholic, he would not consult his priests about his politics.

If we seek to assess the general effect of Catholic social teaching, again the truthful answer seems complex. On the one hand, since Leo XIII issued the Encyclical *Rerum Novarum* in 1891 an impressive body of teaching has been built up. That Encyclical, which was reaffirmed forty and seventy years later (*Quadragesimo Anno*, 1931, and *Mater et Magistra*, 1961) defended the "natural" right to private property, it praised the family and the Church as the chief educators, and it denounced the growing power of the state; on the other hand, it also defended the right of workers to organise themselves in order to obtain a "just" wage related to the needs of the worker's family. The ideal held up by these Encyclicals, and by many Roman Catholic writers who applied their principles to economic problems, was that of co-operation between capital and labour in running an industry

[1] For a favourable account, see Michael Fogarty, *Christian Democracy in Western Europe 1820-1953* (London, 1957). A well-documented example of a hostile view is G. Poggi, *Catholic Action in Italy* (Stanford, 1967), but the clergy's electoral work for the Christian Democratic Party in Italy after the Second World War was perhaps the century's most striking example of clericalism in politics.

or the benefit of all. Not the bureaucracy of the state, but a "guild" of those who worked with hand or brain within the industry itself was to be the guardian of social justice and the architect of distributed prosperity.[1] This solution for the internal problems of industrial democracies was followed up under John XXIII (*Pacem in Terris*, 1963) and Paul VI (*Populorum Progressio*, 1967); these Encyclicals pleaded for peace in the nuclear age and for justice for the under-nourished masses of the underdeveloped nations. Such guidance from the Popes has maintained the courage of Roman Catholics who have offered radical criticism of the selfishness and brutality of the West in this century. Papal leadership has provided a charter for the participation of working-class Roman Catholics in the cause of their own class, and has probably made many other religious believers pause before a too complete identification with the cause of social reaction.

On the other hand, there has been a gap between the ideals of these Papal Encyclicals and the realities of Roman Catholic involvement in the often sordid life of our time. In the eyes of many, the Papacy itself has been prevented from rising to the full height of its prophetic stature by its obligation to put first the Roman Catholic Church's own freedom. The Popes have been Italians, and Vatican City has been a small state within Rome; the Popes have been fathers to millions of Catholics living under tyrannies; and it is not surprising that Pius XI and Pius XII sought to get along with Mussolini and Hitler. When the Fascists and Nazis denied freedom to the Church, and in particular when they claimed sole control over the education of the young, the Popes protested vigorously, but it is significant that Pius XI never plainly condemned the Italian invasion of Abyssinia, while his Encyclical *Mit Brennender Sorge*, denouncing the neo-paganism of the Nazis, was less thorough than his condemnation of Communism, issued five days later in 1937 (*Divini Redemptoris*). Pius XII was essentially a diplomat; he spent the years 1917-29 as Papal nuncio in Germany, and was then Secretary of State at the Vatican for nine years. He has been accused of cowardice in not protesting publicly against the Nazis' extermination of the Jews, and the debate about that charge is worth considering because it shows up a widespread uneasiness about the role of the Papacy. It can be replied that Catholics (including Pope Pius) rescued many Jews, and that a more general protest would almost certainly not have rescued any more.

[1] Catholic Distribution was preached by, e.g., Hilaire Belloc in *The Servile State* (London, 1912).

But the very ugly fact remains that German Catholics generally applauded Hitler's policies except when these damaged the Church. Only seven of them sought exemption from military service on grounds of conscience. Dr. Guenter Lewy, after a carefully documented study, concludes that the general silence of the neutral Pope and the patriotic bishops about the iniquities of Nazism "reflected not so much a personal failure to be courageous and to uphold the cause of justice, but the demands of an institution which for close on two thousand years has put its survival as a channel in the salvation of individual souls before the moral demands of its own Gospel."[1] The Catholic Church has seldom hesitated to "interfere" in politics when urgent moral or spiritual questions have seemed to be at stake—and has on occasion used its weapons very severely (for example, in Italy against the anti-clericals before 1929 and against the Communists under Pius XII). The Catholic Church in Germany in 1933 possessed great resources for influencing public opinion, and although gradually deprived of these it had enough influence left in the 1940s to make a difference. What might have been done may be seen from the sermon of Bishop (later Cardinal) Galen which in 1941 stopped the Nazis' euthanasia of non-Jewish "defectives". About eight hundred Catholic priests perished in German concentration camps for offences against the Nazis; there were some heroes.

During and after 1945 the crucial moral challenge concerned the use of weapons of indiscriminate destruction. Here again the Papacy was tame, and no lead came from the American Catholic bishops; and the financial reliance of the Church on American public opinion cannot be ruled out as irrelevant. Not until the Encyclical *Pacem in Terris* and Chapter V of the Second Vatican Council's Pastoral Constitution on the Church in the Modern World did the Roman Catholic Church go beyond a generalised condemnation of war, and even then American Catholic leadership made no effective move to alert the public to the moral aspects of the possession of a nuclear arsenal and the use of savage weapons in Vietnam.[2] The contrast with the condemnation of contraceptives was striking. All this is understandable in the harsh conditions which have existed for the diplomacy of the Papacy and the Catholic Church since 1914, but the practical compromises may be remembered more vividly than the eloquent appeals. It is monstrously unjust to put the blame on Pope Pius personally; in two world wars he led massive relief pro-

[1] *The Catholic Church and Nazi Germany* (New York, 1964), p. 244.
[2] I tried to sum up the pre-Council discussion about the idea of a "just war" under modern circumstances in my *Withdrawing from the Brink* (London, 1963).

grammes which made Vatican City a symbol of hope to the distressed, and he never lacked either the courage or the perseverance to hold up the moral standards which accorded with the tradition which he expounded. Few fashions contain more cant than the fashion of the 1960s to denigrate this Pope, after the adulation which he received in his life. But the fashion may itself be excused, to some extent, by recalling the unctuous tone of superiority which has marked the Papacy's ethical pronouncements.

In the Roman Catholic Church's contribution to the problems of the underdeveloped countries, a compassion for the poor, accompanied by much missionary self-sacrifice, has been evident. But most students of these problems hold that the compassion for the poor would have been infinitely more effective if it had been accompanied by encouragement to limit families, and by the active participation of the higher clergy in the struggle of the peasants against poverty, disease, squalor and ignorance. Tragically, the Church by its fight against public money for family planning facilities, by its lack of enthusiasm for public education, and by its blessings on some of the worst exploiters (we think of Sicily and Latin America), may be judged by history to have impeded the progress of those peoples whose needs have been stated eloquently by recent Popes.

It is difficult to be sure just what has been the effect on Western industrial and political life of the Popes' social ideals. Christian Democratic governments in Europe have not effectively applied them when they have had their opportunities, and in the United States the National Catholic Welfare Conference, despite some excellent statements, has not been as consistently courageous in achieving social justice as in denouncing immoral films. As for "social action" by Catholics: the development of specifically "Christian" trade unions in some countries may have weakened, by dividing, the working-class protest. Many Catholics have looked nostalgically back at the peasants and craft-guilds of the Middle Ages, and realistic comment on contemporary industry has been rare. The small minority of "the Catholic Left" may be justified in arguing that only a massive extension of State power can secure social justice in practice. If that is so, then the great suspicion of socialism which marked the Papal Encyclicals—at least before John XXIII's blessing on "socialisation"—may have been a disastrous discouragement of what was really needed: Christian Socialism.

Perhaps a just verdict on the social record of the Roman Catholic Church in the twentieth century cannot be reached without using paradoxes. On the one hand, the emphasis was right—international peace, justice for the workers, co-operation between labour and management, justice for the poor nations, co-operation between them and the rich—and it was authentically prophetic to proclaim this emphasis through tragic days when nations, classes and races seemed determined on each other's ruin. On the other hand, the rhetoric of the Papal Encyclicals, and of lesser Roman Catholic writing, could suitably have been made rather less grand, for much of its commentary on social problems was unrealistic and its influence on the course of the century was small.[1]

Protestant Social Thought

However, the classic example in the twentieth century of a "Christian" attempt to force some debatable opinions on society at large arose not from Roman Catholicism but from American Protestantism. The prohibition of alcoholic liquor sprang directly from church-inspired crusades for temperance. It was enacted as an Amendment to the Constitution in 1919, and not repealed until 1933. Prohibition, although it was an intolerable interference with liberty and although it led to many social evils by driving the drink trade underground, was part of an idealism which should not be despised. Drunkenness among industrial workers had been both a symptom of their "alienation"—to use the Marxist analysis of that ruthless stage of capitalism—and a contribution to the plight of themselves and their families. The American churches had given far less support to labour's protest than the workers had wanted; the churches had been sadly dependent on the support of the capitalists.[2] But the history of the time shows that the churches' fight against liquor was accompanied by some prophetic attacks by their leaders and assemblies on brutalities of the industrial system. The Social Creed of the Churches, adopted by the Federal Council of Churches in 1908 and strengthened by revision in 1912 and 1932, included warnings against specific policies or acts of injustice; and a similar statement came from the National Catholic Welfare Conference. The controversial Christian report on the steel strike of 1919 was by no means an isolated case of church spokesmen standing up for labour's right to unionism and

---

[1] For a more favourable estimate, see Roman Catholic literature such as Orazio Premoli, *Contemporary Church History, 1900-1925* (1925; Eng. trans., London, 1932), or the symposium on *The Catholic Church in World Affairs*, ed. W. Gurian and M. A. Fitzsimons (Notre Dame, 1954).

[2] The classic study was Liston Pope, *Millhands and Preachers* (New Haven, 1942).

ollective action in days when such things were liable to be denounced
s creeping Bolshevism.[1]

The main motive which led to the "noble experiment" of
'rohibition was, however, a naive belief that the machinery of the
tate could be used to enforce righteousness. The same criminal
nnocence in the assessment of human nature and of political reality
ay behind the (admittedly short-lived) Inter-Church World
Aovement in 1919 with a billion-dollar programme to survey "all
he facts about the religious, social, moral, physical and economic
nvironments of humanity throughout the world", so that "from
hese facts a unified program shall be worked out in which all can
oncur".[2] Innocence inspired the American churches in their
indiscriminating endorsement of the war in 1917.[3] Innocence also
nspired their pacifism which encouraged their country's holier-than-
hou isolation from the problems of the world until the world, derived of effective American influence, drifted through the agonies
f Manchuria and China, Ethiopia and Spain, to the Nazi conquest
f Europe and the Japanese sinking of the American fleet in Pearl
Iarbour. And much innocence has continued through the bitterly
old war against Communism, leading many American Christians
nto a dangerous identification of American foreign policy with the
ause of the Kingdom of God.[4]

It was against the danger of such romanticism that Reinhold
Niebuhr protested. The most mature Christian commentator on the
ocial agonies and dilemmas of twentieth century, he made his name
y his warning in his book *Moral Man and Immoral Society* (New York,
932) that the conflicts of power needed more than optimism about
he power of ideals to counteract vested interests.[5] At first Niebuhr
ised the Marxist critique of conflict and change in society, toying
vith the belief that the proletariat might be exempt from the
mmorality of social groups. As a minister in industrial Detroit he
iad come to see that all the well-known philanthropy of a Henry
'ord was in vain if Ford's automobile factories could be closed for

---

[1] The "Social Gospel" was given its finest expression in the books by Walter
Rauschenbusch, *Christianity and the Social Crisis* (New York, 1907) and *A Theology for the
Social Gospel* (New York, 1917).

[2] Donald B. Meyer, *The Protestant Search for Political Realism, 1919-1941* (New York,
960), p. 9.

[3] The classic study was Ray H. Abrams, *Preachers Present Arms* (New York, 1933).

[4] See Paul A. Carter, *The Decline and Revival of the Social Gospel* (New York, 1954).

[5] Because British publishers in the 1930s considered this book neither Christian nor
political, I had the curious privilege of publishing the first British edition of *Moral Man
and Immoral Society* in 1963, together with the biography of Reinhold Niebuhr by June
Bingham, *Courage to Change* (New York, 1961).

"retooling" without care for the destitution to which many fathers
of families were reduced by this economic action; and he had
gradually broken with the pacifism of the main "Social Gospel"
movement because he believed that the possessors of such power
could not be dispossessed without militant unionism in a class
struggle.[1] But gradually Niebuhr also saw through Socialism's
illusions about the perfectibility of human nature, and turning from
all dreams of Utopia in his 1939-40 Gifford Lectures on *The Nature
and Destiny of Man* he explored the classic themes of sin and salvation.
Man's dignity, Niebuhr came to teach, lay in his freedom. Man is
"subject to the necessities of nature, of sexual and racial limitation,
of geography and climate, and of the dominant drives of his own
creaturely nature;" but "when man rises above the necessities and
limits of nature he is not inevitably bound in his actions to the norms
and universalities of 'reason'." Man is *free*: free to love, to worship,
to dream and to create beyond reason, but also free to grab, hate and
destroy. His dignity has the same ground as his sin. Thus Niebuhr
could joke that his early book should have been entitled *Immoral Man
and Even More Immoral Society*.[2] Applying this profound analysis of
human sinfulness to the problems of establishing social justice through
a long period which has brought one unprecedented problem after
another to the intelligence and conscience of his people, Niebuhr
directed the eyes of many in the intellectual community in America
to a God who alone is free from the ambiguities of historical movements, and who alone is above sin and "beyond tragedy". But it is a
sign of his greatness in the essays which have come from his old age
that he has shown a willingness to re-think the classical Christian
concepts such as "Original Sin" which are unintelligible to most of
the laymen whom he would wish to reach.[3]

Reinhold Niebuhr, for all his awareness of the limitations of
historical movements, has never contracted out of the intellectual and
political work involved in them. He came to support Roosevelt's
New Deal for the United States, and to urge a decisive stand against
both Nazism and Stalinism abroad, without the illusion that success
over poverty at home or tyranny abroad would usher in Paradise.
He proclaimed the duties of the American government, but also
advocated many restraints on it. His sober interpretation of the

[1] See his *Leaves from the Notebook of a Tamed Cynic* (Chicago, 1929).
[2] See, e.g., Niebuhr's intellectual autobiography in *Reinhold Niebuhr: His Religious,
Social and Political Thought*, ed. C. W. Kegley and R. W. Bretall (New York, 1961),
especially p. 10.
[3] Some of Reinhold Niebuhr's later essays were collected in *Christian Realism and Political
Problems* (New York, 1954) and *Man's Nature and his Communities* (New York, 1965).

responsibilities of the United States in the era of nuclear power has helped many less articulate fellow-Americans to a greater restraint, and has consoled some observers abroad for the North American dominance of the non-Communist world. Recent American policies can, of course, be criticised on many grounds, but in restraint and altruism they compare favourably with America's post-1917 oscillation between the innocent crusade to build a democratic peace and the withdrawal into pacifist isolationism when the United States left the League of Nations to its fate. Niebuhr's rejection of pacifism, his acceptance of power despite its sinfulness, and his profound meditation on the connections between "pragmatic" justice and the "impossible" ethic of love, were first inspired by his acceptance of the Marxist insistence on the power of the workers as the one remedy for the evils of American capitalism; but these teachings reached the height of their influence in relation to international affairs, and specially in relation to America's cold war against Communism.

Niebuhr's style is marked by a relish for paradox. He has frequently pointed out how, thanks to the presence of sin everywhere, no cause on earth can be trusted utterly—not even the cause of American democracy, not even the cause of the institutional Church. This realism has been a major contribution to an age which (particularly among Americans and among Christians) has often seen moralising used as a screen to cover unpleasant facts—and which (as in Communism) has been burdened by violent tyrannies motivated by puritanical ethics. Ruthlessness in the cause of morality has been a nauseating characteristic of the twentieth century. Much sentimentality or hypocrisy might have been checked among moralists, and much misery might have been spared to the masses who have been the victims of various moralising panaceas imposed by force of arms or public opinion, if a realistic analysis of the kind offered by Niebuhr had more widely taken the place of the simple-minded application of "morality" to politics too often urged by preachers and publicists in the name of Christ. If this insistence on paradox and subtlety has sometimes made Niebuhr's eloquence obscure to the simple-minded, it is precisely this wrestling with the obstinate facts that has commended this thought to the sophisticated, including many intellectuals who do not share his Christian faith in an eternal absolute beyond the temporal paradoxes. And the influence of Niebuhr has been great on the fairly sophisticated churchmen who have commented on our troubled age through the various Councils of Churches—although the study of Christian ethics has been starved in the Protestant churches outside the United States, and it has been given to tragically few (if any) ecclesiastics or theologians to speak to men of affairs with anything like Reinhold Niebuhr's effectiveness.

History may judge that the best comment on our age has come from the assemblies and agencies of the World Council of Churches and from the national councils associated with it. In part this comment has been in the shape of a costly concern for the relief of the victims of wars and disasters and for the resettlement of refugees. In part it has come as the churches have provided a platform for the legitimate aspirations of the Afro-Asian Revolution. In the areas of "rapid social change" in the 1950s and 1960s the World Council of Churches has sponsored an intensive programme of study and action intended to equip Christians to enter more fully into the tasks of building modern nations; and in the richer countries the World Council, with its associated national councils notably in the United States and Britain, has put its influence behind the fights for civil rights for coloured minorities, and for greater economic equality for the coloured and hungry majority of the peoples of the world.[1] Here are crusades which, being solely concerned for justice, seem to be exempt from most of the follies (although not, of course, from all the limitations) of the moral causes which absorbed the enthusiasm of previous generations in the churches. Together with this emphasis on the supreme importance of the tension between the "haves" and the "have-nots" of the world, there has gone a constant warning against the total horrors of nuclear, bacteriological or chemical war and a constant pressure in favour of risky initiatives in disarmament. This pressure against war has (unlike the pacifism of the 1920s and 1930s) sympathised with the dilemmas of the statesmen who are caught in an evil situation for which they are not entirely to blame; and it has been backed up by a consistent argument that the ideological conflict between capitalism and Communism, the West and the East of the world, was not serious enough to justify the use of the Bomb. Ever since John Foster Dulles and the Czech theologian Josef Hromadka clashed at its inaugural Assembly in 1948, the World Council of Churches has tried to work out the idea of the "responsible society", avoiding the brutalities of both individualism and collectivism and governed by the role of the state in giving service to citizens. But underneath these great causes there has been a concern for the rights of minorities, for unspectacular experiments in racial

---

[1] See Paul Abrecht, *The Churches and Rapid Social Change* (New York, 1961), and Richard Dickinson, *Line and Plummet: The Churches and Development* (Geneva, 1968).

artnership or in the reconciliation of rival groups in industry, and or other efforts to emphasise the dignity and freedom of the individual in his inescapably social context. Here, in struggles to make nd keep human society human, are the "middle axioms" which relate he great visions of Christian idealism to the everyday tasks of political realism.[1] Here, worked out in some detail, is the "planning or freedom" to which the sociologist Karl Mannheim challenged Christians as they looked forward to the post-war reconstruction.[2]

A striking development of the 1960s was an outburst of bold thinking by Protestant Christians about the character and content of their ethical decisions in the personal problems of life. This new crisis in ethics had been building up because Christians had noticed—some more acutely than others—that new decisions had been demanded by new situations created by scientific progress. The dominance of power politics by nuclear weapons forced the old issues of pacificism or patriotism with a new intensity for many consciences and led to a new debate about whether those weapons should be "renounced", or kept as a deterrent against aggression, or wielded as instruments of war against military forces, or even, at the last extreme of horror, hurled like obscene parodies of the thunderbolts of Zeus to punish civilian populations. Some of the new situations posed the most intimate of questions. The advance of medical science's capacity to alter the course of nature caused many to wonder whether personality should be regarded as sacred in all circumstances, or whether, in the interests of those around them, people might legitimately be conceived by artificial insemination, or aborted before birth, or altered in their characters by brain surgery or drugs, or killed when judged to be too old or weak. Even the comparatively trivial ethical problems involved in heart transplants caused many to discuss the meaning of personality in the surgeon's age of miracles. The availability of contraceptives produced another debate about whether sexual intercourse could now be treated as hand-shakes had been in the old Western society, or whether it should be tolerated or encouraged between homosexuals, or whether it should be confined to men and women who might marry, or whether, within marriage, it could be enjoyed for years without any thought of rearing children. From the nuclear graves of an overmighty civilisation to the cradles of a scientifically planned family, modern progress thus threw down new challenges to traditional ethics, changing patterns of work and family life, politics

[1] See Edward Duff, *The Social Thought of the World Council of Churches* (London, 1956), and Alan R. Booth, *Not Only Peace* (London, 1967).
[2] Karl Mannheim, *Diagnosis of Our Time* (London, 1943), pp. 144, etc.

and social security, recreation and transport, reminded people that all ethical codes have been relative to their social environment; and these new situations caused many to probe the ethical dimensions of *all* situations in real life. Many Protestants asked: do we now need a "situation ethics"? They meant by this: do modern people need a "new morality" in which personal decisions are taken not by referring to long-established rules but by fresh choices inspired by the wish to find the most "loving" or the most "sensitive" or the most "authentic" action?

In this debate, some agreements seem to be emerging from the smoke of a wordy battle. One agreement is that action guided by love is certainly nearer to Christian ethics than is an unthinking or unfeeling obedience to a moral code which may be irrelevant to the situation in which action is needed. Another agreement is that a humble concern to "do the loving thing" for the benefit of one's neighbour is nearer to Christian discipleship than is the Pharisaism which is the constant temptation of those who righteously adhere to the laws laid down in a text book. If the freshness of love, with its honesty, courage and creative power, can be recovered for a Christianity grown stale cold and irrelevant, then the challenge of "situation ethics" will generally be thought to have been not only healthy but also vital to the maintenance of religious inspiration for the conduct of the free adult. But, perhaps inevitably, much that has been said under the banner of the "new morality" has been said in such a way as to suggest a view of human nature which is pathetically irrelevant to the stuff of life. "The new morality" has often seemed to be based on an optimism about the power of individuals to love intelligently—a view no less disastrous than was the optimism of the social Gospel about the power of societies to establish the reign of love. An analysis of this new phase in Christian ethics no less devastating than Niebuhr's in the 1930s is widely seen to be needed. That analysis, when it comes, is likely to proceed by asking the question: *what is the real situation in* which a decision about the use of nuclear weapons or contraceptives about the transformation or termination of a human life, must be made? And the real situation is likely to be seen as involving more than the emotions of the principal actors in the immediate drama. The interests of society and of future generations will almost always deserve extremely serious consideration, and the wisdom of society and of past generations will almost always deserve more attention than the individual in his enthusiasm is liable to offer at once. Above all, a believer in God will say on reflection (or under the pressure of

)ther believers) that the will of God should be reckoned the decisive actor in the real situation; for putting God first is the heart of what it neans to be ethical in a Christian context, with the aid of the Christian community. Such deeper considerations will not necessarily restore old patterns of ethical behaviour; new situations may indeed call for new decisions. But they will deepen the debate, by doing what the Bible does, by reminding optimists of the depth and breadth of sinful selfishness, by pointing to the mystery of man as the son of God, and by disclosing the mystery of the real world as the scene of the coming of the Kingdom of God.[1]

"To Keep the Mystery Present"

For Britain the focus of a concerned, and on the whole a realistic, approach by Christians to social problems was provided by the work of Archbishop William Temple.[2] Specially influential were the carefully prepared Conference on Politics, Economics and Citizenship over which he presided in Birmingham in 1924 with its war-time sequel at Malvern, and his small books, notably his *Christianity and Social Order* (London, 1941) which argued that shareholders' profits from companies should be limited as their liabilities already were. Since Temple's death in 1944 no prophet of equal calibre has arisen in Britain.[3]

Post-war Germany has witnessed the spectacle of—and has learned some lessons from—a mass movement of Protestant laymen, the *Kirchentag*. Amid many problems of national reconstruction including the division of Germany, the *Kirchentag* has tried to combine biblical insights with social responsibilities, under the leadership of Reinold von Thadden-Trieglaff.[4] Martin Niemöller, the German pastor imprisoned by Hitler, has since 1945 used his great moral authority to plead for pacifism.[5]

Examples could be quoted from elsewhere in the world, but it

[1] The best introduction to this debate is provided in the two books by Joseph Fletcher, *Situation Ethics* and *Moral Responsibility* (Philadelphia, 1966-67), and the best presentation of the resources of ethical thinking by Christians of various schools is that made in *A Dictionary of Christian Ethics*, ed. John Macquarrie (London, 1967).
[2] See Robert Craig, *The Social Thought of William Temple* (London, 1964).
[3] In a history of modern Britain tribute would be due to Bishop George Bell of Chichester, who in the House of Lords denounced the Royal Air Force's "obliteration" bombing of German cities (see the biography by Ronald Jasper, London, 1967), and to Dr. (later Lord) MacLeod, founder of the Iona Communiity in the Church of Scotland and an eloquent advocate of the Christian conscience in politics (see his *Only One Way Left*, Glasgow, 1956).
[4] See Werner Hühne and Mark Gibbs, *A Man to be Reckoned With* (London, 1962).
[5] See Dietmar Schmidt, *Pastor Niemöller* (London, 1959).

should not be pretended that Christian conferences, books and
speeches have to date made a major impact on the world's affairs
What has been contributed has been the more modest gift of an army
of men and women willing to spend their lives in Christian service o
the modern world. Most of such contemporary Christians have been
lay people, but the army has included many priests and ministers
acting in accordance with the vision held out by the great Cardinal
Suhard of Paris: "It is a good thing if priests become witnesses once
more, less to conquer than to be a 'sign'. It has been well said that to
bear witness to God does not mean to make propaganda, nor to evoke
violent emotion, but rather to 'keep the mystery of God present to
men'. But this means so to live that one's life would be inexplicable if
God did not exist."[1]

The mature, equipped and disciplined willingness to be present in
the world without looking for recognition or for results may make
clear the evolution of Christianity away from its identification with
capitalism and colonialism, away from its "triumphalist" self-
satisfaction and ecclesiastical rigidity. That is why Christians who
have been martyred under Communism or in the anti-colonialist
crises of Kenya and the Congo have meant more than the proud
achievements of the rich Church in Russia, China or Africa.[2] That is
why Charles de Foucauld in his hut at Nazareth or at his post in the
desert, and Sadhu Sundar Singh as a holy man on the Indian road
disappearing on his last evangelistic journey, and Toyohiko Kagawa
going to the slums of Kobe and from there organising the first labour
protests in Japanese history, are perhaps the three men who have
most deeply stirred the Christian world in our time—together with
Albert Schweitzer in his jungle hospital, Dietrich Bonhoeffer in his
prison, and Teilhard de Chardin the scientist who saw nature aflame
with the glory which had Christ at its heart.[3] And among the leaders
of the Church, none has commanded a deeper loyalty than those
genial prelates who were always concerned for the secular life
around them, John XXIII and William Temple.[4]

[1] Quoted from the last of the Cardinal's three great Lenten Pastorals of 1947-9. An
English translation is E. Suhard, *The Church Today* (Chicago, 1955).
[2] One of the most moving accounts is that given by his widow of Dr. Paul Carson's
medical mission in the Congo: Lois Carson, *Monganga Paul* (New York, 1966). But the
stories of missionary heroism are innumerable.
[3] See E. Garnett Burns, *Charles de Foucauld* (London, 1962) and René Voillaume, *Seeds
of the Desert* (1952; Eng. trans., London, 1955). The best biography of *Sundar Singh* was by
A. J. Appasamy (London, 1958), and the best introduction to Kagawa was C. M. Simon,
A Seed Shall Serve (New York, 1965).
[4] Pope John's own *Journal of a Soul* (1964; Eng. trans., London, 1965) should be
supplemented by an assessment of his less conservative actions. See Meriol Trevor, *Pope
John* (London, 1967).

In a way which we cannot yet foresee, the sheer attractiveness of uch saints, and of thousands of less public Christians, may draw ion-Christians into a desire to know more about Christ and Christ's Church. For these twentieth-century saints, differing so profoundly n their situations and theologies, had two things in common. First, hey were all trained within the Church, within the great tradition; nd second, they were all willing to discard the weapons and uniforms f Christianity's past—like St. Francis of Assisi when he stepped into new world, "nakedly following the naked Christ".

CHAPTER EIGHT

A New Statement of Christian Belief

Communicating with the Modern World

A new humility leading to a new flexibility—that, we have seen, i
what is desired by many voices which have been raised in angry c
sad, despairing or constructive, comment on the state of the Christia
Church in the twentieth century. A new humility and a new flexibilit
in the Church's organised life seem to be the necessary conditions of
new Reformation. But what matters even more: *a new humility and
new flexibility seem to be the necessary conditions of receiving more truth*
enlighten Christians in the basic questions of religious belief. A number c
points may be made rapidly in this connection, as preliminar
observations.

First, let us say something about the new mood of Christia
humility. The refusal of Pope John and the Second Vatican Counc
to add fresh dogmas and anathemas to the stockpile in Christia
history may turn out to be a decisive gift by the 1960s to the future
The patient courtesy with which Christians from divided denomina
tions are learning to treat each other "in Christ" is slowly bein
extended; it begins to bridge the deeper divisions which exist betwee
Christians of conservative and radical temperaments, and betwee
believers prone to belief and those for whom faith is a hard-wo
victory in a personal battle which may go the other way tomorrow
Each side, conservative or radical, in the theological debate is liabl
to misrepresent and abuse the other. Such insults may be an inevitabl
part of controversy, but they must be transcended if the truth is to b
reached and if the public which seeks a true religion is to be servec

This is not to say that no limits at all should be set to the Christia
Church's comprehensiveness. A society has a right to be itself whic
must be weighed against an individual's right to dissent, and th
right may be claimed by the Christian society. Public opinion outsid
the Church would probably agree with the New Testament's ow
insistence that at the heart of the Christian society there must be
unity of faith in God through Christ. If Christians come to think th

ιey are at liberty to teach *anything* while remaining spokesmen of the
hurch, they rapidly lose touch with the education which is given
ɔ the individual who does acknowledge an obligation to take
ɛriously the convictions, or common-sense, of his fellow-churchmen.
he twentieth century has afforded a number of examples of eminent
ιctims of this spiritual disaster. In the last resort, the Church's
ɩberty to dissociate itself from the opinions of clearly heretical
fficers or members must, it seems, be preserved by disciplinary
rocedures, along with the individual's liberty to leave the Church
ɹietly and honourably. But by the 1960s it seems to have been
greed by those with the deepest sense of responsibility for the
ɛelfare of the Church that disciplinary procedures are justified only
s the very last resort. Normally a heresy trial does more harm than
ɔod. A rebel must be expected either to put himself out of touch with
ɩs church (as hundreds of clergy and millions of laity have done in
ɩis century) or to continue to educate himself within his church's
ɛllowship by exposure to his church's mind; and the choice is usually
ɛst left to him.

It is not yet clear what the Roman Catholic Church will look like
ɹhen the theological storms now brewing have burst. Very serious
ɛnsions between the senior bishops and the advanced theologians
lready exist, and perhaps a major schism cannot be avoided. But
ɛrtainly the idea of imposing discipline on theological thinkers by
ɩeans of an elaborate syllabus of errors to be renounced (such as the
nti-Modernist oath imposed on Roman Catholic priests since 1910)
ffends, or at least embarrasses, many who hold responsible positions
ɩ church life. A major heresy hunt has been avoided even in the
itter controversies which have divided the German Lutherans since
ɩe war about Bultmann's "demythologising" of the New Testament.
ʌost of the new statements of belief which have emerged from
'rotestant churches in this century (examples from the 1960s are the
tatements of the English Congregationalists and Presbyterians, and
ɩe Confession of the United Presbyterian Church in the United
tates) have not attempted to enforce conservative positions at
ɩsputed points. Instead of being primarily concerned to discipline
ɛeretics within the Church, such statements have attempted to help
ɔhristians to speak about what is essential in their faith to a world
ɹhich cannot understand that faith's old expressions.[1]

[1] Charges of heresy against Bishop James Pike in the Protestant Episcopal Church in the
Jnited States have recently resulted in a debate which has been dramatic, and which at
ɩe time of writing (1968) seems to have had two useful consequences of general interest.
'irst: many have agreed that a bishop should not be so immature, careless and unbalanced

The point that these statements of the Christian Gospel are outward-looking may conveniently connect with some other points to be made briefly about Christian theology's relations with the natural world. We must hope that as Christians turn to the world they may learn some of the lessons to be derived from the errors made by previous theological generations in adjusting the Gospel too rapidly and thoroughly to the temporarily fashionable philosophy; *but turn to the world they must.* If they remain barricaded in the citadel of ecclesiastical orthodoxy or biblical theology and isolated from the world, Christian theologians will end by talking to themselves. A remark by W. R. Inge to the effect that the theologian who marries the spirit of the age is soon left bereaved was much quoted in the days when ecclesiastical orthodoxy or biblical theology seemed the only safe way of presenting the Gospel; but Inge "married" *some* parts of his culture and that was why, although he made mistakes, he made an impact on his time.[1] Inge's own enthusiasms for political and philosophical movements now outdated should remind us that the theologian has really no alternative to marriage if he is to be fertile— and that what a virile theology needs is discrimination in living with a succession of secular mates. For the world has concerns far removed from those which supply the domestic gossip of the Church, and if Christians do not speak of their God in terms of those concerns they will not effectively speak at all; so that if the Christian message is to be understood, the challenge and risk of a conversation between Christian theology and secular philosophy must be accepted afresh in every generation.

To plead for a more natural and relevant, less exclusive and rigid style in Christian theology is, however, not to say that the old style of "natural" religion can now be resumed. We saw in Chapter 4 how with a diluted but real dogmatism, "natural" religion attempted to provide "an amazing wealth of external evidence by which the divine origin of the Christian religion can be brought home beyond question even by the unaided light of reason."[2] Or at least, "natural" religion

in his theological teaching as Bishop Pike has been, and therefore many are relieved that by his own choice, Dr. Pike no longer works as a diocesan bishop. But second: many are glad that the Protestant Episcopal Church refused to conduct an official heresy-hunt, and that leaders and theologians of the Church produced some memorable statements justifying the risks taken by the Church in upholding the freedom of earnest seekers after truth such as Dr. Pike. The passions surrounding this case have been recorded by William Stringfellow and Anthony Towne in *The Bishop Pike Affair* (New York, 1967). Hysteria is shown by what those authors say, almost as much as by what they quote.

[1] Inge opposed democratic progressivism, but endorsed a Platonic aristocracy. See above pp. 149-50.

[2] Pope Pius X , in his Encyclical *Humani Generis* (1950).

tried to argue that "probability" was on the side of "revealed" religion.[1] But we must insist once again that the unaided light of reason shows to the religious questioner a universe which is from first to last ambiguous. Faith in God is not compulsory—nor, if purified, is it stupid. In this universe a man must choose; and God (if God is) must value the freedom of a man's choice more highly than he values certainty or accuracy in religious doctrines. What Christians who choose to believe in God as a result of their own experience are summoned to do is to take the stuff of the world, and to interpret its ambiguities as disclosures of God. This is a work not of scientific or semi-scientific demonstration, but of poetic or mystic insight; and it results not in proud dogmas, but in a humble faith which can communicate its convictions only to those who have "ears to hear" because they, too, are humble.[2]

Conversions, then, will come only through genuine conversations. What will the conversations be about? Although we might not suspect this when reading most Christian theology, most of the raw material used by the Christian Church's only ultimate Master was not philosophical or doctrinal or ecclesiastical, but was the life of plants and birds, shepherds and merchants, kings and children. The parables of Jesus belong to a Palestine which is remote from the modern town-dweller, and the Spirit promised by Jesus to his disciples has to be claimed to inspire parables and symbols for the modern world. One necessary task of the Christian imagination is to relate old parables or symbols to new questions (or to old questions in a new dress), but the creation of new parables or symbols cannot be shirked by Christians who would continue the prophetic and artistic courage of their Master. The renewal of the Christian imagination is thus an urgent priority if the Church is to communicate with our time. Already the twentieth century has so developed that the most distinguished poets in the English language in the age of Eliot and Auden are Christian believers.[3] New hymns have been sung, and new religious plays performed; and a renaissance in church architecture (specially in France and Sweden), with some first-class painting or tapestry design or stained glass, have opened up the hope of new arts.

[1] As in Bishop Joseph Butler's *The Analogy of Religion, Natural and Revealed, to the Constitution and Course of Nature* (London, 1736).
[2] See the essay in which H. E. Root calls for a new style in "natural" theology, in *Soundings*, ed. A. R. Vidler (Cambridge, 1962).
[3] The struggles of poets to reach a clear vision in an age of disillusioned materialism, their guilt, dread, rejections and waiting, and their affirmations of Christian images old and new in order that their personal vision might be expressed with integrity, were studied by Kathleen Morgan in *Christian Themes in Contemporary Poets* (London, 1965).

The communication of the Christian Gospel will remain excessively academic until these arts, and the art of new speech, sweep over the living Church—and out of it to reach the everyday life of the people. Only in this way can the Church repeat what Jesus did: which was, not to lay down for all to accept a dogmatic proposition about an experience, but by means of popular art to intensify the experience itself. By telling parables, Jesus opened the eyes of some to look for themselves on nature as the good work of God, and on life as a drama in which people act as they do because people are in some ways like God (fathers like the Father, etc.). Only in this *earthed* style of teaching can the Church, like Jesus, begin where people are, and thus slowly lead people into a creative conversation.

It is, therefore, of much more than academic interest that the reconstruction of the parables of Jesus in their original setting, and the detection of the detailed changes which these parables underwent as the early Christians pondered and expounded them afresh, have been among the positive achievements of the modern critical study of the New Testament.[1] Discussing the dynamic and endlessly fertile art of Jesus, based as this was on loving observation of daily life, Professor Amos Wilder wrote: "In the Jesus of the parables we have a humanity in which uniquely the heart of man is recognised, as is not the case in all such humanisms, and yet in a way which is universal."[2] And Professor Gerhard Ebeling has summed up this humanism of the parables: "The art of the parable is none other than that of bringing the hearer face to face with what it is to be human and thereby to make clear what it means for God to draw near."[3] Professor Ebeling faces the question: how can the Church of our time speak with power about God in the world? How can the words of Christians once more become *events*, as the words of Jesus were events? His answer is that the words must be concrete, clear and active. Such language arises out of the willingness to share the world's experience, and out of the willingness to concentrate and take time. Thus the humility and the flexibility of the parable-teller can lead to the power of the prophet; and this power can drive men to choose, to say yes or no. Those who hear the parables become involved as actors in the drama brought before them.[4]

[1] The best summary of this achievement is in Joachim Jeremias, *Rediscovering the Parable* (1965; Eng. trans., London, 1966), although some scholars reckon that Professor Jeremias is too confident in his reconstruction of the original meaning of the parables.
[2] A. N. Wilder, *Early Christian Rhetoric* (London, 1964), p. 96.
[3] Quoted by Wilder, *op. cit.*, p. 79.
[4] See, e.g., Gerhard Ebeling's essay on "Worldly Talk of God", reprinted in his *Word and Faith* (1960; Eng. trans., London, 1963).

t this stage we had better pause to say that we are not meaning to commend a pious sentimentality or a new vintage of theological rgon. Two warnings by sociologists may be cited here. Peter Berger rites about the secularisation of the West: "Religion manifests itself public rhetoric and private virtue. In other words, in so far as ligion is common it lacks 'reality', and in so far as it is 'real' it lacks ommonality. This situation represents a severe rupture of the aditional task of religion, which was precisely the establishment of a integrated set of definitions of reality that could serve as a common niverse of meaning for the members of a society."[1] And from the eological ferment earlier in the century, there survives this warning om Max Weber: "The need of literary, academic or café-society tellectuals to include religious feelings in the inventory of their urces of impressions and sensations, and among their topics for scussion, has never yet given rise to a new religion. Nor can a ligious renascence be generated by the need of authors to compose ooks, or by the far more effective need of clever publishers to sell ooks."[2]

The communication of Christianity must take place in a period hen the West's intellectual life is dominated by *science*. If Christian elievers are to be at all numerous and at all intelligent, they must clude many whose minds have been shaped by science. Even hristian theologians, who are usually (but not always) without a ientific background, tend to be conscious of the scientific atmo- ohere of the intellectual world around them. It is natural that ymen and theologians alike should often think it necessary to relate ligion to science, as ways of knowing and speaking.

Clearly, the attitudes, procedures and languages of science and ligion are very different. Science forms theories and tests them by operiments. Its language is public; anyone with sufficient patience, telligence and knowledge may rethink the theories and repeat the operiments. Brave talk by religious believers about theology as a ience betrays an inadequate understanding of the profound ontrast between science and religious language, between the disci- line of the scientist and the discipline of the man of God. For ligious language is essentially a personal language. It is one man's, r one society's, interpretation of an event as a disclosure of the ivine. The interpretation is made in terms of the rest of that one

[1] *The Sacred Canopy*, p. 133.
[2] *The Sociology of Religion*, p. 137.

man's experience. Even the social character of religion does not mak
it truly public, for societies differ greatly in their religious traditior
which influence their members. Even the event which is interprete
by religion may not be a public event, at least not in the form in whic
religion claims that it took place. It may be a private ecstasy; or
may be an everyday event which only the prophet has seen as "charg
ed with the grandeur of God"; or it may be a miracle which can b
proclaimed in the witness of the believer but which cannot b
admitted into scientific history-writing. Religious language come
alive for a hearer when that hearer decides to accept the event whic
it interprets as connecting momentously with lesser events which h
has already interpreted out of his own experience, and the decisio
must always be with the hearer (influenced by the community aroun
him). Something of all this highly emotional process is preserved fror
generation to generation by the models or symbols in a religiou
tradition, and because they have such an emotional content thes
models and symbols come to be regarded as sacred. Religious believer
come to feel that the symbols which are dear to them should not b
compared with everyday objects, and any proposal to replace ther
by fresh symbols is liable to be regarded as blasphemous, wherea
science makes progress by its willingness to scrap old theories. Scienc
and religion are very different ways of describing the world.[1]

Yet the difference between religion and science, although profound
can never be complete. Religion attempts to describe an unearthl
and therefore largely unknowable source of light for the world, and i
shows the world as mysteriously bathed in that light, looking the sam
and yet different in comparison with the world as seen and describe
in the light of the common day. But the world cannot be completel
divided. It remains one world, seen in these sacred and secular lights
and therefore religious believers who are also intelligent thinkers ca
never give up the attempt to compare the two views, religious an
scientific, in order to see the one world with the fullest possible clarity

It is healthy that there has recently been some discussion of religio
and science among religious believers who are also trained scientists
Since we have already confessed the average theologian's ignorance c
science, we may add that not many scientists have taken theology'
discipline seriously enough. Among scientists religion is often lef

---

[1] The difference may be brought out by comparing C. H. Waddington, *The Scientifi
Attitude* (London, 1941), with W. A. Whitehouse, *Christian Faith and the Scientific Attitua*
(London, 1952). Readers may remember that the integrity of the scientific attitude ha
been defended already in this book, both against "natural" theologians (above, pp
177-86) and against "religious" humanists (above, pp. 237-243).

nexamined; for most scientists, this neglect amounts to the rejection
of traditional religion, but among some scientists who are religious
believers their lack of time for theology may result in an almost
childishly naïve traditionalism—or in a faith so vague that it is not in
conflict with knowledge because not in contact with it. But some
effort has recently been put into the difficult comparison by suitably
equipped thinkers.

One theme which often emerges is that both the religious and the
scientific communities demand that candidates for entry should be
initiated into that community's customs. Sympathetic humility and
self-forgetful perseverance are indispensable if any newcomer is to
gain access to the secrets of either religion or science.[1] And another
frequent theme in this well-informed comparison is that, when its
secrets have been penetrated, neither religion nor science turns out
to be a straightforward account of the obviously real world. Each
discipline, into which the newcomer must be initiated by stages, at
the end confesses that it is unable to picture its world with complete
accuracy. For the sake of its own thought and for the sake of communication, each discipline therefore uses *models* which can represent
intelligibly some aspects of the mysterious reality. The use of the idea
of fatherhood to describe God in religion is the use of one model;
another model is the scientific picture of the atom as (in the
nineteenth century) as a hard billiard ball or (in our time) a
miniature planetary system. And the willingness to study such models
humbly, with the intention of learning from them, may be the greatest
test of the newcomer's desire to become mature in the discipline.

Both science and religion can to some extent overcome the
inadequacy of any one model by "qualifying" that model—that is,
by placing it alongside others; and both science and religion often
expect the vital disclosure to come to a humble student only through
his study of a combination of models. Thus the physicist studies an
electron by means of mental models which describe it as behaving
now like a particle, and now like a wave; the truth about the electron
cannot be expressed more simply. Not only the electron but light
itself is said to have some particle-like and some wave-like qualities,
and the physicist cannot say anything simpler about it. The student
of science has to accept this situation and proceed through it. In a
way not altogether dissimilar, the religious believer may find it
necessary to use a combination of models in order to express a truth

[1] This experience is reflected in William Pollard, *Physicist and Christian* (New York, 1961),
and John Habgood, *Religion and Science* (London, 1965). Both scientists have become
Anglican priests.

greater than any one of them. For example, light has often been used as a symbol in religion. It may be pictured as the light of a growing dawn, or as the light of a threatened candle, meaning that the light which comes from God begins to illuminate the world (the world being either responsive or hostile). But light may also be pictured as the noonday brightness suffusing the world, meaning that the light comes from a God who is open to the world and reaches a world which is open to God. Thus God's transcendence over nature and men, yet also his being in everything and everyone, may be pictured by a union of apparently contradictory symbols.[1]

These are examples of the inadequacies in single models being corrected, but the student must be prepared for some hard thought before the disclosure will come. He must make sure that the two models, placed side by side, are not *essentially* contradictory; and having ascertained that he must discover what exactly are the features in the different models which are most useful in the task of understanding the total truth. We cannot wonder that, in religion as in science, no impatient person stands a chance.[2]

But while we grant that both religion and science use models, we may still hesitate to say that religious models are useful instruments in a true description of the real world. We have so many warnings from the past that religious doctrines may be used as substitutes for science, or as denials of science. It is therefore necessary to affirm that no proposition should be regarded as authoritative for science simply because religion claims that it has been "revealed", and that no proposition, however sacred it may be for religion, should be preserved when it has been disproved by science. Such affirmations are not only necessary in logic; they are also needed in practice, for many Christians in the twentieth century have continued to exalt a dogmatic system over science. The conflicts of religion and science are not yet over. However, the crucial question for religion is not the occurrence of this or that event which religion may have affirmed and science may have denied (such as the creation of the world in 4004 B.C., or the "special" creation of Adam from whom all men are descended). The crucial question is: *what is the character of reality as a whole?*

To this question about reality as a whole science provides no

[1] An excellent study of light as a religious symbol forms Chapter 9 of John Macquarrie *God-Talk* (London, 1967). But the classic modern treatment of imagery in religion remains Edwyn Bevan, *Symbolism and Belief* (London, 1938).
[2] Some elements in a comparison of religious with scientific models were suggested by Ian T. Ramsey in *Religious Language* (London, 1957) and *Models and Mystery* (London, 1964).

answer, for science is the study of particular events or objects. The scientist is no more (and no less) qualified than the non-scientist in discussing "the riddle of the universe". Ernst Haeckel's widely influential book of that title, translated in 1900, was not science, although it used much evidence from Darwinian biology and other science. It was a controversially philosophical work, tracing the iron laws which controlled the evolution of the universe and denouncing the idea of an active God as a "gaseous vertebrate"; and it explicitly advocated a new quasi-religion, "monism". *The Survival of God in the Scientific Age* by Alan Isaacs may be cited as a popular book of 1966 which also made no secret of its atheistic interpretation of the evidence provided by science.[1] But after working through the evidence about the evolution of matter, the evolution of mind and the evolution of the concept of God, Dr. Isaacs conceded the vital point that the basic interpretation of it by religion cannot be disproved, however many mistakes religious teachers can be shown to have made. "The religious organizations," Dr. Isaacs wrote, "being committed to 'truth' by revelation, find it impossible to see themselves as a temporary bridging operation between the emotional past and the rational future—or as an extra branch of the secular social services. And they may, of course, be right—the agnostic has no grounds for ruling out the truth of revelation. All that he can be certain of is that in the present context of the nuclear age the religions are rapidly losing their support."[2] By Haeckel's standards, the anti-religious conclusion reached by Dr. Isaacs was no conclusion at all: "Perhaps our greatest gift to posterity is that we have released our children from the fear of the supernatural. The concept of God is still available for those who need it—and those who do not, have no longer to be ashamed, and no longer to be afraid."[3]

We must therefore state here that the uncertainty of science destroys only the attempt to prove God from nature; it does *not* destroy belief in God as a valid option. Some "natural" religion has to be rejected as claiming too much; but precisely because nature is ambiguous, atheism also deserves to be checked if it dogmatically claims to be the only possible "scientific" attitude. The thoughtful believer is allowed the same freedom which the agnostic rightly claims for himself.[4] And the believer's is a more honourable freedom

---

[1] It was published in London as a Pelican paperback.
[2] See p. 207.
[3] See p. 215.
[4] For a fine statement of this by one of the most sensitive of the British philosophers who advance an agnostic view of religion, see the essay by R. W. Hepburn, cited above, p. 266.

than Dr. Isaacs implies. The thoughtful believer is the man who gives his support to religion not because it is fashionable, but because it seems true to him; and he believes religion to be essentially true because he needs the concept of God (or its equivalent in Eastern religion) *in order to interpret his own experience.*

Religion is therefore associated with a world-view which is different from the scientific attitude, although not essentially incompatible with it—just as atheism is different from the scientific attitude, although the same person can, of course, be both an atheist and a scientist. The believer chooses to view reality in one way, although when he is acting as a scientist he is as ready as the next man to pursue his investigations so far as possible "without bringing religion into it". His choice is neither arbitrary nor irrational, for it results from his thinking about his experience. Even in a laboratory experiment, the personal factor enters into scientific work, for many scientific theories are born in "hunches" and are only slowly formulated and tested. But a closer analogy to religious faith within science arises out of the status of a scientist as a human being, who has to choose whether or not he is to work on a particular project, serve a particular company, university or government, or to marry a particular girl; in these life-determining decisions the scientist, like the next man, has to proceed on the basis of intuitions which he may find it hard to express or to rationalise.[1] And it is in the experience of making such decisions, about religion or about secular life, that a man comes to see most clearly where freedom is left in the age of science. There has been something ludicrous about the enthusiasm with which religious believers have greeted various developments in modern physics, believing that this or that new model in science allowed room for the freedom of man's mind or of God's will. For example, Heisenberg's "indeterminacy principle"—his discovery that the elementary particles of the atom behaved in ways which could not be predicted—was hailed as demonstrating the freedom of God to act providentially in an otherwise law-abiding world. But such descriptions of matter at its most microscopic (descriptions which may one day be improved) have nothing to do with the decision for or against a religious interpretation of the whole of reality. The freedom that can be known in the world is the freedom experienced by the person who decides, and this freedom is real amid many factors which profoundly influence personal decisions. Here is the freedom

[1] The classic statement of this has been made by a Professor of Chemistry who became a Professor of Philosophy. See Michael Polanyi, *Personal Knowledge* (London, 1958) and *The Tacit Dimension* (New Haven, 1966).

with which a scientist decides whether or not to make the atomic bomb; and here is the freedom with which an individual challenged by a religion decides whether or not to accept its claims.

The decision for or against religious faith is made by the total person, and however reasonable it may be it arises from levels of the personality deeper than the reason. *In this choice, the total person takes a view of total reality.* Religious believers, in addition to jumping at the latest developments in physics, have often made themselves ridiculous by finding gaps, especially in biology, into which their God could be inserted while the rest was left to science. For example, there has often been a religious emphasis on an alleged lack of continuity between mind and matter, so that mind could be described as a miraculous creation by God. But the advance of science is constantly filling in such gaps, so that the God of the gaps quickly becomes redundant. Instead of thinking of *gaps*, it seems to be more useful to think of *levels* in nature. At one level, the parts go their separate ways, but at the next level, the parts combine into a system, and it is out of that organisation—not out of the introduction of a totally new part— that novelty emerges. Nature is increasingly studied as a continuous whole, as a system of systems from the smallest to the greatest. Organic life, for example, or mental activity, while each is seen to be distinctive, is each regarded from a scientific point of view as matter organised at a new level of complexity: "life" or "mind" is not a totally new miracle. It is always possible for the scientist to emphasise the old level at the expense of the new, and to reduce the whole system to the alliance of its parts, forgetting that the system works in a new way. Thus biology need not be pursued as the study of living organisms as they exist and behave; it may be reduced to the levels of physics and chemistry, and it often has been. Psychology need not be pursued as the study of the mind of man; it, too, may be reduced to lower scientific levels, as it was by J. B. Watson and other "behaviourists". Such "reductionism" can, of course, be criticised on strictly scientific grounds. The religious believer may or may not be a reductionist when studying any one level in science, but he is a man who sees, beyond all the levels described by science, a level which may be pictured, with the aid of symbols or models, as the level of the activity of God.

This level beyond science is the level of "miracle". The true miracle for the believer who accepts the scientific attitude while going beyond it is not the sudden entry of God into the world, reversing in a special case the operation of a "natural law" which is otherwise inflexible.

The believer is content to leave each allegedly special case to a specially careful study of the evidence. The believer may well interpret his own experience of God in such a way that the possibility of God altering normal procedures is not ruled out, and the believer who has such an understanding of God may rightly point out that the so-called "laws" of nature need not be inflexible, for they really express the norms in the statistics of humanly observed phenomena, not unchanging decrees issued by nature. But all believers hold that God normally works through normal procedures rather than emergency actions, and the believer if he is sensitive to the possibility of error in claims about "miracles" will not rest his whole faith on one special case proving to be utterly abnormal. The great miracle for the believer in the age of science is *reality as a whole.* "Miracle" comes from the Latin for "wonder". Reality as a whole is wonderful to the believer, for the mystery of its source, character and destiny is illuminated for him by the models provided by his religion.[1]

Christian Faith and Current Philosophies

The religion which is communicated by parables or models must also be interpreted by a philosophy which is as clear and convincing as possible. Jesus himself was no philosopher, and no philosophical system can be an essential consequence of his teaching—certainly not the philosophy of St. Thomas Aquinas, which was a brilliant but temporary feat of the Middle Ages, seeking to harmonise the God of Jesus with the God of Aristotle. A. N. Whitehead was surely right in his famous description of Christianity (here contrasted with Buddhism) as "a religion seeking a metaphysic".[2] The Christian religion can awaken personal faith by the appeal of its symbols, supremely by the symbol which is provided by the whole life of Jesus; and the intellectual arguments follow the impact of these symbols on the whole person. Faith, in brief, is existential (and so is unbelief). But some genuinely intellectual arguments there must be, specially as society becomes more educated. "Faith" must, in St. Anselm's famous phrase, "seek understanding"—analysing itself, drawing conclusions from its intuitions, and testing itself against all other ways of looking at the evidence. A philosophy which follows faith must also examine the

[1] The best modern introduction to the field, which has here been sketched so unsatisfactorily is Ian Barbour, *Issues in Science and Religion* (New York, 1966). Professor Barbour is a physicist and Protestant theologian. Other recent treatments include *Christian Theology and Natural Science*, Bampton Lectures by E. L. Mascall (London, 1956), and Harold K. Schilling's more deeply existentialist *Science and Religion* (New York, 1962).

[2] *Religion in the Making* (New York, 1926), p. 50.

ecular philosophy of the day—regarding this as the intellectual
xpression of the attitudes which, largely because of facts which
ociology or psychology may usefully analyse, are dominant in the
eriod.

In the twentieth century there has been a series of dialogues
etween Christian theology and secular philosophy. At first the
onversation was between a "Christocentric metaphysic" of the kind
which William Temple embodied, and the philosophical idealism
hen reigning in the universities with its confident talk about the
volution of mind, value and God; then the conversation was
etween a "biblical realism" of the kind proclaimed in Europe by
Karl Barth and in America by Reinhold Niebuhr, and the existen-
ialism which studied the nature of the person's decision for or against
uch a faith; and more recently the dialogue has been between a
ather less confident faith, founded on a critical understanding of the
Bible, and the philosophy which coldly analyses the language of
metaphysical claims.[1] When we see what nonsense is still paraded as
wisdom in our world, we need not regret that most of the energy of
he professional philosophers, at least in the English-speaking
niversities, has recently been devoted to this analysis of words,
ather than to a love of the higher-flying wisdom. But there are signs
hat a new phase in the endless dialogue is about to begin, and that in
his phase Christian faith will seek a more constructive and articulate
nderstanding of what it wishes positively to say in the modern world.

Some theologians, sensitive to the social and psychological impact
f our century, have tried to work out a way of talking about God
which is not metaphysical at all, even not "religious", but which is,
n their favourite word, "secular"—more secular than the anti-God
hilosophy of secularism, because more open to the realities of
xperience. In a sketch for a book which he did not live to write,
Dietrich Bonhoeffer mentioned that "the transcendental is not
nfinite and unattainable tasks, but the neighbour who is within
each in any given situation."[2] Followers of Bonhoeffer have tried to
evelop an understanding of transcendence as the encounter with the
eighbour, and these attempts have healthily recognised the truth, as
ld as Christianity, that we cannot claim to know or love the trans-
endent God unless we know and love the human neighbour. Such
wareness of the independent, and to the end mysterious, reality of the

---

[1] John Macquarrie's masterly survey of *Twentieth-Century Religious Thought* may be supplemented by a summary of the most recent phase: J. A. Martin, *The New Dialogue between
Philosophy and Theology* (New York, 1966).
[2] *Letters and Papers from Prison*, p. 210.

other person is specially valuable in the age of technology, when personal relations may be atrophied by our concentration on our masterly manipulation of inanimate objects. Thus a student of science may need reminding that his girl is not like his test-tubes.[1] But encounter with the neighbour cannot be the *total* content of transcendence, unless we really are going to reduce theology to anthropology, stopping with man as well as starting with him.[2] Professor Ronald Gregor Smith, whose book on *Secular Christianity* was one of the most thorough attempts to follow Bonhoeffer along this line, has in another recent book recorded an occasion when he put the crucial question, in a conversation with Martin Buber. "I said something to the effect that it was not clear to me how 'the eternal Thou' was to be understood as implicated in each relational event. How could this be proved? 'Proved?' he replied. 'You know that it is so.' Now, long afterwards, I understand that this *knowing* of which he spoke was a trustful, believing knowing."[3] In other words, through the neighbour some of us experience the transcendent God—and others of us (the more thoroughly secular) experience only the neighbour. The division remains between religious faith and religious unbelief. As Professor Gregor Smith says: "If faith cannot be demonstrated, neither can it be disproved. It remains faith, and by its mere existence it involves a total response."[4]

Some recent theologians have sought to present Christianity in a larger, although still "this-worldly", setting—as a political rather than personal matter, as an interpretation of this world's history. One of the most exciting presentations of this thesis was offered by Professor Harvey Cox in *The Secular City*. The prophets of Israel and Jesus himself saw God in the events of history, and not at all in metaphysical speculation—in the events of the world, and not primarily in the rituals of the temple. It is therefore healthy when Christians discern the hand of God in the great drama of our age. Such Christians do not regard the enormous expansions of human intelligence and knowledge, the new freedom of mind and speech and the spread of popular education, the triumphs of the natural and social sciences, and the beginnings of a true psychology, as threats to be denounced and resisted; instead, they regard these things as great new facts in which believers in God should rejoice, as great new acts

[1] John Macmurray's Gifford Lectures on *Persons in Relation* (London, 1961) may be regarded as the crown of personalist philosophy.
[2] See the essay by G. F. Woods on "The Idea of the Transcendent" in *Soundings* chapter 3.
[3] R. Gregor Smith, *Martin Buber* (London, 1966), p. 22.
[4] *Secular Christianity*, p. 58.

in which God has once again "visited and redeemed" his people. The whole modern movement which at present seems to involve a destructive secularism may already be to the believer a demonstration of the lordship and goodness of God, on the ground that it brings a vast new strength to the bodies and minds of men and women who were made "in the image of God". And it may be the unpopular task of the theologian to say so, thus incurring the wrath both of the complete secularist (who deplores any mention of God) and of the conservative churchman (who for practical purposes may seem to identify God with the Church). At least, the theologian may be able to raise his voice against a complete contrast between the will of God and the progress of man. And gradually the theologian may be able to persuade the ordinary believer to share a positive attitude to many aspects of secularisation. If this human advance out of superstition and misery could not have been achieved without damage to the high religions including Christianity, the devout believer who endorses "the humanity of God"—the breathtakingly high value placed on men by their Father and Maker, extending to incarnation in a man— may gradually learn not to quarrel with God's own acceptance of the cost of human progress. In this Christian light, the whole modern movement may itself be seen as a miracle from God, as a foretaste of the revelation which the living God may grant to the modern world.

This modern civilisation originated in Christian Europe, and has been carried by Christians or ex-Christians to the other continents; and to contribute to its progress seems a clear enough call to Christians today. But we must add that in what remains of the twentieth century Christians should make their contributions with their eyes open—unless all the reminders by Reinhold Niebuhr and others about the distinctiveness of Christianity's realistic insights are to be abandoned as if the 1930s had never happened. The modern city does not escape from the ambiguity and the tragedy of all history, and our secular civilisation should not be idolised. In fact, many of Professor Harvey Cox's fellow-Americans (the rich as well as the poor among them) have found life in the city hellish, or at least disappointing, and going to church has been one of their ways of escaping from the secular city, or at least of finding courage to live in it. If the happiness of mankind is our criterion, then we must, it seems, judge that the world-wide spread of our secular, urban, commercial, technological civilisation is no more unambiguously beneficial than was the previous phase of unbridled capitalism at home and imperialism abroad; and it begins to be apparent that the real progress of our civilisation—its true humanism, in the sense of serving the full development and deep happiness of the human race —will demand that more people in the secular city face openly the question of what their humanity means. This must include the question whether they and their neighbours are, or are not, meant to live in the light of a destiny as citizens of the eternal City of God. The Christian in John Bunyan's seventeenth-century *Pilgrim's Progress* made the mistake of dismissing the world which included his wife, children and neighbours as "the City of Destruction", but a twentieth-century Christian has still to regard the path of life as in some sense a road which takes himself, his family, his neighbours and the whole human race to a destination which he believes to be the Celestial City. Others will not share his belief, and the debate between faith and unbelief is likely to continue until the Celestial City is reached (or turns out to be a mirage in the desert of a pointless universe). But if one thing is clear as the believing pilgrim struggles along the road, it is that secular urban planning is not the same activity as theology's quest for the ultimate.

Religious belief may, therefore, legitimately protest that the object of its concern is really *ultimate*: it is more than the human neighbour, and more than the secular city. Religious faith may also rightly affirm that its object is more than the sum total of the natural world already around us. Sometimes religion in our time has been reduced to little more than a sense of perspective. Religion has been described as urging us not to be anxious about the details, but instead to "see life steadily and see it whole". In our century's more optimistic moments, such a religion has been presented as a vision of the glorious whole; and in our century's blacker moods, it has been presented as liberation from narrow cares or temporary despairs. These elements are certainly present in religion as most believers in the modern West would understand religion; but, when all this has been said in praise of religion, most believers will still feel that religion's grand object has been left out of such descriptions. The vision offered by the Western religious tradition to perplexed or despairing minds is a vision of a power which is greater than any person or object in the universe, and greater even than the sum total of objects and people; and in the long run the value of this religious tradition stands or falls with the truth of this vision. It is necessary to emphasise this point, which seems obvious enough to almost all those who look at religion from outside, because in our time a number of those standing within the religious world, including theologians, have obscured it; they

have argued that religion may rightly claim to provide emotional reassurance or ethical inspiration, but not information about what really is.[1]

Most of those who stand outside religion, as well as most of those
who worship within it, would suppose that the vision just mentioned
does constitute religion's central claim to truthfulness and therefore
to usefulness. But in our time the word "God" has lost much of its
former power, not only for those who have been thoroughly secularised, but also for many of those who have felt the psychological
impact of our secular century while remaining in the religious
tradition. It is not surprising that some theologians have wished to
show afresh the basic strength of the idea of God, but to discard
outmoded elements in traditional talk about God. Such theologians
have turned to current philosophical movements for help. Here,
however, we shall not offer an elaborate exposition of the philosophical
school in question; we shall merely provide the briefest outline of how
the philosophical tradition is likely to be relevant to the fundamental
problems of the person who is interested in religion without being a
professional philosopher. We may excuse ourselves for our lack of
philosophical refinement by recalling that our purpose is to see the
broad relevance of these ideas to theology and through theology to
the religious life of the age. The philosophies which we have in mind
are the philosophy of Being, associated with the German thinker,
Martin Heidegger, and the philosophy of Process, associated with
the Anglo-American thinker, A. N. Whitehead.

Being and Process

For the philosophy of Being—which is extremely hard to state clearly
—the clue may be provided by Wittgenstein's remark that "not *how*
the world is, is the mystical, but *that* it is."[2] As Leibniz asked in the
eighteenth century: "Why are there entities at all, and not just
nothing?" Any observation of nature, or any incident in life, may
awaken that question in us, but the wonder of sheer Being may be
experienced most sharply when we consider its alternative: the
destruction of what was. Since we are samples of Being, the wonder
may come home to us by meditation on our own deaths, when "to
be or not to be" becomes for us the question of all questions. Man

[1] E.g., a Cambridge philosopher, R. B. Braithwaite, presented the Christian religion as a
way of life, but not as a vision of ultimate reality, in a famous lecture on "An Empiricist's
View of the Nature of Religious Belief" reprinted with comments in *Christian Ethics and
Contemporary Philosophy*, ed. Ian T. Ramsey (London, 1966). But that lecture of 1955 does
not fully represent Professor Braithwaite's position.

[2] *Tractatus Logico-Philosophicus*, p. 187.

knows that he has been thrown into life, and man knows that he will die, and man wonders whether he will die entirely—and man asks whether there is any point in it all. Such questions may lead the questioner to meditate on the mystery of the "Being" which all existent things and persons have in common; and so the questioner may be led to sense, and to contemplate, what is in the mystical tradition called the source of Being, or the power of Being, or the ground of Being, or Being itself. According to most parts of the great mystical tradition, Being itself may be deeper than all things, and stronger than all their deaths. The religious name for "Being itself" is "God"; but it is impossible to answer the question "What is Being?", for Being is not a "what" or something, and "Being itself" cannot be expressed except through symbols or models. Even to say that "Being exists" suggests a confusion between Being and mere existence. Yet Being may be revealed. Anything in the universe can become a symbol or model for the mystery of "Being itself"; any "what" can disclose it to us; at any moment the discovery of the deep truth may occur; and the greatest symbol is a rational, spiritual person—a person who bears the mystery of Being in his existence, a person who may learn what it means *to be* by looking into himself.

Paul Tillich in his *Systematic Theology* (3 vols., New York, 1951-63), and John Macquarrie in his *Principles of Christian Theology* (New York, 1966), related this philosophy of Being to traditional Christianity's doctrines, and the passionately eloquent and deeply moving sermons of Tillich[1] and of Rudolf Bultmann[2] related it to the doubts and anxieties of twentieth-century man. Such books show how this basically mystical or aesthetic understanding of existence can bring out the deep reality of many of the affirmations which the Christian wishes to make about God and about Jesus. Theology when preached in this way can help a modern man towards "authentic existence". Courage can replace despair arising from a sense of meaninglessness, and concern for what ultimately matters can replace a man's temporary, illusory satisfactions provided by trivial, material objects.

The philosophy of Process is definitely interested in *how* the world is—although it, too, is basically mystical or aesthetic.[3]

[1] *The Shaking of the Foundations, The New Being* and *The Eternal Now* (New York, 1948-63).
[2] *This World and Beyond* (1956; Eng. trans., New York, 1958).
[3] The relevance of this philosophy for Christians was summed up in two short books, *God in Process* by Norman Pittenger and *Exploration into God* by John Robinson (both London, 1967). See also the longer books by John Cobb, *A Christian Natural Theology* (Philadelphia, 1965), and Peter Hamilton, *The Living God and the Modern World* (London, 1967); and *Philosophers Speak of God* (Chicago, 1953), where Charles Hartshorne and William L. Reese compare Whitehead's philosophy (to its advantage) with a wide variety of other attempts to speak.

It begins with the failure of science to detect a purpose in every part of the universe. Modern science in its early days struck up a friendship with Christian theology on the basis of an agreement that the beauty of a designed order could be seen in every part of creation; but the experience of the limitations of purpose, or at least of the limitations of science, has become an overwhelming psychological fact in the nineteenth and twentieth centuries. The Process philosophy starts from that experience, and it is perhaps not too fanciful to say that this philosophy interprets the whole of reality through using a model provided by the achievements of modern science: the model of the successful experiment. The whole universe is interpreted as a process where failures or accidents apparently occur, but where gradually these failures and accidents are seen to be less significant than the victory at the end. The ultimate victory comes with the coming of that beauty of order, which "natural" theology used to teach was present from the beginning.

This Process philosophy sees a beauty and a goodness in the world. And it sees this beauty and goodness as more significant than the disorder and evil which are also in the world; for in the world it sees human intelligence and love, and it sees that these mental or spiritual activities of man are, at least in their essential physical basis, continuous with the rest of the universe, mind emerging out of matter. The philosophy of Process therefore interprets the whole of reality in the light of the fact that evolution has produced thought and love in man. Such a philosophy can have a very powerful religious significance, interpreting all the universe. For if the power of intelligent love is taken as the clue to the meaning of this whole vast process, then the power which runs through evolution (and through the whole universe) can itself be understood as persuasive and not coercive. In other words, God (or whatever other name we may give to the ultimate reality) may be seen as the supreme example—the "chief exemplification" in Whitehead's phrase—of intelligence and love, not of mere power.

The relevance of this Process philosophy to the idea of God has been seen by Process philosophers in at least two ways—ways which are essentially different. Some philosophers of this school equate God with the natural process itself, either as this process already is or as it is coming to be. Such philosophers belong to a tradition at least as old as the seventeenth-century Spinoza. On this showing, God *is* the universe as the spiritual power of love prevails in the universe. But others (and Whitehead was among them) think that the reality of

God is greater than the reality of the natural process. They find room —even if to some it may appear a rather obscure room—for the transcendence of God (who to Whitehead was a "real entity"). On the basis of either understanding of the meaning of the word "God", Process philosophers can suggest a picture of nature as God's growing body, but the second, fuller, understanding of the nature of God is more satisfying religiously to those brought up in the Western tradition, for it sees God as the transcendent Lover and the whole process of the universe as the expression of this divine Love. A vision of God such as we find in Whitehead seems rooted in the essential validity of the West's traditional religious vision. Bertrand Russell has written many memorable affirmations that the universe should be faced as meaningless;[1] but it indicates the continuance of the religious vision in our time that Whitehead, who in the early years of the twentieth century was Russell's collaborator in mathematical work of immense originality and distinction, thought that the religious vision yielded some reliable information about the natural process. "The fact of the religious vision, and its history of persistent expansion," he wrote, "is our one ground for optimism. Without it human life is a flash of occasional enjoyments lighting up a mass of pain and misery."[2] Whitehead therefore respected the West's religious vision of the transcendent God, whether or not his philosophy found adequate room for it.

Both the philosophy of Being and the philosophy of Process deserve to be taken seriously, for they are twentieth-century expansions of older styles of philosophical or religious argument. They both appeal to the new self-consciousness of twentieth-century man, who is aware of the wonder of his existence, and of the power of his mind, against a background which often tempts him to despair. The philosophy of Being, with its deep emphasis on a static peace and perfection at the heart of things, seems likely to appeal more to a deeply disturbed society, and the philosophy of Process, which emphasises "becoming" and tends to view change as progress, seems likely to appeal to a society which is cautiously optimistic; and in fact we do find that Martin Heidegger the German, and Paul Tillich the German-American, wrote and spoke about Being in the period from 1914 to around 1960, when Germany was in the throes of a destructive crisis and when the United States was under the threat of total war, whereas Whitehead and his disciples have emerged as the apostles

[1] See above, pp. 36, 265.
[2] *Science and the Modern World*, p. 275.

of Process from more peacefully academic (and scientifically minded) circles in Britain or America. But both philosophies have in common a concern to relate twentieth-century man to his total environment. They seek to show modern man his roots; and in this they fulfil one of the age-old tasks of religion. They try to demonstrate that man is not a lonely stranger in the universe; on the contrary, his life is united with all that is, and his mind is at home in the evolution out of which it came.

Such philosophies may in their different ways give a contemporary significance to the mythical account of the creation at the beginning of the Bible. That account has often been regarded as arising out of a pseudo-scientific knowledge of the origins of the universe, or out of a religious speculation about them. But the first chapter of the Old Testament seems to have been one of the last chapters to be written, and it seems to have arisen not out of science or out of speculation but out of the experience of Israel. That experience had a double climax: the Exodus from Egypt, and the Exile in Babylon. In those crises, Israel was confronted by two great empires, and Yahweh the one God of Israel was pitted against strange, mighty gods. Under immense pressures the faith of Israel held fast. Moses in relation to Egypt, and the unknown prophet known as Second Isaiah in relation to Babylon, interpreted the people's experience so as to disclose to them the unique Lordship of the one God, and the *Genesis* model of God the Creator survives to embody that crisis in religion. This model will not help the twentieth century to decide whether the universe began with one primeval nucleus and a "big bang", or whether the creation of atoms is steady and continuous; that is a question best left to the astronomers. But the ancient model may help the twentieth century to see whether it, too, discovers the God of the Bible to be the conqueror in its own tribulations because he is the source of its own existence. As Bultmann wrote, "the affirmation that God is Creator . . . cannot be made as a neutral statement, but only as thanksgiving and surrender."[1]

The age of science has to ask what in its own experience is similar to the experience which created the biblical myth. The philosophies of Being and of Process point to the answer, which is that estrangement or alienation, although felt in our time as perhaps never before, is not the deepest experience of modern man. Paul Tillich in particular has seen the grace of God ("Being itself") as coming to

[1] *Jesus Christ and Mythology*, p. 69. The biblical doctrine of Creation was discussed by Langdon Gilkey, *Maker of Heaven and Earth* (New York, 1959), and more philosophically by Donald Evans, *The Logic of Self-Involvement* (London, 1963).

modern man in every moment when man feels that there is an infinite power in the universe which accepts and sustains his finitude, and an inexhaustible love which accepts and transforms his anxiety; and Professor Macquarrie's large-scale reconstruction of Christian doctrine is made on the simple basis that God is Being experienced as gracious. Without this basis, Macquarrie argues, a Christian existentialist's analysis of human existence cannot be a Gospel; for without this basis, the last word about the human situation is a word of anxiety.[1]

This experience of communion with a goodness at the heart of life comes to people in moments of intensely personal joy such as the delights of marriage or parenthood, or in aesthetic ecstasies such as a full response to great music—rather than in the routine of intellectual work; but there is an aspect of science which can help intellectuals whose personal life may be impoverished to appreciate what is being said in these philosophies. Science may itself provide this relevant experience, for science is the correspondence between the mind of man and external reality. There are limits to the capacity of the mind, and one of these limits is the "givenness" of the whole universe (no one can tell how the primeval nucleus came to be); another of the limits is the unpredictability of the behaviour of the most elementary particles; but the mind can travel far before it comes up against such a limit. Up the telescope or down the microscope, the material of science seems to be orderly and responsive to the mind of man. The universe expands continuously at a speed which is faster than the speed of light, yet the mind of man can reach where even his aided eye cannot. At a level humbler than the microscope can reveal, the dance of the atoms in the stream of energy still seems to have a pattern which the mind can grasp. After its fantastic adventures, the inquiring mind still seems to be at home. This experience does not automatically produce religious orthodoxy, but it appears to have played a part in making a considerable number of the century's distinguished scientists religiously sensitive. In a period when the artists have normally felt angry because they have been isolated rebels against society, many of the scientists who have most effectively applied their intellects to nature have been most profoundly moved to a contented humility before the miracle of their success.[2]

[1] Perhaps with some unfairness, John Macquarrie criticises Rudolf Bultmann for not being explicit enough about this, in *An Existentialist Theology* (London, 1955) and *The Scope of Demythologizing* (London, 1960).

[2] F. R. Tennant's major work, *Philosophical Theology* (2 vols., Cambridge, 1928-30), was perhaps the century's most subtle study, from a religious angle, of the correspondence between the mind and reality at the basis of modern science. Tennant found evidence for

Evil and the Sovereign God

The philosophies of Being and of Process have been subjected to many intellectual attacks. They have often been expounded in a far from simple style, and critics, perhaps after a period of embarrassment at not being able to understand all this impressive writing, have tended to conclude that at least part of the fault lies in the philosophers' own confusion. But the protest has been against the religious as well as against the rhetorical character of such philosophy. It has been alleged that a half-concealed religious motive accounts for the fondness of philosophers such as Heidegger and Whitehead for grand ideas such as those of Being and Process. Are these somewhat cloudy metaphysical notions substitutes for God in the minds of intellectuals who are unable either to accept or to forget religious orthodoxy? When openly religious believers have used these philosophies in the defence of their faith, the criticism has been that here faith has concealed the depth of the abyss which separates it from reason. Is a theology which is in fact Christian once again pretending to be "natural" by employing philosophical fashions as weapons (or defences)? However, since we have already described these philosophies as basically mystical or aesthetic, we may dwell here—however briefly—on their religious (rather than on their intellectual) inadequacy. This we can do by relating these philosophies of Being and Process to *the problem of evil*.

These philosophies can be so expounded that they do not take evil seriously enough, yet in our time the problem of evil is the greatest stumbling block to religious faith. Is evil merely an aspect of the "non-being" which is necessary for Being to be? Or is it an accidental quirk which shows the power of the ultimately victorious Process to use everything? Or does it simply happen, without God being able to either stop it or to cure it? Some in our time have minimised evil in such ways. But Hebrew, Christian and Muslim monotheism declares: the death of a sparrow is evil, and the Lord of heaven and earth has to permit it before it can happen. If evil is a real and important part of the world, is it somehow part of the God who is the soul of the world? Some in our time think so. Thus a Christian writer, H. A. Williams, recently referred to the problem of evil "which has defeated the monotheistic centuries". He quoted the

the ordering of nature by God within the scientific activity itself, although, in his new and broader version of the old argument from the design of the world to the existence of the divine Designer, he also stressed the aesthetic appeal of nature, the fitness of the environment for human life, and the suitability of the world as a training-school in morality. These facts cumulatively produced a religious "certitude"—at least for him.

saying of Amos: "Is there evil in the city, and the Lord has not done it?" He related this to our experience of our own evil as part of our vitality. On the saying of Amos, he commented: "This rings truer to my experience than the unacknowledged polytheism of the Christian tradition where the Devil is really a god in disguise—a descendent probably of a Persian Zoroastrian deity." About his own experience, he said: "There I find both God and Devil, and I cannot put asunder what I find joined together. My experience will not allow me to believe in two gods, and the result is all but intolerable."[1]

Here Mr. Williams bravely voiced a problem which goes very deep. Yet his joining of God and the Devil really belongs to the Hindu tradition, which in philosophy declares that ultimate reality is "beyond good and evil" and which in religion worships the destructive as well as the creative in the goddess Kali. A different solution is offered in the great prophetic tradition of the monotheistic centuries: the tradition of Judaism and Islam which is also the tradition of Christianity. Plainly, however, the prophetic tradition needs to be restated for our time.

This prophetic tradition—in which Amos did not speak the last word—affirms that God is perfect. God is unlimited in his power and God is utterly good, and it is only because God is thus perfect in power and goodness that the prophetic tradition proclaims that he deserves man's total self-surrender in worship and love. Why then, does the perfect God, the Sovereign Father, permit evil? Mr. Williams is surely right to observe that this is the problem which has fascinated, and (if what we seek is a tidy intellectual system) has defeated, all who have adhered to the tradition; but we must add that if the problem is solved by the admission of imperfection into God, *the tradition ceases*. It is only out of the agony of this problem of evil that the glory of Jewish, Muslim or Christian belief in God can arise, for it is precisely the fact that the creation is partly evil that most sharply distinguishes the Creator in his perfect being from the worlds which he has chosen to call into existence, and from the men on whom he has chosen to bestow the gift of life.

Much of twentieth-century theology, discussing the problem of evil, has been concerned with the rejection of one solution. The rejection has consumed so much energy because, at least from St. Augustine onwards, this solution has usually been taken to be the doctrine of Christian orthodoxy. It is the solution which traces the existence of evil to the rebellion or fall of man, or of the angels, or

[1] *The God I Want*, ed. James Mitchell (London, 1967), pp. 186-8.

of the "world-soul". The creation was perfect before this fall, so that the evil in it has been caused by the wickedness of the creature, and the Creator is not to blame. One trouble about this solution to the problem is that the scientific study of evolution disproves the existence of any golden age in which the nature and environment of men were perfect. The biblical picture of the fall of Adam is myth, not history. To transfer the blame to the angels or to the "world-soul" seems ingenious but implausible, since both angels and the "world-soul" seem to be models which may assist the religious believer's imagination, rather than actual entities with wills of their own.[1]

When it advances beyond such negative criticisms, a theology which wishes to restate the faith of the monotheistic centuries for our own time finds the problem of evil largely baffling; for if theology confines itself (as it should) to affirmations which interpret actual experience, theology has to confess that it has no clue showing what purpose may be served by many events in the universe. Nothing in human experience enables man to interpret these events, which seem to come out of pure chance, although their randomness may be an illusion which a fuller experience and understanding will one day pierce. The contemporary experience of randomness is a psychological fact on which the religious philosophy of Process is erected; for that philosophy refrains from claiming that all events are designed or controlled by God. A reverent agnosticism will not go so far as to deny purpose in such events, however; it will simply say that we do not know.

But theology can be helped by contemporary religious experience to make a few affirmations of faith. One such affirmation is that the grace of God can supply strength in which the sufferer can live with the fact of evil; and another is that God can enable the sufferer to accept and use his bitter ordeal as a discipline which leads to spiritual progress. Such affirmations cannot be made cheaply. The courage of personal faith must be wrung out of the hard, often cruel, experience of living men and women, as their experience confirms the faith of history's saints. Such affirmations about how evil is to be overcome in the individual's experience cannot fully answer the question why evil is permitted at all, since the weight of suffering in the world often seems out of proportion with the benefits gained from it. Yet these affirmations about personal experience can be strengthened by the

[1] For the fall of the angels see, e.g., E. L. Mascall, *Christian Theology and Natural Science*, chapter 8; for the fall of the world-soul see, e.g., N. P. Williams, *The Ideas of the Fall and of Original Sin* (London, 1927), chapter 8; and for criticism of such speculations see, e.g., F. R. Tennant's Hulsean Lectures on *The Origin and Propagation of Sin* (Cambridge, 1902).

faith that God, the Sovereign Father, is overcoming the total fact of evil. *Precisely in relation to the problem of evil,* the faith of monotheism in our time proclaims the triumph of God.

This faith, however, does not claim that God's triumph is already complete in the creation as it is. This faith, rather, is the faith that at the consummation of his work the Creator will bring to order, and will justify, all that he has done in his previously imperfect creation. The faith of monotheism in our time therefore looks, as the faith of the Bible did, towards "the last things" (in Greek, *ta eschata*). This faith interprets reality as an eschatological process; and it does so because faith's vision of the history of salvation shows a history which gives the clue to all history, but also a history which has not yet reached the final climax towards which it moves. In no other way can the problem of evil be reconciled with belief in one, good God.[1]

Contemporary theology in its rejection of inadequate or unworthy images of God can reduce the transcendence of this one, good God by treating the word "God" as a poetic way of describing the transcendence of one's neighbour in a world which remains aimless or evil. But this is not the inevitable consequence of theology's purification of the images of God. It is also possible for theologians to adhere to the biblical doctrine that the love of the neighbour is only a road to the love of God, whom alone we are to love with all our being; and such theologians can reaffirm for our time the inexhaustible mystery of the God whom the Bible presents as the King who is transcendent over all evil, as the Lord of heaven and earth. And this leads us to study some of the other teachings by recent theologians about the mystery of God.

The Reality of the Mysterious God

At the end of his book on the possible answers to contemporary anxiety, *The Courage to Be* (New York, 1952), Paul Tillich wrote: "The courage to be is rooted in the God who appears when God has disappeared in the anxiety of doubt." We need to sense the force of this insistence by a great theologian that the real God is beyond all the images of God which are liable to disappear once questioned. Tillich's philosophical way of speaking should not conceal his intention of continuing the protest of the Bible. Included in his

---

[1] The best recent discussions of the problem of evil are by two English theologians: Austin Farrer, *Love Almighty and Ills Unlimited* (London, 1962), and John Hick, *Evil and the God of Love* (London, 1966). For a summary of the (mainly European) theological debate about eschatology, see Oscar Cullmann, *Salvation in History* (1965; Eng. trans., London, 1967).

prophetic distrust of all images was a specially powerful protest against one particular form of religious triviality: the sentimental tendency to regard God as *one person among others*, the childish tendency which ends in the picture (still popular among many adults) of God as the "Old Man in the Sky". Tillich here supplied the austere correction which both the prophets and the mystics have always offered to the simple sentimentality of the devout, but in fairness to him we should see that he was not undevout himself. He did address his prayers to God as "Father", and his protest against a trivial conception of the divine personality arose out of a desire to stress the power of God. God, Tillich taught, cannot be merely one person among others—because God is in every person. Implied in Tillich's protest against the sentimental picture of the Old Man in the Sky was also a rejection of the more intellectual tendency to regard God as *one object among others*—the highest part of the universe, but only a part. This tendency can result in the philosophical concept of God as the First Cause. The First Cause is an object in philosophical speculation which may or may not be there in actual reality (it is hard to tell); but anyway the First Cause is inert and remote. Or this tendency can result in the acknowledgement of God's presence only in a series of fitful interventions from the supernatural sphere, as when a watchmaker corrects a watch which normally he leaves alone, or as when in a Greek tragedy a god appears at the end to clear up the man-made mess (*deus ex machina*). Even orthodox and devout Christians may reveal a trivial conception of God when they speak of God "entering history" at the incarnation. God, Tillich taught, is everywhere; God is in all that is. As a Protestant prophet, Tillich taught that religious faith must be deepened in sensitivity to the depths of the mystery of Being. Such a purifying insistence on the wonder of God's reality seems now absolutely vital to the future of faith in God.

From its negative protest, however, modern theology may be emerging into a few positive affirmations. Faith in our time meets God's presence in this life, for no other life is yet available to us—*and faith finds God to be not a mere aspect or part of this existence but the inexhaustible mystery of "Being itself"*. Faith watches God's work in history, and gains through this work a vision of eternity. Thus the "high" God—high in the sense that this God is "Being itself"—is also near; and yet when he is near, God is known as "high" above all persons and all things. Faith declares that we may sense the presence of this God anywhere, in the secular world primarily, but also within religion. God shows himself to us, and we are grasped by him. We can answer him and obey him, but we can never fully describe how he has come to us, and still less can we describe him as he really is. In our time as for Moses in the Old Testament, the secret of the Lord remains with the Lord; his full name is not given to us, and his nature will be revealed only as he will gradually show himself more fully to us when we obey him.[1] And what is even more astonishing for faith: God treats us as adults, we can easily escape from his grasp, and again and again, even when we obey him as sons, he withdraws in order to teach us to stand on our own feet and not to cling to him in childish dependence. In our time, therefore, faith does not reach certainty; faith experiences much of that sense of godlessness which is described as the "death" of God; yet faith perseveres.

Faith in God perseveres, for, despite the validity of the protest against the idolatrous tendency to reduce the Creator to the level of being one person among many other people, the faith of Western monotheism finds itself still compelled to affirm that God cannot be *less* than personal. The Source and Ground of all that is cannot be inferior to any person in intelligence or will, freedom or love. Despite the inability of any symbolism to reveal perfectly the perfect Being, this faith still finds that personality is the key symbol in beginning to understand God; and one of the reasons for using this personal category in the language of faith is the experience of faith that God, who is more than personal, becomes "a person" when he comes to meet us. Existence now seems to be the sphere of the one great meeting for which all personal encounters are mere preparations, as when W. H. Auden has this vision:

> Space is the Whom our loves are needed by,
> Time is our choice of How to love and Why.[2]

Faith perseveres, because the man of faith has been grasped by his vision of a reality which he must name as God. This holds true, although part of the problem of evil—and for many it is the hardest part to bear of the whole colossal burden—is the evil which religion itself has sheltered or encouraged or caused. One summer's morning in Germany, Martin Buber was asked by a friend why he continued to use the word "God" to describe the reality about which he was attempting to speak. For this friend, the evil which had been done in the name of "God" had ruined the word. In his reply, Buber summed

[1] For a fine statement of this experience from a Roman Catholic background, see Leslie Dewart, *The Future of Belief: Theism in a World Come of Age* (New York, 1966).
[2] *For the Time Being* (London, 1941).

up the prophetic faith of the monotheistic centuries, as this faith has confronted the mystery of the reality of evil and the mystery of the reality of God.

"Yes"—so Buber reconstructs the reply which he then gave spontaneously to his critic—"it is the most heavy-laden of all human words. None has become so soiled, so mutilated. Just for this reason I may not abandon it. Generations of men have laid the burden of their anxious lives upon this word and weighed it to the ground; it lies in the dust and bears their whole burden. The races of men with their religious factions have torn the word to pieces; they have killed for it and died for it, and it bears their finger-marks and their blood. Where might I find a word like it to describe the highest? If I took the purest, most sparkling concept from the inner treasure-chamber of the philosopher, I could only capture thereby an unbinding product of thought. I could not capture the presence of Him whom the generations of men have honoured and degraded with their awesome living and dying. I do indeed mean Him whom the hell-tormented and heaven-storming generations of men mean. Certainly, they draw caricatures and write 'God' underneath; they murder one another and say 'in God's name'. But when all madness and delusion fall to dust, when they stand over against Him in the loneliest darkness and no longer say 'He, He', but rather sigh 'Thou', shout 'Thou', all of them the one word, and when they then add 'God', is it not the real God whom they implore, the One Living God, the God of the children of men? Is it not He who *hears* them? And just for this reason is it not the word 'God', the word of appeal, the word which has become a *name*, consecrated in all human tongues for all times? We must esteem those who interdict it because they rebel against the injustice and wrong which are so readily referred to 'God' for authorization. But we may not give it up. How understandable it is that some suggest that we should remain silent about the 'last things' for a time in order that the misused words may be redeemed! But they are not to be redeemed *thus*. We cannot cleanse the word 'God' and we cannot make it whole; but, defiled and mutilated as it is, we can raise it from the ground and set over it an hour of great care."[1]

The Centrality of the Credible Christ

Dare we go further than this modern prophet of Israel, Martin Buber? Dare we say more?

[1] Martin Buber, *The Eclipse of God* (New York, 1952), pp. 7-8.

It is the belief of Judaism that the Messiah has *not* come; for if the Messiah had come, the Kingdom of God would have come, and of all the peoples of the earth the Jews have the best of reasons for knowing that the Kingdom of God has not come. On many occasions Martin Buber protested out of the tragic experience of his race and of mankind in this century that Christians were mistaken to name Jesus as the Messiah. But the Jewish protest, although right to bind Jesus to the idea of the Kingdom of God, would seem to be wrong if it claimed that Christians believe that the Kingdom of God has come. What Christians believe is that Jesus announced that the Kingdom of God would come—and inaugurated its coming. It seems right that the heirs of the Christian tradition should in our time turn again to examine this teaching of Jesus, remembering that Christians up to the present day have been extraordinarily reluctant to base their theology on the teaching given by the Jesus whom they have described as the Word of God. As Dr. Daniel Jenkins has observed (in a remark which will seem a platitude only to those unacquainted with the uninhibited originality of much thought which seeks a Christian label): "Those who are prepared to accept Christ but not to accept his central message have, at least, the obligation to recognize that they are asserting that he is radically mistaken . . . The question of belief in the Christian God cannot be decided unless a determined effort is made, with a full awareness of the complexity of the task, to discover what Jesus Christ would have us believe about that God."[1]

But *how* can this effort be made with this awareness of the complexity of the task? The centrality of Jesus Christ for Christianity has been expressed for many twentieth-century Christians largely in terms of their response to the revolution in theology effected by Karl Barth, who declared that the one task of a really Christian theology was to study, proclaim and interpret the event of Jesus Christ as the Word of God.[2] Thus "the Gospel-character of the Gospel" has been restated with great force by Helmut Gollwitzer, a disciple of Karl Barth who has been much exposed to the storms of our time as an opponent of Hitler, as a prisoner in Stalin's Russia, and as a professor in West Berlin determined to keep open lines of sympathy and communication with the Communist East.[3] "The Gospel-character of the Gospel," Dr. Gollwitzer has written, "depends entirely on the fact that we may

[1] *The Christian Belief in God* (London, 1964), p. 45.
[2] See above, pp. 171-4.
[3] For the personal background, see Helmut Gollwitzer, *The Demands of Freedom* (London, 1965). Gollwitzer, who edited a useful paperback of selections from Barth's *Dogmatics*, was chosen to succeed Barth as Professor of Theology at Basle, but his appointment was vetoed by the Swiss authorities since he was politically controversial.

and must say: God is. Because he is, he can be for us as what he is and with all that he is."[1] That is a sentence which might not have been written, had it not been for Karl Barth.

Gollwitzer knows from his wide and harsh experience of the twentieth-century world that Jesus Christ's Gospel of God is very definitely *not* a philosophy which every man can reach for himself without needing a teacher. In a review of *Honest to God* which was very sympathetic with the wish of Bishop John Robinson to give Christianity a modern expression, Gollwitzer warned the Bishop that the secular man of the 1960s was not so familiar as the Bishop was with "love" in the "depths" of reality. "Whatever depths he plumbs ... he [the secular man] finds the loneliness and lostness of the person amid the horrifying indifference of nature towards it, but of love he finds at the ground of being not a trace; the frightfulness of nature and of history is brought home to him by every newspaper, but neither by looking around nor by looking deep does he find any reason at all to trust in the ground of being." "The only way of making Christian faith worth noticing again," Gollwitzer concluded, "is not to obscure its rough edges, but to emphasise them."[2]

Thus Christian theology seems bound to take with utter seriousness Karl Barth's proclamation of the centrality of Jesus Christ and of the holy Father who is revealed by Jesus Christ. But the fact remains that only a small minority has found Karl Barth's own way of "making the Christian faith worth noticing again" to be permanently convincing. Barth's failure may be attributed partly to his style, which has always been the eloquence of an excited preacher—a style which in our time falls strangely on the ears both of the intelligentsia and of the intellectually simple. But about Barth supremely it is true to say that the style is the man. In his fully developed and academically supported *Church Dogmatics* as in his moving addresses to the inmates of Basle Prison,[3] Barth deliberately began not with a discussion of the possibility of Christian faith in terms of the hearer's own experience, but with an announcement of a fact repeated from the Bible. He scorned to discuss possibilities; he was gripped by what for him was the all-embracing and all-deciding reality, the glorious reality of God in Jesus Christ. He believed that single-minded concentration on the Word of God as the one object to be considered in preaching or theology is what could deliver those human activities from speculation

---

[1] *The Existence of God as Confessed by Faith* (1964; Eng. trans., London, 1965), p. 235.
[2] *Ibid.*, pp. 252-3.
[3] *Deliverance to the Captives* (1959; Eng. trans., London, 1961); *Call for God* (1965; Eng. trans., London, 1967).

and sentimentality. Thus, and only thus, the task of the preacher or the theologian could become manly and joyous. The scientist studies one object; and Barth called on the preacher or the theologian to be disciplined and objective in something like the same way. Up to a point, this approach is successful. Barth's own torrential eloquence *is* manly and joyous, and the truth to which he is devoted may appeal through his personality. This impact is the equivalent—at a far more intelligent level—of the effect on a mass audience of the evangelism conducted by Billy Graham in Barth's later years. But not everyone will be attracted by such self-confidence. Many people will continue to ask questions which they cannot abandon without denying all their life to this date. Karl Barth (like Billy Graham) is not so helpful there.

For all its many merits, Barth's presentation of Christ suffers from his dogmatic approach. Great emphasis is placed for example, on, the eternal decree of God the Father to be "with men" and "for men" through God the Son, who is called "Jesus Christ" even before the birth of the "God-Man". The purpose behind the whole created universe is that it should be a theatre for the fulfilment of this decree, and the meaning of all history is that in history a People of God should respond to God's choice of them (their "election"). This divine decree has the incidental merit of ruling out the speculation of the sixteenth-century John Calvin (who is greatly honoured by Barth in other connections) that God had predestined some to everlasting damnation. According to Barth, the decree was revealed during the days in which the risen Christ taught his disciples, before his ascension. In those great days the first Christians also learned *how* God had been "with men" and "for men". Here Barth does mainly echo Calvin, for his presentation of the saving act of God is made through an emphasis on Jesus Christ's sufferings on the cross under "the wrath of God". But *all* men, Barth says, were loved by God from the beginning; *all* men sinned and therefore deserved damnation; Jesus Christ when he suffered and died bore the punishment on behalf of *all*, and therefore *all* have been reconciled to God, whether they accept it or not. On the cross God took man's place; therefore, in heaven man may share God's place. For Barth, this is the "incomprehensible miracle" at the heart of the Gospel.[1] Barth differs significantly from Calvin in a clearer stress on God's love as the centre of the cross. God for him is by no means a remote judge, for God is fully in the Crucified; indeed, God the Son, the eternal Second

[1] E.g., *Dogmatics in Outline*, p. 115.

Person of the Trinity, is "the Subject" who is the centre of the manhood of Jesus.

Let us be candid: the trouble about this whole proclamation of Jesus Christ by Karl Barth is that it means little or nothing to modern men whose minds do not move in response to talk about religious metaphysics and religious sacrifices. Not even the genius and attractiveness of Barth can permanently remedy this basic defect. The language of Barth can be deeply meaningful to minds formed by the orthodox tradition of Christianity, and such believers may compare Barth's theology to its advantage with the theology of Calvin, etc. But to those who begin at another place, Barth offers no concessions and no connections. He frankly speaks of faith as a miracle, and his sole concern is that the faith should not be betrayed in the attempt to make it palatable. And many Christians who in our time share Barth's desire to witness to the God of the Bible find that the basic arrogance in such theology is an arrogance which is essentially different in its whole mood from the Bible's firm and unsentimental teaching. The Christ they know did not dismiss the earthy, doubting layman with the "Take it or leave it" of Karl Barth. And they agree with Dietrich Bonhoeffer's letter of 5 May, 1944: "Barth was the first theologian to begin the criticism of religion, and that remains his really great merit; but he put in its place a positivist doctrine of revelation which says, in effect, 'Like it or lump it': virgin birth, Trinity, or anything else; each is an equally significant and necessary part of the whole, which must simply be swallowed as a whole or not at all. That is not biblical."[1]

By inferring that he did not "like" the virginal conception of Jesus, Bonhoeffer indicated his agreement with Rudolf Bultmann and with many others that St. Luke's and St. Matthew's story telling, however beautiful it is in the setting of Christmas, does not strike us as being compatible with our biological knowledge—or even (and this is more serious, for previous generations accepted this miracle while also regarding it as "against nature") as being compatible with the New Testament's portrait of Jesus. The biblical portrait seems to give us a man among men, a royal man "of the seed of David", but nevertheless a man subject to the normal fate of prophets including the misunderstanding of his family. When Albert Schweitzer was a boy, he shocked his elders by asking why the family of Jesus was so poor if the infant had been presented with priceless gifts, and why the shepherds did not become disciples. In our time fewer young minds

[1] *Letters and Papers from Prison*, p. 157.

need be burdened by such doubts, for fewer scholars and preachers of integrity are prepared to teach the Christmas stories literally.[1] Other "nature miracles" in the gospels are also criticised. Faith-healing and the psychical phenomena of the resurrection appearances are accepted (although not necessarily with the details which clothed these stories as told in the early Church), but the raisings from the dead (Lazarus, etc.) and the biggest miracle of all, Jesus's empty tomb, are discarded by many theologians who cannot be accused of a lack of reverent scholarship or of a failure to appreciate the transformation of the apostles which was accomplished by the appearances of the risen Lord.[2] Today it seems right to keep an open mind about the empty tomb, and it seems possible that by the end of this century most Christian theologians will be agnostics on the subject of what happened to the body of Jesus after his crucifixion. At any rate, confidence such as has marked Karl Barth is now rare among theologians outside Roman Catholicism, Eastern Orthodoxy and Protestant Fundamentalism. Outside those circles, not many theologians would see the intellectual situation in Professor E. L. Mascall's complacent way: "Whether or not it was necessary to liberalise theology in order to meet the demands of science yesterday, it is certainly not necessary to do so today."[3] Few theologians not openly dedicated to a dogmatic system would write sentences such as these, again by Professor Mascall: "The human organism which the Son of God took from his Virgin Mother and in which he died and rose from the dead was not destroyed by his resurrection and ascension; it was transfigured and glorified and made accessible to men. By baptism a man or woman is incorporated into this glorified humanity of the Word-made-flesh . . ."[4] But questioning among theologians about the physical aspects of the doctrines of the incarnation and the resurrection need not mean the abandonment of the faith on which the Church has depended for its life since its earliest days. Essentially, this is the faith that in Jesus the Word of God to men was truly embodied and "enmanned" and "historicised" —and that the Jesus who was crucified is the risen Lord, now in the

---

[1] See Thomas Boslooper, *The Virgin Birth* (Philadelphia, 1962).
[2] The weighty historical arguments were summed up by G. W. H. Lampe in *The Resurrection* (London, 1966); but the contributions by D. M. MacKinnon in that book will remind the reader of the spiritual dimensions of any doctrine of the resurrection. See also the German discussion in *The Significance of the Message of the Resurrection for Faith in Jesus Christ*, ed. C. F. D. Moule (London, 1968). Earlier discussion included P. Gardner-Smith, *The Narratives of the Resurrection* (London, 1926), mainly critical, and A. M. Ramsey, *The Resurrection of Christ* (London, 1946), mainly devotional.
[3] *Christian Theology and Natural Science*, p. 46.
[4] *Ibid.*, p. 314.

glory of his Father and at the centre of his Church. The physical details do not matter in comparison with those tremendous affirmations.

By referring to the doctrine of the Holy Trinity, Bonhoeffer (whose own academic writing on the problem of the nature of Christ can scarcely be described as unsophisticated) was indicating his great sympathy with many modern questioners. If they are agnostic about many of the details in the earthly life of Jesus, such questioners are even more sceptical about the ability of human minds to describe with precision the links between that life and the home life (in technical theology, the "aseity") of God. Bultmann's contention seems likely to prevail that theology "cannot speak of God as he is in himself, but only what he does for us."[1] Among many theologians there is an impatience with the metaphysical dogmas of the past. This leads to a questioning of the contemporary relevance of the fifth-century Chalcedonian Definition of the divine and human natures in Christ, and it leads also to an ashamed disgust with the virtual tritheism (three gods) of much popular Trinitarianism. When Barth tells us that the Word of God was "the Subject" in the person of Jesus, and that the Word derives from the communion of the Three Persons of the Trinity with each other in eternity, such theologians dare to ask: does even Barth know what he is talking about? How can any mortal man be confident that he has understood the unique personality of Jesus? How dare he seem to be at home in the home life of God?

Theologians who confess their ignorance about most aspects of this mystery may, however, believe and teach that in an utterly unique manner "God was in Christ"; that God was present in Jesus without removing that Son of God from among the sons of men; that God acting mightily through that holy, loving life, so as to reveal his glory and so as to save the world.[2] Thus H. W. Montefiore writes: "His knowledge was human knowledge, his actions were human actions. Yet in Jesus the divine activity was fully present so far as is possible to human personality . . . We are exactly translating the essence of Chalcedon into a different thought-form. We have not rid ourselves altogether of the concept of substance, but we cannot

---

[1] *The Theology of Rudolf Bultmann*, ed. C. W. Kegley, p. 273.
[2] Examples of recent discussion are J. M. Creed's Hulsean Lectures on *The Divinity of Jesus Christ* (Cambridge, 1938), mainly historical; Donald Baillie, *God Was in Christ* (London, 1948), comparing the presence of God in Christ with the experience of God's grace in the Christian; Norman Pittenger, *The Word Incarnate* (London, 1959), presenting Christ as "that One in whom God actualized in a living human personality the potential God-man relationship which is the divinely intended truth about every man" (p. 285); and John Knox, *The Humanity and Divinity of Jesus Christ*, distinguishing speculation about Christ from the experienced fact of Christ.

theologize about it, since the Being of God is transcendent to our existence."[1] Or Professor John Hick writes that the Divine Love "caused" the love of Jesus, much as the radiant energy of the sun causes the light which falls on the earth, so that "Jesus was God's attitude to mankind incarnate".[2] Jesus seems to have been extremely reticent about his self-consciousness, and no doubt he was sharply aware of the inadequacy of all the traditional titles which his followers were to apply to him.[3] But Jesus did believe that his mission was unique and all-important, so that the simple Christology which we have just outlined may be considered both necessary and enough. In Dr. Norman Pittenger's words, "one group of Christians has tended to say that this person is God living and acting humanly. Another has tended to say that this person is the Man in whom God lives and acts. The difference between the two ways of phrasing the fact which Christians have encountered has led to almost interminable theological argument, which has been as little enlightening as it has been little edifying."[4]

What our time needs, therefore, in the reconstruction of a distinctively Christian faith is the centrality of a *credible* Christ as the enfleshed Word of God. This recovery must take account of biblical scholarship, which with its patient learning and courageous honesty has been one of the most strenuous forms taken by the free intellectual life of our century; and it must be patient to relate itself to all our century's difficulties with Christian orthodoxy. Much has been questioned or destroyed by modern biblical scholarship, but what remains? We need to try to answer Dietrich Bonhoeffer's question: *Who is Christ for us today?*[5]

At least since Albert Schweitzer's *Quest of the Historical Jesus*, it has been generally acknowledged by scholars that Jesus taught about the supernatural and world-transforming Kingdom of God, and that he lived and died in order that this Kingdom might come on earth as in heaven. The supreme question has been what this message and life can mean for an age which does not think in the language of the first-century Jewish apocalyptic hope. The facts that Schweitzer grossly exaggerated Jesus's identification with the cruder forms of

[1] *Soundings*, p. 171.
[2] In *Prospect for Theology*, ed. F. G. Healey (London, 1967), p. 164.
[3] A survey of the historical evidence was provided by Gunther Bornkamm, *Jesus of Nazareth* (1956; Eng. trans., London, 1960). But even that masterly book did not stop scholarly discussion of the problems involved for biblical criticism.
[4] *The Word Incarnate*, p. 12.
[5] See the symposium sponsored by the Modern Churchmen's Union, *Christ for Us Today*, ed. Norman Pittenger (London, 1968).

hat hope, and that he failed to work out for himself a philosophy
vith any real resemblance to the teaching of Jesus about God, have
ot blinded the more thoughtful to the urgency of the challenge.
What has begun to emerge from the massive debate among the
heologians has been a consensus that the Kingdom means the fully
cknowledged sovereignty of God, and that Jesus regarded his work
s the decisive stage in the inauguration of this Kingdom. That was
vhy in so many of his parables he warned his original hearers that
he greatest conceivable crisis was upon them. It is also agreed that
esus summoned men to enter the Kingdom by following him along
he way of the cross, and promised them that God would bring in his
wn Kingdom fully in his own way and at his own time.[1] Finally, it is
greed that after the death of Jesus his resurrection became for
Christians *the* sign that the Kingdom of which he had spoken had
een inaugurated, and was triumphing.

Because other words have to be produced to express this message
oday, we may refer to some of the preconditions of understanding
his message. Here we must agree with the insistence of Karl Barth
hat it is only a new life that will lead to a new understanding of God.
There must be a thorough turning, a conversion; a thorough re-
ewal, a rebirth; for it is only a life of attempted obedience to the
thical teaching of Jesus, lived in spiritual fellowship with him, that
vill give a person in our time a clear enough vision of the world as it
s meant to be, and of the Sovereign Lord who means this. Only the
xperiences of this discipleship will give men a sufficient foretaste of
he victory of God over evil—a victory which is not complete in this
ge of the world but which is surely coming when all the purposes of
God have been worked out. The experiences of the disciple are not
ufficient in themselves to supply this vision; they only become
ufficient when brought to the Master in a continuing and developing
elationship. Thus the centrality of Christ in Christian thought
nvolves the centrality of Christian prayer in Christian life. Nor are
he experiences of the disciple sufficient to satisfy all of a man's
atural curiosity; they are adequate only to sustain the disciple along
he road to the end. And when the disciple has contributed what he
an to the victory of God, he will find that it has been very little, so
hat when Christian prayer moves from communion with God through
Christ to consider the needs of the world, the disciple learns that his chief
ontribution is to express in prayer the world's greatest (although large-

[1] For a study taking account of textual and of "form-critical" scholarship, see Norman
Perrin, *Reconstructing the Teaching of Jesus* (London, 1966).

356 *Religion and Change*

ly unacknowledged) need: "Thy Kingdom come, thy will be done."
In the course of such a discipline, what does the disciple begin to
discover about the significance of the teaching of Jesus about the
Kingdom of God? After all our criticisms of the great theologians of
our century, it would be foolish for us to pretend to possess the
answers to the vast problems at which we have glanced. (Albert
Schweitzer used to say that the day when the meaning of the
Kingdom of God was agreed on would be the day when the two
streams of dogmatic and liberal theology flowed together.[1]) But in
due humility we may mention a few of the discoveries which have
been reflected and vindicated in some recent theology. For in other
hands than ours, under an inspiration greater than any given to our
own age, these themes might become the battlecries of a new Reformation, the affirmations of a faith able to fire the hearts of the millions.

The Message of Hope

First, the disciple learns that the Gospel is a message of hope.[2]
The message of the Kingdom of God, as proclaimed by Jesus,
was the highest humanism, for it taught that the men, women and
children who crowded the parables had a human nature which
reflected the character of God. Jesus added that God may be
addressed on this basis. It was the astonishing intention of Jesus that
the eternal, hallowed, royal God should be addressed as *Abba*, which
(since English-speaking babies seem to mouth different noises) should
be translated as "Dad". Nor was the intimacy intended to be degrading to God's children. *Abba* was a word which adult Jews, as well as
children, used when addressing their fathers.[3] Here was a mature
faith, which St. Paul writing to the Galatians (4. 1-11) was at pains to
distinguish from the time of our minority, when we were not in any
full sense sons but were "slaves to the elemental spirits of the universe".
When St. Paul wrote about God sending "into our hearts the Spirit of
his Son crying, '*Abba*! Father!' ", he did not imply that we were to be
childish. "*Abba* might be responsible for ensconcing at the very heart
of religion a permanent infantilism", yet "the New Testament itself
contains some very severe condemnations of perpetual immaturity".[4]
The adulthood of Christian discipleship, moving to full freedom by

[1] Henry Clark, *The Philosophy of Albert Schweitzer*, p. 210.
[2] I hope to expand this brief section in a book to be published by the SCM Press,
London, under the title of *The Last Things Now*.
[3] See Joachim Jeremias, *The Central Message of the New Testament* (London, 1965),
chapter 1.
[4] C. F. Evans, *The Lord's Prayer* (London, 1963), p. 24.

many "stations" including the stations of powerful activity, mature wisdom, suffering and death, was known by Dietrich Bonhoeffer, as he prayed in his prison, and as he went to his execution. "This is the end," were his last words to his friends. "For me, the beginning of life." Such words imply one decisive answer to Bonhoeffer's own questions about the place of Christianity in a world "come of age". The coming of age of mankind can reach no higher than simple discipleship reaches when a Christian knows the real God as Father and trusts that in whatever may come, including both tribulation and wealth, both life and death, his Father will give him both freedom and help. "If God is what he is," writes Bishop John Robinson, "then death *cannot* have the last word. His love continues to claim men unconditionally, whatever the outcome. But precisely because it is unconditional, it cannot be conditioned by anything; nothing in all creation can separate from it."[1]

If the heart of Christian prayer is the address to God as *Abba*, the heart of the Christian experience that God "is what he is" is a participation in the joy of Easter. Through mechanisms, physical, psychic or visionary, which cannot be completely understood today, this joy came to the first disciples after the crucifixion of the one who had taught them so to pray. Jesus was right; God was, and is, and will be, the unconditional and unconditioned Father. It was in the world transfigured by this Easter light that St. Luke seemed to hear from the cross a prayer which followed the psalm of anguish and the wordless cry recorded by St. Mark—the prayer, "*Abba*, into thy hands I commit my spirit." In the Easter world the mystery of the ultimate reality was seen as the mystery of victorious love, and therefore here man could accept God as Father. In this light at the death of Jesus, St. Luke also seemed to see the Christmas angels with the shepherds at the beginning, and to hear the symphony behind the word *Abba*: the song of glory to God and peace to man.[2]

Christian hope has been a theme of much Christian thought in recent years. This has been the only response possible for Christians in an age which has been dominated by the secular dreams of Utopia. Christian theology, when it has been vital, has had to come to terms with the totalitarianisms of Communism and National Socialism, and with the longer-lived intoxications of technical and social progress in the democratic age of science. The twentieth

[1] *In the End God* (1950; revd. edn., London, 1968), p. 25.
[2] The difference which the story of Jesus makes to the idea of God can be expressed more philosophically, as in D. W. D. Shaw, *Who is God?* (London, 1968).

century has been eschatological in its inner drive, and the twentieth-century Church has had to think about the contemporary relevance of the eschatological myths and symbols which it has inherited from a vanished (but no less turbulent) world. The World Council of Churches, for example, made "hope" the theme of its Assembly at Evanston in 1954, and the Second Vatican Council repeated in a different context many of the agreements of that Assembly. Theologians in their reflections, after many one-sided emphases and mutual accusations, have increasingly come to see that various elements in the Christian hope should be held together in an eschatology for our time.

First, many of the hopes of history can be endorsed, for the energy in such creative hopes should be interpreted as coming from the Creator. In particular, the revolutionary hope of our own time may be seen as connected profoundly with the energetic optimism of the Christian Gospel. Jesus dared to live in joy because he trusted that his Father would show himself as King; and the central inspiration in the progress of the modern world is connected with that confident trust.[1] Christians believe in a progressive and revolutionary God, who is "above" yet who always calls men into a better future on the good earth. As Teilhard de Chardin liked to put it, "the synthesis between the (Christian) God 'above' and the (Marxist) God 'in front': here is the only God whom we can henceforth adore in spirit and in truth."[2]

Second, the hopes of evolution should be endorsed as they hold before us realistic prospects of technical and cultural advance in the two thousand million years ahead of *homo sapiens*. The full emergence of man, his "hominisation" in Teilhard's phrase, is not complete, but a promise of complete "hominisation" may be heard if the hand of God is seen in the processes of evolution to date; and the twentieth-century Christian may set his faith in that perspective.[3] But fearful dangers remain in both contemporary and evolutionary hopes, and the certainty of death—the death of the individual, the death of the race, the death of the planet—lies at the end.

Therefore, Christian theology rightly continues to put its main emphasis on the third great element in Christian hope, which is the confidence that the glory of God will sustain the glory of man through

[1] For an exposition of hope in the Bible in relation to secular hopes, see Hendrikus Berkhof, *Christ the Meaning of History* (1958; Eng. trans., London, 1965).
[2] Quoted in *Evolution, Marxism and Christianity*, ed. B. Towers and A. Dyson (London, 1967), p. 73.
[3] See Ernst Benz, *Evolution and Christian Hope* (1965; Eng. trans., New York, 1966).

the death which comes to every man and to every part of the universe. "The last enemy that shall be destroyed is death . . . that God may be all in all," wrote Teilhard on the last page of his journal before his death in New York on Easter Day, 1955.[1] Here one of the greatest Catholic prophets to the twentieth century is at one with a great Protestant prophet, Bonhoeffer. Here is faith in the eternal "Lord of heaven and earth", who loves the man whom he has made and, having loved him, will not throw him away. This God remains the "Lord of the living"—through death itself. Here, resting man's whole hope on God's reality and rule, is the most sublime affirmation of the destiny of *homo sapiens*. Since Copernicus man has lost his physical centrality in the universe; since Darwin man has lost his uniqueness in creation; since Marx and Freud man has lost his rationality as the control of his conduct; yet here, in the very simple faith that God loves for ever the man whose character has been shaped by all the influences of the world (influences which Darwin, Marx, Freud and a host of others may analyse), is the modern translation of the old myth of the glory of man in the resurrection of the body. Here, all but totally incredible in the splendour of its courage, is faith in eternal life as the consummation of the whole story of the whole man in the whole universe. "The world as we see it is strictly unintelligible," wrote William Temple in a letter when he had just become Archbishop of Canterbury. "We can only have faith that it will become intelligible when the divine purpose, which is the explanation of it, is accomplished."[2]

"Theologically," Temple noted, "this is a greater emphasis on eschatology." One of the most widely discussed of German theological works of the 1960s was summed up by its author as a restatement of "eschatology", and so as an answer to the challenge of Albert Schweitzer: what for us is the Kingdom of God? "The eschatological," writes Jurgen Moltmann, "is not one element of Christianity, but it is the medium of Christian faith as such, the key in which everything is set, the glow that suffuses everything here in the dawn of an expected new day. For Christian faith lives from the raising of the crucified Christ, and strains after the promises of the universal future of Christ . . . Christianity is to be understood as the community of those who on the ground of the resurrection of Christ wait for the Kingdom of God and whose life is determined by this expectation."[3]

[1] Teilhard de Chardin, *The Future of Man* (1959; Eng. trans., London, 1964), p. 309.
[2] F. A. Iremonger, *William Temple*, p. 538.
[3] *Theology of Hope* (1965; Eng. trans., 1967), pp. 16, 326. Moltmann here relates the Gospel to the thought of a philosopher in the tradition of Marxist optimism, Ernst Bloch.

This summary of Christian eschatology by a biblically based theologian may be compared with a famous passage written by A. N. Whitehead, with a significant silence about the resurrection of Christ. "The essence of Christianity," wrote Whitehead, "is the appeal to the life of Christ as a revelation of the nature of God and of his agency in the world"—and for Whitehead, this was the life of Christ: "the Mother, the child, and the bare manger: the lowly man, homeless and self-forgetful, with his message of peace, love and sympathy: the suffering, the agony and the tender words as life ebbed, the final despair: and the whole with the authority of supreme victory." And Whitehead added: "Can there be any doubt that the power of Christianity lies in its revelation in act of that which Plato divined in theory?"[1] Our answer must be that such doubt is possible. What Whitehead called the "persuasive love" revealed by Christ and by Plato as the final power in the world has been for Christians the "revelation in act" of *the living and triumphant God*. A philosophy which ignores the mystery of Easter, and which uses Bethlehem and Calvary as illustrations of Plato's teaching, must be asked whether it has really included in its system the biblical proclamation of this God. Whitehead neglected Easter as a foretaste of the victory of the living God at the End; and this neglect was all the more regrettable because his philosophy suggested important reinterpretations of the traditional ideas or pictures of eternal glory.

We may sum up an austere and subtle philosophy by saying that, according to Whitehead, immortality consists in being remembered by God; and eternity consists in the permanence given in the "consequent nature" of God to the "perishing of occasions".[2] Such reinterpretations may indicate a way for Christian believers to avoid the selfish sentimentality of the idea of heaven as "pie in the sky when I die". Whitehead's theories may seem too close to the nihilism of Gautama's *Nirvana*; they may suggest a view of human destiny which values the personality and its environment less highly than did the traditional Christian doctrines. Christians will wish to insist that the comparison of God's eternity with man's memory provides only one "model" to help us in the exploration of an inexhaustible mystery. But such reinterpretations, if connected with the Easter mystery, might be developed in a way which communicated with a new power the traditional emphasis that the only ultimate hope of man (and the surrounding creation) is of resurrection into the endless glory of God.

[1] *Adventures of Ideas*, pp. 213-14.
[2] See Charles Hartshorne's essay on death in *The Logic of Perfection and Other Essays* (Lasalle, Ill., 1962), Chapter 10.

For if God is the God of Easter, if God is the Father who remembers the crucifixion in order to forgive it, if God is the Lord of history who brings the highest joy out of the deepest tragedy and who pours an invincible assurance into those whose hearts have been broken, if God is the Lover who began the whole process of the universe out of love and who can be trusted to make the best of it, why should the destiny of being remembered *by this God* be less than the destiny of the "survival" claimed by Spiritualism? Why should history as a contribution to the life of this God be less significant than history "going on for ever"? The transforming power of the human memory already foreshadows the glory which could cover the whole story of man in the universe, when God the Creator in his mercy remembers.

A reference by a recent Christian writer to the power of memory is worth quoting here, although it stops short of Whitehead's point that resurrection is like God's memory. "The dullest of us knows how memory can transfigure; how often some momentary glimpse of beauty in boyhood is

> a whisper
> Which memory will warehouse as a shout.

Don't talk to me of the 'illusions' of memory," wrote C. S. Lewis at the end of his life. "Why should what we see at the moment be more real than what we see from ten years' distance? . . . Traherne's 'orient and immortal wheat' or Wordsworth's landscape 'apparelled in celestial light' may not have been so radiant in the past when it was present as in the remembered past. That is the beginning of the glorification. One day they will be more radiant still . . . The new earth and sky, the same yet not the same as these, will rise in us as we have risen in Christ. And once again, after who knows what aeons of the silence and the dark, the birds will sing out and the waters flow, and lights and shadows move across the hills, and the faces of our friends laugh upon us with amazed recognition. Guesses, of course, only guesses. If they are not true, something better will be."[1]

One of the most interesting of contemporary American theologians has offered the following sketch of a "demythologised eschatology", leading to a new vision of the resurrection to eternal life as the greatest hope in the Christian message. "Because God's love, radically unlike ours, is pure and unbounded, and because he therefore can and does

---

[1] C. S. Lewis, *Letters to Malcolm: Chiefly on Prayer* (London, 1964), pp. 156-8. I do not mean to endorse the fantastic suggestion made earlier in this letter that no one has been converted from scepticism to a "liberal" or "demythologised" Christianity (pp. 152-5). Lewis knew well that myths or models or "guesses" must be used to speak about eternity, and in his own bereavement he experienced this: see his *A Grief Observed* (London, 1961).

participate fully in the being of all his creatures, the present moment
for him never slips into the past as it does for us. Instead, every
moment retains its vividness and intensity for ever within his
completely perfect love and judgment. He knows all things for just
what they are, and he continues to know and cherish them throughout the endless ages of the future in all the richness of their actual
being. In other words, because God not only *affects*, but is also
affected by, whatever exists, all things are in every present quite
literally resurrected or restored in his own everlasting life, from which
they can never more be cast out. This, I hold, is the promise of faith:
that, whatever else may befall us and however long or short may be
the span of our lives, either here or hereafter, we are each embraced
in every moment within God's boundless love and thereby have the
ultimate destiny of endless life in and through him. In this sense, the
promise of faith, which is already known to the Christian in his
present encounter with Jesus Christ, is the promise of victory over
death."[1]

The Message of Patience

A message of hope, on earth and in God's eternal life, may be heard
as the message of the Kingdom of God in our time. But Christian
hope cannot be Christian unless it includes some understanding of
the tragedy which culminates in death, for the central Christian
experience is of Easter illuminating Good Friday; and this dimension
of Christianity continues to be relevant in a world "come of age".[2]

Better than any drama written out of twentieth-century despair,
the story of the crucifixion of Jesus teaches the tragic sense of life and
closes the road to Utopia. The cross shows how history with all its
hopes can lead to disaster; Hebrew religion and Roman law,
representing the best in history, tortured to death the embodiment of
God. And now Christians see that in the crimes and follies of history,

[1] Schubert M. Ogden, *The Reality of God* (New York, 1967), p. 226. Professor Ogden's
essays collected in this volume show the illumination provided by Process philosophy in
the tasks of doctrinal reconstruction after his shrewd study of Rudolf Bultmann's thought
in his *Christ without Myth* (New York, 1961). "At the risk of anticlimax" (*The Reality of God*,
p. 229), Professor Ogden adds that "the interpretation of the promise of faith presented
here leaves completely open whether we somehow manage to survive death and continue
to exist as experiencing subjects as is claimed by conventional theories of immortality."
My own view is that it is clearly true that in eternity we cannot "survive" or "experience"
as on earth—but eternal life cannot be less glorious than the life which we have experienced on earth. This seems impossible because the Christian's "present encounter" is
with the Jesus Christ whose "resurrection" was a revelation of the glory at the End (as
John Baillie said so well in his *And the Life Everlasting*, London, 1934).
[2] I tried to work this out in my *God's Cross in Our World* (London, 1963).

he crucifixion of the best goes on. No one who reads history in the light of that cross will be found prophesying a future for man in which human nature will inevitably create and support progress. The crucifixion of Jesus is a tragedy which shows man as too little for his destiny, which shows to what depths human nature can so easily fall, which shows how little the world's pomps and vanities are worth, and which purges our emotions by pity and terror. But the cross is also something more than that, and the message of the cross, the message of Christian patience, is something more than the teaching of the tragic sense of life. Those modern thinkers who have asserted that Christianity is in the last analysis incompatible with tragedy are right, if by Christianity we mean essentially what the New Testament means. According to the New Testament the crucifixion is a revelation not only of the tragedy of mortal man, but also of the victory of the eternal God in this tragic world. Facile optimism stands rebuked; the broad and easy road to a secular Utopia is closed; yet the road to the Kingdom of God is open, *and that road goes through Calvary*.

This, it would seem, is the Christian understanding of the cross. Jesus seems to have gone to his death voluntarily (presumably he could have avoided getting into the situation which brought it about, had he so wished), and the simplest explanation of the attitude of Jesus to his death seems to be the one which the gospels give: which is, that Jesus believed that a life which was so lived as to incur charges of blasphemy and treason, and yet was defenceless—a life which inevitably led to the punishment of crucifixion—had to be lived in that way if the victorious love of God was to be demonstrated in a tragic world. Was that belief right? The correctness of the belief of Jesus will be accepted most readily by those who accept the witness of the New Testament that the crucifixion was followed by a further act, in which God upheld the faith of the crucified Servant by showing him to the faith of the disciples as the risen Lord. If we are to go beyond an interpretation of the cross as a moving tragedy, this will be through accepting the resurrection as a separate event—whatever its mechanism may have been. It is in the light of Easter that the tragic Friday is seen as "Good"; it is in the light of Easter that the whole story of man is seen as a love story with a happy ending, as the Divine Comedy.

A Gospel of the cross built on these New Testament foundations, and shining in that Easter light, will always proclaim a message of hope first; it will preach patience within this hope. It will always be invincibly optimistic. And here we have to note that it is precisely the optimism of Christianity that has dismayed many secular thinkers of our time whose central experience has been one of disillusionment with lesser hopes. Thus Albert Camus made this comment: "There is, of course, an act of metaphysical rebellion at the beginning of Christianity, but the resurrection of Christ and the annunciation of the Kingdom of Heaven interpreted as a promise of eternal life are the answers that render it futile."[1]

A number of religious thinkers influential in our time have seemed to suggest that Christianity should accordingly be refashioned as the Divine Tragedy. It is the defeat of the purposes of the Sovereign Father on the cross, they have implied, that should lead to a deeper understanding of the suffering of God in this tragic world. Such a theology certainly seems to be more Christian than does the doctrine—with a far larger history in Christianity—which complacently declares that God is already completely in control, his Kingdom come, his will done, his glory and power manifest, in every detail of the universe. It also seems preferable to the doctrine—also highly honoured in Christian history, although owing more to Aristotle than to the Bible—that God is affected neither by the tragedies nor by the triumphs of his creatures, but remains the passionless Source, the unmoved Mover. We shall wish to say that the tragedy in life is opposed to God—so that, although every event is permitted by him, not every event equally reflects God's loving will. Here, it may be, is the reality behind the New Testament's myths of the battles with the demons. We shall also wish to say that God is involved in the struggles of his creatures; his infinite being bears a real relationship to their suffering in time, and his perfection includes the triumphant completion of his creation in the perfection of his creatures. Here, it may be, is the truth behind the Bible's naïve pictures of the sorrow, anger and joy of the God who is in covenant with man. But if we are to remain loyal to the message of the Bible, we shall not wish to deny the perfect eternity of God the Creator; nor to deny that this perfect eternity, this source from which creation emerges, is best glimpsed when through the suffering and sorrow, and beyond all the tragedy of history, the last word is joy. We shall wish to affirm as the distinctively Christian understanding of the cross that the transcendent God was in the crucified Christ, triumphantly transforming the suffering to joy.

The cross of Jesus, seen in this Easter light, reveals the inexhaustible

[1] In a footnote in *The Rebel* (Eng. edn., 1962), p. 27.

patience of the transcendent, and in the end victorious, God. For his own purposes, which are beyond our full understanding, the Almighty Father has chosen to postpone his triumph until the incomprehensibly vast and complex process of evolution has reached its goal. God's choice of such a universe costs his children an agony; and this cost we see when there is no miracle to rescue the crucified Jesus. But God's choice also costs him something; and this cost we see in the Jesus who on the cross is the Model or Image or Word of the transcendent, eternal, triumphantly joyful God who now suffers. Jesus spoke of the Father as the One who gives of his own to his children, and who gives his children freedom and lets them be if that is what they want, and who waits, and who in their distress runs to them. Jesus claimed that through his life God was showing this patient love, and as we look back we can see the love shown supremely in the patience to death—the patience which through its humility conquered.

This vision of the patience of the God of Calvary has consequences for our lives, now that we are "come of age", called to live as God's adult sons and fellow-workers. Recent Christian thought has rightly rejoiced over the progress of our time, and has interpreted this rapid change as the means by which God is acting to awaken the world and to confer on all mankind the privileges of adulthood. Many Christians rightly wish to be involved in the thrill of this hope and achievement, for the delight in it has an eternal source. But after all the changes in society human hearts will still be broken; and during and after these changes, the call for human endurance will remain. For many Christians it therefore matters that they should be confident that this patience, like the hope, has its basis in the eternal joy. It matters that the "Lord of heaven and earth" calls men to share not only his continuing creativity, but also the suffering involved, in the cross which, as Pascal said, will remain until the end of the world.

Dietrich Bonhoeffer, whose phrase about man's "coming of age" has run through so much recent Christian thought, was trained in a strictly pious discipline and a rigorously intellectual theology. Much of his adult life was spent as a leader of the Confessing Church. When the war came he found himself involved in the anti-Nazi resistance alongside many men who did not share his ecclesiastical background. For a time this political movement held high promise for Bonhoeffer; it seemed possible that the Nazis could be removed and an honourable peace negotiated. When he was arrested and imprisoned because of his share in this conspiracy, Bonhoeffer still hoped that the evil tyrant might be killed and further tragedy averted; and to the end he did not repent of his involvement in the struggles of political and military power, in the secular hopes of worldly success. But in prison he learned that success was not necessary for the disciple who would, in hope and patience, take his part in God's creativity and suffering. On the day after the unsuccessful attempt of his fellow-conspirators to assassinate Hitler in 1944, when his own doom was now sealed short of a miracle which never came, Bonhoeffer wrote a word for our secular century with its glittering accomplishments but recurrent tragedies, a word about the triumphant God of Calvary. "I am still discovering, right up to this moment, that it is only by living completely in this world that one learns to have faith. One must completely abandon any attempt to make something of oneself . . . By this-worldliness I mean living unreservedly in life's duties, problems, successes and failures, experiences and perplexities. In so doing we throw ourselves completely into the arms of God, taking seriously, not our own suffering, but those of God in the world . . . How can success make us arrogant, or failure lead us astray, when we share in God's sufferings through a life of this kind?"[1]

To share the Christian faith today is therefore nothing else than this: *to choose to share the faith of Jesus Christ in God the Father who cares and suffers, and who will make known his power and joy as King on earth as in heaven.* Such a faith can be shared by modern minds sensitive to all the criticisms of Christianity mentioned in this book, and to all the changes brought about by this largely secular century. To that faith a future generation, inspired by the self-revealing God, may contribute the fresh vitality and power which this chapter has lacked; on that foundation a more stable fellowship of believers may be built in a more creative epoch; and in that fellowship our children or their descendents, while not escaping either the burdens or the excitements of continuous change, may find a greater peace than has marked the religious life of our century so far.

[1] *Letters and Papers from Prison*, p. 202.

Index of Subjects

Titles of books are not listed. See second index for modern authors.

Index of Authors